Learn Programming with Flash MX

Kristian Besley
Ben Renow-Clarke

Apress™

Learn Programming with Flash MX

ISBN (pbk): 1-59059-241-7

Printed and bound in the United States of America 12345678910

Technical Reviewers: Leon Cych, Dan Britton, Chris Crane
Editorial Board: Dan Appleman, Craig Berry, Gary Cornell, Tony Davis, Steven Rycroft, Julian Skinner, Martin Streicher, Jim Sumser, Karen Watterson, Gavin Wray, John Zukowski
Assistant Publisher: Grace Wong
Project Managers: Kylie Johnston, Jenni Harvey, Vicki Idiens
Copy Editor: Nicole LeClerc
Production Manager: Kari Brooks
Production Editor: Kelly Winquist
Proofreader: Lori Bring
Compositor: Katy Freer
Indexer: Jo Crichton
Cover Designer: Kurt Krames
Manufacturing Manager: Tom Debolski

Distributed to the book trade in the United States by Springer-Verlag New York, Inc., 175 Fifth Avenue, New York, NY 10010 and outside the United States by Springer-Verlag GmbH & Co. KG, Tiergartenstr. 17, 69112 Heidelberg, Germany.

In the United States: phone 1-800-SPRINGER, email `orders@springer-ny.com`, or visit `http://www.springer-ny.com`. Outside the United States: fax +49 6221 345229, email `orders@springer.de`, or visit `http://www.springer.de`.

For information on translations, please contact Apress directly at 2560 Ninth Street, Suite 219, Berkeley, CA 94710. Phone 510-549-5930, fax 510-549-5939, email `info@apress.com`, or visit `http://www.apress.com`.

The source code for this book is available to readers at `http://www.apress.com` in the Downloads section. You will need to answer questions pertaining to this book in order to successfully download the code.

Case study photos courtesy of Ellie Cooper (`elle@eleanor-cooper.com`), Jasper Renow-Clarke, and the authors. Wedding photos used with kind permission of Karl and Nia Besley. Kristian Besley bio photo by Simon James.

About the Authors

Kristian Besley is a freelance author and Flash/web developer, specializing in interactivity and dynamic-driven content. He will, however, try his hand at just about anything....

Kristian has written a considerable number of books, including *Foundation Flash MX, Flash MX Video,* and *Learn Design with Flash MX*. He is also a contributor to *Computer Arts* magazine. In 2002, his website graphci.com hosted the first ever worldwide HTML-based Table Art competition. The entries are viewable at www.graphci.com/tableart. The 2003 competition is currently being planned. Willing sponsors please apply to krisbesley@ntlworld.com.

Kristian was born and raised in a city called Swansea in Wales and attended a Welsh-language school.

Many thanks to Ben, Katy, Libby, Andrew, and Steve.

Ben Renow-Clarke has been a writer and editor for a few years now, and spends too much of his time staring at computer screens. He is glad that programs like Flash exists to make this fun at least some of the time. He is currently living and working in the southeast of England, and finding out why Dante's deepest circle of hell should have been populated by herring gulls. He likes it when the sky is blue and sea is close, and he misses his far away friends.

Ben would like to thank K + K, A, C + P, P + K, J + C, and every R-C for just being great really. He would also like thank EC for the photos. (EC can be reached at elle@eleanor-cooper.com, and is open to any comments and questions on the photos. You can view more of her work at www.eleanor-cooper.com.)

Class 3 Programming Concepts 75

Class 4 Symbols and Objects 119

Chapter 5 Interaction 147

Welcome to the class

Step inside the world of the Learn Programming with Flash MX class, where you will meet a group of fellow students and learn alongside them all about programming using ActionScript in Flash MX.

Under instructor Ken Jokol's guidance, you'll learn core programming principles and use them to create an exciting final case study.

What is Flash MX?

Flash is arguably the most exciting and essential web technology of the moment. We've chosen it for this course, not only because of its importance, but also because it's a great tool to teach programming with. If you've never used Flash before, then don't worry – you don't need any prior knowledge and you'll be shown all the basics of the program.

What is ActionScript?

ActionScript is the programming language that you can use within Flash to add greater interactivity to your Flash creations. Don't worry if you've never programmed before (or are even scared by the thought) because this book is all about introducing you to the concepts slowly and with clear examples, so you shouldn't feel lost. Even if you do, remember that there are five other people in the class who have the same problems and are thinking of the same questions as you.

Once you understand the basic concepts behind ActionScript, you'll not only be able to move on and apply these principles to other programming languages, but you'll also be able to make better, more interactive, Flash movies with enhanced functionality. ActionScript is surprisingly easy to learn and will open the door to an enriched Flash experience.

The virtual classroom

This book is unlike most other technical training manuals. The beauty of learning in a virtual classroom is that you can work at a pace that allows you to fully understand and absorb each new concept.

Your fellow students are new to programming, just like you, and they ask the kind of questions that you've been dying to ask as well. Each student has his or her own needs and approach to each class, and hopefully some of the students' interests will match yours.

In this book, you'l find stepped exercises, just as in other technical books, but with the added bonus that the students are there to question the tutor about how and why the exercise works.

Learn Programming with Flash MX allows you to explore ActionScript in such an intuitive and enjoyable way that you won't even notice you're learning.

Meet your teacher

Ken Jokol will be your guide in this book, leading you gently but directly through the maze of Macromedia Flash MX ActionScript programming. He is the teacher of the Flash evening class at the local college, and is just about to start this semester's course.

Ken has been teaching Flash programming and web design since the days of Flash 4, and has been using Flash fanatically since version 3. He fits his teaching around his day-to-day career as a freelance web designer and developer. He started off as a database programmer, but gave this up to pursue a more creative (and certainly more fun) career in web design

Meet your classmates

Throughout this book you'll be studying with five other students who each of whom has a very different personality and perspective to bring to the learning process:

- **Carl** – the youngest of the group, Carl is a high school student who wants to learn about Flash in order to make a website for his band, Mondo.

- **Gemma** – a graphic designer in her early twenties. Gemma has previously used Dreamweaver to build websites, but her boss has sent her to this course to learn about programming in Flash in order to meet his clients' demands. Gemma is reluctant to learn programming at first, until she realizes how it can help with her design work.

- **Jim** – although Jim works for local government, he dreams of one day making it as a web designer. He's had some experience of programming using BASIC, many years ago. Jim has dabbled with Flash 5, but he's new to Flash MX and soon discovers that there have been some big changes in between the two versions.

- **Joe** – a store owner with very little computer experience, Joe uses a kiosk device to advertise products in his store. The kiosk is looking dated now and he's joined the class in the hopes of teaching himself how to make a new version in Flash.

- **Mazzy** – as someone who loves to keep herself busy, Mazzy has already completed a course on HTML and uses these skills to run her local church's website. She's frustrated by the limitations of HTML, however, and now wants to learn about Flash. Mazzy's nephew has told her that ActionScript is easy to pick up, and Mazzy (and the others) are about to learn just how true this is.

Conventions

We've tried to keep this book as clear and easy to follow as possible, so we've only used a few layout styles:

- When you come across an important word or phrase, it will be in **bold** type.

- We'll use a different font to emphasize, `code`, `filenames`, what to hit on the KEYBOARD, and hyperlinks (e.g. www.apress.com)

- Menu commands are written in the form **Menu > Submenu > Submenu.**

- If we're showing you a piece of code, and we can't print it all on one line because it's too long, then we'll use a code continuation character to indicate that this code should be typed in all on one line.

```
thumb = frame.attachMovie("dummyPhoto",
➥ "dummyPhoto"+count, count);
```

Support – we're here to help

All books from Apress aim to be easy to follow and error-free. However, if you do run into problems, don't hesitate to get in touch – our support is fast, friendly, and free.

You can reach us at **support@apress.com**, quoting the last four digits of the ISBN in the subject of the e-mail (that's 2417, just so you know!). If you're having technical problems with a specific file that you've created from an exercise, it can sometimes help to include a copy of that file with your mail.

Even if our dedicated support team is unable to solve your problem immediately, your queries will be passed onto the editors and authors to solve. All Apress authors help with the support on their books, and will either directly mail people with answers, or send their response to an editor to pass on.

We'd love to hear from you, whether it's to request future books, ask about Apress, or tell us about the sites you went on to create after you read this book.

Class 1
Meet the Students

Objectives

In this class, you will

- Meet each of the students and Ken Jokol, the tutor.
- Be introduced to Flash and discover why it is such a useful program.
- Explore the Flash MX interface.
- Start experimenting with Flash's tools.

Introduction

It came time to meet the class. I sat at the front desk and welcomed all the students as they came in, counting four people of various ages. Not my largest class, but small enough to develop an individual relationship with each of them. There had been five registrants, but it was normal to have the odd person drop out every now and then. I stood up and walked around to the front of the desk to introduce myself. “Good evening, and welcome to my class, ‘Learn Programming with Flash MX.’ My name is Ken Jok—”

At that moment the classroom door burst open and a disheveled figure ran in. “Sorry I’m late, sir, one of my wheels popped two blocks back and I had to carry the bike the rest of the way. Phew, I’m beat.” And with that, he collapsed into the nearest chair.

“Don’t worry about it,” I said. “I hope you’ll be all right getting back home after class?”

“I’ll have to pray they let me take my bike on the bus—it’s a fair walk back to Acacia Avenue.” At that, one of the other students, a middle-aged woman, spoke up. “Acacia Avenue’s not far from where I live, I could give you a lift back in my car if you like. I think there will be room for your bike in the back.”

“Hey thanks, that would be cool,” the young man replied.

“Good, I’m glad we got that sorted out,” I said. “Now where was I? Oh yes, my name: I’m Ken Jokol, and this is the first class in ‘Learn Programming with Flash MX.’ We’ll begin by getting to know each other, and then I’ll explain a bit more about the course and its objectives. I work on the LIFE principle: Last In, First Embarrassed, so let’s start with you.” I turned to the young man who had arrived late and said, “Can you tell us a little about yourself and why you chose to take this class?”

“Okay, my name’s Carl, I’m 16 years old, and I guess you already know where I live. I go to this school, and I play bass in a group called ‘Mondo’—you may have seen our name around on flyers. Actually, the practice room’s just at the end of the hall, and we’re here every Wednesday if anyone feels like hanging out. I’ve seen a lot of cool Flash sites on the Web, and I wanted to make something for the band where we can put up gig dates and photos. You know, some way for our fans to get ahold of us easily. I think that’s about it.”

“Thanks, Carl. That was great. I hope I can help you make the website that your fans deserve,” I said. I turned to the young lady sitting a couple of desks over from Carl and gestured for her to continue.

"All right, my name's Gemma, and I have a degree in fine art. I've been working for a few years as a graphic designer for a firm over on Gerard Street. I thought working with Photoshop and Dreamweaver was the furthest I'd get from pens and pencils, but my boss saw fit to send me on this programming course, of all things! Our clients sometimes ask for simple web pages to go with their print work, and up until now they've been happy with what I've been able to do in Dreamweaver. We often do kiosks to go with our print work, but my boss says that the clients want something more dynamic than our current offerings. Personally, I think that a simple improvement to our Dreamweaver work will be enough, but the boss says otherwise, and my job's not secure enough to argue with him."

She folded her arms and shrugged her shoulders in resignation. "Okay, Gemma," I started, "I can see that at the moment you're not entirely happy to be here, but I can promise you that the skills you'll learn in this class will benefit your clients enormously. Turning things the other way around, your design talents will also be of benefit to this class."

"How so?" she asked with mild interest.

"Because Flash is much more than just a programming language, it's a full-strength web-design tool," I replied. "In fact, it began life as purely a design tool, and more and more programming power was added to it in each successive version. One of the things that makes it so powerful is the way in which the design and the programming worlds combine to create something that's accessible to everyone. Anyway, I'm getting ahead of myself. Let's just say that I think—or at least I hope—that you'll surprise yourself by the end of the course with how much you can accomplish by combining your design skills with some simple programming knowledge."

She thought for a moment, and then smiled. "I'll hold you to that. I'm not convinced yet, but I'll give it a shot," she said.

"Thanks," I said. "That's good enough for me. Okay, who's next?"

A young man in the front row offered to say his piece.

"My name's Jim and I'm a desk clerk for the local government," he said. "It's not the most glamorous of jobs and I've got a crazy dream that I can one day leave my current job and become a web designer. This course is my first real step along that road."

"That sounds good, Jim. I hope I can help you with it. Do you use much software in your job as a clerk?" I asked.

"Nothing that really relates to this, no. It's mostly just Access and Excel. The closest I've been to programming is using BASIC on the family VIC-20. I thought I was pretty good at the time, but that was about 15 years ago, so it's not very relevant now."

"Hold on there, I wouldn't be so sure of that," I interjected. "You'll be surprised to see just how useful that knowledge still is nowadays. Of course, a lot has changed, but you'll recognize bits here and there. So, have you had any experience at all with Flash?"

"Well, I downloaded the trial version of Flash 5 a while back," he said. "I liked what I saw, but to be honest I didn't get very far—I was just playing around with it. I guess we'll be studying the newer version of Flash in this class, right? I heard it's got some new video functionality that I'd like to look at."

"That's right," I said, "we'll be studying Flash MX, and we might just have time to look at its video capabilities. I'll have to have a quick chat with you later, Jim, to see what you picked up about Flash 5."

"Why?" Jim asked. "To see if I'm too advanced for the class?"

"No," I replied with a grin, "more to make sure that you haven't learned too many bad habits. There are a lot of differences between the two versions, and you might find that some simple things don't work the way that you remember them."

I turned to the lady who had offered Carl the lift at the beginning of the class and asked if she'd tell us a little more about herself.

"Certainly, Ken," she replied. "My name is Margaret, but all of my friends call me Mazzy. I'm 52 years young, and a great fan of amateur dramatics. I've tinkered with the Internet here and there for a while, and I took a class in basic HTML with Ms. Jeffries—do you know her?"

I nodded to show that I did and she continued, "Well, I use what I learned from my HTML class to run our church website, but I feel like it's not enough. I've seen some of the other sites out there, and frankly, mine looks dull in comparison. I know that the really great sites all use the Flash plug-in to weave their magic, so when I saw this class offered I jumped at the chance to take it. You know, my nephew promised me that Flash is actually quite easy to pick up, so you'd better not prove him wrong!"

"I'll try not to," I laughed. "Actually, I'm sure none of you will believe me, but Mazzy's nephew is right: Flash is a simple program to start out in, and as you improve your skills, it will repay you by opening up a new world of impressive and, dare I say it, fun programming. Okay, I think that leaves only one more." I gestured to the man seated at the desk next to Mazzy.

"Hi. My name's Joe, and I run a shop a couple of blocks away," he said. "Funnily enough, a class like this has already helped my business, but I never went to it."

"We're intrigued, Joe," I said. "Please continue . . . ."

"Well," he went on, "a few years ago, I approached a programmer about writing a simple kiosk application for my shop. It turned out that he taught evening classes in programming, and we struck a deal that I'd get a discount if the program was written by the class as a project for the course. The work that the class did was great, and the program was very popular with the customers and the sales staff, but it's beginning to look a bit long in the tooth now. Rather than hire an expert to write a new program, I thought I might have a go at doing something myself. So I talked to a couple of people about what I could do to update the program a bit. One guy said I could use a program called 'Director' or something, as that was the best for doing kiosks, but the other guy said that this Flash was probably better for me, as it was easier to work with and should be able to do everything I wanted it to. So here I am."

"Thanks, Joe," I responded. "Your friend gave you good advice. A lot of people find Flash easier to learn than Director, and Flash is also very good at handling kiosks. We'll have to talk about exactly what your original kiosk did, but I've a hunch we'll easily be able to match its functionality and give it a graphical makeover too.

"Okay, that's everyone. So, let's see if I can just remember your names . . . Carl, Gemma, Jim, Margaret—sorry, Mazzy—and Joe."

"What about you, sir?" Carl shouted from the back.

"Me? I guess I should tell you a little more about myself," I said. "First of all, please feel free to call me Ken. Although I'm flattered by being addressed as sir, it seems a bit formal for this class."

"Sorry . . . Ken," Carl said, "I'm just used to calling the teachers 'sir' at school."

"No worries," I said, "the reason I objected to it is because I want us all to be equals here. I'm here to teach you Flash, but at the same time, I don't expect you guys to be the only ones learning something. One of the reasons I enjoy teaching is that I always get something back from the class. For instance, in last year's class we had a young lady who was studying geology, and as part of the website project we took a trip up to the hills to look at the rock formations there. We ended up doing an interactive design based on the different strata of rock that we found on one cliff, and I learned some interesting things about different rock formations. In the same way, I'm sure I'll learn something from such an interesting bunch of people as you all. We've already seen that Gemma's design skills will come in handy, and I can guarantee that you'll all bring something to the class."

"I could teach you to play bass," Carl suggested and raised a chuckle from the rest of the room.

"I'm not sure we'll have time for that," I said, "but I'm sure we'll be hearing your music sometime over the next few weeks."

"Cool," he said and sat back with a satisfied grin on his face.

"Okay," I began, "back to the brief history of me. I have a degree in computer science, and I started work programming databases for a local firm where I used to live. I was there for a few years, but it never really grabbed me.

"After that, I took a break and actually spent quite a long time doing dry-stone walling. If I had to tie that back to programming, I'd probably say something like the construction and planning aspects of it were related, but really I just wanted to do something completely different. After that, I got a lucky break when I got to talking with one of my walling clients and he ended up asking me to do some HTML web design work for his firm.

"It was while I was with that firm that I first started teaching. I lectured in basic HTML at a local community college, and luckily that coincided with the rise in popularity and awareness of the Internet. After that, I started another course in advanced HTML, and left the firm to become a freelance web developer. It was about that time that I discovered Flash version 2. I played with it for a bit, but it wasn't until version 3 that I realized what an amazing and revolutionary program it was. I tried holding a course in Flash after a couple of months of using Flash 3, but it was obviously a bit too early for my area, and I didn't get enough students to make the class worthwhile.

"My first successful Flash course came with version 4 when the seeds of Flash programming first began to take root. I've been doing the same things ever since—working as a freelance web designer whenever I get the time, teaching as much as possible, and upgrading my skills with every new release of Flash. I think that about brings me up-to-date, so I'll stop boring you with tales of my past."

"That's nothing, son," said Joe, "just be thankful you don't have to hear mine!" At that, Jim burst out laughing, and the rest of the class soon joined him. When things had calmed down a bit, I carried on.

"Okay, let's see what we'll be covering in this class and make sure you're all aware of what you'll be getting out of it at the end," I said. "This class is about learning to program, and it's about accomplishing that with the help of Flash. This means that although we'll be briefly looking into the other aspects of Flash, its design tools and animation capabilities, we'll be focusing on its use as a programming tool. To some of you," I glanced at Gemma, "that probably sounds like we're leaving all the fun bits and just looking at the boring stuff, but as I've already said, that's certainly not the case. The real power of Flash is only unleashed when we combine the two aspects of design and programming to create a simple but powerfully deep creative environment. Okay, that may sound like a lot of hot air, but after being locked as I was in a static world of cold coding, working with Flash was a liberating experience."

"Well," Jim cut in, "you've certainly convinced me. Much as I loved BASIC, it was always a chore creating things like graphics and sprites."

"Sprites?" queried Mazzy. "I always thoughts sprites were fairies."

"That all depends on the game you're creating," replied Jim.

"Okay you guys, cut it out," came the gruff voice of Joe. "I'm confused enough as it is without all your talk of sprouts and fairies."

"That's 'sprites,' Joe," said Jim.

"Whatever," said Joe.

I intervened, "Actually, the discussion is kinda relevant. Although we won't be discussing sprites as such, they're an example of why Flash is such an advance from the older programming languages. Basically, a sprite in computing terms is a graphic, usually in a game. For example, an alien in the game 'Space Invaders' is a sprite, as are the ghosts, the pills, and the big guy himself in Pac-Man. The thing is, even though they're graphics, they were still created in code. Rather than a game developer just being able to draw the sprites with a mouse or graphics tablet, they had to construct the graphics block by block with a keyboard. This means that rather than being able to see what they were drawing, developers could see only a string of numbers. As you can all see, this isn't an ideal situation to try to be creative in. Flash, though, allows you to draw your graphical elements using traditional drawing tools and then control them using code."

"But I'm not here to make games," interrupted Mazzy. "How's this helpful to me?" I could see another couple of students nod their assent.

"Okay, if I recall correctly, one of the reasons that you took this class was so that you could improve your church website, right?" I asked.

"That's right," Mazzy replied.

"Okay," I said, "I presume that on your site there are some links—possibly even some graphical buttons?"

"Yes, I learned how to take a picture and use it as a button in my HTML course," said Mazzy.

"In Flash, you don't need to know any of that stuff," I said. "You can create your buttons in the program and assign what you want to happen when you click them without leaving the screen. But Flash buttons are way more powerful than normal HTML links—they can do anything that you want them to, they can fire the cannons of Carl's spaceship, play one of Jim's portfolio films, or change the color of one of Mazzy's pictures. Joe's customers could even click just one button to total up their order, apply a discount, calculate sales tax, and then print out a beautifully designed summary sheet."

"Hallelujah!" Joe called out. "That sounds mighty good to me."

"Okay," I said, "I strayed a little from the original argument there, but hopefully you can see how creating your graphical assets and then giving them instructions in the same program is of use to you, no matter what you are doing."

"I think I can, yes," replied Mazzy.

Just then, Gemma piped up with a smile, "Do you think you'll be able to make me a single button that I can just click to make my clients happy?"

"I can't guarantee that," I said, laughing, "but I'll do my best. Now back to what we'll be covering in this course. This course will teach you the fundamentals of programming in Flash. I'll be providing you with the core skills that you need to be able to understand programming, and to know how to plan and write your own programs. The great thing about these core programming principles is that they're not only applicable to Flash. Even though he used a different programming language many years ago, Jim will still probably recognize some of the programming structures that we'll be looking at. In the same way, once you've completed this course, those of you who want to take things further and explore other programming languages will find that a lot of the principles you learn here will help you pick those languages up a lot quicker than you could otherwise. Even if you aren't planning on taking things any further, you'll have enough knowledge to make strides into programming your own Flash creations that will impress even the most hardened of nephews.

"This course won't teach you every single command and how to implement it perfectly—that would take far more time than we have." I then whispered in an overly covert fashion, "*You'll just have to take my advanced Flash programming class for that*. But what this course will give you is a thorough grounding on which to build the rest of your knowledge.

"We'll achieve this grounding by starting from scratch and thoroughly covering all of the basics, and making sure at every step of the way that each of you understands what we're discussing and why we're doing what we're doing. Alongside the theory, we'll also be making a case study—a complete application in Flash that we'll program all of the functionality for. We'll talk more about this next week, but if any of you have any ideas or preferences for things that you want to do, let me know next week and I'll incorporate everybody's ideas with my own thoughts to come up with a case study that will be useful for all of you.

"The case study will be written mostly in class, but there will also be some homework for you to take home and play with." At this, I heard an exasperated sigh from Carl. "Yes, Carl, I'm sorry. There will be homework, but I promise it won't be much," I said.

What is Flash?

"Okay, let's start with a simple question: What is Macromedia Flash MX?" I looked around the class, and they all looked back at me, expecting someone else to answer. "I know that sounded like a trick question, but I promise it wasn't. Jim, you've used Flash 5 before, what's your answer?"

Jim thought for a second, and then spoke. "Flash, as I know it, is an animation tool for the Web . . . although I suppose it doesn't have to be for the Web." He looked over at Joe. "It was just created with that in mind. It creates small files that load quickly on the Web, and an awful lot of people have the player, so you can guarantee that a large proportion of your audience will be able to view your file."

"Thanks, Jim, that was great," I said. Jim looked around the class and smiled. I continued, "You've covered a lot of the basics there, so I'll just recap some of the things that you said. Flash began life as an animation program, and it has evolved over successive versions into a multimedia application tool. It's fundamentally a tool for the Web, and that's where its strengths lie—it creates small files that can be quickly downloaded over the Internet. It manages to create such small files partly because it uses **vectors** instead of **bitmaps**." I looked around the class and was greeted by two rows of blank faces. "Gemma, how's about you let the rest of the class in on the truth behind vectors and bitmaps?"

"Sure," said Gemma, obviously pleased that she had a chance to get involved with the class. "I'm certain you've all come across bitmaps before, even though you might not have known what they were called. Images that you create with programs like Photoshop, such as JPEGs or GIFs, are examples of bitmaps. They can produce very good-quality images, but they also tend to be quite large files. To find out why this is, we need to look a little closer at how a computer monitor works." She turned around to look at me to check if it was okay to continue. I nodded that she was doing fine, and she turned back around to face the class. "Imagine that your computer screen is just a grid," she said, starting to draw out a grid in midair with her fingers. She then spotted the whiteboard at the front of the class and stood up to use it. "Is it all right if I use the board?" she asked.

"Yeah, no problem," I replied. Gemma moved to the front of the class, chose a pen color, and then drew out a quick but precise 6x6 grid on the board. "Okay, imagine this is a zoomed-in part of your monitor," she said and filled in a diagonal line of squares going across the grid.

"Here we have a simple diagonal line. It's not much of a picture, but it's perfect for illustrating what I mean. Each of these squares is called a pixel, and it's basically the building block of an image. Each pixel can be set to be a different color, and that's how images are made. Anyway, in a bitmap image, we have to describe what every pixel is doing, so this line would be:

Black, white, white, white, white, white.
White, black, white, white, white, white.
White, white, black, white, and so on.

"You can see what a tedious process this is. There are various ways of cutting this down, for example by blocks of the same color:

1 black, 5 white.
1 white, 1 black, 4 white, etc.

"But that still takes up a lot of room. With vectors, though, we describe the line mathematically using the screen coordinates." She wrote some numbers by the side of her grid.

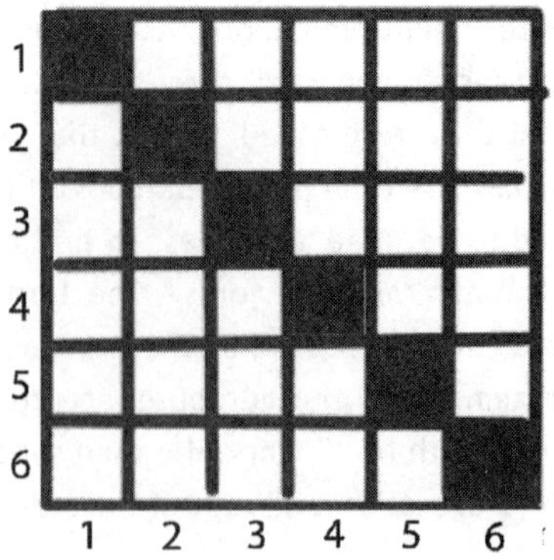

"So all we need to tell the computer here is the color of our line, and the start and end coordinates. So in this example, it's:

Black 1,1 - 6,6

"And that's it. No matter how long the line is, we still only need that much information, but the longer the line is in a bitmap image, the more information we need to store." She turned and looked expectantly at the class, "Any questions?"

There was silence from the class until Carl gave a loud whistle, and they all broke out into impromptu applause. Gemma went an embarrassed shade of red but still managed a theatrical curtsy. When things had died down a bit, Joe raised his hand in the air, "Yes, Joe?" asked Gemma.

"Just a quick question, miss," he said with a grin. "If vectors are so much better than bitmaps, why doesn't everyone use them?"

"That's a fine question, Joe. The reason is that vectors are no good at describing detailed images. If you imagine a photograph with thousands of different colors in it, it's unlikely that you'll have any long strings of sequential color. Let's take a quick example." Gemma drew a line of two red squares, a green square, and a blue square.

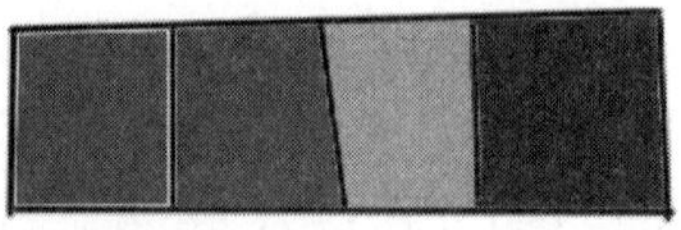

"Okay, in a bitmap, this would be

2 red, 1 green, 1 blue.

"But as a vector, it would be

Red 1,1 - 2,1; green 3,1 - 3,1; blue 4,1 - 4,1.

"That's almost twice as much work for such a simple line. The trick is to play to each format's strengths: photographic images are best described as bitmaps, and images composed of simpler shapes and lines are better as vectors. Does that answer your question, Joe?"

"Yep," said Joe, "that about does it. I'm not sure I'll remember it all, but I think I know what you're getting at." Gemma made her way back to her seat.

"In all honesty," I continued, "this will all become clearer once we start using the program and you can see how things work."

"On that note," called out Carl from the back of the class, "when are we going to start using it? My fingers are itching."

"Okay, okay," I laughed, "hold your horses. I'll just wrap up my quick definition of Flash, and then we'll turn on the computers and get Flashing."

"That sounds awfully rude," said Mazzy under her breath, and the class erupted into laughter once again.

I had noticed that Mazzy had been taking notes throughout the lesson. "Okay, Mazzy, can you quickly recap what we've said about Flash so far?" I asked.

"Yes, certainly," she replied. "Flash is a web animation program with extra bells and whistles, and it creates small files by using vectors instead of bitmaps. How's that?"

"Beautifully succinct," I answered. "And as well as images, you can add sounds and even videos into your Flash files to make some amazing multimedia productions. But we're not really here for the pretty things, we're here for the power that forms the brain of Flash. We're here for the ActionScript." I paused dramatically, but the class didn't take the bait. "ActionScript," I continued, "is the language of Flash. It's what we'll be living and breathing for the rest of the course; it's what will help make your websites, kiosks, and portfolios come alive; and I'm sorry to say that it won't be something that you'll be getting your hands on until next week." I heard a sigh rise from the students, but I couldn't tell if it was from disappointment or relief.

"First of all, we need to get to know the environment that we'll be working in, and I don't just mean this room and where the water cooler is. I mean the *Flash* environment—how to use the various tools to create your assets and how to find your way around the panels to mix gradients, apply transformations, and set text. First things first, though—you need to turn on your computers." Half of the class immediately reached for the power switches. I thought about stopping them so I could finish my instructions, but let them carry on and just called out over the noise of whirring fans, "Your usernames and temporary passwords can be found on your registration forms. You have the option to change your password after the first time you log in. If you don't have your registration form with you, I can give you a temporary username until next week." I was pleasantly surprised to find that everybody had brought their forms with them, so I took my laptop out of my bag and set it up with the projector at the front of the room.

When everybody was logged in, I turned on the projector and let them in on a surprise. "Okay, as you can see, I have the projector hooked up to my laptop so that you can all see what I'm doing, and I can demonstrate the program to you," I said. "There's also another rather interesting feature to the computer network in this room that I think is brilliant, and hopefully you'll come to appreciate it too. By changing this little switch here," I turned a switch by the projector, and the picture changed to show another desktop with Flash open on it, "I can see that Jim has jumped the gun and opened Flash before I asked him to." Everyone turned to look at Jim, who sheepishly closed down Flash, forgetting that everyone could see what he was doing through the projector.

"It's okay, Jim," I said. "I was just about to ask everybody to do that anyway." I addressed the rest of the class.

"This isn't just so that I can persecute you whenever I feel like it, it's actually immensely useful for working through problems that people encounter so that we can all learn from them. The majority of the time, it will just be revealing the contents of my screen—I promise I won't spy on anyone without asking them. Okay, now we're ready to start up Flash and take a look around." I switched the projector back to my screen. "You can find it either through the shortcut icon on the desktop or through the Start menu under **Programs > Macromedia > Macromedia Flash MX**." After a barrage of double-clicks, the monitors were filled with the Flash MX interface.

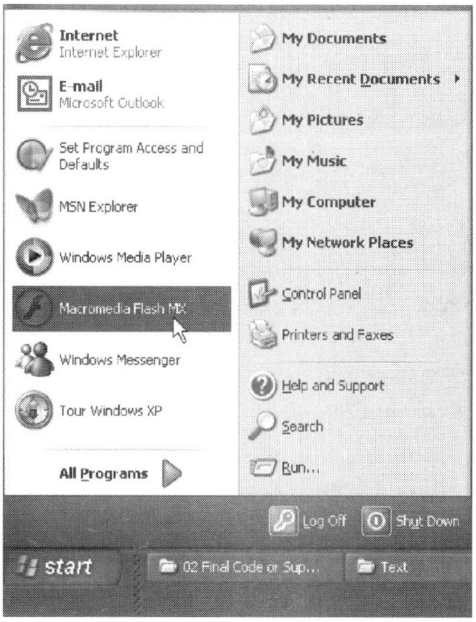

Introducing Flash

"Now that you all know why Flash is suitable for this class," I said, "we're going to take a quick look at the Flash MX program to get you familiar with it. It's important to be comfortable with the program before you can begin learning to program with it.

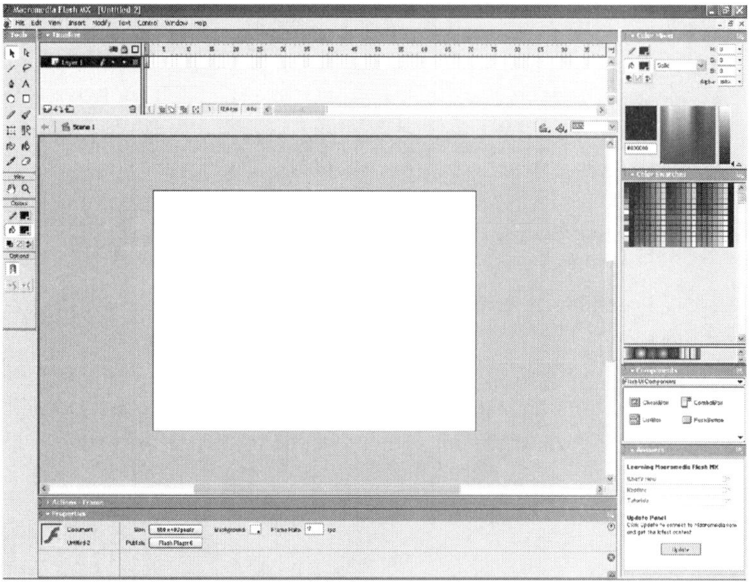

"What you can now see is the main Flash MX interface. This is where we you'll produce all of your websites, animations, or programs—"

Mazzy interrupted, "There's a lot to take in onscreen isn't there? It quite bewildering."

"I'm with Mazzy," Joe added. "There's a lot of information here. I wouldn't know where to start."

"Although it might look complicated right now," I said, "the Flash interface is quite easy to use, having been improved upon with each new edition of the program. We'll spend the rest of today's class exploring the interface and hopefully prove that your initial thoughts of it aren't true."

"That's a deal!" Joe said. Mazzy smiled and nodded in agreement.

"Before we begin, does anyone see anything that they recognize from other programs?" I asked.

Gemma was first to speak. "I can see a few things . . . ."

"Go ahead," I said.

"Well, the first thing I noticed is the toolbar on the left side. Although the tools might be different, it's common in graphic applications to have a toolbar in the same place," she said.

"That's correct, Gemma," I said, "the toolbar is a generic interface feature of most graphic applications, such as Adobe Photoshop or Illustrator. The Flash **toolbar** is where you select a tool for a specific job. This could be anything from the Pencil tool to a tool that draws rectangles or squares. It's Flash's equivalent of the artist's toolbox.

"Is there anything else familiar to anyone?" I asked.

"I'll hazard a guess," Mazzy volunteered. "I presume that the white area in the center of the screen is the page?"

I nodded and said, "Continuing the artist analogy, this area is the artist's canvas. In Flash it's called the **stage**, and it's where our content will be displayed. Let's take a look at all of the interface elements in detail."

I changed the projector to show an annotated screen shot:

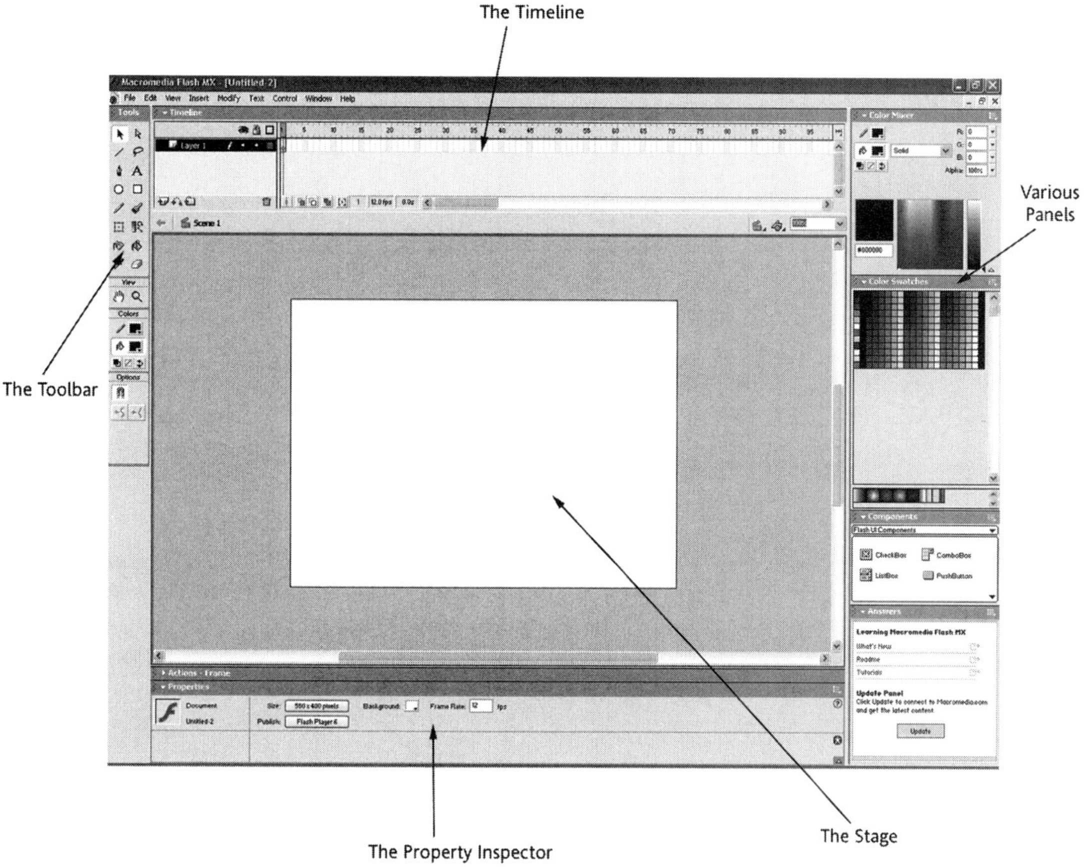

"The Flash interface is made up of five main assets, as you see here. The timeline, the toolbar, the Property inspector, the stage, and a number of different panels. All of these play a different part in the program, and each is just as important as the next one.

"We'll start with the stage."

The stage

"The stage is the viewable area of any Flash presentation. When you want the audience to see something, you'll put it on the stage. If something isn't on stage, then it simply isn't seen."

I changed the image on the projector.

"Notice the grey area around the stage?" Jim nodded, and I continued, "This is known as the work area. If you imagine that the stage is like a theater stage, then the work area is everything that the audience is unable to see from the seats, such as backstage costume changes or the actors waiting to take the stage. So, while the actors are onstage and performing, there is a great deal of activity happening offstage too."

"So, things can be waiting offstage in the work area before coming onto the stage?" Jim asked.

"Sure," I replied, "you might use this tactic when you want to reveal something on the stage later in a Flash movie."

"A bit like the headline band waiting for the warm-up act to finish?" Carl enthused.

I laughed. "Something like that, Carl! We'll learn a little more about how the work area can be useful in later classes. For now, though, it's essential to know that the stage is the one thing that links you to your viewing audience."

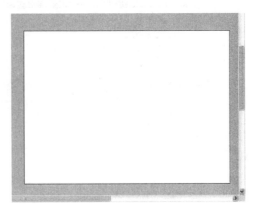

The toolbar

"The toolbar features a variety of tools from drawing tools, such as the Pencil tool, to text and manipulation tools. Every tool has a unique ability which can be used to create or manipulate content," I explained.

"How do we know which tool is which?" Gemma asked.

"An easy way to find out what each icon represents is to hold your mouse cursor over any of them for a little while. A little tooltip will tell you the name of that tool.

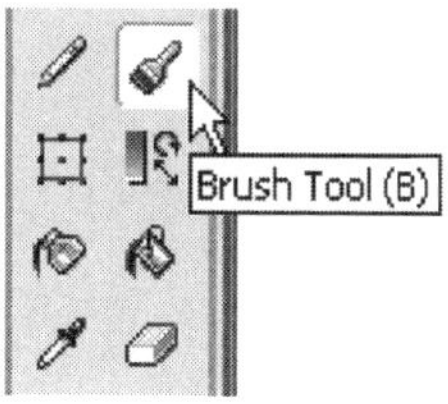

"You'll soon discover that many Flash elements reveal tooltips to help you in the same manner. These will be useful as you familiarize yourself with Flash."

"Great, that means I won't have to write everything down!" Mazzy said, putting her pencil down.

"Do we get to try the tools out now?" Carl asked enthusiastically.

"Not quite yet, Carl," I said. "Let's get an overview of the five interface elements first, and then we can come back and flex some creative muscle later in class. Besides, you'll have plenty of time to try them out outside the class . . . ."

"You don't mean that we'll have homework already do you, Teach? I have enough of that at high school," Carl groaned.

"It depends on how well behaved you are," I joked. The room filled with a short burst of laughter. Once it was over, I proceeded. "For now though, on to the Property inspector."

The Property inspector

I changed the image on the projector and said, "The Property inspector is an extremely useful feature to have. It first appeared with the release of Flash MX."

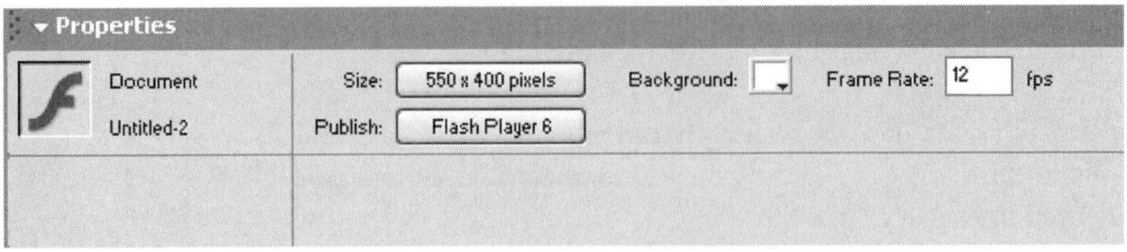

"I didn't think I'd seen that before," Jim said. "Why is it so useful?"

"The Property inspector," I started, "displays information about all content, tools, and anything else in your Flash file. It's the one place you need to look when you require information about anything."

"I don't understand," Mazzy said. She pointed at her monitor. "What information is it showing us now?"

"The true power of the Property inspector will become clear when we get more hands-on with Flash," I said. "In answer to your question, it's simply showing information regarding the Flash document you currently have open.

"When you come to draw or create something later, you'll see that the Property inspector will show you information about whatever object you have selected at that time. Although you might not see its uses now, pretty soon you'll come to rely on it whenever you're working in Flash."

"Is there a Property inspector in Dreamweaver too?" Gemma asked. "Your description sounds familiar."

"Yes there is, Gemma," I replied. "Dreamweaver is made by the same software company that makes Flash: Macromedia. Both have similar interface elements to allow users to easily work and learn from one program to the next."

"That's good to know," Gemma smiled. "At least I won't have to learn Flash from scratch." She paused. "At least until the programming begins, anyhow!"

The timeline

"The next element is essential if our movie is to play smoothly." I changed the projector image to reveal the next element:

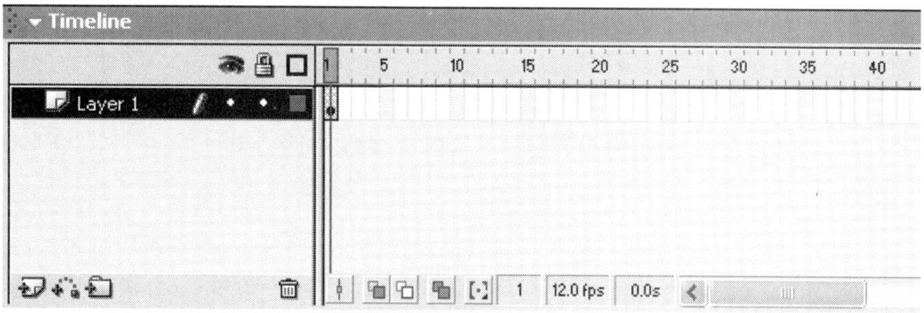

"The timeline in Flash MX relates to the elusive fourth dimension: time. If we use the theater metaphor again, we know that certain things take place at different points in a play, such as actors coming onstage, the curtain being raised or dropped, and so on. The same thing happens in Flash, the only difference is that we're directing the action and we can determine when things happen."

"I've always wanted to be a director," Mazzy said. "Maybe my wish will come true after all." She paused. "Or maybe I just wanted a chair with my name on it and a loudspeaker to control my husband!"

Now that the class had learned a little about some of the interface elements in isolation, I wanted to zoom in on some of them and provide a little context. I started with one of the most important concepts of Flash: the notion of frames.

Frames and keyframes

"The timeline in Flash MX is the very heart of the application," I said. "As with history, the Flash MX timeline is a visual representation of the passing of time. In Flash MX, single units of time are represented as **frames**."

"It's like film and video, Ken," Jim said. "A second of time in film is made up of 24 individual images or frames."

"Jim's right," I replied, "and he's beaten me to it." I reached into my folder and pulled out a strip of film.

"This is a second of film or, for our logic, 24 frames." I passed the strip of celluloid to Carl. "Pass it around and take a look." Carl held it up to the light and squinted his eyes.

"When this strip of film goes through the projector, the quick sequence of images creates the illusion of motion," I began.

"Conceptually, Flash works in the same way, using a number of frames per second to create the illusion of motion or animation. The default number of frames per second, or frame rate, of Flash is 12 frames per second, but this can be changed to anything from 1 to 120."

"A lower frame rate will reduce the fluidity of the motion, though," Jim added. "Cine or Super 8 film runs only at 8 frames per second, and this ruins the illusion for the audience because they're constantly aware of the imperfection of the motion."

"That's dead right, Jim," I responded, "You really know your film. When motion is fluid enough, the movement convinces the eye and a suspension of disbelief is achieved. Conversely, when the frame rate is too low and there are more and more gaps in the fluidity of the motion, the brain is more aware of the gaps because it has to fill in the spaces.

"When it comes to Flash, you can usually get away with the standard 12 frames per second, but for specific, highly animated work, you might need to push it up. For most programming work in this course, 12 frames per second (or 12 fps) will be fine."

I opened a new Flash movie. "Let's turn our attention to a basic Flash movie," I continued. "If you look at the bottom of the timeline section here, you'll see the frame rate represented as 12 fps." The students confirmed this with a gentle nod.

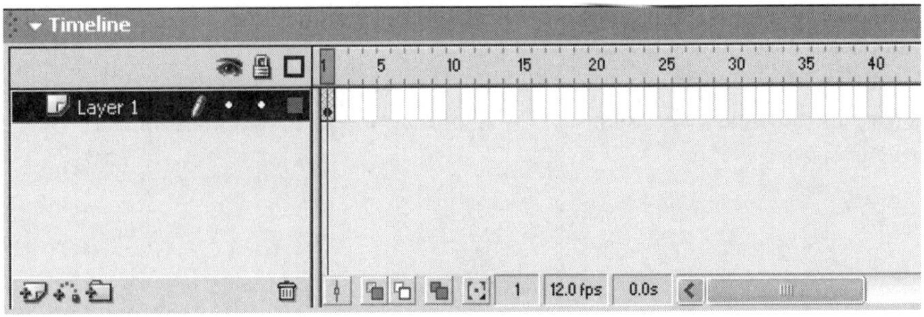

"The numbers at the top of this area represent the frame numbers. Given the frame rate of 12 fps, we can currently see just over 5 seconds of time in the timeline. At the moment, though, because I have no content on my stage, the frames are blank. In a moment I'll fill them with something."

"What's the red thingy highlighting frame 1?" Gemma asked.

"I was just getting to that, Gemma," I said. "That is called the **playhead**. The playhead shows you the current position in the animation. When a Flash movie has a number of frames, the playhead can be dragged along the timeline and the content of that frame is shown on the stage. Let's see how this works."

I opened the Flash movie `lesson01_timeline.fla`. "This timeline has 12 frames, or a second's worth.

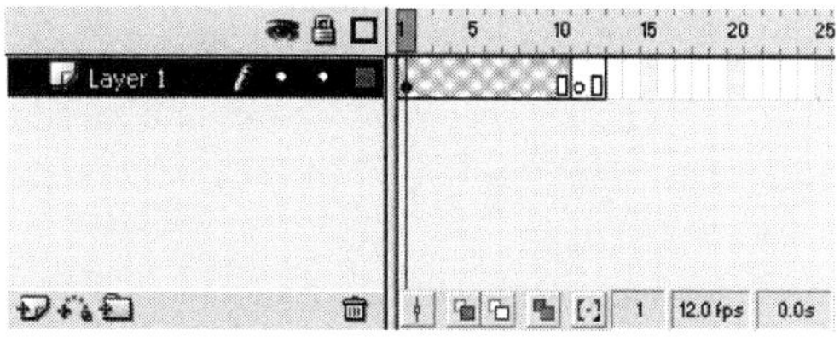

"If I click any of the frames in the timeline, the playhead will move to that frame. Alternatively, you can click and drag the playhead to view the frames." I dragged the playhead over the timeline. "You might have noticed that the content on the stage isn't changing much and that inspiring red square isn't that active."

"You can say that again!" Carl exclaimed. "I was falling asleep back here."

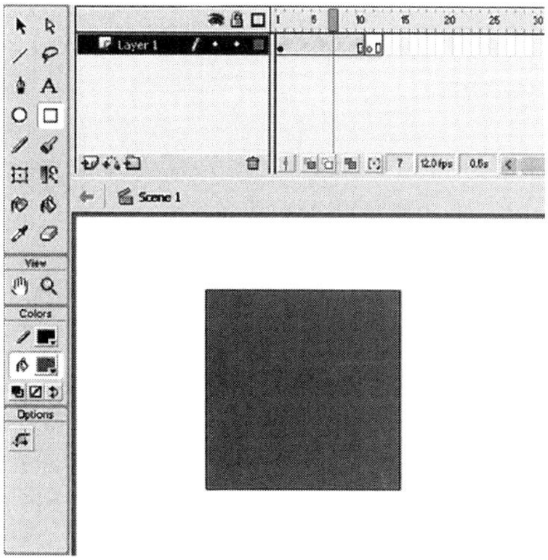

"I'm not going to make it dance just yet, Carl!" I said. "Even though this is by far the most unexciting introduction to Flash, it will help you all to distinguish between the different types of frames in Flash. Frames in Flash come in two main flavors: **keyframes** and normal **frames**."

"You just said frames too many times," Joe said. "I'm confused!"

"Bear with me, Joe, it will all be clear in a moment," I began. "A **keyframe** with content is indicated by a black-filled circle on the timeline, as you can see on frame 1 here. A keyframe is where something significant happens in the Flash timeline, and normal frames are used to prolong the content of the keyframe. In this Flash file, the black circle on frame 1 shows that frame 1 has content, and the following frames, up to frame 10, are gray to show that they've inherited the content of the keyframe.

"An **empty keyframe**, like the one on frame 11, is represented by an unfilled circle. It's very important to know that you can only create or edit content on keyframes. When you first open a blank Flash movie, you'll notice that you're given one blank keyframe to start with. Normal frames are used to extend the content of the keyframes, and they can't be edited.

"Normal frames don't have any signifying icons, but a sequence of them will appear as a gray or white mass, with the end of the sequence signified by a square, as seen on frames 10 or 12. Now, who can tell me what we might see on frame 11?"

I looked at Joe expectantly. After a hesitant pause, he answered, "There isn't anything on frame 11 because it's an unfilled circle." He paused and thought for a moment. "It's an empty keyframe." I nodded to Joe to confirm his answer.

"Mazzy, what do you think would happen to it if we were to place content onto the blank keyframe?" I asked.

"I guess it would be a blank keyframe no longer," Mazzy replied. "Maybe the circle would be filled to show that it had content."

"That's correct," I replied. "Any normal white frames following the keyframe will then turn gray because they're replicating the new content of the keyframe. We'll have a go inserting some keyframes next when we look at the tools."

"Cool!" Carl said. "Let's get stuck in!"

Before I had a chance to move on, Jim spoke. "Ken, are you going to talk about layers now? I guess they're linked to the timeline, right?"

"Why don't you introduce them to the class, Jim?" I said.

"Uh . . . sure, if you think that's okay, Ken," Jim replied. "Feel free to help me out if things have changed since Flash 5 and my memory has given way."

"Just give us an insight," I said.

"Layers are used to separate and organize content on the timeline and stage," Jim said. "They allow you to place content at different depth levels and to have multiple timelines and frame sequences." Jim turned to look at me. "Was that right, Ken?"

"I think that's great for now, Jim," I replied. "We'll cover layers a little later, but it's good to be aware of them for now. It sometimes helps to think of them in an animation sense—like each layer is a separate sheet of acetate."

Various panels

I put the last image on the projector and began, "The final elements of the Flash interface—the panels—are usually located on the right side of the screen.

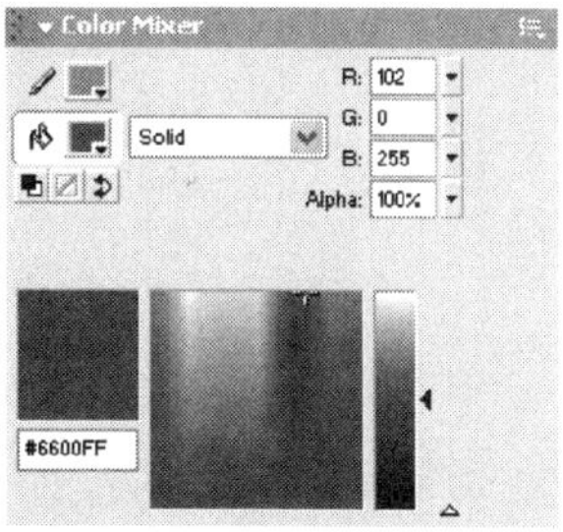

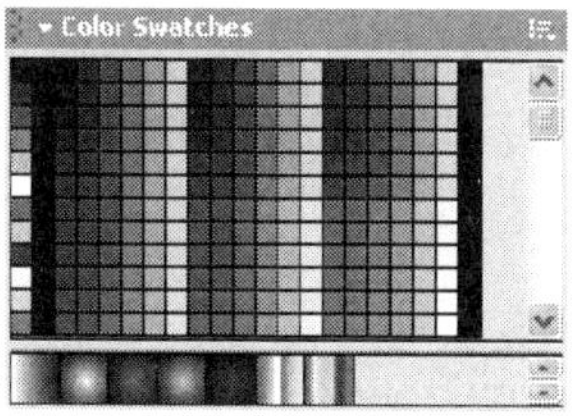

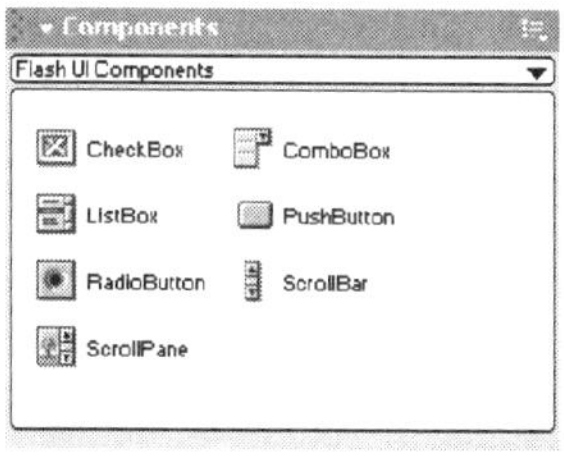

"These panels have many functions to make working in Flash easier. Each panel performs a different task, from resizing an object to mixing some new colors. Although you can only see the default panels now, there are many, many more available."

"How will we know which ones will be of any use?" Joe asked.

"Because the emphasis of this class is programming, we aren't going to cover them all, Joe. But I guarantee that we'll look at a few essential panels later in the class, one of which you will find yourself using more and more throughout the course."

Carl raised his hand. "Which one is that, Teach?" he asked.

"The most important panel for our class, Carl," I started, "is the Actions panel. The Actions panel is the one where we'll do all of our programming and coding."

Carl's eyes focused on the monitor. "I can't see it!" He paused. "I guess it's not a default panel, then."

"That's right," I said. "We'll open the Actions panel in the next class and look at it in considerable detail." Carl nodded.

Tools

For many of the students, this part of the class would be their first hands-on experience with the Flash MX software. I wanted them to feel comfortable enough with it, ready to program with ActionScript in coming classes.

"Now it's your turn to try out a few of the tools in Flash MX," I said. "Although we won't use them all, I want you to experience how they work firsthand and get your hands dirty. Your homework for this week will involve using the toolbar; so if you have any questions, please don't hesitate to ask.

"Open the Flash application if it isn't already open and create a new document with **File > New**. You'll start by drawing a quick shape or two. Before you do, notice how there is a blank keyframe on Layer 1. Now select the Oval tool from the toolbar. The Oval tool is used to draw primitive circular or oval shapes. To use it, press and hold the mouse button to draw a circle on the stage.

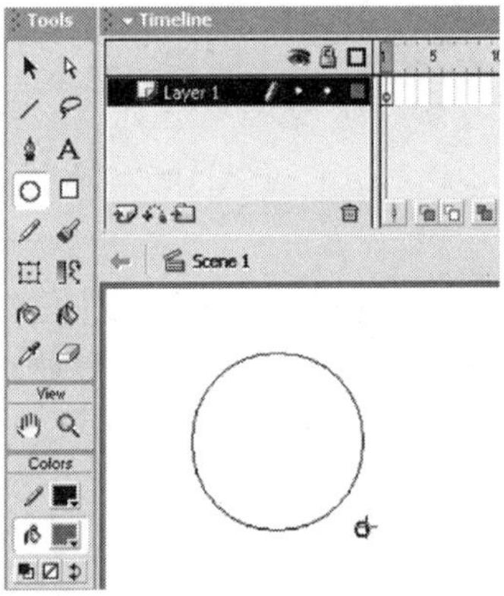

"When you're happy with your shape, release the mouse button and a oval shape is drawn for you. Oval shapes can be drawn with or without fills, or with or without outlines as required. We'll see how in a moment."

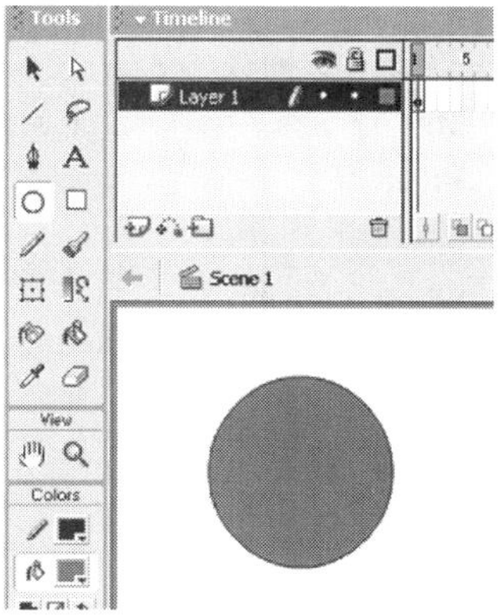

"Wow!" Joe said. "It may only be a circle, but it sure does fill me with a sense of achievement. It beats drawing a circle with a darn protractor or around the edge of a bowl."

"It sure does. Did you all notice that the blank keyframe is now filled? As I mentioned earlier, this has happened because the keyframe now has some much-needed content," I said.

"Even if it is a boring circle," Carl said. "How about showing us where the doodle tool is, Teach?"

"I presume you mean the Pencil tool?" Gemma asked. "It's the next tool down from the Oval tool." Gemma turned to me. "Sorry, Ken, I guess I got carried away trying out all the tools."

"No need to apologize, Gemma. Experimentation is the key," I said. "If you'd all like to try out some of the tools right now, I'll give you a little while to play with them." The students nodded enthusiastically, with the exception of Joe.

"I'd like you to show me some of them, Ken," Joe said. "I don't really know where to start with them, so a few pointers might help."

"Okay, Joe," I said, "but for now, all I want you to do is experiment, so, just as you did with the Oval tool, try clicking some of the tools to select them from the toolbar and then see what they can do. You can change the color of the fill or outline by clicking in the two color boxes at the bottom of the toolbar."

"That sounds easy enough, Ken" said Joe, looking relieved.

"Well, it *is* easy," I said, smiling. "Remember, you don't need to know what all of the tools do. In fact, we could probably get away with using just a couple of them throughout the entire course. The emphasis of this course is programming, not knowing all of Flash MX's capabilities."

The class fell silent as all the students began experimenting with the tools. After a while, I walked over to Joe to see how he was doing.

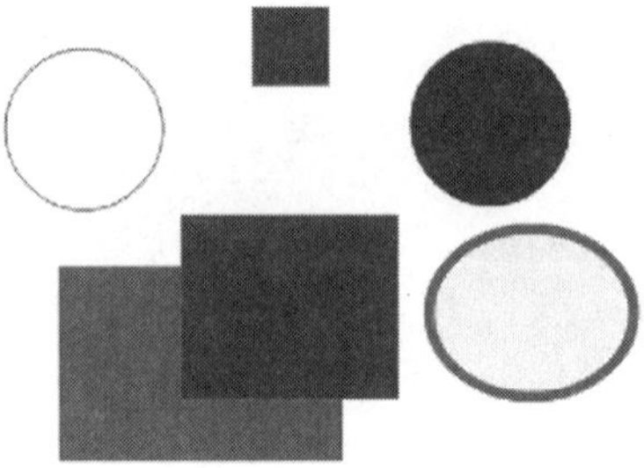

"I've drawn a lot of circles and squares so far!" Joe said. "Some of the tools are a little too cryptic for me to understand."

I leaned down a little and whispered, "Don't worry, I'll be giving out a handout at the end of the class!"

Joe whistled furtively and winked theatrically in my direction. I returned to the head of the class.

"Even if some of you have benefited from that quick bout of freedom, there are a few tools which are essential for all Flash use so I'm going to run through them now," I resumed. "Let's start with arguably the most important: the Arrow tool."

The Arrow tool

I ran my mouse cursor over the Arrow tool in the toolbar.

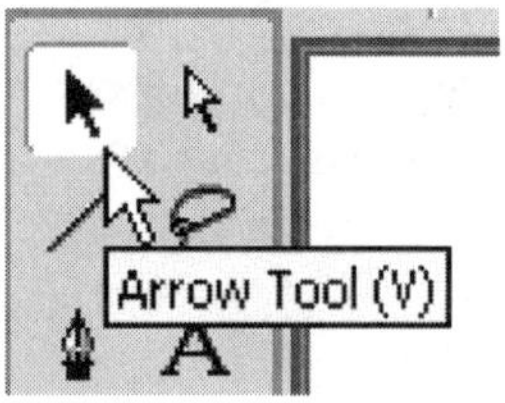

"The Arrow tool is considerably important because it is the Flash selection tool, and to do almost anything in Flash you have to be fully confident of its function. How many of you have selected files on your desktop to move from one place to another?" I asked. Many of the students nodded. I continued, "You might have done this in any number of ways, but the end result is always the same: you select a single file or a number of them.

"In Flash, you need to select items before you can manipulate them, move them, and so on. If you've drawn a square and want to move it later, you need to select it." I opened a new Flash movie and drew a quick square on the stage. "There are a number of ways to do this that we need to look at.

"The first method is to press and drag to draw a selection box. Please give this a try. Draw a shape first, and then drag a selection box to cover the whole shape. It's usually easiest to start dragging from the top left of the shape you want to select.

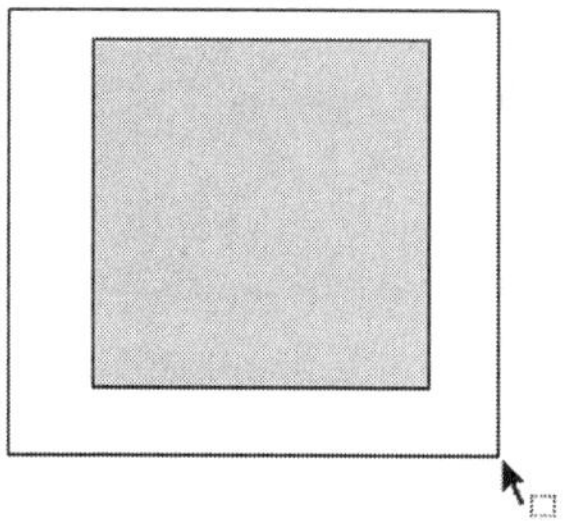

"If you have all done this correctly, the shape will be selected and it will now have a dotted texture like this."

"I got a dotted texture . . ." Joe started.

"It's a Lichtenstein!" Mazzy cried.

Joe continued, "Um . . . only a piece of my square is dotted."

"This might be because you didn't draw a selection box big enough to cover the whole of the square, Joe. Anything captured within the selection box is then selected," I said. "Do you mind if we take a look?" Joe nodded and I switched the projector to show the contents of his monitor.

"Does everyone understand what Joe's problem was here?" I asked.

"By drawing a smaller selection box," Gemma started, "you've selected only a portion of it. To remedy this, draw a selection box bigger than the shape and it will all be selected. Give it a try, Joe." Joe nodded and the rest of the class turned to watch the projector.

"While Joe is trying to master that," I said, "why don't the rest of you try to mimic what Joe has done? Joe has actually preempted the next step of the exercise." Joe smiled proudly.

"The thing to remember is that anything captured within the selection box will become selected," I said.

"Do we make multiple selections using the SHIFT key, Ken?" Gemma asked.

"Yes, Gemma," I replied. "To make more than one selection, hold down the SHIFT key and draw another selection box. When you're done with your next selection box, release the mouse button and you'll have an added selection. Try it out until you're comfortable with it, adding as many new selections as you want."

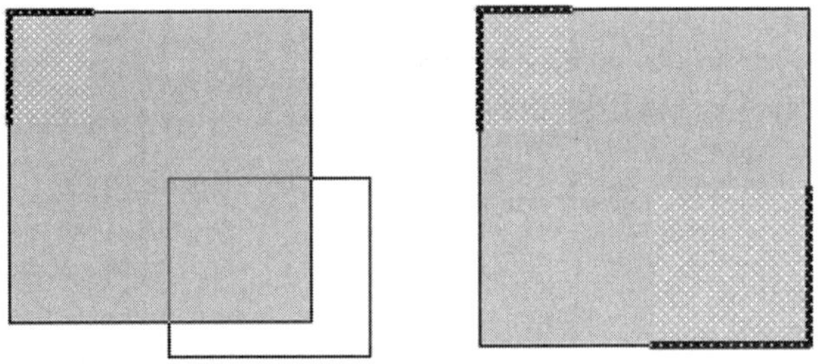

"When can I take my finger off the SHIFT key?" Mazzy asked.

"Once you've released the mouse button, you can let go of SHIFT!" I responded.

"Oh, right!" Mazzy said, freeing her hand and shaking it back to life. "I felt like my finger was glued down for a minute there."

"Now that you all have stiff fingers and experience with the selection box, we'll move on to the next method of selection, click-based selection," I said. "The difference between this method and the previous one is that this tecnique allows you to click any object directly, and it's handy for situations in which you have many objects in the same vicinity.

"First, click away from your shape to deselect it. Now, click once at the center of your shape. The keen-eyed among you might notice that only the inner shape—or fill—is selected, while the shape's outline—or stroke—is deselected. This is because you clicked only once. A double-click will select both the shape and its outline. Try it out now."

"So the shape and outline aren't actually connected?" Carl asked.

"Well Carl, yes and no," I replied. "When your shapes were first drawn using the Oval or Rectangle tool, Flash used a default stroke and fill color. Any primitive shape like this is in fact made of two elements: the stroke or outline, and the fill.

"This is a good time to talk a little about vectors and to show you how the **Property inspector** is useful," I said, and then I switched on the projector and selected my square.

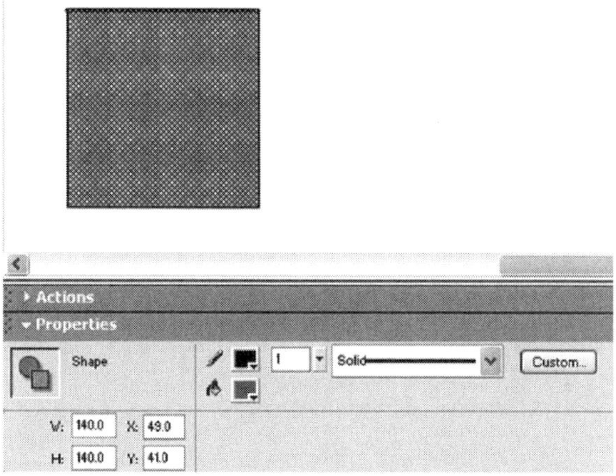

"As soon as I selected the square, the Property inspector immediately changed from its previous state to show me some information about it. Who'd like to tell me what it shows us about the square?"

Gemma volunteered, "It tells us how big the square is, through its width and height."

"That's right, Gemma. The W and H fields here represent the width and height of the shape. This value represents pixels and not any value that we might read off a ruler. What else?"

"It tells us its X and Y position onscreen," Mazzy said.

"That's right, the X and Y in Flash are recorded from the top left of the stage. X represents the horizontal position and Y the vertical position. We're on a roll—who's next?" I looked to Jim.

"It appears to tell us the colors of the square," Jim said.

"That's almost right, Jim," I said. "It doesn't show us the colors of the square as a unit; it shows us the stroke and fill colors independently. A pencil icon represents the stroke color, and the paint bucket shows the fill color.

"If I click the fill color here, I'll be shown a color palette and I'll be able to change the color.

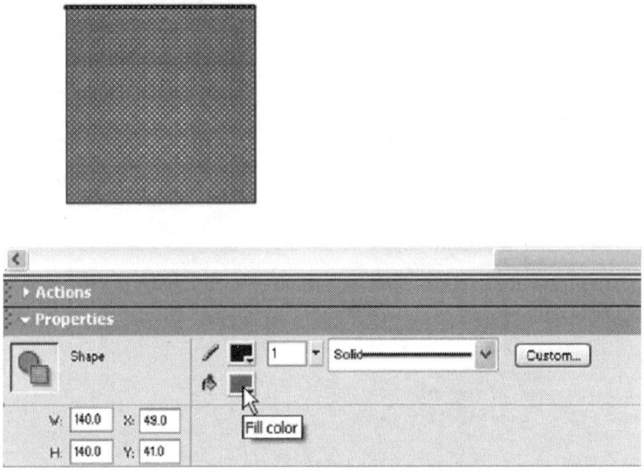

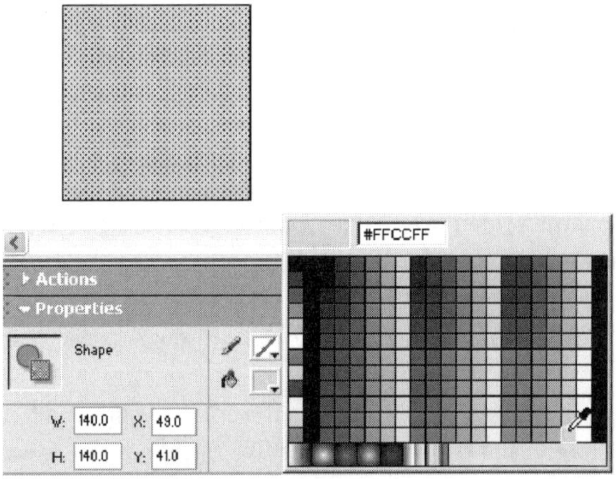

"If I select a different color, the fill color of the square is changed. This is because it functions independently of the stroke. We can change the stroke in the very same way, using the stroke color palette. Who can guess what other options are available for the stroke?"

Gemma looked around and then spoke. "I can tell you, Ken," she said, "but it's only because I know the answer from using vector packages such as Adobe Illustrator. I'm guessing that the number here represents the stroke thickness—is that right?"

"Correct, Gemma!" I said. "A line can be set at any thickness from 0.25 to 10. The default setting here is 1. What else can you tell us about the stroke options, Gemma?"

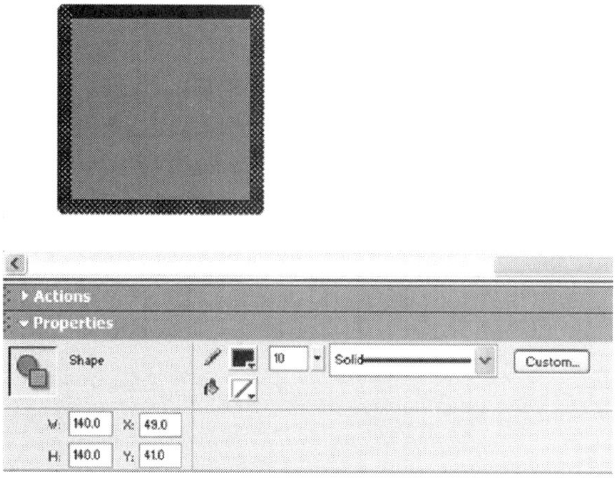

"The stroke type, I guess," Gemma said. "Each stroke can be styled differently, from a dotted line to a jagged line, depending on what you need at the time. Even though there are different options available in Illustrator, I can't say I use anything other than the normal line type. Maybe I'm not that adventurous."

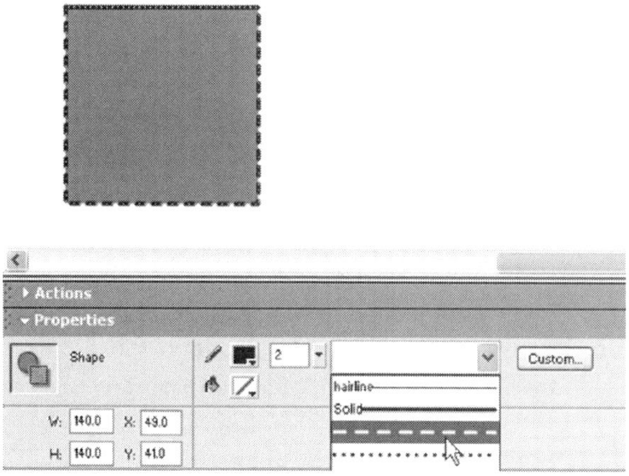

"Not at all, Gemma. For the benefits of the course, we'll stick to the normal line type. It will be more than we need." I paused. "Does anyone have any questions about the Property inspector or strokes or fills?" The class synchronized the shaking of their heads. "If anyone has any problems with vectors during the course, please see Gemma," I laughed. Gemma gave me a pseudo-death stare.

The Text tool

"The next whistle-stop is the Text tool," I started. "Although this tool is pretty straightforward, it does have hidden depths. For now, you only need to be aware of its most basic use, as we'll be using it from time to time during the course. Select the Text tool, which is represented by the letter A, from the toolbar and take a look at the Property inspector.

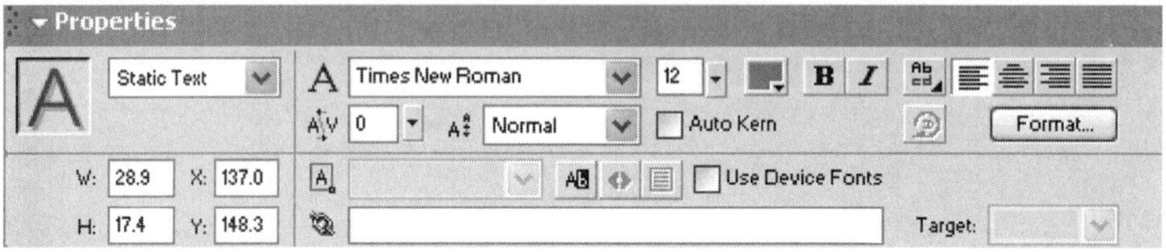

"Not only does the Property inspector show us information about objects, but also it has options for some of the tools in the toolbar. It's **context sensitive**. Hopefully, this will show you its importance within Flash.

"You use the Text tool by clicking anywhere on the stage or work area to create a new text field and just typing into it."

I turned to Carl and asked, "How am I doing, Carl?"

"That's pretty lame, Teach," Carl laughed. "You're a little out of touch with the scene."

I laughed. "Oh well, can't win 'em all." I turned to address the class. "Use the Property inspector to change the font, size, or color of the text. That's about all you need to know about text fields for now—you will learn more about them in future classes."

The muffled sound of drums and electric guitars suddenly filled the air, followed by the screeching of a chair on the floor, and the class turned to observe Carl packing up his bags in speedy fashion.

"We're into overtime now, Teach, and I want to go check out who's playing," Carl groaned, standing up and wearing his backpack. "I should be kicking out the jams about now." Carl attempted a scissors kick, almost falling over in the process.

"One more minute, Carl and we're done, I promise," I said, containing my laughter. "Before you all go, though, I have that homework for you. And anyway, I thought you were getting a lift back with Mazzy?"

Carl sat back down, saying, "Sorry, Mazzy, I'd forgotten about that . . . would it be possible for me to just quickly go and see who's there?"

"That should be fine," said Mazzy with a smile. "I was going to go and see if I could find Professor Jeffries for a quick chat anyway. I'll meet you by the car. It's a green station wagon."

"Okay, for homework," I continued, "I want you all to create a self-portrait in Flash." This was met with an even split of fright and excitement. "You're free to use any of the tools in the toolbar, any of the panels, or anything else you can find. The only restriction is that you keep the portrait as a static image, so for those of you who know how to animate in Flash," I looked at Jim, "stay away from it.

"Once you're happy with your masterpiece, save it using **File > Save** and bring it in on a floppy or zip disk next week, ready for a little show and tell." The same half of the class groaned in unison. "Is that all clear? On your way out, don't forget to pick up a Flash trial CD and, to help you with your homework, I've prepared a handout for you. It's a tools reference sheet with information about all the significant tools." I paused and with relish said, "Class dismissed!"

With that, Carl leapt from his chair and bolted for the door, leaving it flapping in his wake.

"You couldn't take a Flash CD for Carl could you, Mazzy?" I asked.

"No problem," she smiled, and the rest of the class stood and began packing up for the evening.

Summary

Today's lesson was all about introductions: introductions to the students and an introduction to Flash MX.

- You learned that Flash started life as an animation program, but that it has evolved into a powerful web application tool. It creates small files that can load quickly on the Web.

- One of the reasons that Flash files are so small is that Flash uses vector files rather than bitmaps:

  - Vector files are defined by mathematical coordinates.
  - Bitmaps are made up of picture elements or pixels.

- You learned about the Flash MX interface and discovered some of its most important elements, including the following:

  - **The stage:** This is where you place anything that you want to be seen in your Flash presentation.

  - **The Property inspector:** This displays information about whichever object is selected at the time.

  - **The timeline:** This controls the time at which events happen in Flash and is also used to control the navigation of a Flash movie.

  - **Frames and keyframes:** Single units of time are represented in Flash as frames. A keyframe is where something significant happens in the Flash timeline, and normal frames are used to prolong the content of the keyframe.

  - **The Arrow tool:** This is used to select objects so that they can be manipulated. It's possible to select more than one object using the Arrow tool by holding SHIFT as you select.

Class 2
The Kiosk Project

Objectives

In today's class, you'll learn about

- The case study
- The project life cycle
- Interface design

Introduction

I welcomed the class in for their second lesson, and started almost the moment they'd all sat down. "Good evening, everyone. As I mentioned last week, today's class is going to be focused entirely on the case study that we'll be working on for the rest of the course. Normally, this would be a website project that I'd come up with, but this time we have the chance to do something quite different."

I looked around the class to see if I'd piqued anyone's interest, and a few students did look a little intrigued. I was about to reveal my surprise when Carl called out, "This doesn't mean we'll be climbing any mountains like your last class, does it, Teach?"

"You can count me out of that, my boy!" said Mazzy, chuckling. Feeling slightly deflated, I continued, "No Carl, we won't be climbing any mountains, but we won't be making a website either. We'll be doing something a little different, so I wanted to run it by you all first to make sure you agree with it, rather than forcing it on you. So far then, are you with me?"

"Aye, aye, Cap'n!" called out Carl, and the rest of the class started laughing and doing bad pirate impersonations. I could tell this was going to be a long lesson.

The Kiosk project

When they'd calmed down a bit, and the main antics were over, I continued. "Okay, at the end of last week's class, Mazzy approached me and we chatted about a photographer friend of hers who runs a gallery a couple of blocks away." I turned to Mazzy, "Feel free to stop me and fill in any blanks I leave." She nodded her assent. I continued, "The gallery is small . . . ."

"With room for about 10 or maybe 15 pictures without feeling cramped," Mazzy cut in.

". . . and it consists entirely of photographs taken by the owner," I continued. "The problem is that with a gallery this small, there's no room to display the whole collection, so potential buyers won't be able to see all that there is to offer. Knowing that Mazzy had taken a course in HTML, the photographer asked her if she would be able to create a **kiosk** for him that he could have in the middle of the gallery and use to display all of the pictures that he doesn't have room for on the walls." I noticed that Gemma's hand had gone up during that last sentence. "Yes, Gemma?"

"Excuse me, but what is a 'kiosk' in this context?" Gemma asked.

"A kiosk here is a computer display, typically set to run only one program, that the public can use to get information. Usually, a kiosk has a simplified interface—a touch screen for example—but in this case I presume we'll just be using the standard keyboard and mouse, or maybe just a mouse with the keyboard hidden or locked away somewhere."

"Oh, yes, I know what you mean," Gemma replied. "I used a touch screen device at the visitor information center when I was on vacation last summer."

"Good. Is everybody else happy with kiosks and what they are?" I asked, and the class nodded that they were. "Okay, so to recap, the case study would be a browsable gallery of pictures on a kiosk in the shop. Customers would then use this kiosk to view the entire catalog of images, rather than only those that were on display.

"So what do you all think of this case study idea? After all, there's no point doing something if you're not going to get anything out of it in the end. From my point of view, I'm happy that you can learn all the course requirements from it, but in my experience, you guys will be more motivated if you can work on something that is relevant to you."

Accepting the project

I decided to work my way around the class to see if the project met with the approval of all the students. I started with Carl. "The first thing that springs to mind for you, Carl, is that you'll be able create a gallery on your website with pictures of all the killer gigs that your band has played recently. What do you think?"

"Yeah . . . I can see it now," Carl replied, with a faraway look in his eyes, "a virtual gallery that you can walk around and stop and stare at pictures of us in action. We could have our music pumping round the halls too. Cool."

"As cool as that no doubt would be," I cut in, "I think it might be a little too advanced for us at the moment. It's possible to create 3D environments in Flash, but it's a lot easier to create them in a dedicated program. I was thinking of something a little bit simpler—say, a grid of thumbnail-sized images on one half of the screen that you could browse through. Then you could click an image that interests you to see it displayed at a larger size on the other half of the screen. We'll have to get the exact details from the photographer, but this is my general idea."

"I guess that would still be okay," Carl replied. "Will I still be able to have the music playing in the background, though?"

"Yes, that's simple enough to do," I responded. "I guess you could also use the same principles to create a simple jukebox. The songs are displayed on one side, and you click them to have some details about them displayed on the other side and to start the songs playing."

"That *would* be cool," said Carl. "Okay, I'm definitely for this project, and I'll fight anyone who says otherwise!" Carl said with a smile, putting his fists up in a mock boxing pose.

"I was hoping we could settle things more democratically," I replied, "but I'm glad that you want to do the project. Okay, Jim?"

"Well, although I can't see an immediate use for a gallery for me, personally," Jim began, "I can see that it's something that a lot of other people would be interested in, so it's a skill I'd love to be able to add to my portfolio when I become a web designer. So yes, I'm all for it."

"Great. Okay, Gemma?" I asked.

Gemma paused for a while before answering, "I'm afraid I might have to fight things out with Carl. I don't really see how a gallery like this would be useful for my company's clients. But then, as I've said before, I can't really see how Flash is going to be that useful. The great majority of my company's work is still print based, and everything else has been fine in Dreamweaver—I can even see how this gallery could be done in Dreamweaver."

I was about to try and answer some of her worries when she continued, "Although actually . . ." She seemed to be remembering something. "I know that some of the clients have been asking us to make kiosks for them. So, I guess if it's a choice between creating a website, which I know I can make anyway, or making a kiosk, which I've never made before, I'd have to vote for the kiosk."

"Okay, I agree with your ultimate reasoning, though I'm not sure about the method you took to get there," I said with a smile. "I won't try and convince you of the benefits of Flash again, though—I'll just let you find out for yourself.

"Right, Joe, you're up next, and I think you might well be the easiest person to persuade on this."

"Yep," Joe replied, "this would be perfect for me. I want a kiosk to advertise my stock in the store in the same way this photographer does. The only difference for me is that I want to be able to add a little more functionality to it. I'd like people to be able to keep a record of the things that they want and then be able to tally that up at the end."

"Don't forget," I cut in, "that we haven't got all of the details of the case study yet. You may well find that there's more functionality to come."

"Good point," said Joe, "I'll keep mum until all the facts are out."

"Mazzy," I continued, "I know you're keen to do this site for your friend anyway, but is there anything in it that you can think of that would make it useful in your own work?"

"Well, actually, there is something that I've been thinking about recently," Mazzy began. "My local amateur dramatics society is putting on a production of *Oklahoma!* just over a month from now, and I was thinking of putting together a simple information page to go on the community website that I keep. This could be a great method of showing shots from dress rehearsals to get people interested in it."

"Are you part of the production?" I inquired.

"You'll just have to come see it to find out," she said with a grin.

"Go on, just a hint," prompted Jim.

"All I'm going to tell you is that it's quite a big part. If you want to know any more, then tickets are $5 each," she said.

"Aw, come on," Jim pleaded, but Mazzy's lips were sealed.

"No, I can't reveal any more, but there is something I've been wondering about, Ken," Mazzy said. "The pictures from *Oklahoma!* will most likely be quite big, and I don't want people to get frustrated waiting for them to download, but I don't like those little thumbnails you get on so many websites—they seem awfully small to me. Is there a way that we can make the thumbnails big enough so that I can look through them without having to open up the full-size image?"

"Yes, that will be no problem at all," I replied. "We'll be making the thumbnails ourselves, so we can make them whatever size is suitable. We can discuss this in more detail when we start to put the case study together.

"Okay, Mazzy," I continued, "was there anything else that you wanted to add?"

"Actually, there was one more thing that I wanted to ask about. I would be more interested in putting my photos on the Internet rather than having them on a kiosk. Would it still be possible for me to use this kiosk device to display pictures on my home page?"

"Good question," I replied. "The program that we'll be writing will work fine on a web page or a kiosk, but there could be a problem with file size. As you no doubt know, files can take a long time to download over the Internet, and a set of high-quality photographs could take an awfully long time indeed." I paused. "This could get a little confusing, so we can discuss it in a later lesson if you'd prefer?"

Mazzy thought for a second and then replied, "I'm interested in hearing a little more about it now. Could you continue, and I'll stop you if it goes too far over my head?"

"Yep, that would be fine. Okay, one of the big advantages of a kiosk is that everything is stored on the computer, so it's quick and easy to access. We can bundle the program and all of the pictures into one large file and load it all at once. This keeps everything neat and allows us to quickly access the information that we want.

"This method, though, wouldn't work very well on the Internet, because it would take an awfully long time to download the whole program before you could view the pictures. A more sensible strategy for the Internet is to keep all of the pictures separate from the program, and then just download them when they're required. The problem with doing it this way is that it takes some difficult coding, and I think it's more than we can cover in this course. I can certainly provide some pointers at the end of the course if you'd like to explore this option, though." Mazzy and a few other students agreed that this would be useful, so I I made a note to myself that I would discuss this in detail at the end of the course.

The students learn about customizing the kiosk for the Internet in **Class 12.**

I continued, "The other problem with putting all of the images onto the Internet is that we have to look into image compression to get the pictures at the smallest file size without sacrificing the quality too much, and I'm afraid that's beyond the scope of this class. Does that sound okay?" I asked Mazzy.

"Yes, that's understandable," she replied. "I did some experiments with compression in one of my digital photography classes, and that took a long time. I can see why it would take a significant chunk out of our course. Also, the more complicated programming doesn't sound that enticing to me at the moment, but maybe it will at the end of the course. I think if you can give us those pointers then, that would be the best compromise."

"That's fine," I said, "I've made a note so I won't forget. Okay, is that everyone? Any questions? Yes, Jim?" I noticed Jim had his hand up.

"Yes, Ken, something's just occurred to me," said Jim. "One thing that immediately springs to mind is, will I be able to do the same thing, but with animation? I was imagining having a set of thumbnails of stills that, when you click them, play an animation in the main view area. Do you think that would be possible?"

"Yes," I replied, "that should, in fact, be quite easy to achieve. We'll have to make a few small alterations, and add a little bit of extra code, but nothing too difficult."

"Excellent!" said Jim. "That would really make my portfolio stand out from the crowd. This definitely gets my vote."

The project life cycle

"Okay then, that's everyone," I said. "We all seem to be in agreement that this will be an interesting and useful case study.

"Probably without realizing it, what we've done here is complete the first stage of the **project life cycle**. This is simply a structure for ensuring that a project is developed in a methodical and sensible manner. Just as you shouldn't build a house without proper plans, or bake a cake without a recipe in mind, you shouldn't start programming without first planning out what it is the program will do.

"There are six steps in the project life cycle, and we'll be covering all of them in the course of this project. These steps are . . ." I turned and wrote them on the whiteboard as I spoke.

- Accepting the project
- Defining the problem
- Designing the program output
- Breaking the problem into logical steps
- Writing the code
- Testing the code

"As I said, we've just completed the first stage—we've all accepted the project. This may seem like a pointless stage to have, but there's often more to it than we've encountered here. In this stage, you also need to bear in mind whether or not you have the correct tools, enough time, the right budget, and so on. It just so happens that in our case, I know we have all of these things.

"You may also have noticed that the actual programming doesn't take place until the penultimate stage in the cycle. Unfortunately for the hasty among you, this is true. You'll be glad to know, though, that we'll cover the steps in between in no time.

"I'll see if the photographer can come in next week to talk to you all and discuss exactly what it is that he wants us to do. We can then move on to the second stage of the cycle."

"Actually," Mazzy cut in, "he doesn't live far from here. I could give him a call and see if he can come in tonight for a little while if you like."

"That would great," I replied. "Okay, if you can do that now, then in the meantime the rest of us can take a look at some of the faces that I asked you to create for homework last week."

Everyone turned to their bags to retrieve their disks, and I walked over to talk to Mazzy. "You can use the phone in the office just behind this classroom. Do you think he'll be able to come in tonight?"

She replied, "When I spoke to him about it last week, he told me to call him and let him know what our decision was as soon as we made it, so I don't think he has any plans for this evening. And anyway, he's a nice enough guy, so I'm sure he wouldn't mind popping in. What time should I ask him to come over?"

"I've got a couple of things that I want to talk to the class about before he arrives, so do you think 20 to 25 minutes would be okay?" I asked.

"I'll try him and see," Mazzy said. At that moment, there was an explosion of laughter from the back as Jim saw the picture that Carl had drawn. "Let me know how it goes," I said to Mazzy. "I'd better stop a war from breaking out." She left and I turned to face the class.

"Okay everyone, settle down. Jim, what's so funny back there?" Jim tried his best to stifle his laughter and speak. "Nothing, Ken," he said. "I was just marveling at the uncanny likeness between Carl's portrait and the real him."

"It's not a portrait of me now," Carl argued. "It's a picture of what I'm going to look like when my hair is long enough to style properly."

This I couldn't wait to see. "That sounds intriguing, Carl. Would you mind if I put it up on the projector for the rest of the class to see?" I asked.

"Sure, go ahead and laugh," Carl said in a surly tone. "Just as long as I get to laugh at Jim's too." He glared at Jim defiantly.

I addressed the class. "These pictures were only for fun and for you all to familiarize yourselves with Flash's drawing tools. I'm not going to force you to show your pictures if you don't want to, but I'd like a couple of people to volunteer to tell us about the tools and techniques that they used, and to have their picture displayed to the whole class. So, any volunteers?"

Jim immediately spoke out, "I guess I owe it to Carl to go first." I switched the projector to display his monitor, and Carl immediately guffawed. "You look like a girl!" he called out.

"Thanks, Carl," said Jim. "I think it's really good," said Gemma, smiling at Jim. "I like the way that your sweater matches the color of your eyes."

"Why thank you, Gemma," Jim smiled back.

"Okay," I cut in, "would you like to tell us a little about how you drew it, Jim?"

"I found it quite difficult to get the hang of at first," Jim began. "I started off drawing everything on the same layer and soon ran into trouble because I kept trying to move or redraw things and leaving great white gaps where Flash had merged the pieces that I was moving. In the end, I started again, this time keeping the different elements on different layers. "

Jim showed us his Flash timeline over the projector.

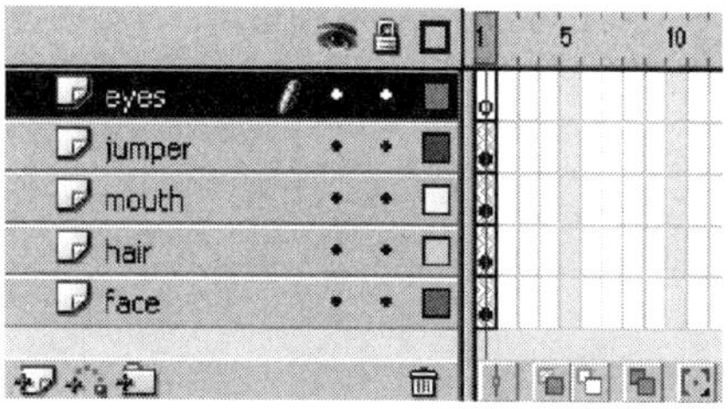

"That worked a lot better, and things soon began to take shape," he continued. "I also played around with the different line styles to try and achieve different textures. There's something not quite right about it that I can't put my finger on, though."

"You've got no ears," Mazzy said bluntly, and the whole class broke out in laughter.

Finally, Jim admitted defeat. "You've got a point there, Mazzy," he conceded. "That may be just what it's missing."

We took a look at Carl's picture.

"I can tell you what's wrong here!" Jim said. Carl sighed. "You don't have a Mohawk haircut! This looks nothing like you."

"It's how I'm hoping to look in 6 months time," Carl said. "It's a future portrait, if you like. At the moment I'm growing it so that it's long enough to get huge spikes."

"I bet your mother won't like it!" Mazzy said. "I can't imagine why anyone would like such a grungy haircut."

"Actually, it would be a punk haircut," I said. "I had one of those myself! It's been a few years since then, though." I laughed. "Carl, would you like to tell us how you made this future portrait?"

Carl nodded. "It might sound lazy, but I just used the Brush tool for this. I liked the way that it's thick and magic-marker-like. My first rendition of this was limited a little using the Oval tool to get the head shape, but I soon found that I preferred the freehand method."

I displayed Joe's portrait on the projector. "I suppose you could say that I stuck with the Oval tool," Joe said.

"As you can see, this picture has ovals and circles all over it," Joe said. "Everything from the pupils to the eyes to the shape of my head."

"I love the way you've drawn the beard," said Jim.

"I did that for posterity," Joe laughed. "My wife keeps getting at me to shave it, so I promised her that I'd get it cut before the end of the month. You never know, you might not recognize me the next time you see me!"

We had just finished discussing the merits of Joe's beard when Mazzy walked back into the room. "How'd it go?" I asked. "Pretty good," she replied. "He'll be over in 5 to 10 minutes or so."

The requirements document

"That doesn't give us very long. No problem, thanks Mazzy." I waited for Mazzy to take her seat again and then continued, "Right, everyone. There are a couple of things that I want to talk to you about before the photographer arrives." I paused. "By the way, Mazzy, what is his name? I can't go on calling him 'the photographer' forever."

"It's Randall," she replied.

"Okay," I continued, "before Randall turns up, we have to decide what it is that we're going to ask him. This is the second stage of our project life cycle: defining the problem. We do this by compiling what's known as a **requirements document**. This is basically a statement of what the program will do and, for a real-world commission, how much it will cost and when it will be completed by. So, for starters, I would like you all to make notes of any important facts that you think Randall mentions when he comes in to talk to us. We'll then compile all of this information at the end of class and make sure that we're happy with the information that we have. We'll then pass our requirements document on to Randall for him to check and make sure that we're covering everything that he wants us to. In a large project, this document can pass back and forth between the client and the programmer many times before both parties agree to it and sign it.

"So, what sort of things do we think we need to get out of him?"

"How about a brief description of what he envisions the program doing, or is that too broad?" Jim asked.

"No," I replied, "it's often worth starting with the simplest questions and then burrowing into more detail from there. Okay, what else?"

"What kind of photos he displays?" called out Gemma.

"What kind of customers he usually receives?" asked Joe.

"How he currently deals with pictures that aren't on display?" offered Jim.

We had put together a list of about ten questions when there was a knock on the classroom door.

"Come in," I called. The door opened, and a man poked his head around the door. "Is this the programming class?" he asked. "Indeed it is," I replied and walked over to meet him. "You must be Randall. My name's Ken," I said, shaking his hand, "and let me introduce you to the class." I walked him to the front of the class, and then pointed out the various names and faces. "Don't worry if you forget them all," I said. "It took me a good couple of years of new classes before I perfected the necessary Jedi mind trick to put names to faces the first time." He chuckled as I continued, "Can I get you a cup of coffee or something?"

"No thanks," he replied, "The reason I came over so quickly is because I need to get away quite soon. It's a full moon tonight, and I want to drive over to the hills and see if I can get some good pictures."

"We'll try not to keep you too long," I told him, "We only need some preliminary information from you, and then you're free to go. If it's okay with you, can we compile the information that we gather tonight and then you can check it and make sure we've got everything right before we go any further?" He nodded his agreement.

"Okay then, Randall, let's begin," I said. "We've heard a little bit about what you do from Mazzy, but it might be best to hear a little more from you in person. Tell us something about your business."

"Sure thing. Well, first things first, I guess," Randall said, clearing his throat. "My name's Randall Holmes and my photography business is called Randall Holmes Photography. Before you get comfortable with that, most friends and clients call me Randy, so I expect you all to start using that name. Or else! I run the business with my assistant, Jess, who helps out occasionally in the gallery and on some shoots.

"As you might have guessed, my place isn't far from here. Business is pretty good, but the rent for my space on the main street is expensive, so the premises are small. In this space, I have both the gallery and my studio, so the gallery area is limited and there's only room for a small number of pictures on the wall."

"This is where the kiosk comes in, then?" I asked.

"Sure, Ken," Randy said. "Because of the small display space and the number of photos I'd like to show off, I asked Mazzy if she would create some kind of presentation to put on a computer screen so that it could run in the gallery."

"What type of photos do you currently display in your gallery?" Gemma asked.

"Well, all sorts to be honest," Randy replied. "The range of work I do is so diverse that it's impossible to showcase them all in such a small space." Randall paused. "I suppose the work that I have on the walls probably falls into weddings and other events . . . and portraits—mostly private work. Private clients usually come into the gallery."

"Besides work for private clients, what other work do you do?" Jim asked.

"I work in all fields, from corporate and private photography to landscapes and artistic prints," said Randy.

"How do you show your work to potential corporate clients?" Jim asked.

"Unless they call into the gallery, I usually send a new set of prints to them," Randy replied. "However, it's a little expensive to do this."

"That's interesting, Randy," I said. "I think that we can probably find a way to accommodate that in our project. Maybe you could send the kiosk to clients on a CD, or it could be put on the Web."

"I'm sure that would be far less intensive than my current system. I'd definitely be interested," Randy said.

"It might be useful if you could bring us a list of all the different types of work that you undertake, so that we have an idea of all the fields we have to cover," I said. "Could you drop that by sometime this week, so we have it ready for the next class?" Randy nodded. "Please tell us something about the image of the kiosk that you have in mind, Randy."

"I guess I'm open to suggestions from you and the class here," Randy said.

"It just so happens we've already had a quick chat about this," I said. "We came up with the concept of an interactive image gallery, featuring a grid of small images that are selected to be shown at a much larger size."

"A little like a contact sheet?" Randy asked. "How appropriate!"

"I guess it does sound that way, doesn't it?" Mazzy said. "Maybe that's an angle to follow for the design of the Flash movie?"

"Certainly, Mazzy, it's definitely worth making a note of," I said. "It sits very well in the photographic context."

"I like the idea already," Randy said.

As I talked, I sketched the basic layout on the whiteboard. "I guess the contact sheet grid would be on the left, and the enlarged image would appear on the right side of the screen.

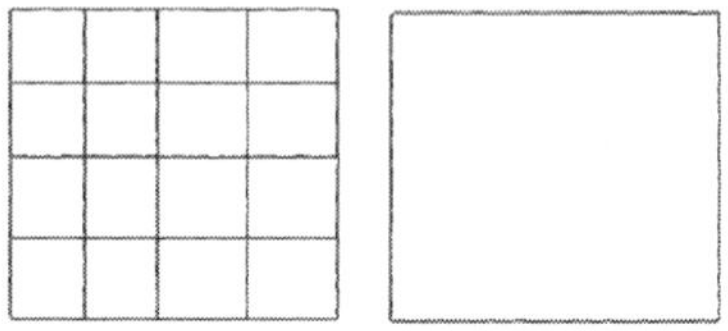

"Something simple like this I guess," I said. Randy looked concerned. "What's the problem, Randy?"

"You've got a grid of only four by four," Randy said. "I know that's just a brief sketch, but will I be limited by the number of photographs I can show?"

"Not if we allow you to show more," Gemma said. "We should be able to consider that in the construction, shouldn't we, Ken?"

"Sure, Gemma," I said. "I guess there are a number of ways that we could do this. We'll talk about this a little later in class and let you know what tactic we think is best. Is that okay, Randy?"

Randy nodded. "Because I have many different types of clients and styles of work, it would make sense to put the different types of picture together. I guess that's feasible, isn't it?"

"No problem," Carl said. "That'd work nicely for my band website too. Each member of the band could have his own set of images."

"Although that sounds like a great idea, Carl," Jim said, "I'm not sure how many photos of sweaty drummers even hard-core fans could take."

"Well, yeah. You're right there," Carl said, laughing. "It would be interesting to see which photos are most popular, though, to see if the myths about lead guitarists being sexy are true."

"What instrument do you play?" Randy asked.

Carl groaned. "Bass." He paused. "I'm the one alongside the drummer." The students, with the exception of Carl, laughed.

"Even though Carl's motives are a little questionable," I started, "I think he might have hit on something for your kiosk, Randy. If we program the kiosk to record every single photo selection, you could find out the most popular image at the end of each day."

"I could use that information to change the images on the wall and in the shop window," Randy said. "I've always wondered which photographs entice people into the shop. Even though I have my favorites from a technical point of view, they're usually not my clients' favorites. Sometimes I have to rely on my instinct."

"How often do you change the images on the walls and in the window?" I asked.

"Depending on how busy I am, usually once a week. With this information, I can show the most popular images of each week," Randy said.

"That sounds great," I said. "It might help us with the recording if you let us know what information you keep for each image. Such as name, index number, that kind of thing."

"Sure, I keep quite a strict database, but I'll get you a list of the ones you might need before next week. The most important ones I can think of right now are index, type, name, and description," said Randy.

"Can you talk us through them?" I asked.

"Sure," Randy replied. "The index is just the individual code of each printed image. It usually refers to the negative roll and individual shot.

"The type refers to the category of work that the image falls under. These types can range from weddings to family portraits to commercial work.

"The name is pretty self-explanatory—it just indicates the name of the photo if it requires one. This is important for landscapes and other images that I sell in the shop.

"The description is used for stating the content of the photo in a sentence or two. Sometimes this will describe the action in the photo, and it helps my clients describe their requirements to me."

While Randy was talking I was making some notes on the whiteboard:

*index no - code (neg roll + shot no.)
*type - category (weddings etc)
*name -
*description

When Randy had finished I asked, "What types of photos do you sell in the shop, Randy?"

"I suppose you could call them arty photos," Randy replied. "I take a camera with me everywhere, and whenever something catches my eye, I capture it. These photos can be anything from mountain ranges at dusk to a broken-down old fire engine. If I develop any of them and think they're saleable, I'll put them in the gallery and sell prints of them. I've got some examples here, actually," he said, pulling some prints out of a bag. "These are some shots I took during a day at the beach."

I passed the pictures around so that the students could all get a good look. Carl whistled appreciatively.

"Wow, these are great," Gemma said. "I might have to pop down to your gallery over the next few days."

"Please do," Randy said. "I'll show you some of my newest works, hot from the darkroom!"

"And still wet, I bet!" Jim said. "I hate the smell of developing fluids."

"It's innate, I think. You either love it or hate it," Randy laughed. "That, or extreme exposure to it dulls your sense of smell."

"Maybe that's it," Jim replied. "I'll stick to digital photography or getting my photos developed in an hour, I think."

"I think we have enough information to work through," I said. "If no one has any other questions, you're free to go, Randy."

"Okay," Randy said. "I'll get those lists to you as soon as possible. Do all feel free to come to the gallery whenever you like. I'm sure I can sort you all out with some prints as a thank you."

"I'll hold you to that!" Gemma warned.

Randy laughed. "Thanks for dropping in, Randy," I said, handing back the photos. "We'll let you know how everything is progressing or if we have any other questions. Is that all right with you?"

"Sure is," Randy said, walking to the door. "Bye, all!"

The class unified in a big "Bye!" and Randy was out of sight.

Breaking down the requirements

Now that the class had some idea of what they should look for, it was time to note the client's requirements from the discussion on paper. Performing this exercise would also identify any holes that we had missed from the conversation with Randy.

"Okay, class, who'd like to start us off?" I asked. "Who'd like to outline the main reason why Randy wants a kiosk in the first place?"

Joe raised his hand and spoke. "Randy wants a kiosk because he has limited gallery wall space, and he would like to show a few more of his photographs to potential gallery clients. The kiosk would enable him to show a lot more images on a computer screen in his gallery."

"That sounds about right, Joe, thanks," I said. "One thing that Randy might have overlooked is related to the space problem in the gallery. To have a kiosk running, he'll need space for a computer monitor. It will be of benefit to us to find out how big the monitor is going to be, because this might limit the resolution at which we can work. This is something we'll have to find out from Randy."

"In many ways," Jim started, "the size of the monitor is a catch-22. A bigger monitor might mean less wall space and clearer quality images onscreen, whereas a smaller monitor will give Randy back some wall space but might potentially strain his clients' eyes."

"Randy might have a pedestal in mind!" Joe laughed.

"Quite, Joe," I said. "The first task on our list then is to find out how Randy aims to display the Flash movie." I marked the task on the board:

Questions for the client:

Where do you intend to place the kiosk?
How big will the kiosk monitor be?

"What's next?" I asked. "Now, we know *why* Randy wants a kiosk—the next question to answer is *what* he wants."

"I think I can answer that, Teach," Carl said. "Randy wants to show off some of his photographs through an interface that enables his clients to select which images they want to look at in detail."

"Why does Randy want his users to select images?" I queried. "Why doesn't he have a timed sequential loop of images?"

"Because passive is bad," Jim replied. "Engagement is the key. If the photographs were to loop over and over they'd almost sink into the wallpaper. Not only that, but if the client makes a selection by looking at the thumbnails, he's looking at what he wants to look at, not what he might happen to see at that moment. This choice is the key."

"It also hooks the client in, Jim," I said. "Once the user clicks one thumbnail, if the interface is responsive enough, he'll undoubtedly click another and another. Mazzy, would you like to talk about the thumbnails?"

Mazzy nodded. "The grid of thumbnails links to their enlarged versions. Once a thumbnail is clicked, an enlarged version of it is shown in the main image area."

"Does anything else happen?" I asked.

"At the moment, that seems to be the only thing that happens," Mazzy replied. "But I have a feeling that Randy might want the client to see some information about each photograph. In his gallery, the photos are mounted with various information such as locations and clients."

"How would that be displayed?" asked Gemma. "Would the information appear somewhere when you clicked the thumbnail to get the full-size image?"

"Yes, that's an option," I replied. "We could have an information box underneath the image to hold that data."

"Does that mean that you would have to select an image every time you wanted to see its title?" asked Mazzy. "That seems tedious."

"I agree," Jim said with a chuckle. "Could we have tooltips, or something like them, to display some short piece of information whenever you hold the mouse over a thumbnail?"

"Yes," I agreed, "we could certainly do that. We'd then get a chance to see how Flash handles time, as we'd want to have a short delay between moving the mouse over a thumbnail and the tooltip appearing."

"Why would we want a delay?" asked Joe. "It's customary to have a short delay," I replied, "because if you're just skimming over something on the screen, it can be a bit annoying and intrusive to have lots of additional boxes pop up at you that you didn't ask for. It's more polite to the user to give her the option of viewing the information, but at the minimum amount of effort if she does want it. In this case, all she has to do is move the mouse cursor over the thumbnail and leave it there for a second or so."

"That sound reasonable to me," said Joe. "Delayed tooltips it is . . . as long as that's what Randy wants."

"Okay, so that's another answer we need from Randy," I said. I wrote on the board:

What other information will be displayed with the enlarged photographs?

"If any textual information needs to be displayed, we can use text fields to do the job for us. I'll show you a little more about this in the next class.

"So far we have a grid of thumbnails. What else does Randy require?" I asked.

"More grids to show more photos," Mazzy started. "Randy wanted the images categorized so that he could expand the number of images available on the kiosk."

"Correct," I said. "Depending on the size of the thumbnails, it's unlikely that there will be enough space to link to a great number of images. Luckily, Randy's different types of work will allow him to neatly categorize his content into succinct grids."

"Can pictures be in more than one category?" asked Jim.

"That's a good question," I replied. "We'll have to check with Randy on that one." I added it to the board:

Can pictures be part of more than one category?

"From a development point of view, we need to decide how the viewer will make the transition from category to category. Although it might not sound like a difficult decision to make, you must consider how the viewer will interact with the application, and therefore you must make it as easy to use as possible.

"The subject of the user experience is much debated and is referred to as **usability**, but I won't be covering it in too much detail in this class. For this project, the main consideration is that the person on the street should be able to use our kiosk easily. Remember that we should never assume a degree of user knowledge—the potential client might not be tech-savvy."

> *You can find out more about usability in the* Flash Usability Guide *from friends of ED (ISBN: 1-903450-25-X).*

"Okay. Let's imagine now that you're using the kiosk and you change the category. What should happen?" I asked.

"Two things, I guess," said Jim. "First, the thumbnail grid for the newly selected category must be shown, and second," Jim paused, "somehow the current selected category will have to be shown."

Carl and Joe looked at each other with puzzlement. "I think I know exactly what Jim means," Mazzy said. "Do you mind if I use the board?" I passed Mazzy the magic marker.

Mazzy wrote a few words on the board. "Imagine you're visiting a website. When you first arrive, you're immediately sent to the home page." Mazzy drew an arrow next to the Home text:

> Home
News
Links
Contact
About

"Even though you're aware of being on the home page, you're still usually provided with some visual clue." Mazzy made some changes on the board. "If you select a link to a different page of the website—say, Links here—the new page will load and the arrow will move to show you your new position:

Home
News
> Links
Contact
About

"Even though this is a pretty simple concept, it helps the user know what he is looking at or where he is. It also prevents him from reselecting the same page because the link is usually frozen out.

"For Randy's kiosk, the same visual cue needs to be present or the viewer won't know if he is looking at this category or the next."

"I'd say it's more difficult to work out where you are from a grid of thumbnails," Jim said.

"You've both made an important decision on behalf of the user," I said. "If the user could thank you for it, I'm sure he would. I'd say a navigation cue is definitely required."

"We'll need to find out how many categories Randy wants," Mazzy said, "and what they are. Each category will need a limit of thumbnails too, won't it?"

"Absolutely, Mazzy." I wrote some more questions on the board:

How many categories of photographs do you want?

What is the maximum number of photographs for any one category?

"What's the next requirement?" I looked to Mazzy, who had been taking notes throughout the class.

"A way of monitoring the number of times a photo is viewed," Mazzy answered. "This is so Randy is aware of what interests or stands out to his clients. Once Randy has the most popular list, he can change the images in the window and on the wall to reflect the most popular selection.

"We know that Randy wants a record of the selected images, but we have no idea of what information he wants to collect and retain, or how often he wants it."

"It might help to think of the information that Randy requires as a report," I said. "All we know about the report so far is that it has to collect the number of hits on the thumbnails. We don't know if the report lists all individual hits, or if it compiles and processes the information.

"For now we'll work on the premise that the report lists each different hit and displays it. For ease of reference from Randy's point of view, this information could be ordered according to the number of hits, so the most popular photograph tops the report each time."

"How often would the report run?" Jim asked.

"It's easiest for this class if the report is run each day and is printed out or noted by Randy," I answered. "Accumulating information over a number of days would involve processes beyond the scope of this class. This is the kind of detail covered in my advanced programming classes."

"I guess we'll have to go with a daily report for now," Carl said. "I think you'd better add a question for Randy on the board, Teach."

"The report doesn't have to be limited to individual hits," I said. "For example, we could process the information to show Randy the most popular category or type of images of that day. Randy might find that wedding photographs are more popular on the weekend and would benefit from a window change over those couple of days.

"Collated information would give Randy a greater summary of information and would save him from having to go through all of the individual image data. We could offer a number of report types." I wrote on the board:

Other than an individual thumbnail report, how would you like the information processed?

"Before I send the questions to Randy, I'll add some of the suggested categories to see if they would be of any benefit to him," I said. "The most important thing is for the information to be presented in the most useful way for him to use."

"How would the report know when to run?" Jim asked.

"Another good question, Jim," I responded. "My immediate thoughts are to set the report to run at a certain time of day—say, closing time—or alternatively for it to be accessed by Randy whenever he wants a report. The best way to allow hidden access to a page is to detect a key press and have a login screen to ensure that only Randy or his assistant can access the information."

Jim nodded. "The login system sounds like the best option of the two. Being controlled by time is a bad idea, because we don't know which hours Randy runs his gallery."

"I know for a fact that Randy sometimes closes the gallery early," Mazzy said. "Having his reports controlled by a timer is maybe not as wise as it sounds."

"Why can I see a flashing screen with the words 'Manual Override Failed' on it?" Carl asked. Carl had his eyes shut tight and his hands were furiously pressing imaginary buttons.

"I think we've agreed that a timer isn't such a good idea, so you can quit the drama, Carl!" I said. "Okay, so the reports are triggered by a key press and are accessed via a login screen for Randy and his assistant. This will also mean that Randy can lock away the keyboard to ensure that only he and his assistant can access it.

"The last remaining aspect of the project we need to talk about is the portfolio CD."

"Aren't we creating the same project for the kiosk and the CD?" Joe asked. "I can't see why we'd need to make it different."

"I think I can," Gemma said. "The first thing that comes to mind is that Randy will need to have his contact details on the CD version. If it isn't in the presentation, then no one will know how to get ahold of him. I made the same mistake with my first portfolio . . . ." Gemma coughed awkwardly.

"So, we'd need to supply his gallery address, telephone number, and fax number and, most important, an e-mail link," Jim said.

"You're both right," I said. "Randy's promotion is extremely important, and providing contact information on the CD is the way to do it. An About page that details Randy's work and expertise might also be in order.

"However, Contact and About pages aren't required on the gallery kiosk. A tiny modification to the Flash file will allow us to distinguish between the CD and kiosk versions of the presentation. Don't worry about building two presentations because we only need to build one."

"Eventually, we'll require the Contact and About details from Randy," Jim said. "I guess we have other things to worry about before that, though!" I nodded in agreement.

"Okay," I said, "let's sum up what we've got, and what information we still need to get from Randy." I turned on the projector and typed up the notes that I had made:

*** Where in the store will the kiosk be placed, and at what kind of resolution will the monitor be set?**
Randy does:
Mostly private client work
With some corporate work
He usually sends out a set of prints to corporate clients, so being able to send a copy of the kiosk on CD to them will be a lot cheaper and easier.
His photos fall into the following categories:

Weddings and events
Portraits
Landscapes
"Artistic"

* He will send a complete list of client types and categories for next week's class. Also, we need to check if a picture can belong to more than one category and the maximum number of pictures that can be in a category.

The attributes needed for each picture:
Index number
Category
Name
Short description

* He will send a complete list of attributes for next week.

Some of this information will need to be displayed in a text box after a thumbnail image is clicked.

There could also be tooltips for users to see some information without having to click every thumbnail.

* We need to check with Randy about whether or not he wants to have the tooltips.

We need a way of indicating which category users are in and which thumbnail is currently selected,

Randy's information report:
Must collect the number of "hits" on the thumbnails and display them in some way
Records individual hits listed by popularity
Printed/noted by Randy once per day
Need to record and order by category as well
Accessed by a keyboard-activated password login screen

* Check with Randy to see how he wants the report displayed.

Portfolio CD needs:

Contact details
An About page
Turn off login page

*** Need Contact and About page details from Randy.**

"Does anybody have anything else to add to the list?" I asked. Everybody shook their heads. "Okay then, Mazzy, are you okay to deliver the list to Randy and to ask him if he can get us the answers to our questions by next week? I'll give you my e-mail address at the end of the class, so he can send the answers directly to me if he prefers."

"That would be fine," replied Mazzy.

I continued, "Now that we know what the requirements are, we can sketch out a quick interface or design. We can then attach a copy of our initial design to the questions and let Randy take a look at it and tell us what he thinks."

Interface design

"Now that we've sketched out some of the requirements for the kiosk, we can sketch out the interface elements," I said. "This will help us spot anything we might have forgotten, and also we can then show the interface plan to Randall and see if he approves of the layout and design.

"As well as being aesthetically pleasing, designing our interface should take ease of use into consideration. Given everything that we've discussed so far, would anyone like to create a quick sketch of the main gallery interface?"

"I think I know how it might look," Mazzy said. "I did something similar in HTML for the church website." Mazzy began drawing.

"On one page you have the thumbnail grid, and this links to a larger version of the picture on the next page.

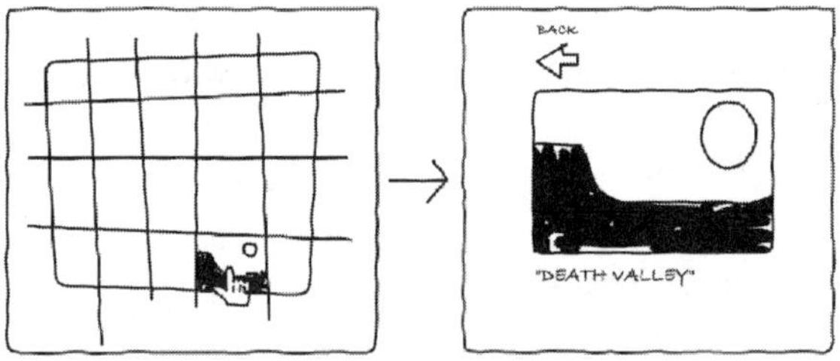

"On the full-size picture page, a Back button leads you back to the grid. This way, you have access both ways—to and from the grid."

"That's a lovely sketch of Death Valley," Carl said. "All that's missing are the vultures and skeletons." Mazzy laughed.

"Okay, artistic judgement aside, what does everyone think of this sketch?" I asked.

"I think it's a little too much like how old web pages work," Jim said. "I've seen many galleries like this, and even though they do the job, Flash seems to allow a greater degree of flexibility. I think we should use the advantages of the package."

"Jim is right," I said. "Although this sketch would be ideal for a non-Flash website, Flash allows you to present information differently through programming. We'll learn more about how it does this in the classes to come.

"As you already know, Mazzy, HTML pages are stored separately, and one page links to another. Traditionally, an HTML website is made up of many HTML files." I quickly sketched on the board.

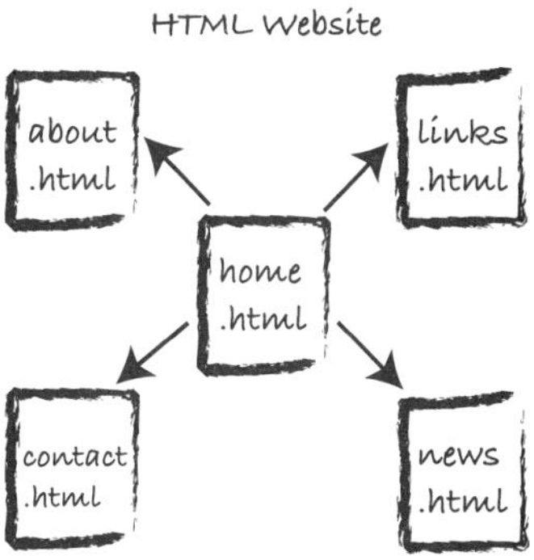

"In this website, each page is linked to from the home page," I said. "When a link is selected, a new page is loaded into the browser window, replacing the previous one. Because HTML sites are constructed like this, it places certain limitations on how interfaces or pages are created."

I drew some more on the board. "Flash websites are traditionally constructed from one Flash **SWF** file. This file can contain all of the required pages, graphics, and other elements.

"In this class, you'll soon discover some of the interactive options available with Flash and you'll see how pages and website elements can be represented within this one compact file."

"What do the letters S-W-F stand for?" Joe asked. "Computers and abbreviations! I can't keep up!"

"These letters stand for Shockwave Flash," I said. "It's just the extension of published Flash files. The extension SWF is pronounced 'swiff.' You'll get used to hearing this as we proceed through the course.

"Who else would like to try to draw an interface?" I asked.

"I'd like to have a try," Gemma said, getting up from her seat.

Gemma began drawing on the whiteboard:

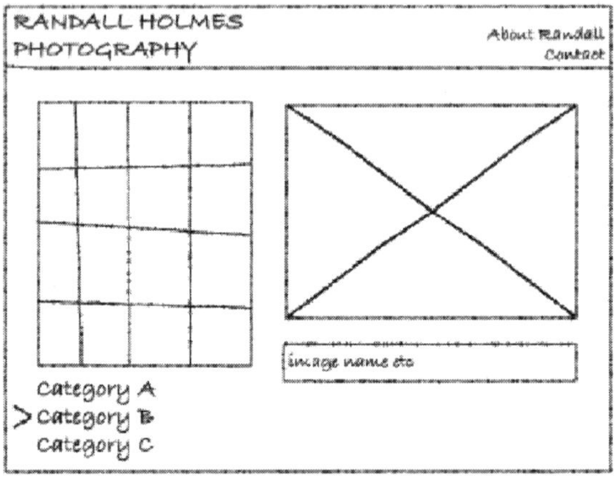

"I'm not really sure how it would work," Gemma said. "But on the left here might be the thumbnail grid, and the enlarged images and text information would appear on the right. It's hardly cutting-edge design, but it seems logical to me."

"So if I clicked a thumbnail, it would appear in the big box on the right?" Mazzy asked.

"Sure," Gemma said. "This way, you can see the grid and the selected image at the same time. I must admit that I'm not keen on going back and forth in websites."

"Can I ask why you chose to place the grid on the left side?" I asked.

"I designed it that way because of the Western direction of reading a page or layout. Top left to bottom right," Gemma replied. "I've always adhered to this rule in my design work, and the same thing feels right here."

"What does everyone think of Gemma's design?" I asked.

"I think it's almost there," Jim said. "I'm not sure about the position of the rest of the assets—the categories, for instance—but the grid and its relationship to the main image area is really neat. I can imagine that it will work really well.

"Although it might be too soon to think about it, how about continuing the contact sheet theme and placing the categories at the top or side of the page as file tabs?" Jim asked.

Mazzy looked puzzled. "I'm not sure I'm with you, Jim."

"Me neither," Joe said. "I guess I'm more of a visual person. How about a quick sketch on the board?"

Jim nodded and approached the board. "I guess I'm thinking of a photographer's file or ring binder. Each category is represented by one tab." Jim drew frantically on the board. He turned to me and asked, "Do you have any other color markers, Ken?" I opened my bag and passed him a few.

Jim stepped back and admired his masterpiece. He smiled with glee.

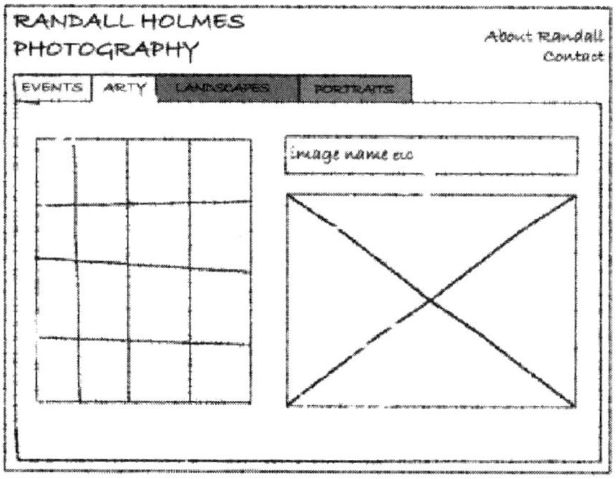

"As with normal tabs, the selected tab comes to the front, and so does the grid for that category. I guess this is just an aesthetic solution, but it covers the need for a visual navigation indicator." Mazzy nodded.

"Is there anything else that we need to sketch in?" I asked.

Mazzy looked down and spoke. "I have a few more things down, Ken, starting with tooltips. How are we going to show them?"

"After a slight delay when the cursor is over the grid thumbnails, the tooltip should be displayed just below the cursor," I said. "Do you mind if I make an amendment, Gemma?" Gemma smiled and shook her head.

I added a cursor and tooltip to the diagram.

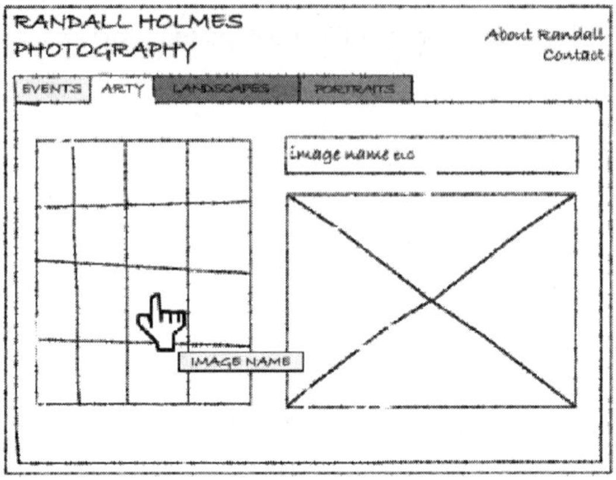

"The last two things are the Contact and About pages," Gemma added. "I've put these links in already, but I have no idea how they'll work."

"I imagine these will be pages or sheets that appear above the rest of the content," Jim started. "I like the idea of slightly opaque sheets—like acetate. The pages will have only a little information, so I guess there isn't much to them."

"No, the Contact page would just need a mailto, Jim," Mazzy said, "an e-mail link to Randy that opens your set e-mail application."

"Randy might also want a self-portrait, of course," I added. "Being a photographer and all that, I'm sure he has a few good ones hanging around that no one gets to see.

“Okay, now that we’ve run out of things on the list, is there anything else we need to include?” I asked. The class was filled with shaking heads. I smiled. “There is one thing I’ve noticed that we haven’t addressed: the combination of portrait and landscape format images in the grid.

“Our assumption has been that the grid is full of landscape-oriented images, and the reality is that Randy probably has many portrait images for all of the categories too. Unless we know that we’ll have a full row of portrait or landscape images, the grid might not turn out as we planned.”

“How about if all image formats are displayed in landscape?” Joe asked.

“Well, Joe, although that would mimic a contact sheet pretty well, it wouldn’t be of much use to users because they’d have to squint or tilt their heads.”

“I’ve just thought about something else,” Mazzy said. “What if the images are all a different size?”

“That’s not a problem, Mazzy. The standard photo format is 4:3 for landscape or 3:4 for portrait images,” I said. “All of the images should conform to this format, and if they come in at different sizes based on this format, we’ll just have to resize them in an application such as Adobe Photoshop.” Mazzy nodded.

“Back to the tilting heads!” I said. “I don’t think that’s really an option, Joe. It’s not the best consideration from a user perspective—but it sure would be easy for us.”

“The other alternative is to only allow Randy to use landscape images!” Mazzy exclaimed.

“That’s even less of an option, Mazzy! Randy—the client—has the right to use whatever he wishes to use, and we as programmers have to find a way to do the best according to his requirements.

“We could simplify things by using a square frame and by centering the thumbnails within it.” I drew on the board. “This way our grid could be drawn in the same way, and we could incorporate landscape and portrait format images.

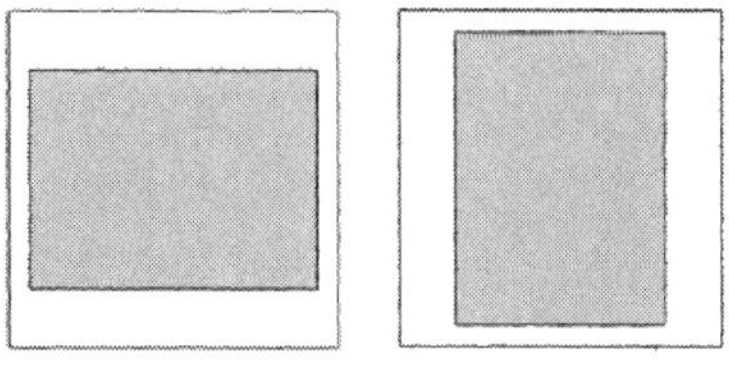

"In these sketches, the outside frame is a square, and the inside thumbnails conform to the 4:3 image ratio. Both thumbnails are centered within the outer frame. A typical grid of frames and thumbnails might look something like this."

"They look more like a set of slides now than a contact sheet," Jim said. "I guess that still fits into the photography theme, though, and it solves the grid problem.

"On a positive note, slides appear to be more professional than a contact sheet. A contact sheet is the middle state when the photographer tends to select which images to process. They often have a number of bad photos!"

I made some changes to Gemma's design, adding the slide grid:

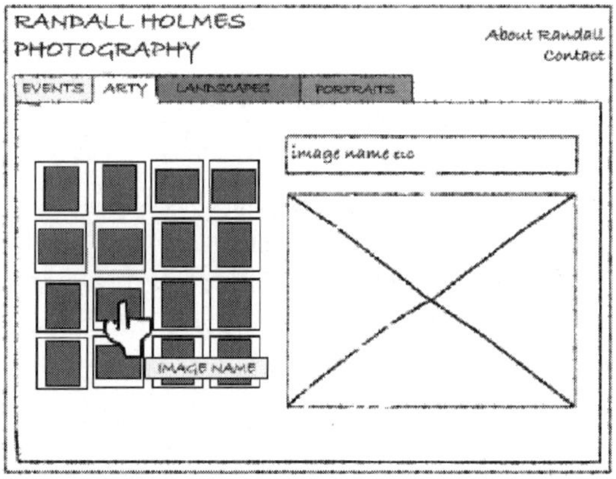

"Okay. Is everyone happy with the current state of the interface?" I asked. The students nodded. "Unless anyone has anything else to add, we appear to be done for today. Today's lesson has been rather intense, but we've covered a lot of the questions that needed asking regarding Randy's website. If we were to leave these questions down to chance, we'd run into trouble somewhere during its development."

"You're not going to wipe that off the board are you, Teach?" Carl said. "I haven't copied it down yet!"

"Not to worry, Carl, I've got a digital camera here to take a shot of the board. Would you like to do the honors?" I asked.

Carl stood up and took a photo with the digital camera. "I'll print out the image Carl's taken and hand it to you next week," I said.

"You'll all be glad to know that I've decided to let you go home this week without any homework." Carl whooped. Mazzy poked him. "You'll need the energy for next week's class, when we start looking at programming concepts.

"Class dismissed!" I said, wiping the board. Before I could even turn around, most of the students were already out of the door.

Summary

In this lesson you were introduced to the idea of creating a kiosk project as a case study.

- You learned that a kiosk is a useful way to display images and information in an interactive setting.
- You covered the ways that a kiosk project can be customised to suit the needs of individual clients. You can add sound to create an interactive jukebox, or you can optimize the images and use the same interface as a website.
- You learned about the project life cycle, which is the number of steps necessary to go through when contemplating a project of this kind. The project life cycle steps are as follows:
    - Accept the project.
    - Define the problem.
    - Design the project output.
    - Break the problem into logical steps.
    - Write the code.
    - Test the code.
- You discovered that a good way to define the problem is to write a requirements document for the client. You use your initial conversation with the client as the basis for this document and then write a list of additional questions that need to be answered to fully understand the needs of the client.
- Finally, you learned that you should consider how the kiosk will look and work, bearing in mind the importance of usability and ensuring that the user finds the kiosk's navigation as intuitive as possible.

In the next class you'll start to come to grips with programming by examining some basic programming concepts.

Class 3
Programming Concepts

Objectives

In today's class, you'll learn about

Programs

- What a program is
- How you can put a program into Flash

Variables

- Storing information in a program
- Picking good names for variables
- Keeping track of information in a program

Operators and expressions

- Using and modifying information in a program
- Understanding which operators take precedence over others

Introduction

I received an e-mail from Randy just a couple of days before the class, so as soon as the students had all arrived, I let them know what it said.

"You'll be glad to know that Randy has answered all of your questions concerning the case study. There may be a few places where you need some additional information, but in general I think his replies are sound. Also, he's happy with our initial sketch of the interface, and he likes the suggestions we made. So all in all, a completely successful start."

An assortment of whoops and hollers came from certain members of the class, while certain others looked around at them and shook their heads.

"But," I continued, "we won't continue with the case study until the end of the class. It's time to take your first real step into what you all came here for: programming."

What's a program?

"Okay, what is a computer program?" I asked. "This isn't a trick question—it's important that we all start off from the same point. I'll offer my basic definition first, and you can let me know if you agree with it or not. A program is simply a set of instructions given to a computer to achieve an aim." I stopped and looked around the class, and every face looked back at me expectantly.

"That's it," I said. "Do you all agree with that definition?"

Everybody looked slightly puzzled and wary, until finally Jim spoke up, "Umm, should there be something in the definition about the instructions needing to be given to the computer in a language that it understands?"

"Yes, that would certainly help," I replied. "It would be no good for me to just ask my computer to make a photo gallery, and then go off to fetch a cup of coffee and expect it to be done by the time I get back. The computer doesn't understand plain English, so we need to give it instructions in a form that it understands.

"Now, computers speak in a series of 1s and 0s called binary, but before you get too worried, we certainly won't be communicating with the computer in binary, and there are very few people in the world that would. The next step up from binary is something called machine code. Machine code is the closest that most programmers will get to talking to a computer, but it's still too obscure and, let's face it, difficult for most people to understand.

"We'll be starting from the next step up with a form that's more readily understandable by humans. The common name for this form is **high-level programming language**—'high' because of its distance from the natural computer language, binary. A great many programming languages are in use around the world, ranging from all-purpose languages to ones focused on specific tasks such as creating graphics or databases. The language that Flash speaks in is called ActionScript, and that's the language you'll be learning and using throughout this course."

Joe's hand went up. "Yes Joe?" I asked.

"If these high-level languages are so much easier for us to use," Jim said, "then why would anyone ever bother using the other, more difficult stuff?"

"Good question," I replied. "The answer is speed. High-level languages may be a lot simpler for *us* to understand, but the computer still speaks in binary. Before it's able to understand the commands that we're giving it, those commands must be translated, and that takes time. Nowadays, computers are fast enough that most people doing most tasks don't need to worry about it—right now, that includes us. All we need to know is that we can give ActionScript commands to the computer, and the computer will follow them.

"Okay, so let's change our definition of a computer program." I turned and wrote on the board:

A computer program is a set of instructions written in a programming language, and given to a computer to achieve an aim.

"Is there anything else we need to add to that?" I asked.

"Do we need to say anything *about* the aim?" asked Gemma. "I mean, do we need to qualify that at all?"

"I don't know, really," I replied, "the aim changes depending on what sort of program you're writing. What kind of thing were you thinking of?"

"Well," she replied, "you wouldn't be writing a program to make a cup of coffee, for example."

"Why not?" I said. "There's a vending machine out in the hall that can make you a cup of coffee. All it's doing is following a simple set of instructions."

"Good point. I'd never thought of it like that," she said. "Maybe we don't need to qualify the aim. Okay then, I think I'm happy with that definition."

"All right then," I went on, "we know what a program is in its most basic form, but what does one look like? To answer that, we'll have to open up Flash."

The Actions panel

There was a shuffling, clicking, and whirring as the class woke their computers out of their slumber and started Flash. I did the same and set the projector to display the image on my monitor.

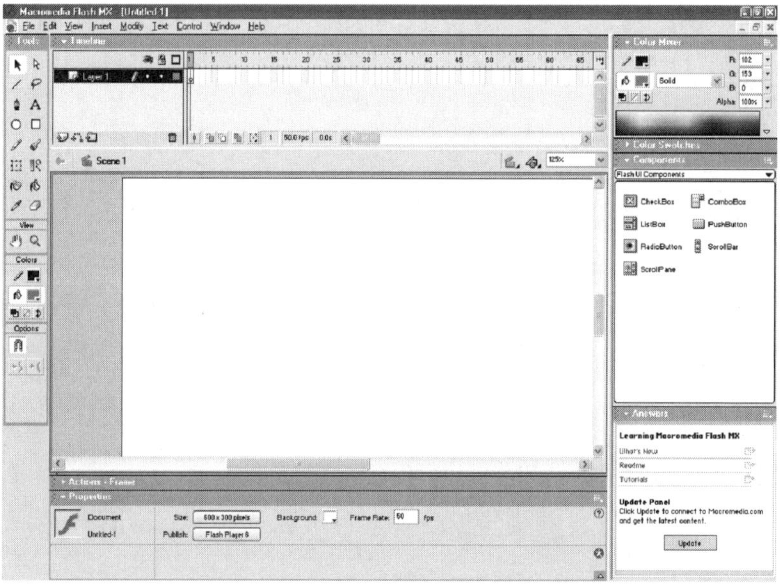

"You've already taken a look around the interface, and you know that the Actions panel is located just above the Properties inspector. If you ever can't find it, you can make it appear by going into the **Windows** menu and making sure there is a check mark next to **Actions**."

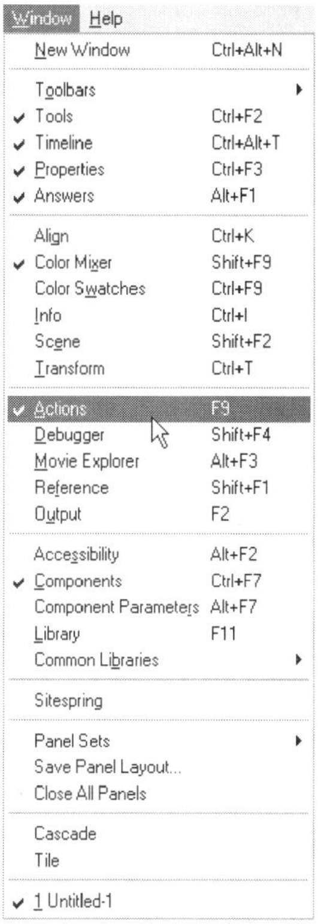

I noticed a puzzled look on Carl's face. "I bet I can guess what you're thinking," I told him. "Why is it that there's no check mark next to it in the menu, but you can see the panel bar on your screen?"

"You're right," he said. "So what's the answer?"

"The reason is that the panel is currently minimized, and it counts as not being open," I responded. "If you check the Actions option in the menu, then you'll see the panel open up as normal. If you then uncheck it again, it will minimize itself back to where it was. Okay everyone, please open the Actions panel and we'll take a look at what it has to offer:

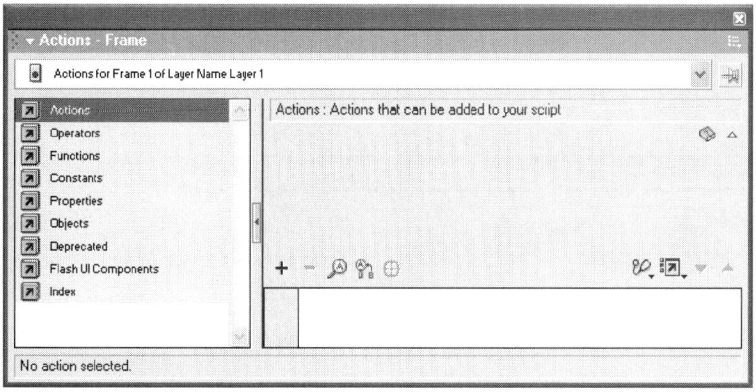

"First of all, before you get too comfortable with what you see here, note that there are two modes for entering ActionScript commands, **Normal** and **Expert**. What you see here is Normal mode, which isn't the one we'll be using. We're going to jump straight into Expert mode."

"Our first look at it and already we're experts," said Mazzy. "It's certainly quicker than painting!"

"I wouldn't go as far as saying *that* just yet," I chuckled, "but by making this change, you'll be going further than a lot of Flash users ever do."

"So why can't we start with Normal?" Joe asked. "I don't think I'm ready to be an expert yet."

"Trust me, it's okay," I said. "The biggest difference between the modes is that in Normal mode you enter commands by selecting them from a list, but in Expert mode you type them in yourself. It gives you a lot more flexibility, and you'll find that it's quicker in the long run."

"But what if we type something in wrong?" Joe asked.

"That does happen," I replied, "but as you'll see later, Flash has ways of letting you know when you've made mistakes. Okay, without any further ado, let's switch into Expert mode. Click the little options icon in the top right of the panel, and select **Expert Mode** from the drop-down menu that appears.

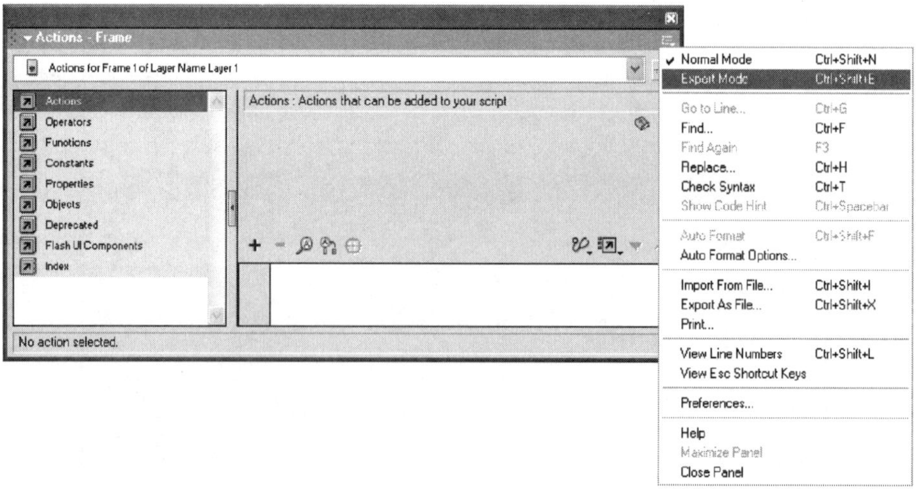

"What you'll see isn't really that different from what we were looking at initially. The biggest difference is that there's a lot more white space."

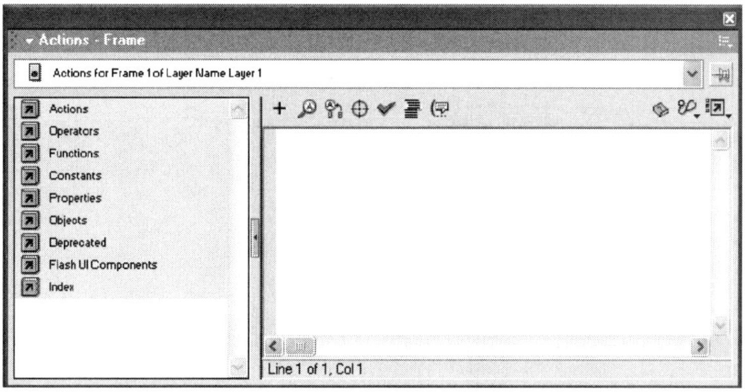

"It actually looks a bit more welcoming to me than the last one did," remarked Jim.

"I'm glad of that," I replied. "Okay, let's take a look around.

"On the left, you'll see a group of what looks like books with arrows on them. These hold lists of all of the commands you can possibly give to Flash, split up into related topics. We'll take a look inside them in a minute.

"Above that, there's a bar with 'Actions for Frame 1 of Layer Name Layer 1' written in it. This is like the address bar in your web browser. It tells you where you are at the moment.

"Below that is a set of funny-looking icons that you'll look at in detail later, and below that is a big white box. This box, called the **code window**, is where you'll be typing all of your code, and if you click it you'll see a flashing prompt, just like you would in a word processing package."

What does a program look like?

"Now you know what a program is, and you know where a program goes in Flash, but what does a program look like?" I opened a Flash file from my computer and showed the Actions panel on the screen. "This is a simple program."

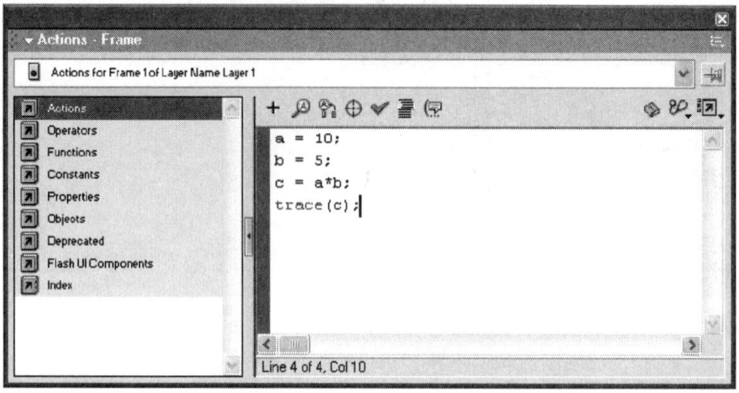

"Don't worry about what it says for the moment—only look at its form," I said. "The first thing to notice is that the program is on four separate lines. If we were to equate it to standard English grammar, then each line is like a sentence. A line in Flash usually contains one complete command. What else do you notice about it?"

"There aren't any line numbers," said Jim. "I remember in BASIC every line was numbered sequentially in tens, but Flash doesn't have that."

"Well, yes and no," I said. "There aren't any line numbers visible at the moment, but take a look at that line right at the bottom of the panel. You'll see that it tells you which line you're on. Actually, I'm glad you brought that up—it's probably better if you do choose to show the line numbers now, as it will make it easier for you as you go on. Okay, if you all go back to the menu where you switched to Expert mode, you'll see an option called **View Line Numbers**. Check that, and the line numbers should appear in the code window:

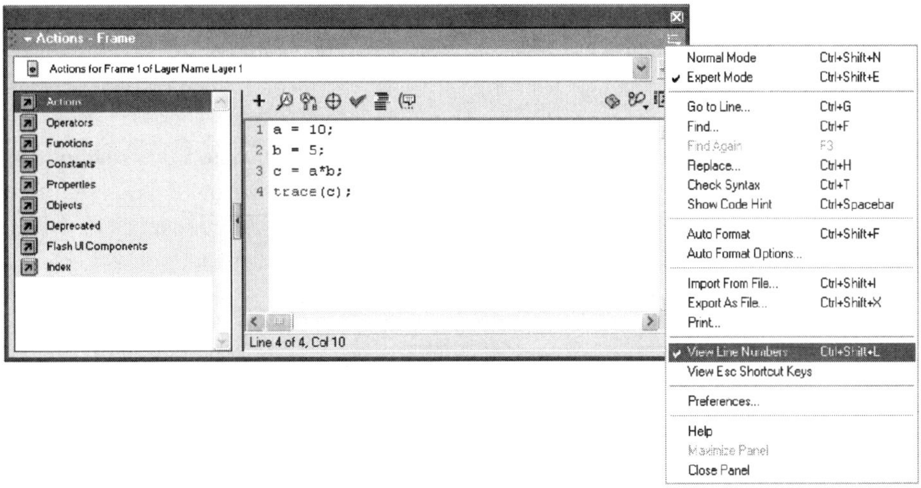

"Do you feel a little more at home now?" I asked Jim. "Much better," he replied with a grin.

"Okay, is there anything else that you notice about the form of the code?" I asked.

"Each line ends with a semicolon?" suggested Mazzy.

"Just what I was looking for," I replied. "In the same way that in English we use a period to mark the end of a sentence, a 'sentence,' or **statement**, in Flash, and in many other programming languages, ends with a semicolon."

"Why's that?" asked Carl. "It seems like these programmers are determined to make things difficult for people trying to learn. If it's so similar to English, then why not just make it the same and use a period? It would save on all this confusion."

"Hear, hear!" exclaimed Mazzy.

"It seems I have a mutiny on my hands," I muttered grimly, prompting a few chuckles. "Seriously, though, can anyone tell me why we *couldn't* use a period to mark the end of the line?" The class fell silent. "Can anyone think of anywhere else where we use a period? Think of numbers, especially prices."

"Ah, because it's also used as a decimal point," Jim said. "But still," Carl argued, "surely computers are clever enough to know when it's between two numbers and when it's at the end of a line?"

"You're right, Carl," I said, "computers are powerful enough to be able to do that, but the problem is that the lines are mostly there for our benefit, to make the program easier to read. The computer actually ignores most of the white space—that's the spaces and carriage returns—and the program could just as easily be written like this." I made some changes to the program on my screen.

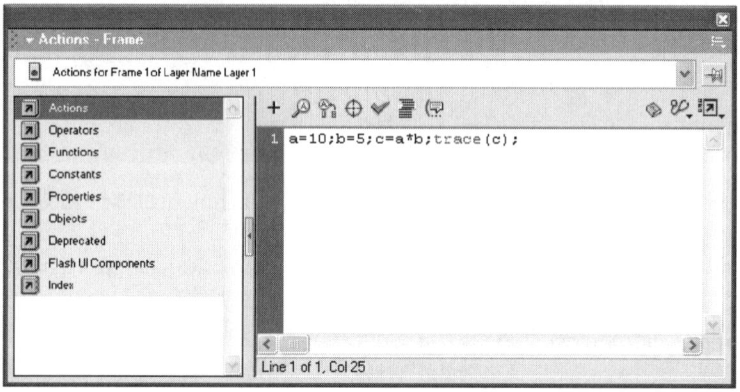

"This would still be the same to the computer, but it looks like a mess to us, and it wouldn't work if we used periods instead of semicolons," I said.

"Okay, okay, I guess you're right," said Carl. "Semicolons at the end of lines it is."

I changed the program back to its original state. "The other thing that you need to know about programs is that they run through from top to bottom. So this program would start on line 1 and finish on line 4." I closed down the program and opened a fresh Flash file.

Variables

"Right then," I began, "I think it's about time for you to learn your first programming concepts. Let's start with **data**. Data is just a fact or a piece of information. For example, I have four pens here for writing on the whiteboard." I held them up. "Let's pull out the basic constituents of that data: We have the *name* of the thing, in this case 'pens,' and the *value* of the thing, in this case 'four.' Now, if we wanted to store this data inside a program, we would store it as a **variable**, which, as its name suggests, is simply 'a thing that can change (or *vary*).' For example, if I lost my red pen, the value of my `pens` variable would change to three.

"So, variables are made up of a pairing of a name and a value, but how does this work with a computer? Well, if I were to tell the computer to remember the fact that I have four pens, then it would set aside a small area of its memory, stick a big flag in it, and mark that area of memory as 'pens.' It would then store the number four in that area.

"Later on, if I asked the computer how many pens I had, it would search through its memory looking for the flag with 'pens' written on it, and look inside the flagged area to see what value it was storing there. Assuming it hadn't been tampered with in the meantime, it ought to find the number four.

"In computer terms then, a variable is a named area of memory, set aside to store a value in. It's a container, and although the contents are free to change, the container itself remains the same. The great thing about this is that whenever I come to use my variable, I only have to mention the name and the computer will instantly pull out the correct value for it.

"This may not seem such a great thing with pens, but consider if you have a program on a handheld computer to work out your finances, and whenever you make any kind of transaction you make a note of it on your computer using the keywords 'add...to...' and 'subtract...from...'

"At the start of the day, you have $1,486.37 in your account. You go to a gas station to fill up your car's gas tank, and while you're there you buy a few candies. The bill comes to $17.75, so you dutifully type into your computer

```
subtract 17.75 from 1486.37
```

"The computer gives you the answer

```
1468.62
```

"Okay, now you drive to work, get out of the car, and see a dollar on the sidewalk. There's no one else around, so you quickly pocket the money and go to your computer:

```
add 1 to ...
```

"For the life of you, you can't remember what the last number was! It would be a whole lot easier to just have the computer remember the data for you.

"If you stored the value of your current finances in a variable called 'current,' you'd only have tell the computer this:

```
add 1 to current
```

"It would do just that, and you'd escape without a headache. Any time that you wanted to know what state your finances were in, you'd just have to ask the computer to display `current` and it would give you the value that was stored there."

Naming variables

"Now there aren't *many* limits on what names you can give to your variables, but you do need to keep one or two important rules in mind," I said.

"The best name for a variable is usually the most descriptive one. That way, you won't have to struggle to remember what information it's meant to be storing. Say you want to define a variable that will keep track of the balance in your current account. What do you think would be the better name for it: `ca` or `CurrentAccount`?"

"Well," said Mazzy, almost immediately, "calling it `CurrentAccount` would make it really clear what information has been stored inside the variable, so that's probably the best one."

"Wait up, though," chipped in Carl, "what's the point in typing out a long variable name like that when you could be using two letters instead? I'd rather use the first one and save my fingers aching! Besides, I already know that ca just stands for 'current account,' so it would be just as clear."

"Maybe it would to you now, Carl," I said, "but what about when you add a load more variables with two-letter names? And what if someone else wants to use your code? For that matter, what if you, in 6 months time, try making changes to the program and can't quite remember what all your short-name variables are for?"

"I guess so . . . ." said Carl, frowning.

"You're right to an extent, though," I said. "There's no point in giving your variable such a long and convoluted name that it takes a week to type out. I mean, who on earth would want to use a variable with a name like this?" I wrote on the board:

BalanceOfKenJokolsCurrentAccountWithTheFirstNationalBank

"Guess it depends on how much you've got in there!" laughed Carl, and I joined in along with the rest of the class. As the noise died down, Jim spoke up. "I meant to ask before, but why have you run all the words together?"

"Yeah, that's a point," said Mazzy. "Where are all the spaces?"

"Funny you should mention that," I said. "That's the next rule of variable names: You aren't allowed to use spaces. The last couple of names I've written out should give you a good idea of how many people get around it—they string all the words together with capital letters at the start of each one. Here's how we might expand the name of our old friend, the pens variable:

numberOfPens

"Another way to get around the 'no spaces' rule is by using underscores:

number_of_pens

"The last rule of variable names is that you can't use any name that's already reserved by Flash as an ActionScript command. You'll see this more later as you encounter the different commands. One easy way to tell if you've picked a reserved name is to go ahead and type it into the Actions panel. If it turns blue, Flash is telling you that it's a command, and you can't use it as a variable name.

"This trick isn't altogether foolproof, but if it does let a bad name slip through, Flash will give you a fairly obvious warning when you test the movie. Here's an example:

```
**Warning** Scene=Scene 1, Layer=Layer 1, Frame=1: Line 1:
Case-insensitive identifier 'date' will obscure built-in
object 'Date'.
```

"Don't worry too much about the details of what it's saying here. Just remember that if you see a warning like this, it's best to change your variable name to something else."

Creating variables

"Okay then, let's look at how to create a variable in Flash," I continued. "Strictly speaking, there are two steps involved. First, you **declare** the variable so that the computer knows to set aside an area of memory and mark it with a specific name, and then you **initialize** the variable by giving the computer a specific value to put inside it. Flash is actually very forgiving about this and will let you use variables even if they haven't been initialized. However, it's still a good idea to try and initialize all your variables by setting them to a definite value *before* you start using them—you'll see why later on.

"So, let's get started. Everyone click inside the code window to make sure that Flash knows that's where you want to be, so that you can name the variable. Now type the following:

```
pens = 4;
```

"There are actually four discrete parts to that simple line, so let's go through them. First off we have the recognizable parts: the *name* of the variable, which in this case is 'pens,' and the *value* that we want to store with it, 4. Between the two, we have an *assignment operator*, or 'equals sign' to you and me. This tells Flash that we want to operate on a variable named `pens`, and assign the value of 4 to it. The last part of the line is, of course, the semicolon that denotes the *end* of our command."

At this point, Jim spoke up. "Didn't you just say we have to *declare* the variable before we put anything inside it? Where does that happen?"

"I did indeed," I responded. "Flash actually makes things very easy for us and will declare the variable automatically when we use the assignment operator on it for the first time. Most of the time we can perform both steps with one line of code.

"Okay then, let's see it in action. Has everyone typed the code into their Actions panel?" Everyone nodded. "Good. The common name for a Flash file like this is a **movie**. A movie contains all of your code and all of your drawings and other things. To run a movie and see what it does, you use the **Test Movie** command. You can find this command in the **Control** menu:

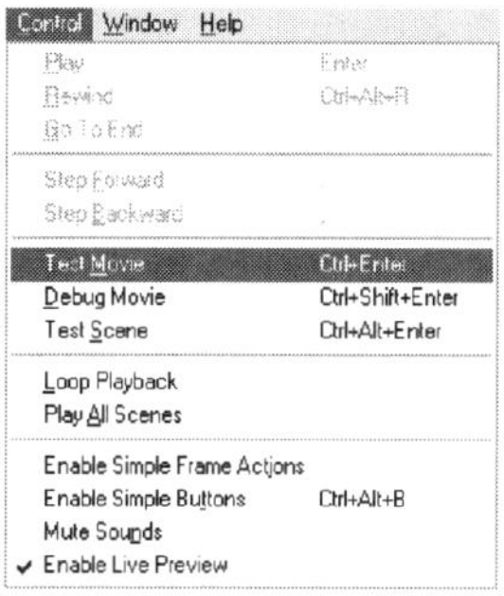

"Alternatively, you can use its shortcut on the keyboard: CTRL/CMD+ENTER. I suggest you write this down somewhere—it's a good one to remember, as it's probably the most common command you'll use in Flash.

"Anyway, use whichever method you're most comfortable with, and test those movies." There was a mass intake of breath as the class ran their movies and waited in anticipation of the wonders that were about to happen. A disappointed exhalation signaled the realization that all that they'd gotten for their troubles was a blank white screen.

"Hey Teach," called out Carl, "I don't think mine's working. Where are the pens?"

"I'm afraid that's it, Carl," I said. "All that we've told Flash to do is create a variable in its memory called `pens` and set it to 4. We haven't told it to do anything with that variable yet."

"But isn't there any way that we can see what it's done?" Carl went on. "If this is all there is to programming, then I'm not sure I want to continue. I thought I'd be saying hello to the world and introducing them to my music, not just staring at a blank screen!"

"Hold your horses there, Carl," I said with a chuckle, "we've only just begun. There is a way that we can see if our code has worked. First let me check, did everybody run their movie?"

Everyone nodded in agreement. "Okay then, if you go to the menu bar at the top of the screen, you'll see a heading called **Debug**. Under this heading, you'll find an option to **List Variables**.

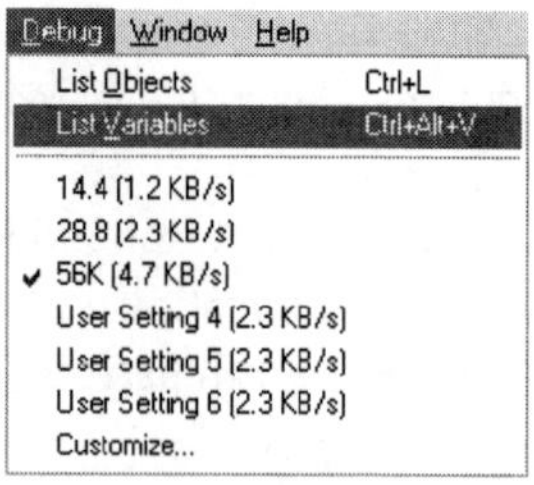

"Sounds promising—why don't we give it a shot?" I clicked the menu, and the class did the same. "You should all now see a panel called Output appear on your screen, with some text like this."

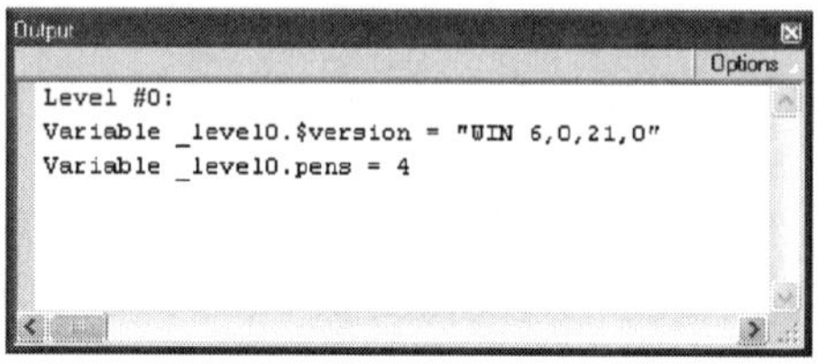

"I see only one line of text," said Joe. I switched the projector to his monitor, and sure enough there was only one line there.

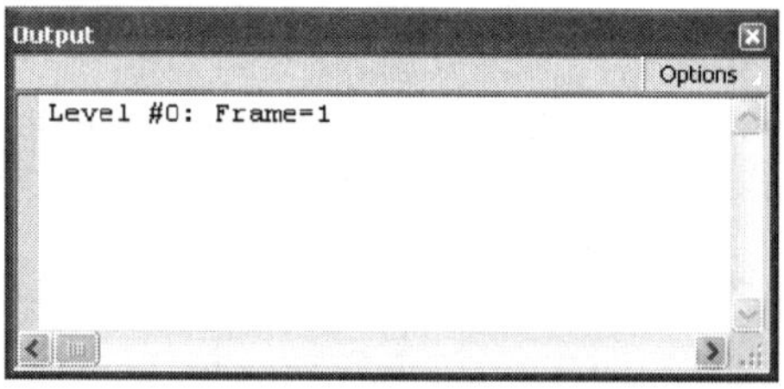

"I think you must have clicked the **List Objects** option instead of **List Variables**. Try selecting it again," I said. He did so, and his screen changed to show the correct information. I switched back to my screen and continued.

"The **Output** panel is where Flash shows you what's going on in the program. Not only can you check it to see what's happening, but also Flash will use it to tell you if there are any problems with the program. Overall, it's quite a handy panel.

"Okay, ignore the first two lines for now. In the third line you should be able to see that Flash has set your `pens` variable correctly."

"What does the 'level zero' bit mean?" asked Jim.

"Right," I began. "I won't go into this in great detail right now, but put very simply, Flash can load movies into other movies. I might have one movie containing video footage of Carl's band, and another containing one of Jim's animations. I have a third 'master' movie with two buttons: one to load Carl's video and one to load Jim's animation. I'll pick one or the other depending on my mood, or on a particularly good day I might choose to play them side by side at the same time.

"If I run the master movie, all the buttons and other stuff in the movie that isn't loaded in from outside will sit on `level0`. When I load another movie in, I have to assign it a level number, so Carl's video could end up on `level1` and Jim's animation on `level2`. By keeping them on different levels, it makes it easier for me, and Flash, to keep track of what's happening in each movie.

"The important thing to remember for now is that everything you create here today will be stored in `level0`.

"Now let's return to the coding environment by closing the Output panel and the blank screen. Just click the cross in the top-right corner to close them both. You can also use the menu command **File > Close** to close your Flash movie."

Tracing variables

"There's another way for you to look at what Flash is doing," I said. "The **`trace`** command is designed to send values to the Output panel while the movie's running. With this technique, you can even tell Flash what to display and when to display it.

"`trace` is a very simple Flash command. To start with, you just need to type the word 'trace' onto a new line in the Actions panel. Note that the word changes color to blue, signaling that Flash has recognized it as a reserved word. If it doesn't, you know you must have done something wrong, though that's most likely to be nothing more than a misspelling.

"You then need to tell Flash what it is that you want it to `trace`, and you do this by putting your variable name in parentheses. As soon as you type the opening bracket, though, you'll see something strange appear:

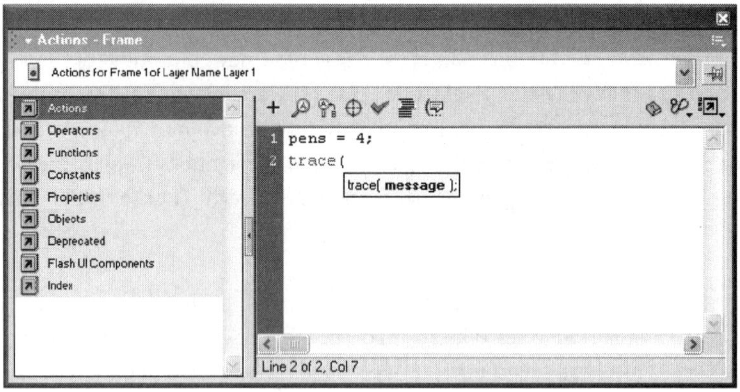

"This is another of Flash's little helping hands, and it's called a **code hint**. Flash tells you what it's expecting you to put after the `trace` command. It's telling you to say what you want it to `trace` and then to finish it off with a closing bracket and a semicolon, so you'd better do as it asks. Type in exactly what Flash is telling you to, but change `message` for your variable name `pens`. Finally, finish off the line with a semicolon like so:

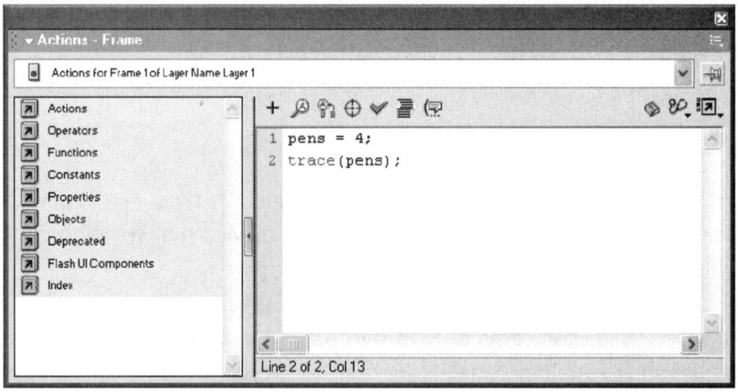

"Any questions?" I asked. Jim raised his hand and said, "I clicked somewhere else on the screen and my code hint thing disappeared. Is there a way I can get it back?"

"Yep, no problem, Jim," I responded. "Remember above the code window there were those two sets of icons that we skipped over earlier? Well, the last icon of the left bunch, the one that looks like a bracket with a speech bubble next to it, will show a code hint that was previously hidden:

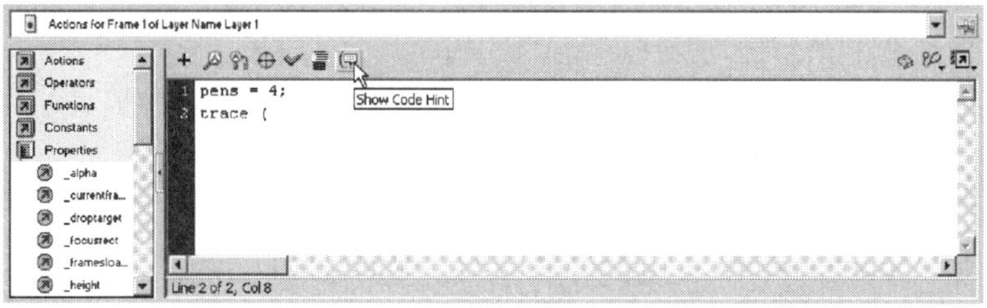

"To use it, the first thing that you have to do is put the cursor back in the position where the code hint originally appeared, so that's just after the opening bracket following 'trace'. Once that's done, just click the button and the code hint will appear again."

"That did it—thanks, Ken," Jim said.

"Okay," I continued, "once you've all finished entering the command . . ." I looked around the class, and they all indicated that they had ". . . you can test the movie again." Everyone did so, and this time they were all greeted with an Output panel containing the number 4:

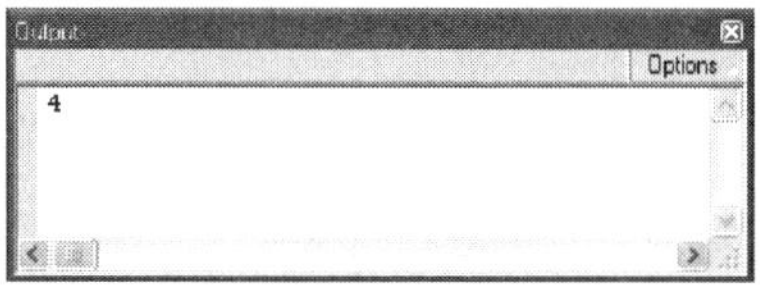

"As I said before, the great thing about the `trace` command is that not only do you control what information the computer gives you, but you also control when the computer gives you that information. For a quick demonstration of what I mean, let's add another couple of lines to the program. Close down the Output panel and return to Flash.

"The lines that you'll be adding are almost exactly the same as the two that you've already written. Luckily, you don't need to type all the words out again—you can simply copy and paste those two lines beneath the originals." I did so on my screen, showing them that they could use the **Edit > Copy** and **Edit > Paste** menu commands, or the keyboard shortcuts CTRL/CMD+C to copy and CTRL/CMD+V to paste.

"Now all you need to do is change the second of your pens variables to a new value, let's say 10. That should leave you with this:

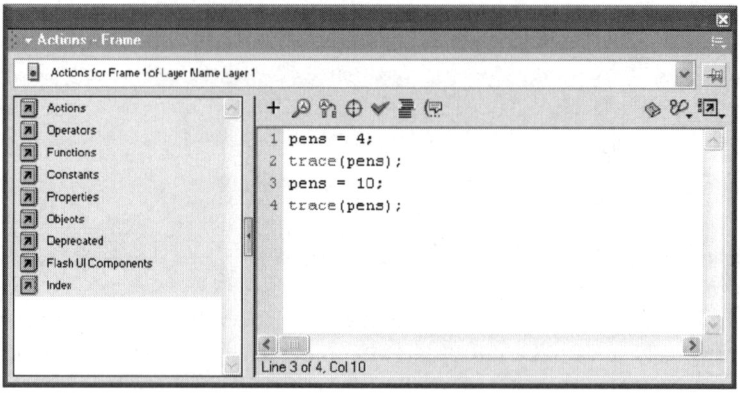

"Variable names are only useful as long as they're unique, so you can't have two of the same. If Flash comes across something like this, it assumes that you're just setting the old pens variable to a new value, and it overwrites the old one. But, as luck would have it, this is exactly what you want it to do!

"Can anyone tell me what we'll see in the Output panel when we run this program?" I asked. Jim spoke out, "I presume that we'll get the number 4, followed by the number 10."

"That's exactly right," I replied. "Let's run it and see.

"Okay, what's so special about this? Well, if you check the **List Variables** menu, you'll see that it only holds the current value of pens:

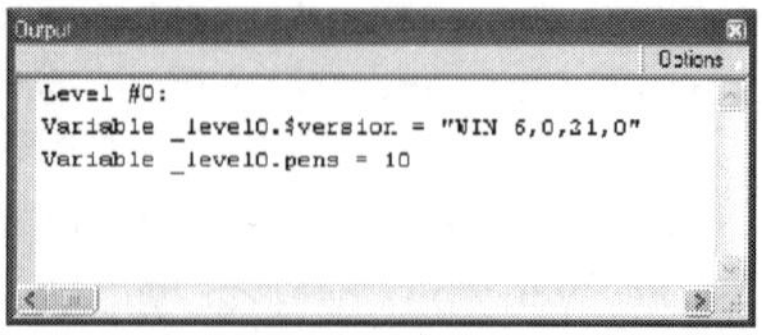

"By using the trace command, you can get information back at any stage of the program, rather than just looking to see that information at the end. Without the benefit of trace, you might never know that the variable had been changed halfway through the program.

This, along with a couple of other tricks that you'll learn later, will be invaluable in helping you test programs and unearth the bugs in them."

"Excuse me," said Mazzy, "but what's a bug?"

"Sorry," I laughed, "I should have explained that. A bug is anything in a program that causes it not to work properly."

"Why call it a 'bug,' though?" Mazzy asked.

"Well, back in the 1940s, computers were great, room-sized beasts that ran on telephone relays," I said. "The programs they ran (*all* written in 0s and 1s!) were very simple—by today's standards, anyway. All the same, they'd sometimes go completely wrong for no obvious reason. When the engineers who ran them snuck a peek inside, they discovered that moths had flown into the computer, gotten themselves caught in the relays, and quite literally blocked them up. Messages couldn't get through from one part of the computer to another, so the program couldn't do what it was meant to do.

"Ever since then, the word 'bug' has stuck. Now, if a program doesn't work, then you say that it has bugs, and you have to fix those bugs to make it run properly."

"Ah," said Mazzy, "that explains the meaning of the Debug menu. I wondered about it earlier, but I didn't have a chance to ask you about it."

"Yep, debugging a program simply means going through it trying to find and fix the problems," I said. "It won't actually track down any moths inside your computer, but with any luck, the only bugs you'll come across are of the code variety.

"Now remember, if there are any times when you don't understand something, then please just throw up your hand and ask away. I don't mind backtracking a bit to answer a question, and I can guarantee that if you don't understand something, it means I haven't explained it properly and there will be others in the class who haven't understood it fully too."

"All right then," said Mazzy, "I promise that in future I'll let you know whenever there are bugs in your teaching."

"Thank you," I said with a chuckle.

"Okay, let's look back over what we've done so far. Carl, I admit it's still not earth shattering, but you've learned some amazingly important things here. You now know how to give information to the computer and how to tell it to store that information under a name that's easy for you to remember.

"You've also learned how you can retrieve that information. You can go to **Debug > List Variables** to peek directly into the computer's information repository for that particular movie. Alternatively, you can use the `trace` command to tell the computer what you're looking for and to make it give you the information when you want it."

Different types of data

"Right, we've now finished with our first type of data," I continued, "and there are a couple more that we still need to look at. What we've covered so far is a number, or numerical variable. So, other than numbers, what other type of information do you think we'll need to use in our programming travels?"

"Umm . . . text?" suggested Gemma.

"That's right, but as I've already discovered, these programmers like to make things difficult, so rather than it being called 'text,' it's called a **string**," I said.

"A *string*?" said Carl, rolling his eyes, "What has string got to do with text? Wait, don't tell me . . . it comes from the days before telephones, when people would use two cans with some string between them to talk, and over the years the words that passed between the cans became known as strings? It's got to be something stupid like that." The class broke out in a rash of laughter.

"If only that were true," I said to Carl. "That's the best explanation I've heard in years. Unfortunately, the real reason is nothing like as romantic. It's called a string simply because it's a load of different characters strung together. For example, 'hello' is a string of five characters. The reason that we say 'characters' and not 'letters' is because strings can contain letters as well as numbers. In fact, strings can contain almost anything that you can find on the keyboard. Let's look at another example."

"Here," I said, writing on the board, "is a string of six characters."

8 cars

"But there are only five characters there," said Joe.

"Ah, but one's hidden," I said. "Can anyone tell me where the sixth character is?"

"Would it be the carriage return at the end of the line?" suggested Mazzy after a few seconds.

"No," I said, "but that's a very good guess. I'll give you a clue: The character isn't invisible. You can see it there on the board." This confused them even more, but then Gemma spoke up. "I know what it is! It's the space between the 8 and the word 'cars.' Am I right?"

"Yes, that's exactly it," I said. "So, whereas a number variable can contain only numbers and certain other special characters such as decimal points, a string variable can contain anything from a single character to the complete works of Shakespeare. Now, without any further ado about anything, let's see how to use these truly flexible variables." I went back to the projector.

"Take a look in the Actions panel. Here you can see that to make a numerical variable, you use the format 'name equals value' and finish it off with a semicolon. Creating a string variable is much the same, but the value needs to be enclosed in quotation marks, like this." I typed another line onto the program on the screen:

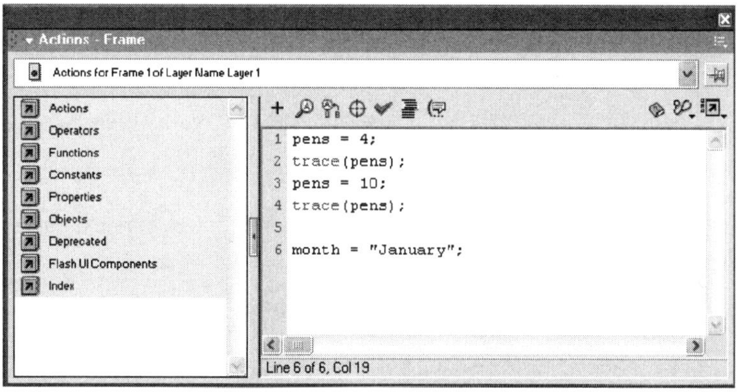

"One thing that you'll notice immediately is that Flash changes the color of strings too. They come out as a lighter blue.

"Strings are as easy to use as numbers, and you can `trace` them in exactly the same way. Okay, I want you all to add a string to your program and `trace` it." The class turned to their computers and started typing. It wasn't long before Carl had his hand up. "Yes, Carl?"

"Just curious, but what would happen if I didn't put the quotation marks in? Would it just blow up?" Carl asked.

"Actually, Carl, you'll be surprised to hear that it wouldn't. You'll see what will happen in just a second," I said.

"Okay," Carl responded.

Copying variables

"Right," I continued, "does everyone have their strings and `traces` working? Good. Remember how I said earlier that whenever Flash sees a variable name, it searches its memory to find the value that's stored with it? Well, this means that we can use a variable name in place of a value, and Flash will treat the variable name as the associated value. Let's look at an example." I cleared what I'd typed so far and started afresh:

```
coffees = 7;
drinks = coffees;
trace(drinks);
```

"Okay, let's walk through what's happening here. Mazzy, can you tell me what we're doing in line 1?"

"No problem," said Mazzy. "In the first line we're initializing a new variable named `coffees` and assigning it a value of 7."

"Thank you, Mazzy," I said. "I couldn't have put it better myself. Okay, Jim, you've got the difficult bit, can you tell us what you think is happening in line 2?"

"I'll give it a go," Jim replied. "I think I understand it—it's a bit like algebra. What we're doing is creating a new variable called `drinks`, and we're assigning it the value of the variable `coffees`. Now we know `coffees` is equal to 7, so we also know that by doing this, `drinks` will be set to 7 too. How's that?"

"Absolutely perfect," I said to him. "In fact, I even think it deserves a round of applause." I started clapping, and the rest of the class followed suit. Jim looked slightly embarrassed but still managed a seated bow. When the applause had died down he continued, "I have to admit that there's something that I'm not sure of, though. What happens to the `coffees` variable? Is it replaced by the new `drinks` variable?"

"No," I replied, "the `coffees` variable is left untouched. All that we're changing is the value of `drinks`. Jim, can you finish up by telling us what the last line will do?"

"Certainly," he replied. "When we run the program, the last line will `trace` the value that's stored in `drinks` and display it in the Output panel."

"And can you tell us what value that will be?" I asked.

"If I understood the last conversation right, it should be 7," he said.

"All right then," I said, "let's try it out and see." I ran the program and when the results appeared on the screen, the class cheered.

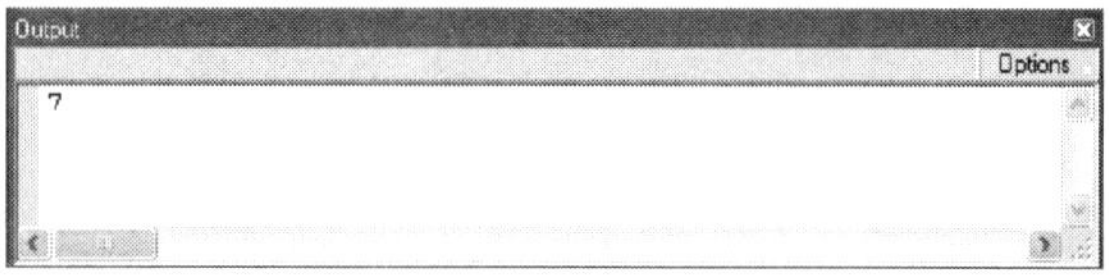

"Congratulations, you were all right," I told them. "So, is everyone happy with the basics of variables so far?"

"One quick question, Ken," Mazzy said. "We've looked at the last couple of examples with numbers, but I presume that the same thing will happen with strings?"

"Yes, Mazzy, it would be exactly the same. Here, I'll give you a quick demonstration." I made a slight amendment to the program and then ran it.

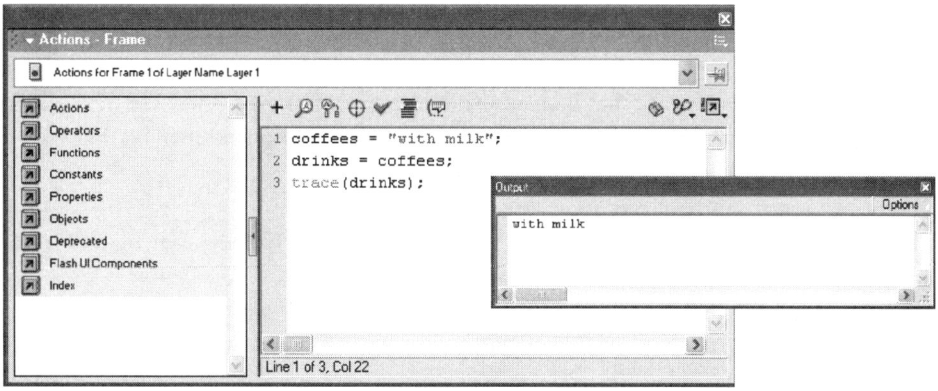

"You can see that we get the same result using a number or a string. With the next few examples that we're going to look at, though, you'll begin to see the differences between them."

Operators and expressions

"You've now seen how to create variables, but you haven't really done anything *with* them," I said. "Now you're going to make them earn their name. What Jim said earlier about variables being a bit like algebra was exactly right. For example, let's take a simple algebraic equation, **`a = b + c`.** In Flash, this is called an **expression**, a statement that can be evaluated to return a value. What do I mean by this? Well, let's take a look back at our algebra and put some numbers in it." I began writing on the board:

$$b = 10$$

$$c = 5$$

$$a = b + c$$

"In the last line, 'b + c' is a statement that we want to evaluate. It's fairly obvious that it will return the value of b *plus* the value of c. So, 'b + c' gives us 14."

"Fifteen!" called out Gemma and Jim in unison. "Just checking to see if you were awake," I said with a wry smile.

"Okay then," I continued, "we went to the statement and evaluated it, and what we returned with was a value. I'd say that fits our definition of an expression pretty well.

"Let's look at our expression. The only thing we haven't seen before is that 'plus' sign in the middle. The correct name for that is an **addition operator**. You may remember that I called the 'equals' sign an *assignment* operator earlier, so what's this operator thing that I keep talking about?"

"Is it the smooth guy on the end of the phone?" asked Carl. This was met by a flurry of giggles.

"Not quite," I said, "an operator is something that performs an operation on something else—in our case, these are mostly mathematical rather than surgical." Carl groaned at my pun, so I went on with the explanation.

"In our simple expression, we have two operators: one to add two values together and one to assign a value to a variable. Other operators that you're no doubt familiar with are the subtraction, multiplication, and division operators.

"Let's see how these can be translated into Flash. Well, in a fine example of how easy it is to translate English into ActionScript, all you have to do is add semicolons to the end of each line and you're done."

"Uh, Teach?" said Carl. "Algebra isn't exactly what I'd call English. I get what you're saying, and I see that it's nice and simple, but algebra's a touchy subject with me at the moment, and the less you say it's easy, the better I'll feel."

"Okay, Carl, I'll stop mentioning the 'A' word," I told him.

"You never know," said Mazzy, "all of this programming might help you with your math. And anyway, if I can follow it in my 50s, then I'm sure you can cope with it too." Carl looked shocked, but Mazzy turned and winked at him with a big smile on her face and he soon softened up. "You're right," he said, "it's just that whenever I hear that word I switch off. I guess the answer would be for me to listen more rather than for you to change. Okay algebra, do your worst, I'm not scared." He pulled a calculator out of his bag and waved it around menacingly to show just how ready he was.

"Right," I said, "after that brief intermission, the main program will resume. We were about to convert our ALGEBRA . . ." (said with menace, and met with furious calculator-waving from Carl) ". . . into code. As I said before, this is as simple as just adding semicolons to the line ends. I also want you to add an extra line to report back and display what the final value of 'a' is. First person to show me the correct Output panel wins a prize. On your marks, get set—GO!"

There was a cacophonous crash of keyboards, and Jim's hand was the first up out of the fray. "Me! Me! ME!" he cried. Carl reached forward and tried to wrestle Jim's arm down while still attempting to type at his own keyboard with his spare hand. Jim foiled him by simply raising his other hand too. "Okay, Jim, I think you were first. Let's take a look at your screen," I said, flicking the projector over to display his monitor.

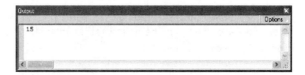

"That's the right result. Let's take a look at the code," I said. Jim closed the Output panel and went back to Flash.

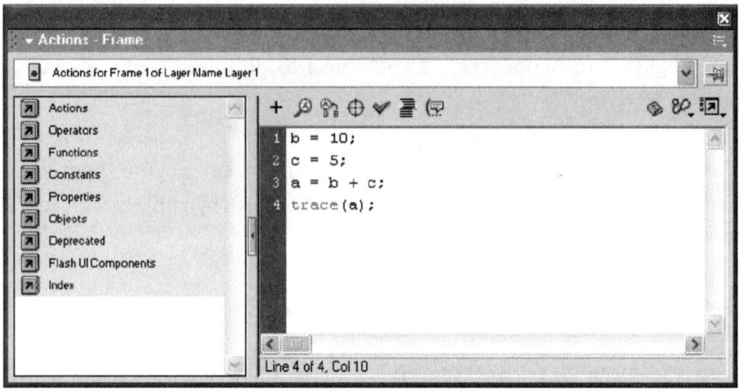

"That looks pretty good to me," I said. "Okay, your prize is to tell us what's happening there in Flash terms." Jim looked at me agog. "You're joking, right?" he asked. Meanwhile, Carl laughed behind him. I reached into my desk, fished out a candy bar that I'd bought from the gas station earlier, and tossed it to him. "All right, there you go, but you still have to tell us what the code means."

Jim thought for a second and carefully arranged the candy on his desk in full view of Carl. "Right, we start by initializing two variables, called `b` and `c`. We then create a new variable and assign it to the value of `b` plus `c`. In our case, `b` and `c` have the values 10 and 5, respectively, so `a` is set to be 10+5, which gives 15. Finally, we `trace` this value to the Output panel."

"Very good," I said. "You also managed to somehow avoid the trap that I had carefully set for you. I was hoping that you'd say we *initialized* the variable `a`, but in fact we don't."

"I guess I'm just too clever for you," smiled Jim.

“I’ll catch you yet,” I replied with a grin. “Okay, do you remember what I said earlier about initializing variables?” Mazzy checked back through her notes and replied, “That it was good form to initialize a variable before you used it and that initialization should be done with a specific value.”

“Thank you, Mazzy,” I said. “Can you all see what I was getting at now? We’ve initialized our first two variables here with very specific ‘hard’ values, but we’ve started using our third variable straight away. It isn’t *so* bad here because we can see what we’re setting it to just above it, but in a larger program we probably wouldn’t have that luxury.

“As you can see here, it isn’t essential to initialize your variables first in Flash, but in some other languages that you might come across, you’ll find that it is. If that were the case, then you’d initialize the variable a first by setting it to an arbitrary number—say, zero—and then use it. Something like this:

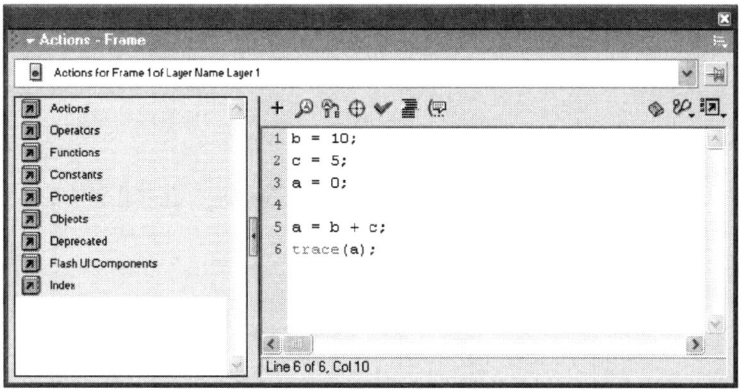

“Remember that we said that numbers and strings were different types of data? Well, in some other languages, you have to declare which type a variable will be before you can use it. So for example, you might have this:

```
string name = "Ken"
```

“This would create a new variable called name, make it a string, and give it a value of ‘Ken.’ Luckily for us, though, Flash is an untyped language, and it decides on the data type that we intend for a variable when we create it. But untyped variables have another interesting fact about them, as you’ll see in a moment: We can change their data type on the fly.

"Right, we've looked at adding two numbers together, but what happens when we add two strings together? Let's create another simple program." I opened a new movie on my computer, and typed out the following:

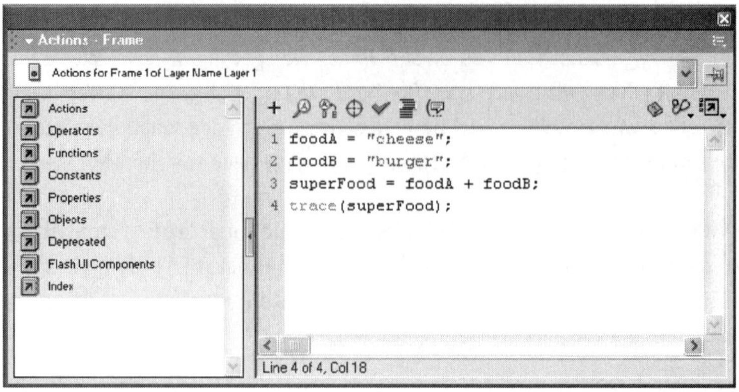

"Can anyone guess what we'll see in the Output panel?" I asked.

"Cheeseburger!" called out the class. I ran the program:

"That's right. When we add two strings together, the first string gets joined to the beginning of the second to create one long string. This process is called **concatenation**."

"Umm, can you spell that?" asked Mazzy. "Of course," I said, and did so.

"Now you'll see the magical changing data types," I continued. "If you add two numbers together, then the answer is another number. If you add two strings together, then the answer is another string, but anything added to a string will also result in a string. Let's take a look." I changed the program:

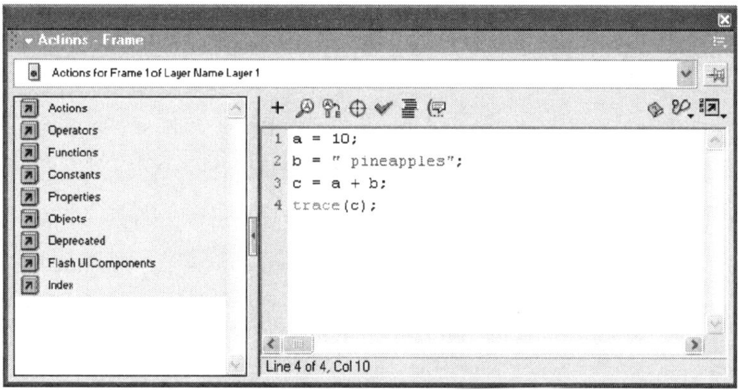

"Notice that I've added a space before 'pineapples.' If I now run the program, I get the following:

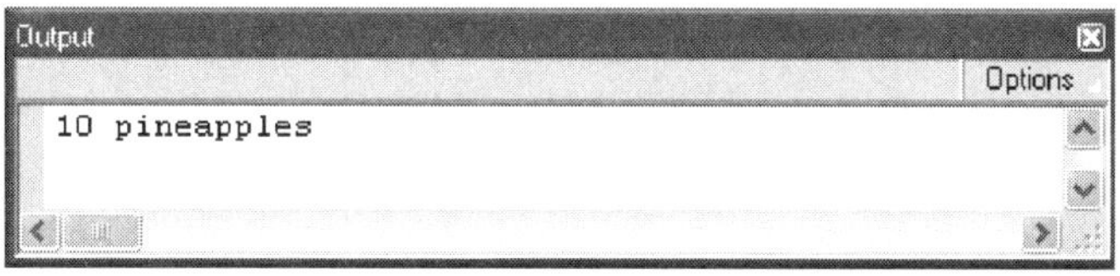

"If I also check the **List Variables** menu, then I can see what type my variables are:

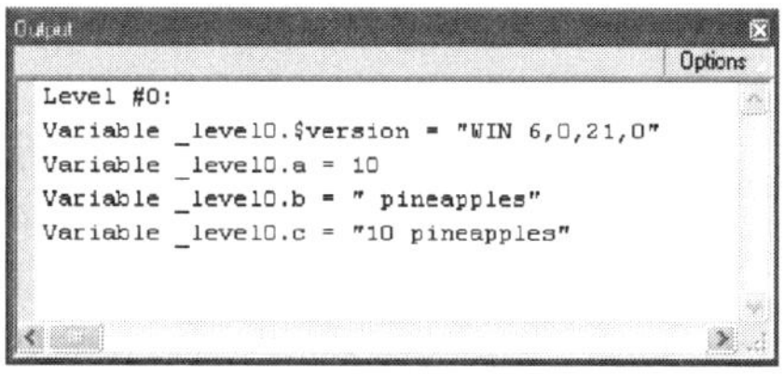

"As you can see, there are quotation marks around the value of variable c, indicating that it's a string. Now a quick test for you all—there's another prize for the first person to tell me what the output from the following program will be."

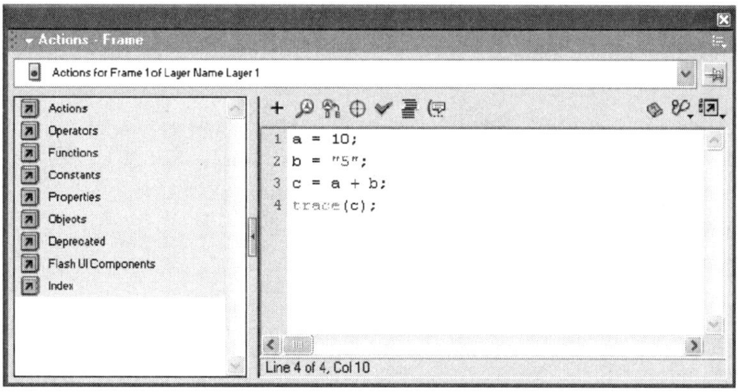

Carl's hand immediately shot up. "You seem pretty confident Carl," I said with a smile. "Okay then, what's the answer?"

"One hundred and five," he replied. It was Carl's turn to smile as he saw the obvious surprise on my face. "I bet you thought I was going to say 15 didn't you?" he taunted me. "I have to admit," I said, "that was what I thought."

"In that case," said Carl, "I think I deserve an extra prize for you not having faith in me. C'mon, pay up." I took two candies from my drawer, walked over to Carl, and handed him the candies. "Congratulations," I told him, "not only have you proved me wrong, but you also proved that you can pay attention to even the most seemingly boring algebra. That's definitely worth this prize. Now how about you tell the rest of the class how you arrived at your answer?"

"Easy," said Carl, looking very pleased with himself. "Although the first variable was a number, the second was a string. You can tell because of the quotes around it. As the good teacher said, anything added to a string gives an answer that's also a string, so I just treated them all as characters rather than numbers, and . . ." he cleared his throat, ". . . concatenated them." Mazzy reached over and patted Carl on the back, and the rest of the class looked at him appreciatively.

"Thank you, Carl," I said. "So does everyone follow that logic?" The class agreed that they did. "In that case," I went on, "let's move on to working with some other operators—the basic set of numerical operators. You'll recognize all of these from basic math." I turned and wrote on the board:

```
+, -, /, *
```

"In case you're not familiar with the last two, we use / instead of ÷ for division and * instead of x for multiplication on computers.

"Okay, we can use these operators with numbers in exactly the same way as we've been using the addition operator, and they behave exactly how we'd expect them to. Say we used any of these expressions in a program:

```
a = 3 + 7;
a = 14 - 4;
a = 5 / 0.5;
a = 2.5 * 4;
```

"All of these would give a the value 10. No big surprise there, but there's something else we need to be aware of."

Operator precedence

"Have any of you come across the idea of **operator precedence** before?" I asked. Jim raised his hand. "If it's what I think it is, then yes," he said.

"Good," I said, "I'm sure it will ring a few bells with more of you as we go through it. Jim, would you like to start us off?"

"All right," Jim began slowly. "Precedence comes into play when we have more than one operator in an expression. Can I use the board, Ken?"

"By all means," I replied. Jim walked over to the board and continued, writing down examples as he discussed them.

10 + 3 + 2 =

"When we have multiple operators, the usual procedure is to work from left to right, so in this example, 10 + 3 = 13, and 13 + 2 = 15. This is all well and good when we have a simple sum containing two addition operators, but it gets confusing when the operators are different. For example:

10 + 3 * 2 =

"Now, if we use the same procedure and work from left to right, then we'd go 10 + 3 = 13 and 13 * 2 = 26. Unfortunately, most math teachers would fail us for that logic, and tell us that the answer was 16. How do we get 16? Well, in the order of precedence, multiplication comes before addition, so we work that out first: 2 * 3 = 6, and then 10 + 6 = 16. It's just a convention to stop people from getting confused, and to make sure that we all get the same results.

"The order of precedence goes like this:

1. multiplication
2. division
3. addition
4. subtraction

"So that's the order in which parts of a sum are worked out." Jim turned to me. "Can I set a quick challenge, Ken?"

"Sure," I replied, "but I don't know how many candy bars I have left, so you might just want to say that the winner gets to be smug for 5 minutes."

"Okay, then, can anyone tell me what the answer to this would be?" Jim asked.

$$9 + 4 * 5 / 10 - 1 = ?$$

The class scratched their heads over it for a while, and it was Mazzy who finally came up with the correct answer: 10. "That's right," said Jim. "Let's quickly work through the sum in the order of precedence to find out why. Multiplication first . . .

$$4 * 5 = 20$$

". . . followed by division . . .

$$20 / 10 = 2$$

". . . then addition . . ."

$$9 + 2 = 11$$

". . . and finally subtraction.

$$11 - 1 = 10$$

"Of course, we'd never normally see a sum written like that." He turned to me and said, "Do you want me to continue?"

"Sure, you're doing great," I told him.

"Normally, we use parentheses to mark out parts of an expression that need to be worked out first. For example:

$$(10 + 3) * 2 =$$

"In this case, the answer really is 26 because whatever's in parentheses is always worked out before everything else. Using parentheses makes everything a lot clearer, so quite a few people will forget about the order of precedence altogether and just use parentheses to denote everything. Although this is perfectly acceptable, I think it's much better to learn the order of precedence, and then use a mix of both that and parentheses to get the best results." Jim took a bow, and returned to his seat.

"Thanks a lot, Jim," I said, "that was very informative. Has everyone jotted down the order of precedence?" The class nodded that they had. I began wiping the board clean when Gemma stopped me with a question. "Before you clean it all off, could you just help me with something?"

"Of course, Gemma, what is it?" I asked.

"I've been playing around with that formula that Jim wrote on the board to show the order of precedence," said Gemma, "and I've been trying to put parentheses in it but having a few problems."

"Okay, was it this one?" I said, pointing at the board. "That's it," she replied.

$$9 + 4 * 5 / 10 - 1 = ?$$

"Well, the easiest way to add the parentheses is to follow the order of precedence," I said. "If you're doing things this way and putting parentheses onto an expression that you've already created, then you'll often find that you have parentheses inside parentheses, and it all gets a bit confusing.

"The rule is, don't put new parentheses inside ones you've already added. Once you've added parentheses, treat them as if they were the number to be solved. Let's take a look. First of all, we put parentheses around the multiplication:

$$9 + (4 * 5) / 10 - 1 = ?$$

"Next is the division, but remember that we can't put parentheses inside ones that we've already created, so our division parentheses go around our earlier multiplication ones:

$$9 + ((4 * 5) / 10) - 1 = ?$$

"Following the same rules, we then need to add our addition parentheses:

$$(9 + ((4 * 5) / 10)) - 1 = ?$$

"We don't need to use parentheses for the last part of the expression because there's nothing else left to get confused with, but for the sake of completeness:

$$((9 + ((4 * 5) / 10)) - 1) = ?$$

"As you can see, this is starting to look a lot more complicated than our original expression. As Jim said earlier, it's better to know the order of precedence and how to use parentheses. Then you have the most freedom to choose whichever you like."

Advanced tracing

"Okay, now that you know how to add things together, you can take another look at your `trace` command and start to get full use out of it," I said.

"All of the times that you've used `trace` so far, you've only ever returned a value in the Output panel. This is fine for short programs or when you're tracing only one thing, but as things begin to get more complicated, then you need more information with your `trace`s. You can achieve this by writing a simple description of the variable that you're tracing and then adding the value to it when you `trace` it. Let's take a look." I wrote on the board:

```
seriesWins = 8;
trace(seriesWins);
```

"If you typed this into Flash and ran it, all you'd get in return would be the number 8. If you forget about the program and just focus on the output for a second, then you can see just how inadequate it is. Eight what? Eight windows? Eight leaves? You need to qualify this information somehow, ideally by having something in the Output panel like this:

```
The number of wins this season is 8
```

"Now there are a couple of ways to achieve this. The one that fits most comfortably into what you've learned so far involves creating another variable with this extra information in. You then add that to your original variable and `trace` the result like this:

```
seriesWins = 8;
extraInfo = "The number of wins this season is " + seriesWins;
trace(extraInfo);
```

"This would give you the answer that you want, but there's a better way. You can dispense with the `extraInfo` variable altogether and add your description inside the `trace` command itself.

"You can include any expression within the parentheses of the `trace` command, and it will evaluate this expression and display the result in the Output panel. So," I turned to Flash, "you could rewrite that earlier program like this:

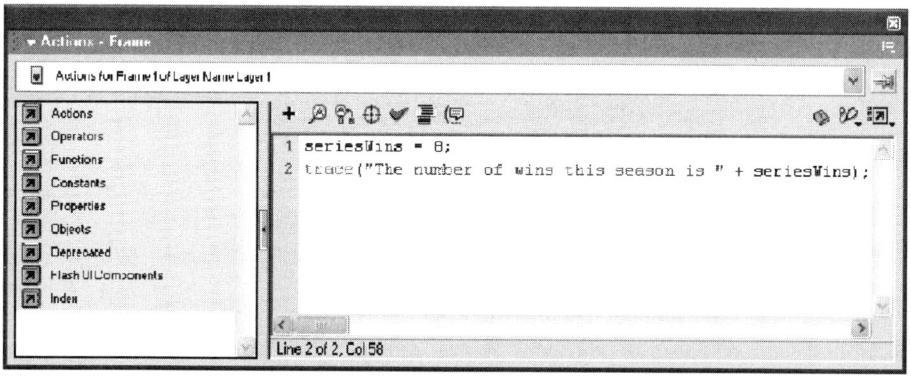

"Run this, and you should get your desired result:

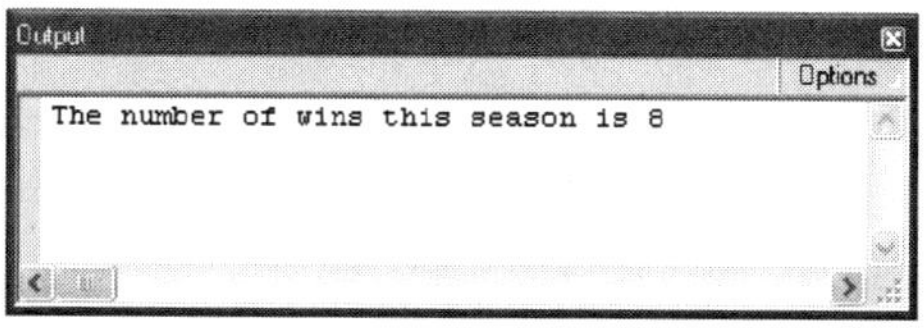

"This is flexible enough to display any string you want. So, for example, you could put the number in the middle of the sentence by simply adding a string on either side of it:

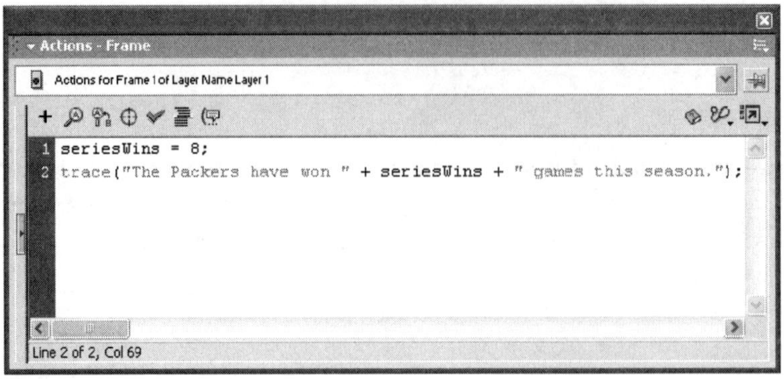

"Notice how I've put spaces in the strings on both sides of the variable to make sure that it displays correctly, like this:

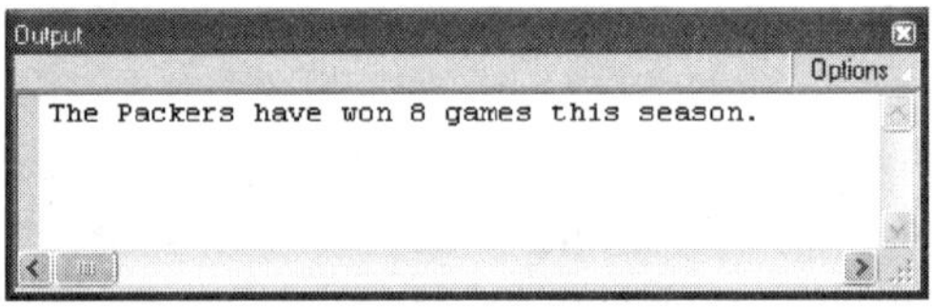

"Without the spaces, you'd just see a mess like this:

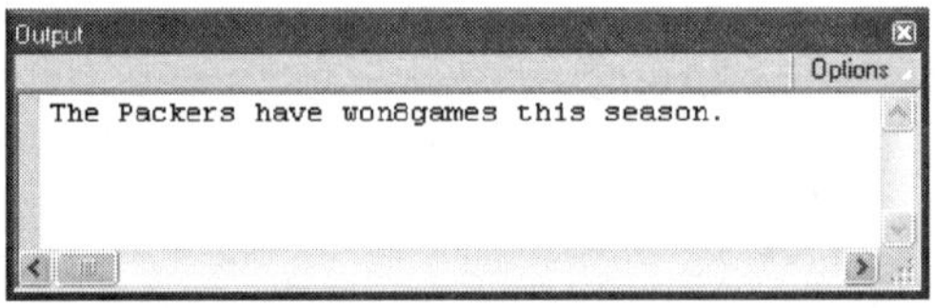

"Okay, you've learned quite a few important concepts today, so let's finish off by thinking about how you could use some of what you've learned to help out Randy."

The case study

"Variables are such basic building blocks of programming that we'll be using them everywhere throughout the case study," I said, "but can anybody think of any specific pieces of data that we could store in variables?"

"How about the total number of pictures?" suggested Jim.

"Or indeed the number of pictures in each category?" said Mazzy.

"And what about the number of categories?" asked Jim.

"And could the names of categories be strings?" Mazzy inquired.

"Would the size of our grid fit into a variable?" Joe pondered.

"What about the volume of the background music?" mused Carl, mostly to himself.

I laughed. "And what about you, Gemma? Can you think of anywhere we could use variables in the case study?"

"I was actually wondering," Gemma began, "whether the `trace` method of data reporting that we've been looking at could be used to display the end of day reports for Randy."

"Swot!" shouted Carl.

I studiously ignored Carl and replied to Gemma, "The method of combining strings and numerical variables that we've been exploring will, indeed, be used a lot in the reports that we'll be preparing. We won't, however, be using `trace` to report the information back to Randy.

"The `trace` command and the Output panel are debugging tools—they're only there for the programmer's benefit. The end user will never see the Output panel or the results of a `trace` at all. We'll be exploring the ways that we can display the reports to Randy in later lessons.

"For now, though, have a good evening, and I'll see you all next week."

After everyone had left, it occurred to me that I'd completely forgotten to show them the e-mail from Randy as I'd promised at the start of the lesson. I quickly forwarded it around the class e-mail addresses, with an apology and a note saying that for their homework this week, they could look over the e-mail and get back to me with any questions ready for next week's class.

```
From: Randall Holmes [mailto:randall@rhphotostudios.inc]
Sent: 25 February 2003 6:37 pm
To: Ken Jokol
Subject: Re: Quick questions for Flash gallery

Hi Ken,

Thanks for your mail. I've answered all of your questions below. Let me
know if you need any more info from me.

Thanks for all your help with this, I appreciate it.

Randy


>> "Can you give us a list of the different types of work that you
>> do, and the categories that you'd like to have displayed?"

Wedding shoots (also studio wedding portraits)
Corporate shoots, both studio and site-based
Arty pictures for sale at the gallery
Nature pictures for sale at the gallery
Family pictures, both studio and site based
Portraits – schools, graduations, etc. both studio and site based

Those are the main areas, but I'm not sure if I'll want to separate them
like that. How about 'Family, Outdoor, Artistic, and Portraits'?

>> "What information do you need to keep with each picture?"

I need:
– a reference number
- the title of the picture
```

- a short description of the picture
- the basic category that the image falls into

I'll send over a list of all of the images and the information to be stored with them as soon as I can.

>> "Where do you intend to place the kiosk?"

I was thinking of having it in the middle of the gallery so that it's immediately visible as clients enter the gallery, and within easy reach no matter where the clients are. I've got a plinth thing that should be suitable to keep it on.

>> "How big will the kiosk monitor be, and what resolution will you
>> be running it in?"

I've got an old monitor here that I don't use any more, which I thought would do. It's a 17" monitor, and I normally run it at 800 x 600 resolution at 96 dpi.

>> "We're thinking of using tooltips with a short delay on them to
>> show the picture title whenever the user rolls over a thumbnail.
>> Does this sound all right to you?"

Yeah, that sounds great. I've seen some image galleries online that did that, and it seemed really intuitive.

>> "What other information needs to be displayed with the enlarged
>> photographs?"

I'll give you a list of the text that I'd like when I send you the pictures. It changes between pictures, but mostly it's just a short description of the picture and sometimes the picture size or a price as well. This can all be in the same block of text, though.

>> "Can pictures be part of more than one category?"

No, I hadn't planned on that. One category per picture is all that's required.

>> "How many categories do you want?"

I was planning on 4 – see one of my earlier answers for the names.

>> "What is the maximum number of photographs for any one category?"

I'm not sure, something like 10 per category would be fine. Maybe a couple more . . . Let me know what looks good, but something around that figure I'd think.

>> "What information would you like to store for the statistics
>> report that we discussed?"

Let me see, I'll need the number of times that the each image has been clicked, the index number of the image, the image name so I can tell which one it is without cross-referencing the index numbers . . . oh, and it might be handy to store the category too so that I can see which is the most popular. Will that be okay?

>> "Will it be okay for the report to run continuously, and then you
>> can check it and reset it whenever you want? I'd have thought
>> something like once a day would be fine. The other option would be
>> to have it run on a timer, but Mazzy informed us that you don't
>> always keep to normal hours."

She's right, I often close early or shut the gallery if I'm the only person there and there's an important shoot to do. Of course, I try to have cover whenever possible, but sometimes I just have to close for a few hours, and if that's toward the end of the day then I'll just close up shop. It would be great for me if I could get the statistics whenever I need to. Will I then be able to simply print them out for my records?

>> "We're thinking of having a keyboard-operated login screen that
>> you'll need a password to access. Also, I suggest that the
>> keyboard is normally kept somewhere that the customers can't

>> reach it, as they'll only need the mouse to navigate the
>> program. This will also prevent any unwanted computer tampering."

Sounds good to me. There's already a lockable drawer in the plinth that I had in mind, so I can just drill a hole in the back of that for the wire and keep the keyboard safely stored in there. I'm not brilliant with passwords, though, so I'll have to get back to you with something that's easy for me to remember.

>> "How would you like the report displayed? Is a table okay, or
>> would you prefer a graph or something more dynamic?"

A list is fine by me. As long as the information is simply laid out and easy to read then I'm happy. I don't want some overly pretty but impossible to read chart, if that's okay.

>> "Finally, we'll need some contact information and some brief
>> information about yourself for the CD version."

Okay, I'll have a think and send it along in a couple of days. How much would you like me to write for the 'about me' bit?

Summary

Today's lesson introduced you to the basic building blocks of programming. You started by thinking about what a computer program actually is:

- "A computer program is a set of instructions written in a programming language and given to a computer to achieve an aim."

You were then introduced to the Actions panel and saw how it enables you to feed instructions into a Flash movie.

The next step was to start coming to grips with the ActionScript language, so that you can write programs that your Flash movies will understand. You learned about

- Variables, which use name/value pairs to store data in the computer's memory. You looked at the rules of good variable naming, including
    - Should be self-explanatory
    - Must not contain spaces
    - Must not be "reserved" words
- The `trace` action, for showing values in the Output panel.
- Operators such as =, +, -, *, and /, which let you control and modify the information in a program.
- Expressions that combine several operators in one command. You looked at rules of precedence that determine the order in which the operators operate and how you can use parentheses to override these rules.

In the next lesson, you'll be looking at symbols in Flash, and you'll see how your programs can start to affect what's on the stage.

Class 4
Symbols and Objects

Objectives

In today's class, you'll learn about

- Symbols
- Movie clips, graphics, and buttons
- Instances
- Object properties and methods

Introduction

Even though the students have worked a little in Flash so far, they have yet to learn about the most important elements for programming in Flash: symbols and instances. In this class the students will learn what symbols are, why they are important, and how they are used with ActionScript.

Symbols

"If you remember back to the first class," I started, "you all had the opportunity to experiment a little with Flash's drawing tools. Even though this might have been important in grounding you in Flash, there's something a lot more significant to your classes and programming: **symbols**. From now on, you'll all use symbols almost every time you use Flash.

"Symbols are, at the most basic level, a way of storing things in Flash so that they can be reused again and again. These things can be animations, graphics, bitmap images, or any other content imaginable within the Flash application. All of the symbols in a Flash file are stored in the Library panel.

"There are endless advantages to using symbols. The first of these is the reusability factor. Once you've made something, such as a graphic, into a symbol, it can be cloned over and over again. The next significant factor that stems from recycling graphics is that Flash files are smaller with reused assets. Besides vector graphics, the other key to Flash's low file sizes relates to symbol reuse.

"The most important factor for using symbols for your classes relates to programming. Using symbols allows you to control them with ActionScript and opens up endless creative and programmatic possibilities. Before I go any further, let's all create a basic symbol so you can see the flexibility that they bring you."

Creating a symbol

"You're going to make a forest," I said. "The reason I've chosen this is because a forest consists of a number of trees. If you draw one tree graphic and convert it into a symbol, you'll have the ability to make the whole forest through some cloning."

"Sounds like great fertilizer," Joe started. "I wish I could get some of that!"

"Me too," I said. "I have black fingers—the touch of death!"

"Wow! Great name for a band, Ken," Carl said, scribbling something down.

"Thanks, Carl," I said. "Now, everyone start Flash MX and draw a simple tree on the stage using the basic tools."

I gave the students a few minutes and went around the class checking if everyone had finished drawing.

"Okay, now that you all have a tree—" I started.

Mazzy interrupted, "Or something resembling one!"

"We need to make it into a symbol," I said. "Before that, who was listening 5 minutes ago and remembers where Flash symbols are stored?"

Gemma raised her hand. "In the Library?" she ventured.

"Correct, Gemma. Symbols are stored in the Library panel." I instructed the class to open the Library from the **Window menu**. "Yours will be empty for now, but in a moment you'll be able to see your tree symbol.

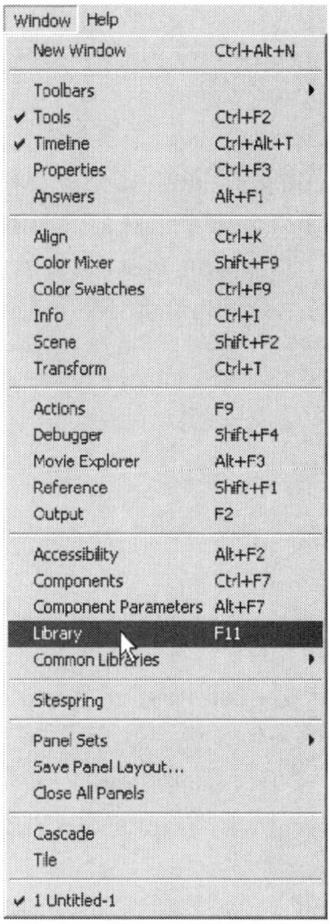

"Okay, select all of the tree using the Arrow tool and select **Convert to Symbol** from the **Insert** menu." I showed the class how to do this over the projector:

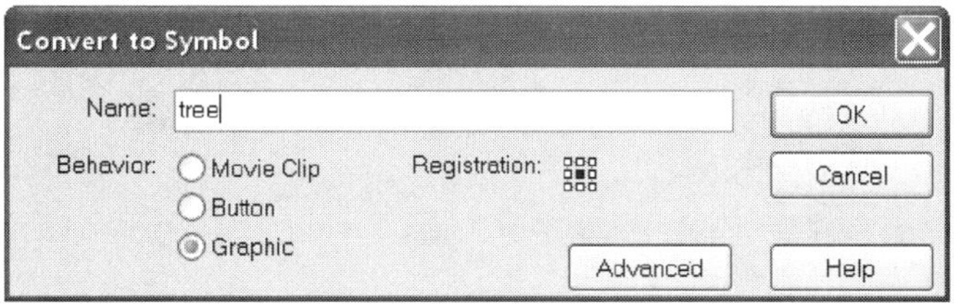

"The dialog box that appears will request a little information about the new symbol that you're creating. For now, give it the name tree, a Graphic behavior, and leave all the other information as it is. Then click **OK**.

"If you look at your tree on the stage now, it's surrounded by a blue box. This is Flash's way of telling you that it's a symbol. You should see the new symbol stored in the Library panel.

"You can now drag and clone as many copies of the tree symbol from the Library onto the stage as you want. Give this a try, creating a small forest with multiple copies. Remember when I talked about recycling and small file sizes? In this case, you would have to load in only one tree graphic, because all of the clones use the same symbol from the Library.

"Each cloned copy of the symbol dragged from the Library is called an **instance**. Each tree, therefore, is an instance of the tree symbol.

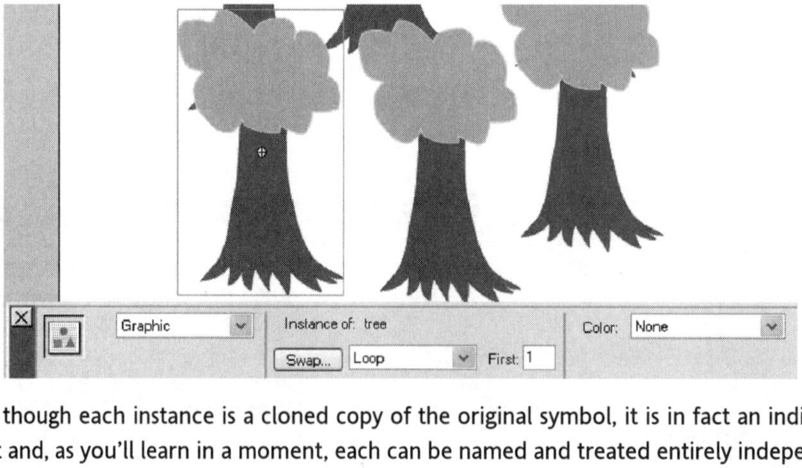

"Even though each instance is a cloned copy of the original symbol, it is in fact an individual object and, as you'll learn in a moment, each can be named and treated entirely independent of the others.

"There is just one catch: Each instance is always directly linked to the parent, and if the appearance or 'behavior' of the parent is changed, all of the cloned instances change too."

"There is no hope for teenage rebels after all," Jim said, winking at Carl. "One day, we all have to don our crisp white shirts and navy suits and head for the office." Carl shivered theatrically as if a draft had suddenly revealed itself.

"Not quite, Jim," I said. "Each instance can be an individual. It might not be able to wear denim to the office, but it sure doesn't have to put on the typical business attire. Even though instances are linked to the appearance of the parent symbol, many of their visual properties can be changed. This includes size, color, and transparency."

"Show me how!" Carl said. "I have a tree that's *growing* apart from the others!"

Many of the students groaned at Carl's dry pun. "Please show him," Joe said, "before we get another one of those crackers!"

"My pleasure, Joe," I said. "Let's start with a little color change. First, select the tree instance you want to change and, in the Property inspector, click the **Color** drop-down menu. Select **Tint** from the menu.

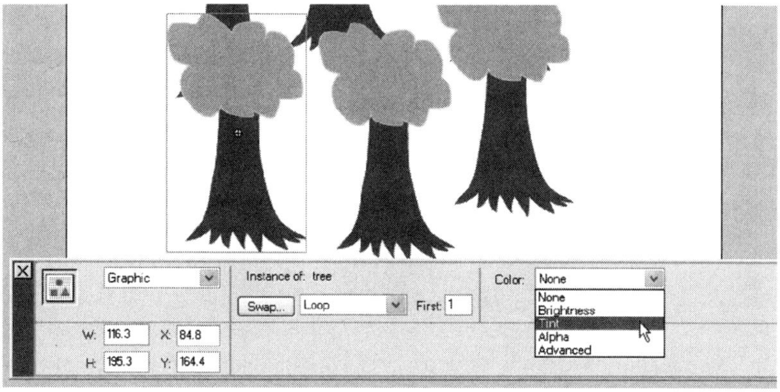

"Changing the input values appears to change the tint color of the selected instance. You can select a color from the palette, and the three RGB values below represent your choice. The percentage value signifies the intensity of the tinting—a 100% tint will remove all definition from your tree, leaving you with a colored silhouette.

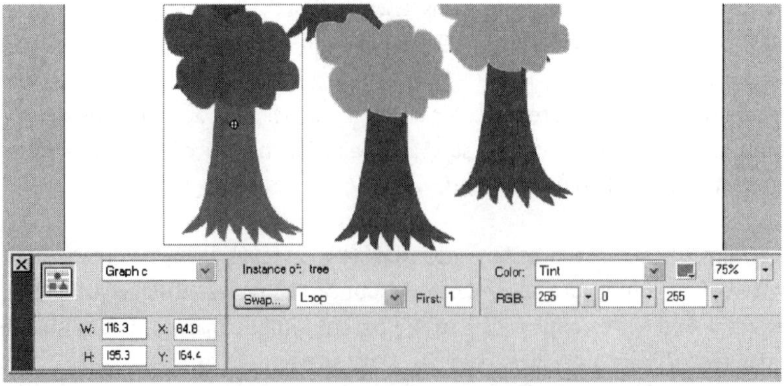

"The second major change that you can make to instances is to change their physical size, rotation, or shape. Select an instance and use the Free Transform tool to distort it a little." I scaled and rotated the tree instance.

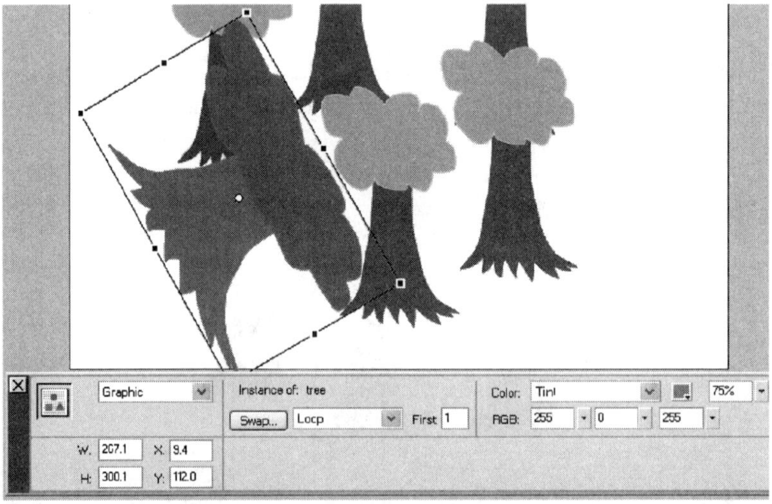

"I hope that's enough individuality for you, Carl," I joked. "Now that we've looked at symbol basics, let's get a little more in depth."

Symbol types

"So far you've used only one symbol type, but there are three in all, one of which you'll use a lot more than the others," I started. "The three available symbol types in Flash are graphic, button, and movie clip." I wrote these on the board:

graphic
button
movie clip

"I'll cut to the chase and reveal that the movie clip symbol type is by far the most important to us, and it's the one that we'll be using time and time again. It will be of most benefit if I cover the movie clip type first and then quickly look at the other two types."

Movie clip symbols

"Movie clip symbols are arguably the most useful type because each movie clip has its own timeline very much like the main timeline," I said. "This makes movie clips extremely useful for storing segments of animation, video, or any other content. In fact, a movie clip is the ultimate Flash container because it's so versatile.

"Say, for example, you want an animated forest. You could create an animated tree and drag multiple instances of it onto the main stage. Let me show you a typical movie clip timeline."

I selected **Insert > New Symbol** and gave the symbol the name a movie clip. I changed the Behavior to **Movie Clip**. Before I had time to click **OK**, Gemma butted in.

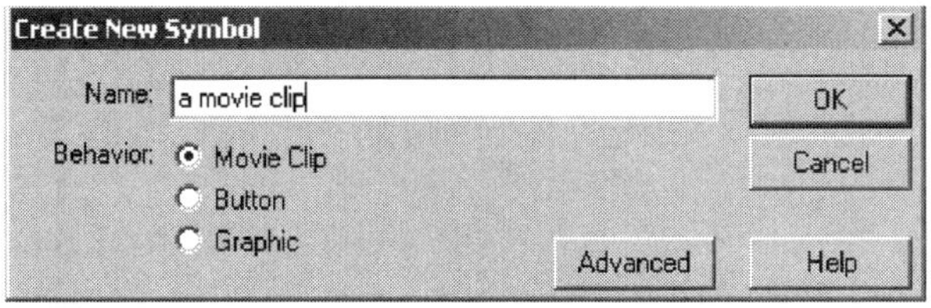

"You did it differently last time," Gemma observed. "You didn't select anything to turn it into a symbol."

"That's because this time I'm making a fresh symbol, so I've chosen **Insert > New Symbol**. Last time I was converting my drawing into a symbol, so I selected **Insert > Convert to Symbol**," I replied. "Once I click **OK**, I'll be transported to the new movie clip timeline so I can put some content in it." I clicked **OK**.

"Now, even though this might look just the same as the main timeline, it is in fact the timeline of a whole new movie clip. If you look just below the timeline, you'll see that the new movie clip name has been added alongside the Scene 1 text."

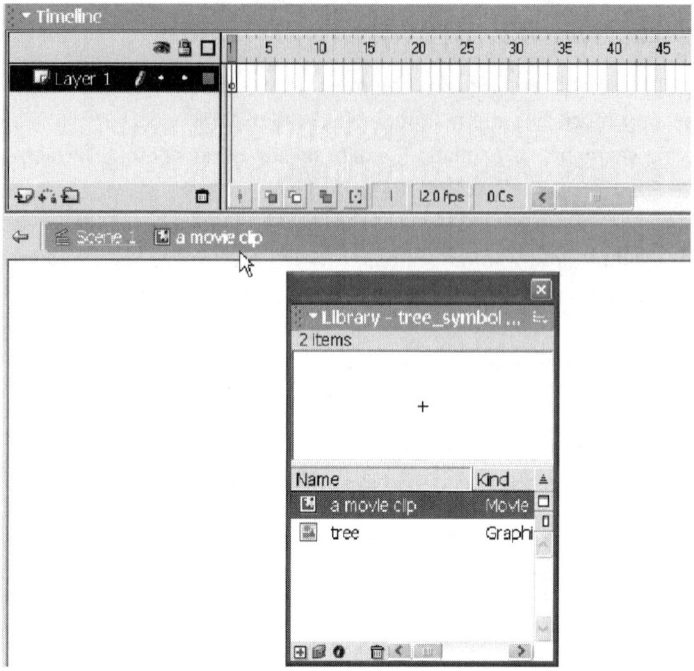

"Scene 1 is the main timeline, right?" Jim asked. "Was that bar always a darker color like that?"

"Scene 1 is the main timeline that we're familiar with, Jim," I said. "Normally, the bar is lighter. What's happening here is that we're in the new movie clip's **symbol-editing mode**. This mode is used to edit or add to a symbol.

"The crosshairs in the center is called the **registration point**. The registration point is the anchor point of the symbol. This is the point that a symbol is rotated around."

"So it's the center point, then?" Joe asked.

"If that's how you'd like to think of it, go ahead," I said. "Later in class, I'll show you how the registration point earns its money. For now, though, I'd like you all to create a new movie clip and to draw some content on two keyframes within the movie clip's timeline. It doesn't matter what you draw, just make sure that the content of the two keyframes is different. I'll come back in a few minutes to see how you're doing."

The students immediately focused on their monitors and I left the class to fetch a cup of coffee. When I returned, many of the students appeared to still be hard at work.

"Don't be fussy about what you're drawing," I said. "The important thing is to have different content over two keyframes." At that, the working students looked up.

Mazzy said, "I couldn't remember how to add an empty keyframe, Ken. Jim straightened me out, though."

"All actions involving frames or keyframes are located on the **Insert** menu," I said. "If you ever get stuck again, chances are you'll find what you want there.

"Do you all have a movie clip in the Library with two keyframes of content?" I asked. The students all nodded. "Now, I'd like you all to return to the main timeline by clicking the Scene 1 button."

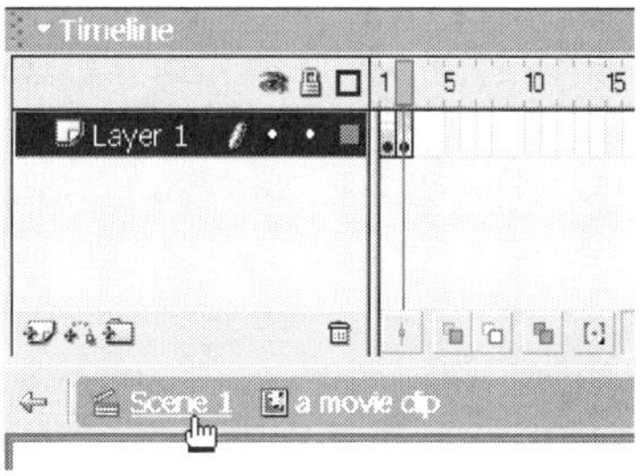

"Can we drag the movie clip out onto the stage now, Ken?" Carl asked.

"You're always one step ahead of me, Carl," I said. "Insert a new layer first, and then go ahead and drag a few copies of the movie clip onto the stage." I gave the students a moment to do this. "When you're done, test the movie and watch what you've just made."

"It's not very pretty," Joe said.

"It's giving me a headache," Mazzy said. Carl laughed. "Yours is enough to give anyone a migraine," he said.

"I appreciate that what you've made isn't award-winning animation," I said, "because it's flickering so fast, but it shows you the power of the movie clip. Each of the movie clip symbols loops and runs at the same frame rate as the main timeline but is independent of it. This shows you how you can create complex animations and movies without cluttering up the main timeline.

"Movie clips help you create animations, and they're also the prime symbol used for control with ActionScript. As you already know, each of the symbols on the stage is an instance of the parent symbol. Movie clip instances can be named and controlled individually.

"Select a single movie clip instance and take a look at the Property inspector:

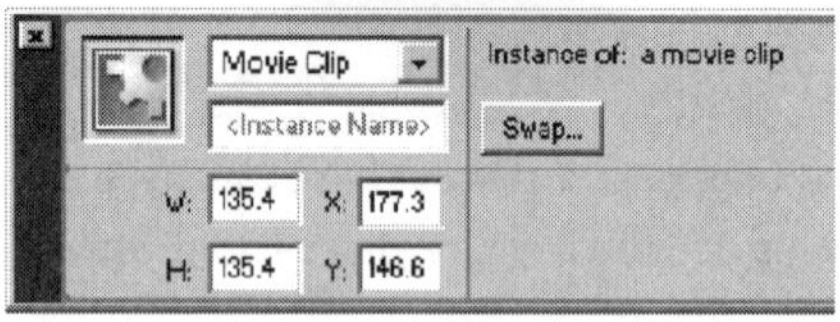

"The Instance Name text field here is where you name movie clip or button instances. Later in the class, you'll see how this can be used to control symbol instances with ActionScript.

"For now, though, let's quickly look at the graphic symbol."

The graphic symbol

"Of the three symbol types, this one is the least useful for our purposes," I said. "The graphic symbol is used for single-frame images or graphics, so the content of graphic symbols is largely static.

"Double-click the tree symbol in the Library to enter symbol-editing mode for it. Even though you might see a timeline like the movie clip timeline, this one doesn't allow for animation:

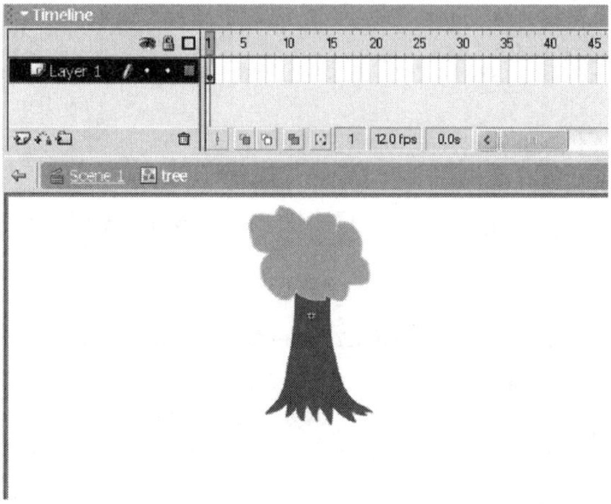

"The major downside to graphic symbols is that their instances can't be given instance names, and therefore they're useless for ActionScript and programming purposes."

"I guess there isn't much point dwelling on these then, is there?" Jim said.

"Not really, Jim," I responded. "But before I move on to tell you about buttons, remember that I talked about the visual link between the parent symbol and its instances? Let's see this in action. Now distort or change the tree in some way and then return to the main timeline.

"You'll quickly notice that all of the instances have been updated too. This is because you changed the original symbol and the instances reflect the current state of their parent."

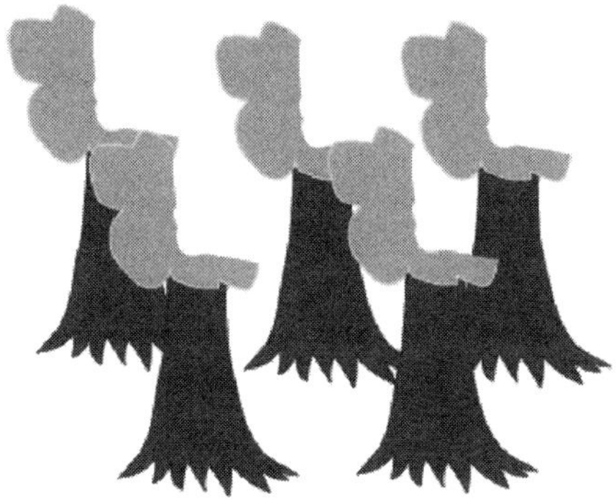

"It's all a bit like pop and fashion," Joe said. "As soon as Britney Spears changes her outfit, my daughter changes her clothes to copy her."

"Thanks for the insight, Joe," I laughed. "Now on to the next type of symbol: the button symbol."

The button symbol

"In previous versions of Flash, the button symbol was pretty important for all interaction," I started. "With the release of Flash MX, buttons have kind of taken a back seat, but they're still often used for simplicity.

"The button symbol is totally different from the other two types because it's used exclusively for cursor-based interaction. A typical button symbol has three graphical states that change depending on cursor interaction: one for the normal button, one for a rollover, and one for a mouse press." I drew a diagram on the board.

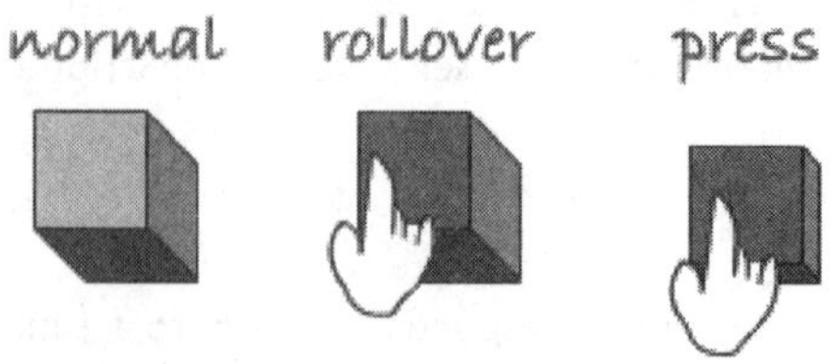

"The difference is noticeable in a button symbol timeline." I selected **Insert > New Symbol** and chose a button type symbol.

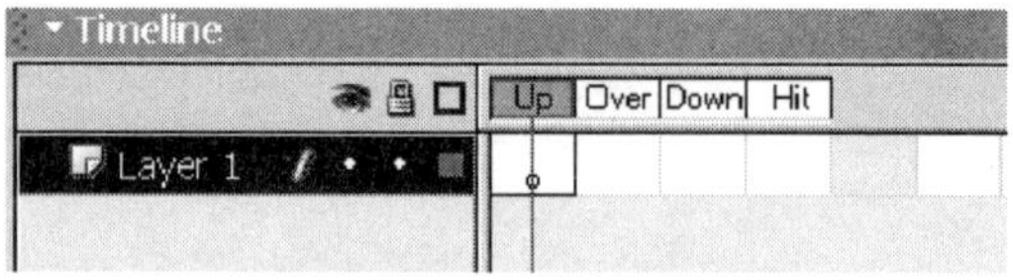

"Immediately, you'll notice a number of differences from the movie clip timeline," I said. "The three visual states are represented here. The **Up** frame represents the normal state, and the **Down** frame represents the press state."

"There is an extra state, Ken," Gemma said. "What's the Hit state for?"

"The **Hit** state defines the actual area of the button," I replied. "If this state is left empty, the Up state is used to define the button area. Defining a hit area is particularly important if your button is an outline or some text, or when the button will be hard to press.

"I'd like you all to quickly try making a text button with four states. Follow my lead."

On the Up keyframe, I wrote the text "Hello" using the Text tool and black ink.

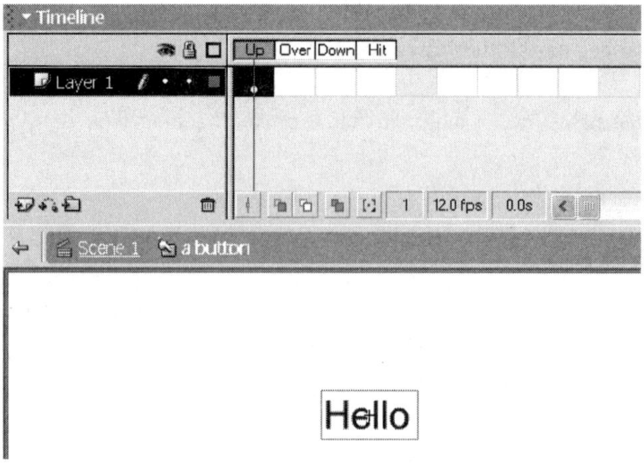

On the Over frame, I selected **Insert > Keyframe** to duplicate the contents of the Up keyframe.

I said, "Change the color of the text on the Over frame to red:

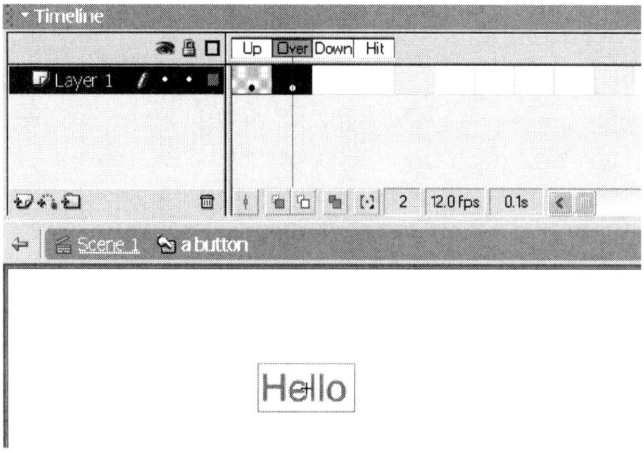

"Repeat the same thing for the Down keyframe, changing the text to green. For the Hit state, insert a keyframe and draw a square to cover the text:

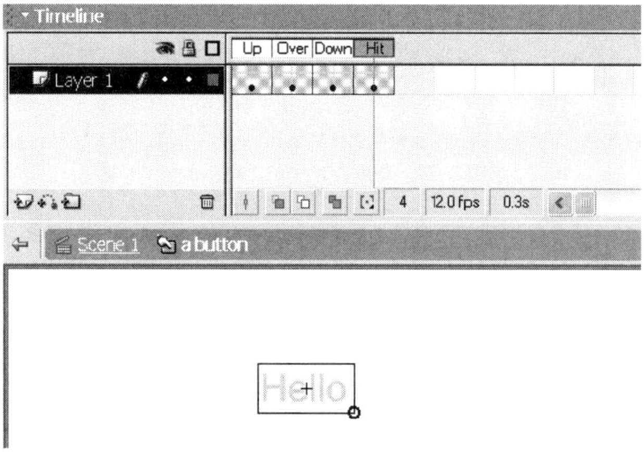

"The reason you do this is to make the button trigger any time the cursor is in the vicinity of the text. As I said before, if you leave the Hit state as text, it will be hard to trigger a rollover. Once you're done, drag a copy of the button from the Library onto the main timeline stage and test the movie.

"When you roll over the text, it will change to red, and when you press the mouse button on it, it will change to green. You'll tell the button what to do when you press the mouse button later using a little ActionScript."

"Oh yes!" Mazzy exclaimed. "It's much easier to do it in Flash than trying to learn lots of JavaScript code."

"It sure is easier than 20 lines of code," I said. "The ease of visual changes is the primary reason you'll want to use button symbols in Flash. In Flash MX, movie clips can function as buttons, and this has led to the button symbol being used less and less."

"Can button instances have instance names like movie clips?" Jim asked.

"In Flash MX, Jim, they can," I said, "so you can control them with ActionScript if need be. I won't totally eradicate button symbols from the class, but you'll use movie clips a lot more. That's it for the three symbol types. Now I'll talk a little about instance names and how Flash works with them."

Instance names and objects

"As I mentioned earlier in class, **instance names** are used in ActionScript to control different symbol instances," I started. "Every instance requires an individual identification, and no two things can be given the same name.

"We're lucky in this class in that we each have a unique name. In previous classes I haven't had such fortune! If I asked Mazzy to open the window, Mazzy might—"

Mazzy interrupted, "If you asked politely, Mr. Jokol."

"I'm sorry, Mazzy!" I laughed. "If I *politely* asked Mazzy to open the window, she would probably open it for me."

"I don't think she would, Ken," Carl said. "Not the way you ask. Didn't your parents teach you any manners?"

"Obviously not, Carl," I laughed. "I used Mazzy's individual identification, her name, to ask her to open the window. If I *politely* asked Jim to close the door, he might get up and do it for me."

"In both situations," I said, "I'm using their unique identification to ask them to do something for me. In ActionScript, the same thing is done with instance names. However, in ActionScript, if it can be done, it will be done. ActionScript doesn't need to say please." I winked at Mazzy.

Giving an instance a name

"Even though I've already hinted at how to give an instance name to an instance, I'd like you to experience it firsthand," I said. "It's probably the most significant thing to remember in Flash, and if you forget to do it, you'll quickly become annoyed when your movie refuses to play ball.

"First, open a new Flash movie using **File > New**, and create a new movie clip symbol with **Insert > New Symbol**. Give it the name arrow and click **OK**."

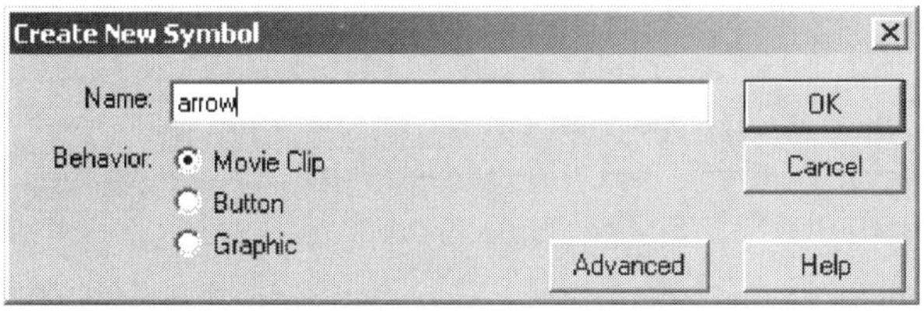

"Do you want us to draw an arrow, perchance?" asked Joe.

I nodded. "Draw an arrow with a long neck facing upward, and let me know when you're all done."

While the students drew their arrows, I made mine. When all the students were ready to proceed, I went on.

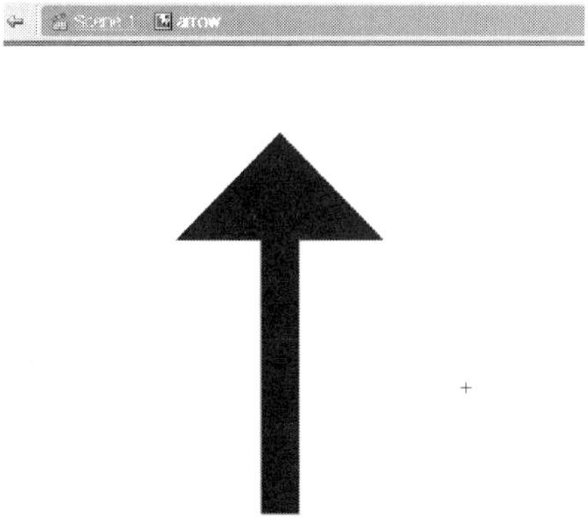

"The purpose of this movie is to show you how ActionScript can be used to control objects with instance names. In this example, you're going to make the arrow rotate a little. Because you need the arrow to rotate around its center axis, you need to center the arrow to the registration point. You can do this using the Align panel.

"Open the Align panel, if you don't already have it onscreen, from the **Window** menu. Once you have it, make sure that **Align/Distribute to Stage** is on. It should look like this."

I clicked the **Align/Distribute to Stage** button. "This option will make sure that all alignments are made according to the center of the stage or the registration point.

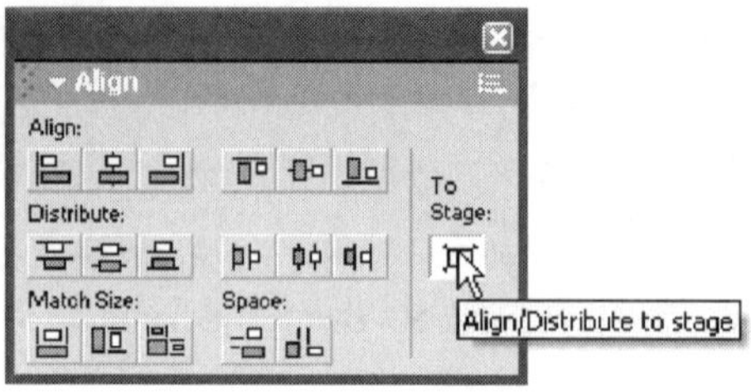

"Next, make sure that the arrow is fully selected and then click the **Align horizontal center** button, followed by the **Align vertical center** button. This will center the arrow to the registration point exactly. If your arrow isn't centered on the registration point, make sure that the **Align/Distribute to Stage** button is clicked.

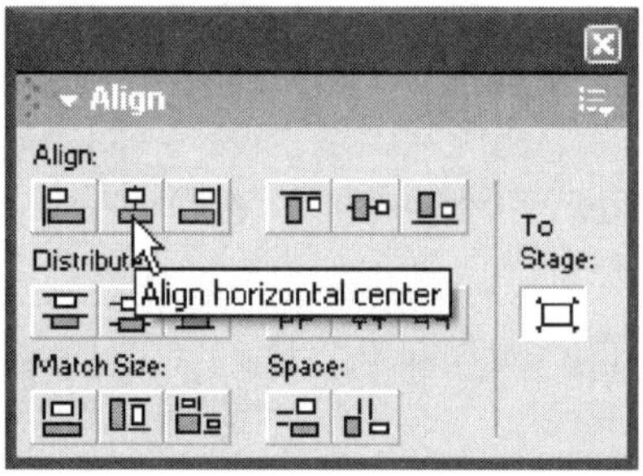

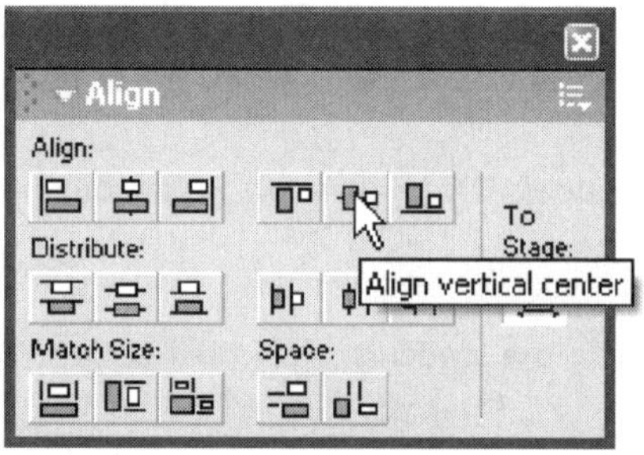

"You should then have something like this," I said. The class looked at my rendition:

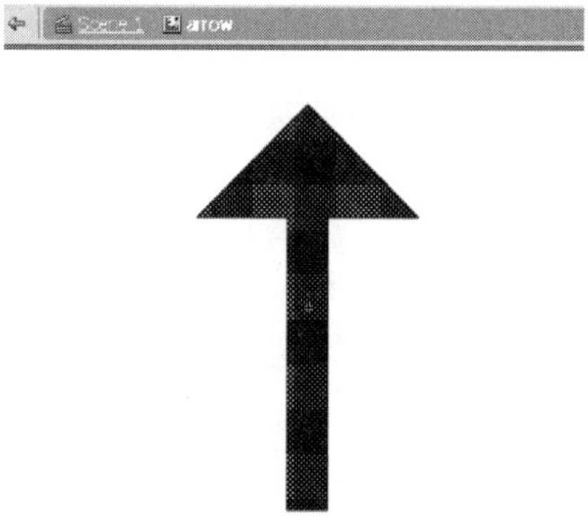

"I drew the type of arrow that native Americans would have used," Carl said.

"As long as it has some form of tip or northern indicator it's fine, Carl," I said. "Now return to the main timeline using the Scene 1 button. On the main timeline, insert a new layer and call it 'actions.' As before, this is where you'll place all your ActionScript code.

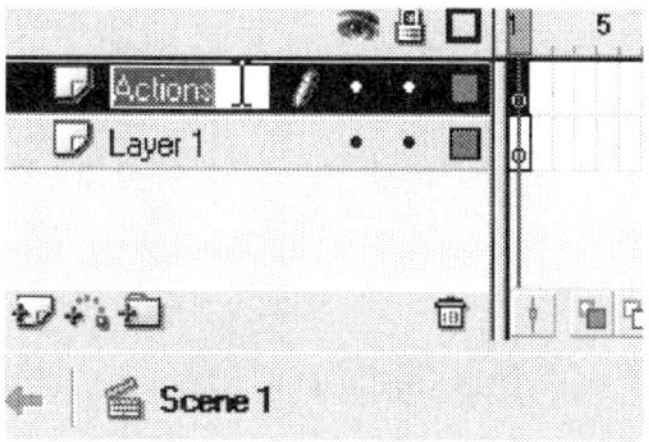

"Before we get to the ActionScript, who can guess what we should do next?" I asked.

Jim stuck his hand up. "We need to place the arrow movie clip on the stage," he said. Before I had a chance to correct him, Carl had done it for me.

"We need to place an *instance* of the arrow movie clip on the stage," Carl said. "Right, Ken?"

"Carl is right, Jim," I said. "Remember that the symbol is the parent and it's exclusive to the Library. Clones of the symbol are known as instances and these are what you use on the stage. Select Layer 1 and drag an instance of your arrow movie clip onto the stage and center it with the Align panel as before.

"Jim, would you like to guess the next step?"

"It needs an instance name," Jim replied. "We give it this using the . . ." Jim spoke slowly, looking around his screen for the answer, ". . . using the Property inspector."

"Correct, Jim," I said. "Select the arrow instance and give it the instance name of `bigcompass`. Make sure this is one word."

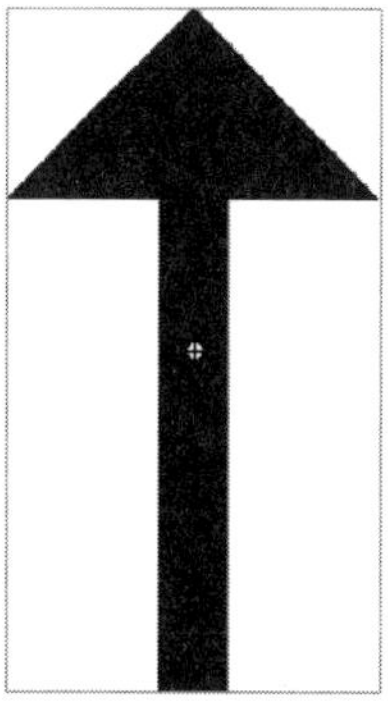

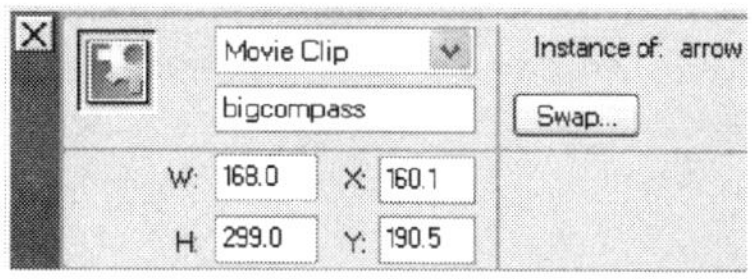

"I'm confused," said Joe. "Why does it have two names?"

"This particular instance, Joe, only has one name: its instance name," I said. "'Arrow' is only the title of the parent symbol. The symbol name is largely irrelevant. However, there's nothing to stop you from giving an instance the same name as the symbol name—but in most cases I'd advise against doing this. Does that answer your question?"

"I guess so," Joe said. "I'll just have to get into that way of thinking."

"I'll just try to remember it through my five cats," Mazzy said, smiling with glee. Joe and the rest of the class looked puzzled. "Even though they're all my darling cats, they have individual names and that's how I call them." Carl banged his head against the table a few times. Mazzy crossed her arms and began to redden.

Carl sat back up. "Mazzy even has a picture of each of them in her wallet!" he said.

"Okay, cats or no cats, try to remember that instance names are what count!" I said. "Now select the keyframe of the Actions layer and open the Actions panel by pressing F9. Type the following into the Actions panel:

```
degree = 90;
bigcompass._rotation = degree;
```

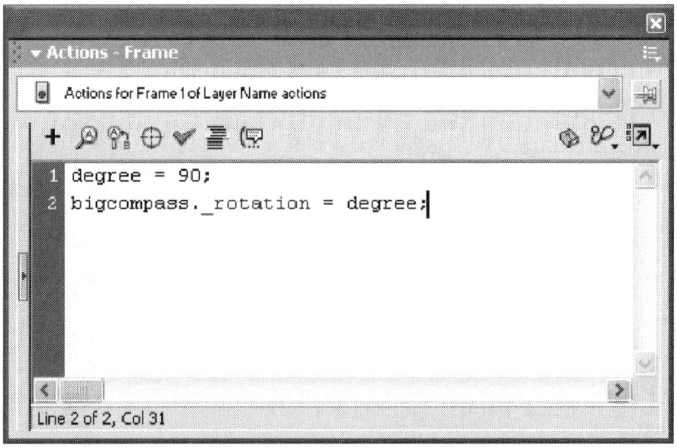

"Who would like to tell me what the first line of ActionScript does?" I asked.

"It sets the variable degree to 90," Joe said. "I guess we're rotating the arrow 90 degrees."

"Sure, Joe," I replied. "The second line of code here uses what is called **dot notation** to change the rotation of bigcompass to the value held in degree.

"The format of dot notation is always written in the same way as this, starting with the instance name and then supplying an action for the instance. In this case, you're changing the rotation property of bigcompass to be equal to 90.

"Run the movie and you'll see what happens. The arrow is set to a 90-degree angle, reading clockwise. If the arrow doesn't rotate at all, check that your instance name is correct and your code is written right."

"Why is rotation preceded by an underscore character?" Gemma asked.

"That's because rotation is a **property**," I responded. "You'll learn about properties in detail later in today's class. For now, though, close the preview and drag another instance of arrow onto the stage. Select it and use the Free Transform tool to make it much smaller. This time, give it an instance name of smallcompass.

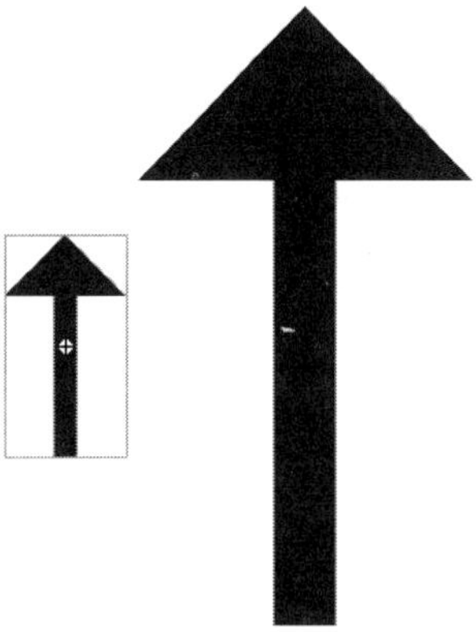

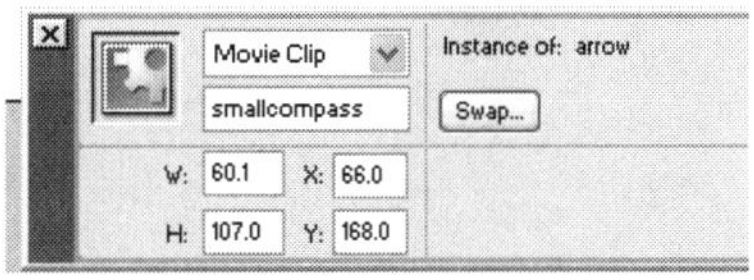

"Select the actions layer, and open the Actions panel again. Add the following line to the end of the code."

```
degree = 90;
bigcompass._rotation = degree;
smallcompass._rotation = degree*2;
```

"I think I can guess what's going to happen," Joe said. "The smaller arrow instance is going to be rotated to 180 degrees. Even with my math I can figure that one out."

"Run the movie to see if you're right, Joe," I said. "Even though you've rotated only two arrows, you can start to see how to control different instances using ActionScript.

"ActionScript is called an **object-oriented programming** language. If you start to think of all instances as objects and imagine that ActionScript controls all the objects, you can begin to understand how it works."

"So ActionScript is like a Greek god," Carl said thoughtfully. "It has the power to move the pieces around the chess board and controls their individual destiny—"

Mazzy interrupted Carl. "Stop right there! In a moment you'll start existentializing and the whole class will spiral out of control."

"Thanks, Mazzy," I laughed. "Even though ActionScript might be omnipotent, it's certainly not godlike. Think of it more as a guiding or aiding force, coordinating the instances and objects. Before we veer too far into analogy-land, let's take a look at something very real: properties."

Object properties

"All objects, such as symbol instances, have different **properties**," I said. "If a human were an object, we'd all have obvious physical properties like height, weight, and clothing size, as well as a property such as age.

"Different Flash objects have different properties available to them. Most of these properties can be changed, but some are read-only. Movie clip instances have a variety of properties available to them, some of which are shared by other instances, but others of which are exclusive to them.

"We'll most commonly use movie clip instances, so it will help if we take a look at some of their basic properties." I wrote at the top of the board:

MOVIE CLIP PROPERTIES

"Movie clips have a number of standard physical properties." I added a category below:

physical

_rotation
_alpha
_visible
_height
_width
_xscale
_yscale

"All of these properties control the physical appearance of movie clip instances and all of them can be changed and read. A couple of them might stand out as being familiar to some of you from your previous web use. You've already seen the `rotation` property in action—it applies to the rotated angle of the instance. Most of the other properties here are quite self-explanatory. I'll quickly run through them, but you'll benefit most from actually experimenting with them.

"The **_alpha** property applies to the opacity or transparency of the instance. This is measured as a percentage, where the default and maximum setting for this is 100%."

"So 100% will show the instance at full transparency?" Mazzy asked. I nodded. "So would a setting of 0% render an instance invisible?"

"Yes it would, Mazzy," I replied. "However, the next property, **_visible**, concerns itself with the visibility or, conversely, invisibility. The `_visible` property is a **Boolean**, meaning it can only be either true or false.

"The next two properties, **_width** and **_height**, are pretty obvious—they represent the physical size of the object. Both are measured in pixels.

"**_xscale** and **_yscale** are a little more complicated because they're concerned with the scaled size of the instance. Every object's original scale is 100%. x represents the width, and y represents the height. The size of objects can be changed with either of these properties.

"So far, you've seen how object's properties can be changed using the rotation example, but it's important for you to all know how to work with properties." I wrote on the whiteboard:

```
square._alpha = 50;
```

"In this line of ActionScript, the `_alpha` property of the instance called `square` is set to 50, or 50% opacity, in layman's terms. In many ways, this looks like how you set a variable, except that, in this case, you're setting the value of the property.

"If you wanted to return the alpha value for any reason, you could do so like this:

opacity = square._alpha;

"In this code, I'm setting the opacity variable to equal the alpha value of the square instance."

"Why might you want to get a property value?" Jim asked.

"There are endless reasons why you would, Jim," I said. "For example, say you wanted to toggle the visibility of an instance using the _visible property. First, you'd need to know if the instance was currently visible or invisible before you could invert it. I'll cover situations like this in a couple of weeks.

"For now, I'd just like you all to add a line of code to the compass example. Add the following to it." I added some code to my Flash file. "This will change the _alpha property of the bigcompass instance to 20.

```
degree = 90;
bigcompass._rotation = degree;
smallcompass._rotation = degree*2;
bigcompass._alpha = 20;
```

"Given the ability to read and change properties, who would like to take a bold gamble at how you would set the _alpha of smallcompass to three times that of bigcompass?"

Carl raised his hand. "Uh . . . smallcompass._alpha = 60, " Carl said quickly.

Mazzy swiped Carl. "smallcompass._alpha = bigcompass._alpha *3?" Mazzy guessed.

"Well done, Mazzy," I said. "I'm glad you took into consideration that the _alpha value of bigcompass could change at any time. Carl, I'm afraid you hard-coded the _alpha value of smallcompass. In your case, you'd need to make two changes to your code—not very efficient."

I wrote a new category of properties on the board. "This next set of properties is exclusive to movie clip instances and the main timeline, allowing you to read frame-based information.

<u>frames (read-only)</u>

_currentframe
_totalframes

"The first property here, **_currentframe**, allows you to read the current frame position of the playhead within a movie clip instance. **_totalframes** returns the total number of frames within an instance timeline. Although these properties might not seem too useful at the moment, they might make sense when you come to use them with methods."

Methods

"If properties are the attributes of an instance or object, **methods** are actions that you perform on them," I said. "If height and age are human properties, then speak and walk are human methods. In Flash, methods are used to perform particular actions on instances and objects, from copying an instance to making one move. In short, they help get things done.

"Movie clip instances have a number of available methods, including a couple of frame-based methods." I wrote on the board:

MOVIE CLIP METHODS

frame methods

```
play();
stop();
gotoAndPlay (framenumber)
gotoAndStop (framenumber)
nextFrame();
prevFrame();
```

"The first method here will make the playhead play, and the next one will make it stop.

"The **gotoAndPlay** method will send the timeline playhead to the specified frame and will play from there. **gotoAndStop** will send and halt the playhead at the required frame. The next two methods will send the playhead to the next or previous frame from its current position."

"Flash's equivalent of frame forward or frame reverse," Carl said. "Cool!"

"Even though they might not sound as cool, the gotoAndPlay or gotoAndStop methods here are far more useful because they allow you to skip to any frame you want to," I said.

"Before we go on to a short exercise using methods, one important thing to know about methods is that sometimes they require an inputted value, and other times they don't. It all depends on what the action actually is and whether there are different ways to do it.

"For example, if someone tells you to jump, you might ask 'How high?' and the person might tell you. But if that same annoying person tells you to switch the kettle on, you only have to go ahead and switch it on."

"What about asking them how much water the person wants in the kettle?" Gemma asked.

"Well, Gemma, that's a different task altogether," Jim said. "That's called filling the kettle. Ken asked us to switch it on!" Jim looked to me.

"In reality, you both have a fair point," I said. "Putting the kettle on might involve more processes than simply switching the kettle on. Being an optimist, Gemma, I was assuming that the kettle was half full!"

"If someone is asking you to jump, that person must be military personnel," Gemma said. "I'd assume that you were making tea for everyone in the mess tent!"

"Who said we were making tea?" Jim asked.

Carl reddened. "Who cares about hot beverages anyway?" he roared. "Can't we just move on, Ken?"

"It's all my fault, Carl," I said. "Maybe the sergeant should tell you to make your bed! I'm assuming there's only one way to make an army bed, of course."

"Who said you were in the army?" Joe joked.

Before Carl had the chance to explode, I stepped in. "As you learned the hard way, some methods require input and some don't. In the methods on the board, only the middle two require any values—the frame number to send the playhead to.

"A method is called using dot notation. A method that doesn't require any values is called like this:

```
cartoon.play ();
```

"In this example, a movie clip with the instance name of `cartoon` is told to play. This means it will play from its current position." I wrote some more on the board:

```
cartoon.gotoAndStop (4);
```

"Here, the playhead of `cartoon` is sent to frame 4 and is halted there."

"If the play method doesn't require any input value," Mazzy started, "why does it have parentheses?"

"It all relates to how methods are created," I said. "I don't think there's much point going into detail about this right now. You'll learn exactly why in a later class. For now, it's best to remember that all methods require parentheses, whether or not they require any input.

"Who'd like to do a short exercise to see methods at work?" I asked.

"I'm sure I speak for us all," Gemma started, "when I say that a practical exercise is definitely in order."

I asked the class to open a new Flash movie and to create a new movie clip called `counting` with five blank keyframes. On each frame I asked them to center a text field with text from frame 1 to frame 5.

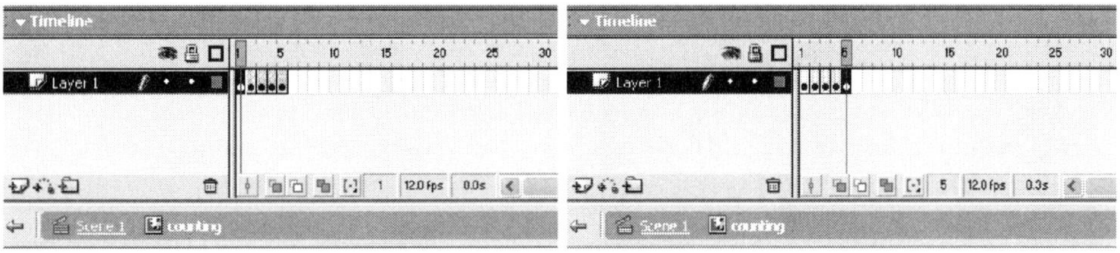

"Once you've done that, return to the main timeline and drag two copies of the new movie clip onto the stage. Tint one of them red with the Property inspector, and name them `blackcount` and `redcount`, accordingly.

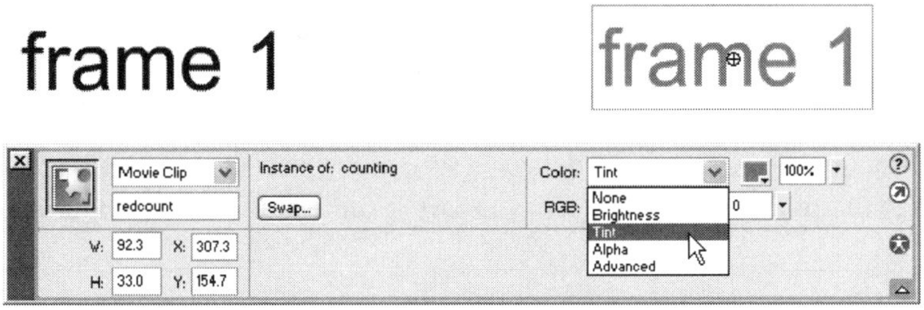

"If you test the movie as it is, you'll notice that both instances loop continually over and over at breakneck speed. It's time to control them a little with ActionScript. Close the test movie for now and insert a new layer called actions.

"As before, the keyframe on the actions layer will store all the ActionScript that we need. Add the following code.

```
redcount.gotoAndStop (3);
blackcount.gotoAndStop (blackcount._totalframes);
```

"The first line of code will send the `redcount` instance to frame 3 and stop it. Simple enough? The second line of code uses the `_totalframes` property and will send the playhead to that frame. Who'd like to guess what text it will display?"

"It should show *frame 5*, Ken," Joe said. "There are five frames in the timeline of the movie clip, so `_totalframes` should give us 5." I asked the class to test the movie to see if Joe was right.

frame 5   frame 3

"Congratulations, Joe," Mazzy said.

"Can anyone tell me how we can send—and stop—the `redcount` instance to the next frame in the sequence?"

"There are two ways you could do it," Gemma said. "The first is to cheat and to use a `gotoAndStop` method to frame 4, and the other is to use `nextFrame`, I think." Gemma paused. "I'm not sure if `nextFrame` stops the timeline though. . . ."

"Just remember the still frame advance and review," Carl said. "The video stays on pause, but you just go backwards or forwards a frame."

"Both your answers were right, Gemma," I said, "but `nextFrame` was what I was looking for. Using a `gotoAndStop` was very much like cheating!

"Okay, I'd like you all to go to **File > Save**, and save this file so you can experiment with some of the properties and methods you've seen in the class in your own time. We will use this FLA in future classes, so make sure you save it somewhere ready for future use!

"We've covered a lot of subjects in this class, and although you still might be itching to get interactive with Flash, I promise you that the next class will finally give you what you need to go ahead and make something interactive. All of the things you've learned today will benefit you greatly in the coming weeks. Class dismissed! Go home and rest, you've all earned it!"

Summary

In this week's class, we learned about the following:

- **Symbols**: The method by which elements of your Flash movie can be created so that they can be used over and over again.

- The three different types of symbols—movie clip, graphic and button—and how movie clips are the most versatile and useful of the three.

- **Instances**: How each copy of a symbol that is dragged onto the stage, is given its own unique identifier – an instance name.

- How these instances can be thought of as objects that can be controlled using ActionScript.

- **Object properties and methods**: The way in which ActionScript controls instances.

In the next class you'll learn how to make their movies more interactive using the power of ActionScript.

Class 5
Interaction

Objectives

In today's class, you'll learn about

- Events
  - Timed events
  - Button events
  - Thumbnail events

- Using events in ActionScript

- Altering the position of an instance on stage using _x and _y object properties

- Attaching instances from the Library using the `attachMovie` method

Introduction

In this week's class, the students will learn all about interaction. Before they can begin working on the case study, they must know how to detect and react to user interactions in Flash. Interactivity is the difference between an active and a passive viewer.

When I arrived in class, Carl was already seated quietly. "I decided to fix my bike," he said, "and I'm really keen on getting interactive."

"I'm glad to see you taking such a strong interest. You can help me by switching on all the computers if you like," I said. Carl jumped up and started helping.

Events

"In today's class, we're going to come to grips with interaction," I said. "ActionScript is an **event**-driven programming language, responding to things happening within a Flash movie. These happenings, or **events**, as they are called, can be anything from a mouse click to a lapse of time.

"In real life, we're constantly acting on events. For example, imagine that you're in your car and you're stuck at a red light. Before driving forward, you have to wait for the light to turn green." I turned to Carl. "Or Carl, imagine you're waiting for the latest Metallica release to hit the stores."

"Rock on, Ken!" Carl said, giving me a thumbs-up and a significant nod.

I laughed. "In both those scenarios, you have to wait for something to happen before acting. The event in the traffic example is when the light turns green. The event for Metallica fans is the release and sale of the new album. When the event happens, we act on it, driving on down the road and buying the latest CD. In both those example events, timing is key.

"Besides timed events, interaction can also make things happen. For example, when you turn the key in a lock, you're unlocking a door. The event here is the turning of the key, and the end result is that the door is unlocked.

"Flash relies on a number of different events to tell it when to do things. This could be the passing of 10 seconds, a key press, or the movement of the mouse. Events will form the basis of interaction in our case study, and later in today's class we can detail the events that we need to use for Randy's kiosk.

"For every required event, an action is set up to tell Flash what to do next. The action performed following an event is called an **event handler**. The event handler is the action instigated by the event—for example, in a scenario where an About button is clicked, the About page is then displayed."

"How would an event and its handler be written in ActionScript, Ken?" Jim asked.

"Well, right now, I think we might benefit from using pseudo-code, Jim," I said. "Pseudo-code is a way of writing code using plain English rather than actual code." I wrote on the board. "If we want to express something in code, without actually using code syntax, we can use pseudo-code.

```
when the doorbell sounds {
   open the door
}
```

"This pseudo-code shows the event and the event handler. The first line is the event, and everything inside the curly brackets is the action that you take. Although you've not seen curly brackets yet, these are used in ActionScript, as you'll see in a moment. The chunk of code in a set of curly brackets should all be run line by line.

"If you change the event handler code within the curly brackets . . ." I wiped the second bracket off the whiteboard and added some more text to the board, before rewriting the second bracket at the end, ". . . then you're adding more actions to be performed."

```
when the doorbell sounds {
   open the door
   greet your visitor
}
```

Mazzy laughed. "If my doorbell rings," Mazzy said, "I'm more likely to chase the visitor away. Most of the time they're trying to sell me something!"

"We'll be able to change this pseudo-code to consider the type of visitor in the next class, Mazzy. That way you won't be forced to greet them all!" I said. "Now we'll look at some of the most common event types in Flash MX. Along the way, I'll show you the pseudo-code for each event type, before you get to use them later in class."

Event types

"The number of event types in Flash MX is huge and ever increasing, because new objects are being created regularly. There are, though, a few basic events that you'll use almost every time you write any ActionScript. All of these events are applicable to movie clip instances.

"The majority of these are cursor-based events," I continued, "but the first event uses the frame rate as a measure."

Timed events

onEnterFrame

"The `onEnterFrame` event is triggered every frame of the movie, so if your movie rate is 12 fps, this event will trigger 12 times every second."

"Why isn't it called `onEveryFrame`?" Joe asked. "Seems like an illogical event name."

"I suppose it might seem a little strange, Joe," I replied. "The event name `onEnterFrame` is simply saying 'every time I enter a frame.' Many programming terms are derived from other programming languages, and sometimes they might not exactly fit into everyday terminology." Joe nodded.

"The `onEnterFrame` event is ubiquitous, because it's used for checking information regularly. In programming games, such as *Space Invaders*, `onEnterFrame` is used to check if bullets collide with alien craft. Because this event is so frequent, it's ideal for intense interactivity.

"The pseudo-code for this event is pretty straightforward." I wrote it on the board.

```
every frame of the movie {
    do this;
}
```

"As I mentioned earlier, this pseudo-code shows the event and its handler. Whatever is in the curly brackets is performed when the event becomes true."

"Where will we use this event for Randall's kiosk?" Mazzy asked. "We don't have any intense interactivity, Ken."

"How about clicking the thumbnails?" Jim said.

"We won't need to use the `onEnterFrame` event for Randall's kiosk," I replied. "I'm only showing it to you because it's a key event in Flash. Clicking thumbnails and other buttons,

Jim, will require use of button events." I informed the class that we would leave the `onEnterFrame` event at this point, and we would return to it for a short exercise a little later.

Button Events

"Because buttons are greatly important to Flash presentations, websites, and kiosks, knowledge of standard button-based events is essential for anyone learning Flash programming," I said.

"There are a number of button-based events that all react to different cursor interaction with the button instance. These range from a mouse rollover to a mouse button release, with all sorts of different events inbetween." I started with a simple button click.

onRelease

"`onRelease` is the first button-based event. It detects a mouse button click or the release of a mouse button."

"Can you tell me the difference between a click and a press, Ken?" Gemma said. "I know I do them both, but it's an innate ability perhaps. I don't even know what I'm doing half the time."

"A mouse button press is the initial button press, so when your finger pushes the mouse button from up to down. This counts as a press," I said. I saw Mazzy trying this out.

"A mouse button click or release is when you lift your finger off the button, releasing it. The mouse button then goes from down to up. This is usually what you do when you're releasing a dragged object or clicking a link," I said. "This is the most common event for mouse interaction. All web hyperlinks are triggered by a mouse release. In essence, the release is used most commonly because it's a confirmation of your intentions.

"We'll use this event to detect interaction with the thumbnail grid," I said. "When the user has clicked a thumbnail image, the full-size image will load in the set place and the information for that image will be shown." I wrote the pseudo-code for this event on the board:

```
when the user clicks on a thumbnail {
    load full size image;
}
```

"This event will also be used for the About and Contact pages linked to from the main menu. Generally, when you're creating a link to a different frame or page, you should use this event type." I decided to proceed to the next events.

`onRollOver` and `onRollOut`

"The `onRollOver` events detect a button rollover," I started. "When the cursor first rolls over the button, the event is triggered. When the cursor rolls off the button, the `onRollOut` event is triggered."

"Why would we need to know when the user rolls off something?" Gemma said.

"In most cases, you wouldn't actually use `onRollOver` without `onRollOut`," I said. "If the rollover changes a visual state, the rollout will return it to the original state. All website elements that you see changing when you roll over them also change back when you roll off them." I drew a diagram on the board:

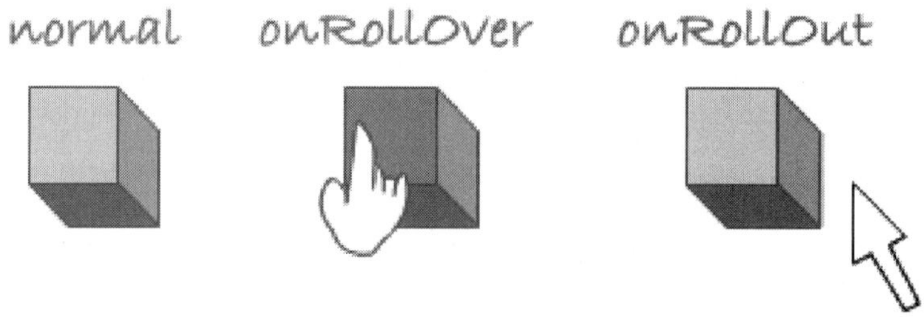

"This is a typical roll-on/roll-off button reacting to two different events: the rollover and rollout. The same graphic is used for the first and last states here, but this is only because we revert to the normal state."

"When we saw button symbols, we didn't need to program a rollout state," Jim said. "How is this different with movie clip instances?"

"Button symbols, as you saw, don't require any scripting to change their visual state because it's already done behind the scenes," I said. "Because movie clips don't have this, you need to explicitly program each event. In essence, you're causing a movie clip instance to mimic a button. The actions that the instance performs are more important than changes in visual state. You could program a button symbol in a similar way, but movie clip symbols are more flexible, as they can act on more events.

"Maybe it will help if we think about Randy's kiosk and what benefits these events will have for it. Let's consider the actions for a thumbnail. Who can guess how we can use these events for a thumbnail?"

The students all appeared to freeze. Carl began to whistle and look to the ceiling. "Okay, let me break it down a little," I said. "How could we use these events to display our tooltips?"

After a short while, Jim broke the silence. "Are we programming the events for each thumbnail?"

"Just go with a single thumbnail for now, Jim," I said.

"Okay, the typical activity for each thumbnail is to show a tooltip on cursor rollover, and to remove it from the screen when the cursor goes off the thumbnail." Jim paused. "That's your rollover and rollout, Ken." I nodded.

"Thanks for having a go, Jim," I said. "You're absolutely right. Each thumbnail should show the relevant tooltip on rollover and, when the cursor rolls out, it should be hidden. Each thumbnail then has the two events attached to it." I wrote the pseudo-code on the board:

```
when the cursor rolls over a thumbnail {
    show its tooltip;
}
when the cursor rolls off a thumbnail {
    hide its tooltip;
}
```

"The same code would be attached to each thumbnail," I said. "You might have noticed that these blocks of code are separate. This is because both events function individually, even though they're attached to the same thumbnail image. Instances can have many events attached to them because each event can be triggered without the knowledge or approval of any other event.

"Later in today's class we'll have the typical list of events for each thumbnail set up, ready to put into practice in the next class. For now, though, there is one more event to look at."

onPress

"You might already be able to guess what the `onPress` event does," I said. The students nodded. "The `onPress` event is triggered by a mouse button press.

"One useful application of this event is for dragging items. Typically, to drag an item, the mouse button is pressed to begin moving it, held while the item is in transit, and released to drop the item." I prompted the students to try dragging a file around on their desktop. "Even though the actual process will come naturally to you, I urge you to seek out the events involved in a typical drag process." I showed the class the events involved using a file on my desktop:

"The initial button press (`onPress` event):

"While the button press is held, the file is dragged (no event).

"The button is released and so is the file (`onRelease` event)."

"Can you show us how we'd do this in Flash MX?" Mazzy asked. "It looks very useful, because it's a common action."

"We can take a look at it in a moment, Mazzy," I replied. "Before we break into Flash MX coding, I'd like someone to write a typical drag in pseudo-code for me." I looked around the class. "Who'd like to volunteer?"

Carl stood up and walked to the front of the class. "I'll give it a go, Teach," he said. I passed him the magic marker and stood back. Carl wrote on the board.

```
button press {
   drag file;
}
button release {
   drop file;
}
```

"Does that look right, Teach?" Carl asked. I nodded.

"That's pretty good, Carl," I replied. "But you've not given any context to the button press and release. If you were to look at this with no knowledge of what we were just talking about, it would be easy to assume that a button press anywhere would allow you to drag a file." I made some changes to Carl's pseudo-code:

```
when an item is pressed {
   drag it;
}
when an item is released {
   drop it;
}
```

"The difference here is that I've contextualized the event with the instance," I said. "Every event must be assigned to an instance or object. Now I'm going to show you how this pseudo-code might look in Flash ActionScript."

Events in ActionScript

"Pseudo-code is useful for visualizing code before you actually get your hands dirty in Flash," I continued. "In most cases, you might spend a little time refining your pseudo-code, but this example is pretty simple, so we can't take it any further.

"The Flash code for the last chunk of pseudo-code looks like this." I typed the following into the Actions panel:

```
item.onPress = function () {
      startDrag (true);
}

item.onRelease = function () {
      stopDrag ();
}
```

"Whoa! That's a little nuts!" Gemma said. "Where did all the extra bits come from?"

"Under the hood, this is the same as the pseudo-code you just saw. ActionScript simply requires it to be in its syntax," I replied.

"Event handlers, as you already know, are written as a chunk of code. In ActionScript, this chunk is defined within what is known as a **function**. I'm not going to go into much detail about functions in this class, but within this context, it's just a subsection of code.

"As you already know, the event handler (or function) here is triggered by the event. When the event happens, the block of code is run."

"It looks like a property or variable declaration." Joe said.

"That's right, Joe," I said. "In this instance, though, with an event, the declaration is called a **callback**. In previous versions of Flash, event code was attached directly to movie clip instances, but in Flash MX, instances can be referred to from anywhere in the movie, hence the name callbacks."

"What are the empty brackets after the function?" Mazzy asked.

"For now, Mazzy, these brackets aren't that important to us because they'll always be empty for callbacks and events," I said. "When we look at functions in a future class, you'll come to understand what these are."

Dragging exercise

Now that you know how events and their handlers are constructed, you can create the dragging. For this example, you'll mimic the desktop and drag a file graphic.

1. Open a new Flash movie and give it a pale blue background (#00FFFF). This color is known as Aqua.

2. Create a new movie clip symbol called **file movie clip** and draw a file icon. Center the graphic.

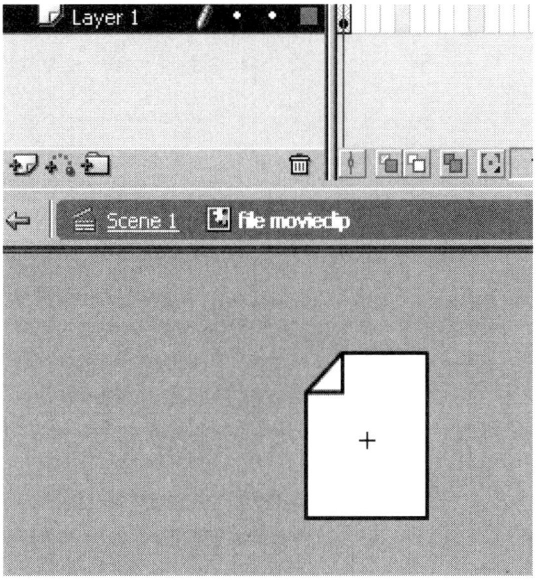

3. Use the Text tool below the graphic to give the file a name.

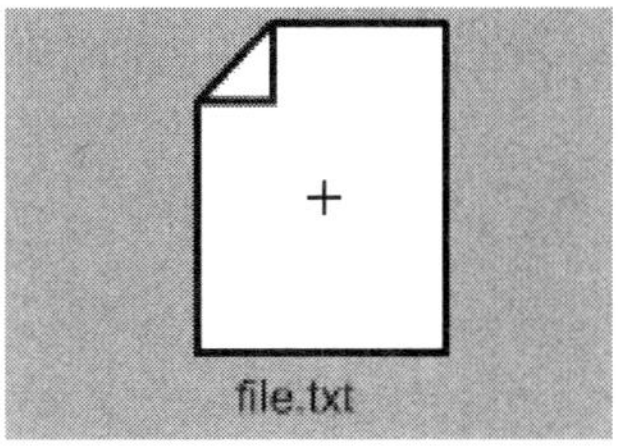

4. Return to the main timeline and drag a copy of the file movie clip onto the stage. Give it an instance name of **file**.

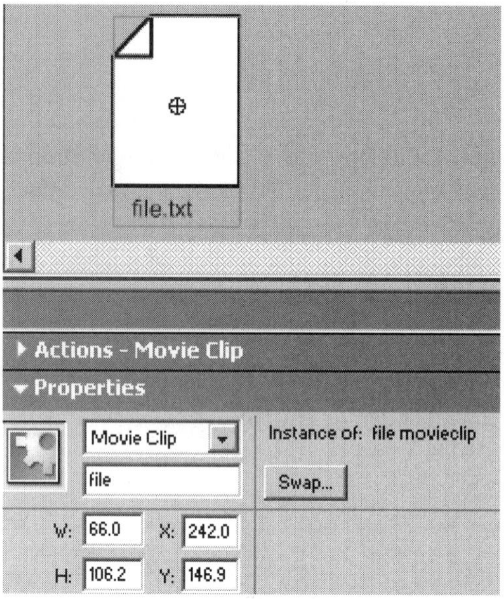

5. Insert a new layer called Actions. Select frame 1 of the Actions layer and open the Actions panel.

6. Add the following code:

```
file.onPress = function () {
      this.startDrag(true);
      this._alpha = 60;
};
file.onRelease = function () {
      this.stopDrag();
      this._alpha = 100;
};
```

7. Test the movie by pressing and dragging the file. Release the mouse button to stop dragging it.

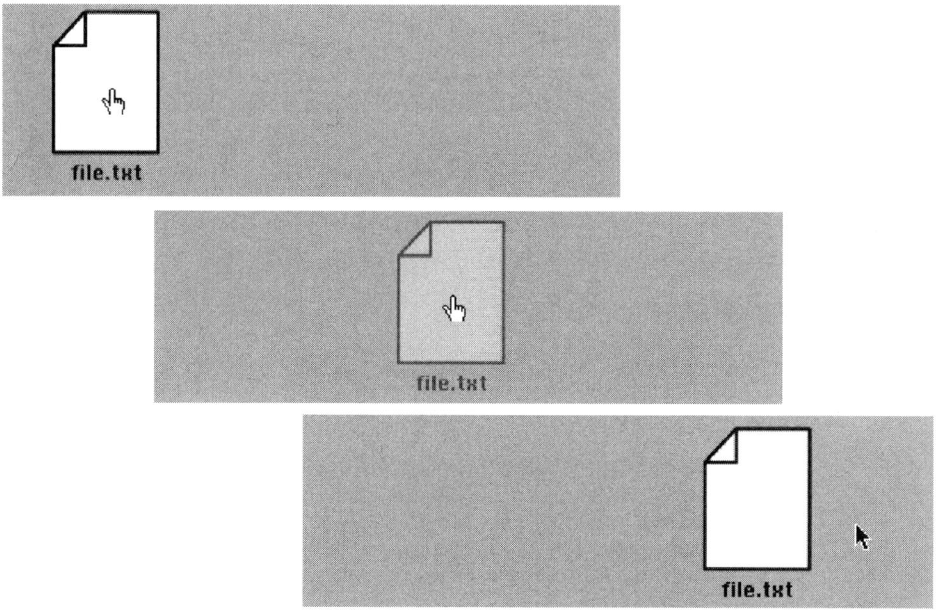

"Let's talk a little about the ActionScript involved in this movie," I said. I pulled up the Actions window onscreen.

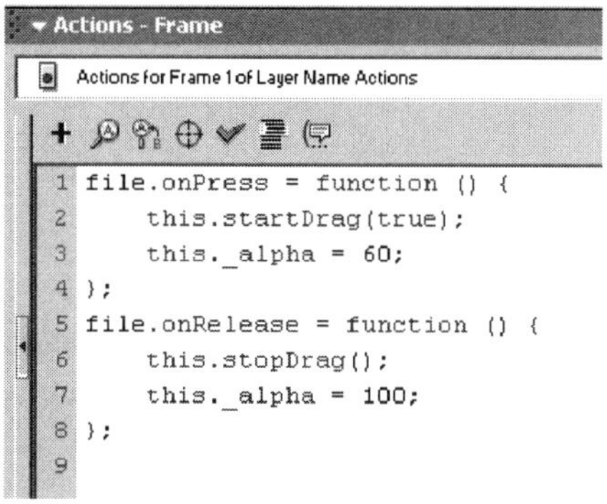

"On line 1 you define the `onPress` event for the `file` instance:

```
file.onPress
```

"Then you declare the event handler as a function—or a block of code. This block of code starts and ends with a curly bracket."

```
file.onPress = function () {
```

"Line 2 uses the movie clip method startDrag applied to the keyword this. this is an ActionScript keyword that acts as a reference to the movie clip instance that the callback is linked to. For example, in this script, this is the equivalent of _level0.file. You can find out what 'this' is referring to by simply tracing it like so:

```
file.onPress = function () {
      this.startDrag(true);
      this._alpha = 60;
      trace(this);
};
```

"If you test this now and press the button, then you should see that Flash reports what you expect: '_level0.file'."

"So this is file?" Joe asked. "Why not use file.startDrag?"

"I used this because it keeps the code modular," I said. "If anything is moved around in the code, I don't have to change all the targeting every time."

"I have a question, Teach," Carl said. I nodded. "What is the argument for startDrag? It appears to be set to true."

"The argument set to true is lock. lock is an optional parameter of the startDrag method—it's a Boolean value that specifies whether the registration point of the dragged object sticks to the mouse cursor, which in this case it does. The startDrag method has a few other optional arguments. To find out more about them, you can take a look in the Reference panel.

"The onRelease event code follows the same structure as the onPress. The only difference here is the stopDrag method. stopDrag reverses the action of startDrag, releasing the instance. What do you think would happen if you removed the onRelease event altogether?"

"If the dragging isn't stopped," Mazzy said, "I imagine the file would stick to the cursor forever."

"That's right," I said. "If the `stopDrag` method isn't called, the file will continue to be dragged by the cursor, even if the mouse button is released.

"Okay, before I move on to the next subject in this class, I'd like to get a handle on the case study. I'm off for a cup of coffee," I said. "While I'm out, I'd like you all to come up with the number of events required for each thumbnail and what the action should be for each event. Nominate someone to whiteboard duty, and get that person to write the answers on it in pseudo-code." Before they could get a chance to copy the notes from earlier in the class, I wiped the board clean, giving them an evil smirk.

Thumbnail events

When I arrived back at class, the students were all seated, chattering away. On the board was an impressive display of pseudo-code.

"Okay, who copied my board notes today?" I asked.

```
thumbnail.onRollOver {
    show tooltip;
}
thumbnail.onRollOut {
    hide tooltip;
}
thumbnail.onRelease {
    show fullsize photo;
    show photo information;
}
```

"No one, sir," Carl said, sitting upright and proud. "The class triumphed through teamwork."

Mazzy sniggered, trying hard to hold it back. "He's right," Mazzy said.

"Okay, I'll let you all get away with it this time, but next time I'll set you a more difficult challenge!" I said. "Did you have any problems with it?" I laughed. "Obviously not!"

"There was one thing, Ken," Jim said. "We weren't quite sure of the order they should be in."

"The order doesn't matter," I said. "Each event is registered individually, and it doesn't rely on any of the others." Jim nodded. "On that bombshell, we'll proceed!"

Screen coordinates

"In this part of the class, you'll learn about Flash's screen positioning," I said.

"The reason you need to learn this now is so that you're ready to go in the next class. In next week's class, you'll begin programming the case study, specifically the thumbnail grid. So in the last half of this class, you'll learn some fundamentals for the job.

"Who remembers any math from school?" I asked. Carl nodded. "I'll rephrase that—who, with the exception of Carl, remembers much math from school?" A couple of heads bobbed. "I've got you down as a math expert, Carl, I do hope you don't let me down.

"In the last class there were a couple of key object properties that I didn't talk about: the x and y properties. Even though I talked about physical properties, I declined to mention these two beauties."

"Why did you skip them?" Jim asked. "They're pretty important, aren't they?"

"Yes, they are, Jim, but I saved them for now so that we could talk about them within the context of Flash's screen or stage coordinates." Jim nodded. "So far you've all seen x and y positions and readings shown through the Property inspector and the Info panel. In these dimensions, x represents an object's horizontal position, and y represents its vertical reading."

"Z is the depth position, isn't it?" Joe asked.

"It sure is, Joe, but luckily for us we only need to work with two dimensions, x and y," I said. "The reason I asked you all about math is to break some bad news to all of you." Mazzy began to look worried.

"You're not going to give us a math test, are you?" Mazzy asked.

"No, not at all," I replied. "The reason I mentioned math is because of Flash's screen coordinates. Well . . ." I paused, ". . . one axis, y, is upside-down from the norm. If you've forgotten about math, then this won't make much of a difference to you, but if you're used to reading the y from the bottom corner, then you'll have to remember that Flash works differently."

"I do math at school," Carl started, "but I still don't know what you're talking about."

"Okay, Carl, I was going to cover it anyhow," I said. I opened a Flash movie showing Flash's screen coordinates. I made clear to the class that the stage size was set to the default of 550 (width) x 400 (height) pixels.

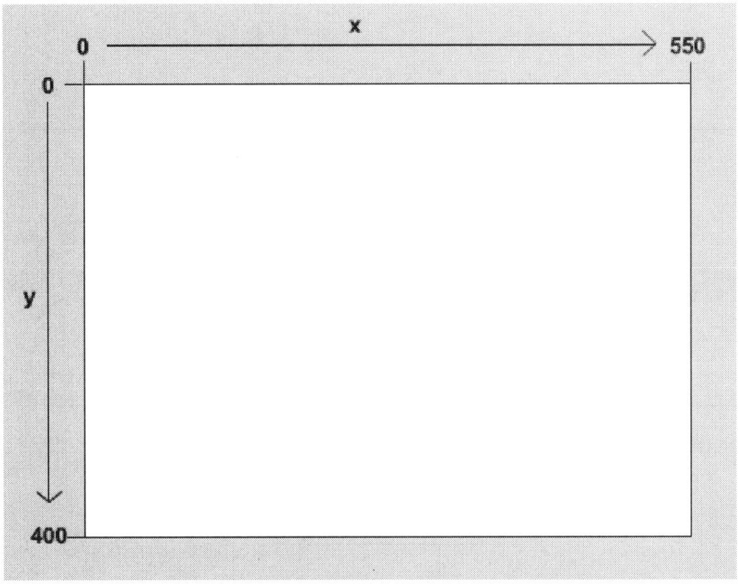

"Flash reads the x and y coordinates from the top-left corner. The pixel location of the top-left corner then is 0,0. x then increases to the right, and y increases down the page. The location of the bottom-right pixel would be 550x and 400y."

Jim sat up. "I think I'm with you, Ken," Jim said. "I remember that the y axis in BASIC reads from the bottom of the screen to the top."

"I'm sure the print applications that I use do the same," Gemma said. "This might take a little while to get used to!"

"Once you've got it in your head that it works in reverse," I said, "you should be okay. It's important that you're aware of it, though; otherwise, you'll never figure out why your code doesn't work!" I opened a saved Flash movie.

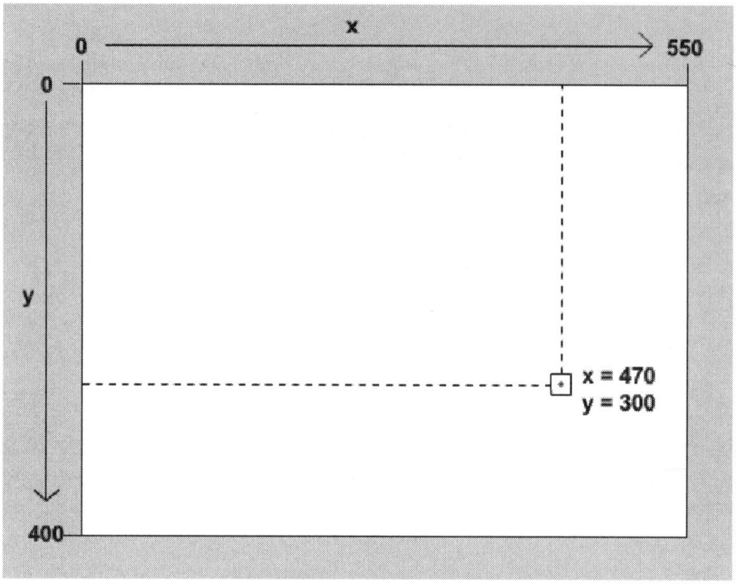

"In this movie, I've just placed an object on the stage at a fairly random position to show you its readings. Remember that x reads the horizontal position from left to right, with the left edge starting at 0. The y axis starts from the top to the bottom, with the top edge registering as 0.

"Given all this, the position of the square object is an x position of 470 and a y position of 300. Is this clear to everyone?" The students all agreed. "Okay, now we can move on to the _x and _y properties."

The _x and _y properties

"In the last class, you learned about common movie clip properties, and how to change and read them. Who'd like to refresh the memories of the rest of the class?" I asked.

"I'd find it easier to write an example down on the board," Joe said. "But I can't remember any properties right now!"

"How about the `_alpha` property, Joe?" I said. "It might help everyone with their homework too!" Joe came to the board and wrote:

```
instance._alpha = 40;
```


"This is how to set the `_alpha` of an instance," Joe said. "I can't remember how we read a property."

"Great, Joe," I said. "Reading the property is simply a case of reversing this a little." I added to the board. "On this occasion, I'm setting the variable degree to be equal to the value of the `_rotation` property of `instance`.

```
degree = instance._rotation;
```

"Okay, the `_x` and `_y` properties pertain to the position of an instance on the stage. This position, by the way, is read from the registration point of the object. Using the `_x` and `_y` properties is just the same as using any of the other properties. You might set the position of the above square using ActionScript like this." I wrote on the board:

```
square._x = 470;
square._y = 300;
```

"This would position the square at a stage `_x` position of 470 and a `_y` position of 300, mimicking the previous diagram. In the next class, you'll use the `_x` and `_y` properties to draw the grid."

Mazzy got my attention. "This might seem like a stupid question, Ken, but what if something goes outside the perimeter of the stage?"

"If something goes offstage below zero, then it will run into a minus figure," I said. "Otherwise, if it goes past the maximum boundaries, the figure will continue to grow. However, in both cases, you won't be able to see the objects because they're outside the viewable area.

"Sometimes, Flashers use the offstage area to temporarily house things outside the regular view rather than hiding the object using the `_visible` property." I paused. "Right now, you're going to use all of the lessons that you've learned in today's class to make an instance move left or right on demand.

"You'll do this using two buttons—one each for left and right—which will control the `_x` position of an instance on the stage. So, in the event that the left button is clicked, the instance will move a set number of pixels to the left."

Controlling the _x position of an instance

1. Open a new Flash movie and insert three new layers. Name the layers **Actions**, **square**, **button text**, and **buttons**.

2. Insert a new movie clip symbol called **square shape** and draw a simple square using the Rectangle tool. Center the square using the Align panel.

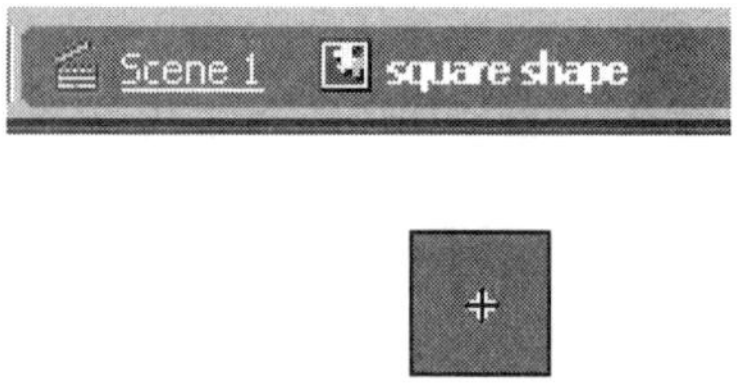

3. Return to the main timeline and drag a copy of the **square shape** movie clip onto the **square** layer. Give it an instance name of **square**.

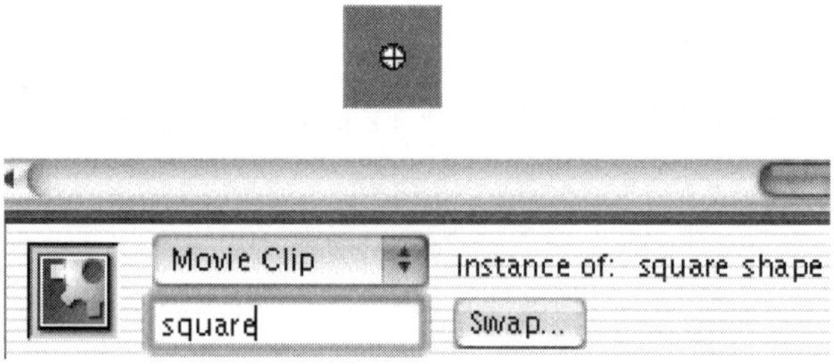

4. Insert a new movie clip symbol called **common button**. Draw and center a circular shape.

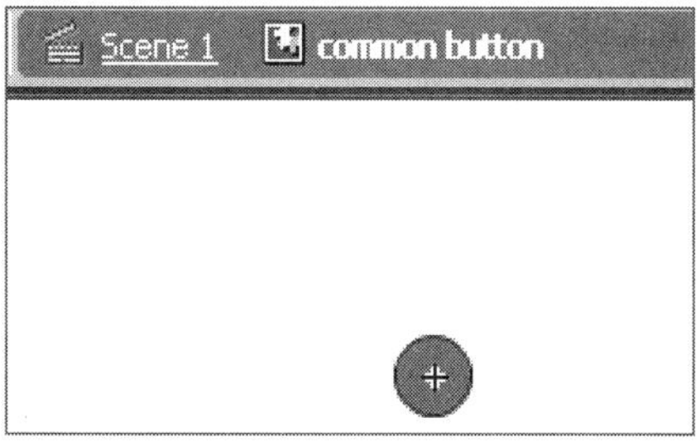

5. On the **buttons** layer of the main timeline, drag two copies—one for left and one for right—of the **common button** movie clip and position them below the square.

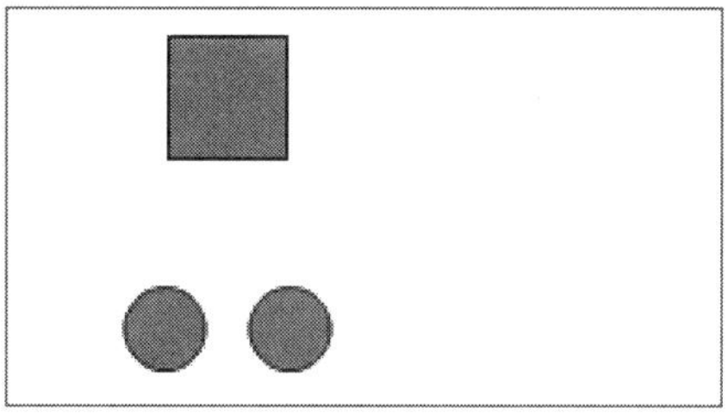

6. Select the leftmost button and give it the instance name **leftButton**.

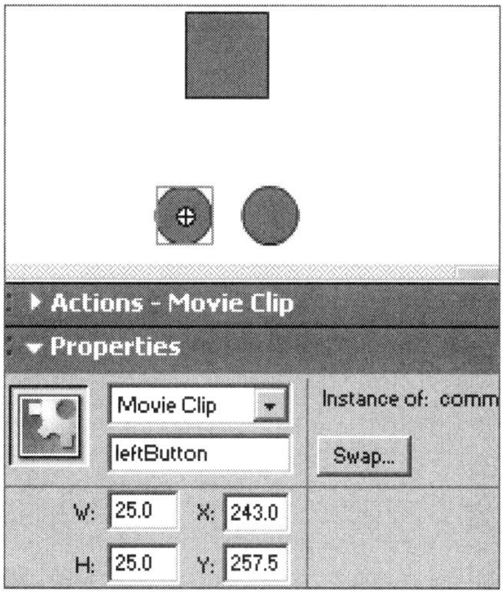

7. Give the right button the instance name **rightButton**.

8. On the **buttons text** layer, use the Text tool to place an L at the center of the leftmost button.

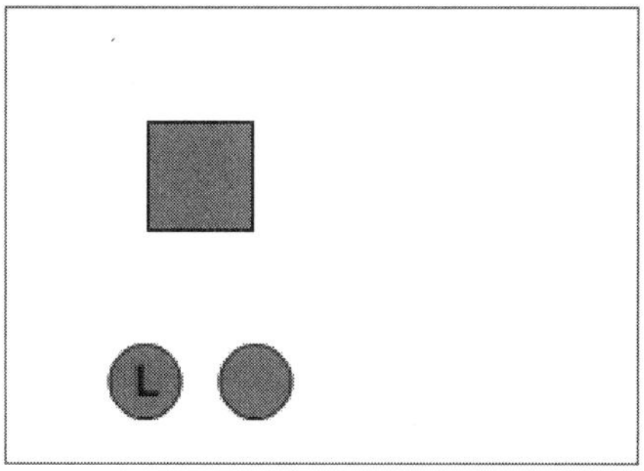

9. Repeat the same for the other button, using an R character.

10. Add the following code:

```
// initialize speed variable
speed = 10;
// button events
leftButton.onRelease = function() {
      square._x = square._x-speed;
};
rightButton.onRelease = function() {
      square._x = square._x+speed;
};
```

11. Test the movie. Use the left and right buttons to move the square horizontally on the screen.

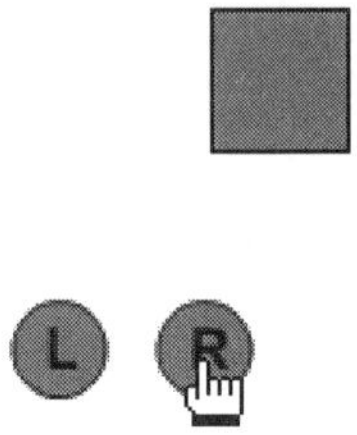

"Okay, the first thing we did here was create an instance to be moved—in this case, it's the square, which isn't a terribly exciting asset to work with, but it will do the job for now. After naming the square instance—a momentously important action—you created a button symbol. The reason you made one button rather than two is simply because one button will do the job! The most important part of the buttons, after all, is the code given to them.

"Once you gave both the buttons instance names, you then entered a little ActionScript. The code that you entered should be familiar to you all from earlier in class, but just in case you were watching Jim doodle or you fell asleep, I'll go over it now.

"First, I decided to mark the code with some comments, so on line 1 and line 3, you have comments relating to the code to follow it. The code here is distinctly in two sections: the initialization and the events:

```
// initialize speed variable
speed = 10;
// button events
```

"The initialization here on line 2 just sets up a variable called speed. The speed variable defines how far in pixels the square will move on every button click. If you want the square to move more or less, this is where you would change this. The reason you have this variable is not only for economizing on changes, but also for keeping it away from the bulk of the code for ease of reference.

```
leftButton.onRelease = function() {
```

"Line 4 begins the `onRelease` event for the leftButton instance. This line, as you've seen before, simply sets up the event and sets its handler as a function. The code on line 5 might look new to you.

```
square._x = square._x - speed;
```

"This code sets out to change the value of the `_x` property of `square`. Its value is set to be equal to its current value minus the value of `speed`." I saw some blank faces in the class. "What you're doing here is simply updating the _x position. By making it equal to itself minus `speed`, it's actually taking the previous value and subtracting from it. It's a little bit like algebra." I wrote an equation on the board.

$$x = 5$$

"How many of you remember algebra?" I asked. I saw more shakes than nods. "Okay, say that x is equal to 5. How much is x?" I placed my hand to my ear. The class united with a "FIVE!"

"So if I were to say, given that x was equal to 5, x is now equal to x + 10, how much is x now? If you all write it down, replacing the second x with its value, you'll find out. It might also help if you cover over the x and equals sign.

$$x = x + 10$$

$$x = 5 + 10$$

"So how much is x now, Joe?" I asked.

"Fifteen. Even my math isn't that bad," Joe said.

"I got it, too," Mazzy started. "If I can guess it, I suppose anyone can."

"Okay, now that you've got that," I said, "let's return to the _x property:

```
square._x = square._x - speed;
```

"Remember that square._x will return its current _x property on the stage, and you're subtracting the value of speed from its current value. So in a scenario where the _x property of square is 180, and you're subtracting speed — 10 from it, the new _x position of square will be 170. Is that clear to everyone?"

"Sure," said Joe. "I'll just remember the algebra."

"It's easier if you cover up the first half of the code," Gemma said. "Otherwise it gets me a little flummoxed!"

"I'll help you out if you get confused, Gemma," Jim said. Carl nudged him and he reddened.

"Okay y'all, returning to the code," I said. "I guess you can all tell me what happens in the second event now?" The students all agreed. "I'll spare you the description of it then. Before I go on, I want to make a couple of adjustments to the code."

I asked the students to change the code so that it looked like this:

```
// initialize speed variable
speed = 10;
// button events
leftButton.onRelease = function () {
      square._x -= speed;
}
rightButton.onRelease = function () {
      square._x += speed;
}
```

"What just happened to our algebra?" Joe asked.

"The values are still the same," I said. "I've just written the code in a shortened version. Where you previously used square._x = square._x + speed, you now have square._x += speed. The += operator tells Flash to increment the value or variable." I wrote a couple of equations on the board.

```
x = x + 10;

x += 10;
```


"Both of these lines do the same thing, in slightly different ways. If you don't get this right away, you'll become familiar with it over the next few weeks when we start using it."

"How about subtraction?" Jim asked. "I guess -= is the short version of a subtraction?" I nodded to confirm Jim's comment.

Incrementing or decrementing a variable or property

"If that wasn't enough," I started, "there's also a shorthand version of an increment or decrement of 1. Where you might be tempted to think that x += 1 is the way to do it, x++ is the most efficient way."

Joe sighed. "Just when I was starting to think this was all easy," he said. I wrote a few equations on the board:

```
x=x+1;

x += 1;

x++;
```

"You can see the three stages of shorthand evolution here!" I said. "Even though all of these equations simply add 1 to the value of x, the last of these is by far the quickest to write. In a similar way, x- - will remove 1 from the value of x. As with the last form of shorthand, if you don't find yourself using this right away, don't worry because it will come to you. As you'll learn next week, incrementing a value by 1 is a very common action, so you'll soon get the hang of it."

Attaching instances from the Library

"Even though there isn't much time left in today's class, I think it's important to touch on this one last subject," I said. "So far, whenever you've needed any graphic elements or assets in the stage, you've dragged a copy of them from the Library and given them instance names.

"With ActionScript, however, there's a less manual way using a method called **`attachMovie`**. The `attachMovie` method will allow you to grab an instance from the Library at any time. In reality, using `attachMovie`, your stage could be totally empty to start with, and all of the necessary graphics and instances could be placed using `attachMovie` methods.

"However, I'm not saying that this is what we're going to do!" I paused. "Otherwise, you might end up with a massive load of ActionScript that doesn't do that much. A method like `attachMovie` is useful for creating a dynamic interface—an interface in which elements change often.

"Randy's grid is one such scenario. Because the grid of thumbnails will change, the grid will need to be redrawn with the correct thumbnails. In next week's class, we'll use `attachMovie` to pull the thumbnails from the library and help us draw the grid.

"Before we can pull anything from the Library, the symbols need to be given a unique identifier called a **linkage name**. This is given to any symbol by right-clicking the symbol in the Library and selecting **Linkage** from the context menu."

> *Mac users should* Ctrl*-click where any right-clicking is required.*

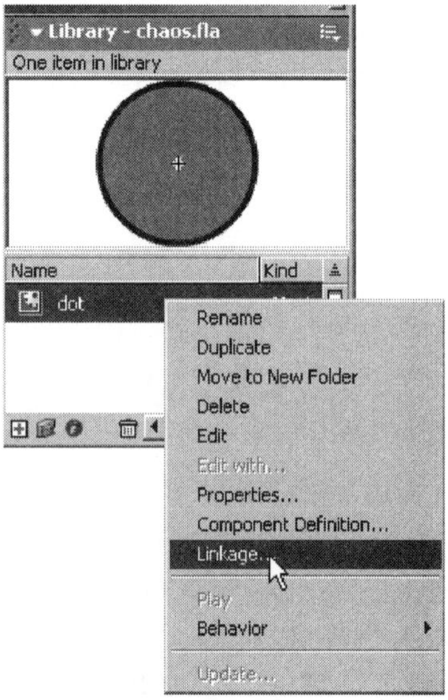

"You then need to click **Export for ActionScript** and give it an identifier name. It's then available to attach dynamically using `attachMovie`."

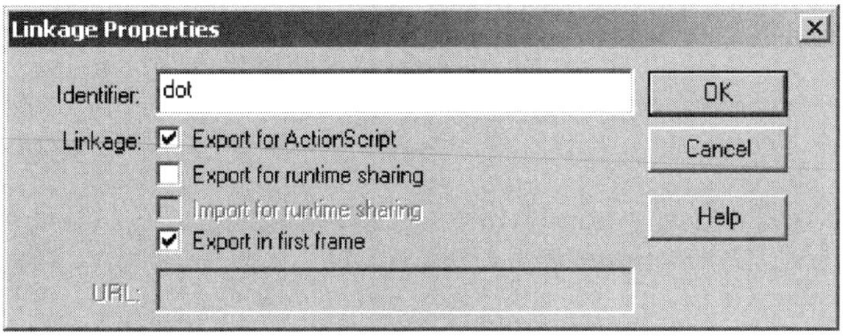

"So how does this `attachMovie` method work, Teach?" Carl asked.

"The `attachMovie` method requires three parameters, Carl," I said. I wrote on the board.

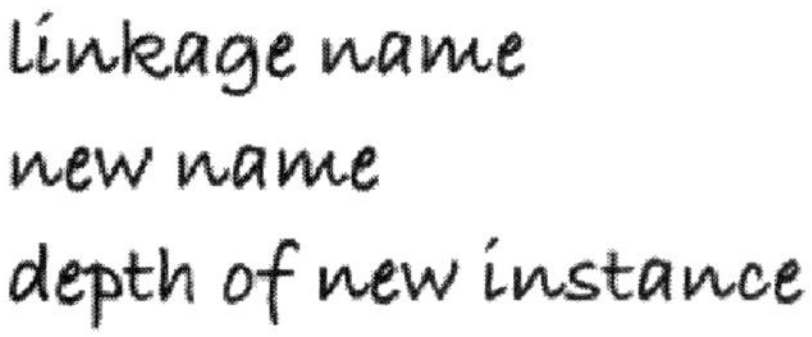

"The first of these is the identifier or linkage name that you've just given it." Carl nodded. "The next parameter is a name for the new instance. `attachMovie` creates a new instance of a symbol, and as you've learned already, each instance requires a unique name; this is where you provide it.

"The last parameter covers something you've yet to see: depth. As well as an individual name, each instance on the Flash stage physically has its own individual depth. This level determines the stacking order of an instance. Depth levels start from 0—the lowest stacking position—and count upward.

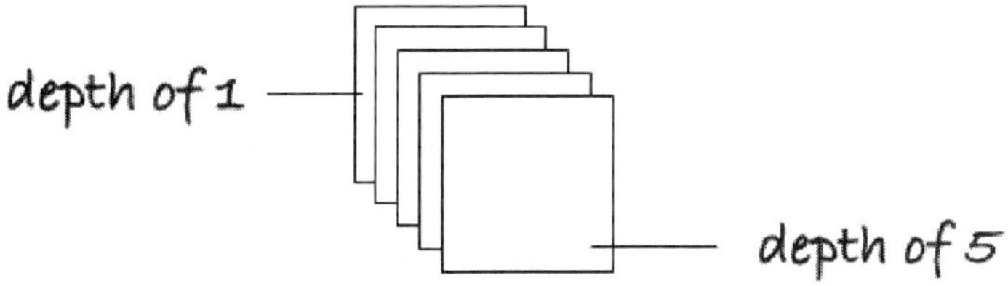

"No two instances can occupy the same depth level. If a second instance is attached at the same depth as another one, the original instance is removed and replaced by the second one."

"So the depth here applies to the new instance we've created?" Carl asked.

"Yes, it does," I replied. "Let's see how it works with a quick demonstration."

Using the attachMovie method

1. Open a new Flash movie. Create a new movie clip called **dot** and draw a single small circle.

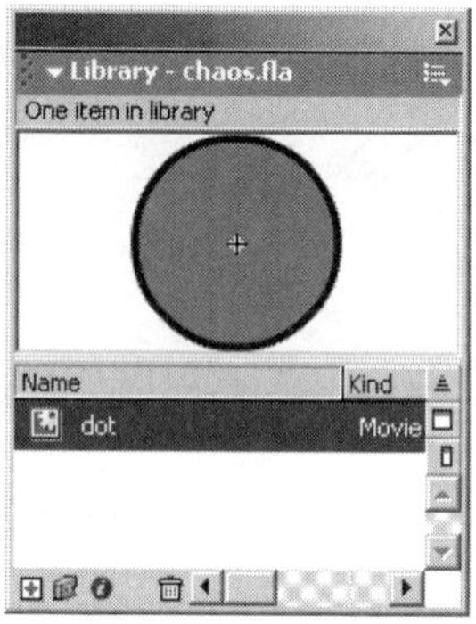

2. RIGHT/CTRL-click the **dot** symbol in the Library and select **Linkage** from the menu.

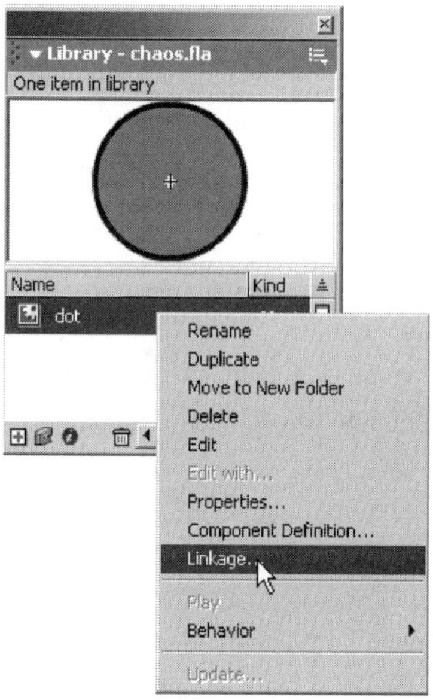

3. Click Export for ActionScript and give it the name 'dot.' Then click **OK** to confirm it.

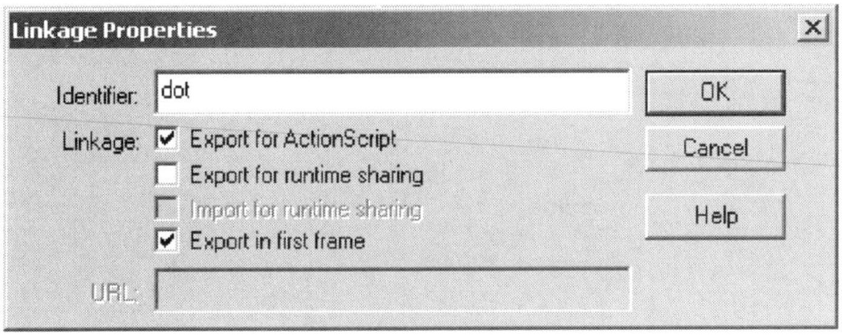

4. On the main timeline, select the keyframe on the existing layer and open the Actions panel. Enter the following ActionScript:

```
// initialize variables
depthCount = 0;
// code to run every frame
_root.onEnterFrame = function () {
    newdot = _root.attachMovie("dot", "dot_"+depthCount, depthCount);
    newdot._x = Math.random ()*550;
    newdot._y = Math.random ()*400;
    depthCount++;
}
```

5. Test the movie and watch the dots fill the screen:

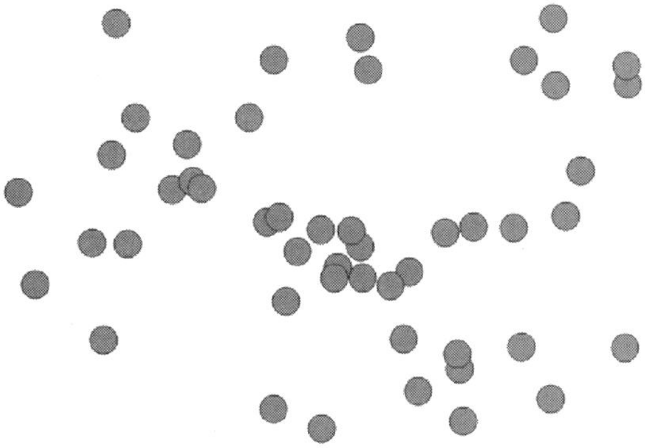

"Wow!" Carl enthused. "It looks like someone is getting the measles!" The students all laughed.

"You kill me, Carl!" Jim said.

“Okay, who would like to guess what’s happening here?” I asked.

“Besides the measles spreading?” Mazzy asked. “I’d say that a new dot appears regularly. I’m guessing from the code that one new dot appears every frame because of the `onEnterFrame` event.”

“That’s right, Mazzy, you have the general gist of it,” I said. “There is a little bit more code here, so I’ll run through it line by line.” I paused. “I’ll start with line 2:

```
depthCount = 0;
```

“Here, we initialize a variable called **`depthCount`**. This variable will be incremented every frame to ensure that the depth level of each new dot is different.

“On line 4, we set up an `onEnterFrame` event using the _root level:

```
_root.onEnterFrame = function() {
```

“Although this might seem strange, we can use the `_root` level for a lot of different things. Remember that the `_root` level is just a huge container for all of the instances and content on the stage, therefore it has properties and values like anything else. Line 5 is a little different from what you’ve seen so far:

```
newdot = _root.attachMovie("dot", "dot_"+depthCount,
➥ depthCount);
```

“Let’s break this line down, piece by piece. First, we’re creating a variable called `newdot`. `newdot` is used to reference the newly attached dot instance, and you’ll see the benefit of it on the next two lines. Then, the actual **`attachMovie`** method is called for. It’s preceded by **`_root`**, which means that the attached instance will be positioned within the _root level. The arguments then follow—what three parameters do we need for the `attachMovie` method, Carl?”

“Linkage name, new name, and depth of new instance,” replied Carl, sneakily reading from the whiteboard.

“Thanks, Carl,” I said. “So, to continue with this knotty line of code, here you see these three parameters. First to come is the linkage identifier, **`"dot,"`** followed by the new name for the instance. The new name is set as 'dot' with the addition of the value of depthCount: **"dot_"+depthCount,**

"This means that the instance names will come out individually like this:

dot_0, dot_1, dot_2, dot_3, dot_4, dot_5....

"The final argument is the depth, which is set to **depthCount**." I paused. "On lines 6 and 7, the new instances are positioned using the _x and _y properties. The newdot variable is used here because it refers to the newest instance created every frame:

```
newdot._x = Math.random()*550;
newdot._y = Math.random()*400;
```

"Use of the Math.random methods here creates a random number from 0 to the multiplied value. In the case of line 6, 550 is used to represent the maximum width and 400 is used on line 7 for the height of the stage. This means that the dots will be positioned randomly on the stage.

"Finally, line 8 increments the depthCount variable by 1 using the shorter ++ operator, ready for the next time the event is run:

```
depthCount++;
```

"Now I see why we might need to increase a variable by 1," Joe said. "I guess we'll use something similar next week."

"Sure, Joe," I said, "the latter part of this class has been to prepare you for the dynamite class next week!" Carl cheered. "For now, though, I think you'll all find that we've ended the class a few minutes late. Please feel free to go. I'll stay behind for a moment to switch off all your computers."

"Thanks, Ken," Joe said. "I have to dash or my dinner will be in the dog!" On that, Joe ran out of the class. The rest of the class followed him, tired and, judging by most of them, ready for bed.

Summary

In this lesson, you learned the following:

- ActionScript is an event-driven language, which means that it responds to things that happen in the Flash movie These things that happen in Flash movies are known as **events**, and the action performed following an event is called an **event handler**.

- There are many different types of event in Flash MX. Some important ones to note are as follows:

  - **onEnterFrame** is a **timed event**. It's triggered every frame of the movie, rather than by a cursor move or mouse activity. As this event is triggered every frame, it's used to check information regularly and is ideal for intense interactivity.

  - **onRelease** is a **button event** that detects the button click or release of a mouse button.

  - **onRollover** detects when a cursor rolls over a button, and **onRollout** is triggered by the cursor rolling off the button.

  - **onPress** is triggered by a mouse button being pressed, such as in drag-and-drop movements.

- Event handlers are defined by callback functions. Functions are blocks of code.

- Flash reads x coordinates from left to right and y coordinates from top to bottom.

- **_x** and **_y** are object properties that define the position of an instant on the stage.

- **attachMovie** is used to take a movie from the Library and place it onstage. A movie clip instance can only be attached from the Library if it has a linkage identifier.

- Dynamically attached instances are organized by depth. Instances added to the stage with the `attachMovie` method must all be placed on their own individual depth level.

Class 6
Programming Structures

Objectives

In today's class, you'll learn about

- **If** statements, which are the way in which Flash movies can choose between two different paths.
- **Switch** statements, which work as a series of **if** statements, enabling you to choose among many different outcomes.
- **Loops**, which save time by letting Flash do the hard work. You can create loops to set up repetitive tasks with a minimum of fuss.

Introduction

It's a shortened class this week, but I've given the students some information to work through beforehand to get them started. Let's eavesdrop on two of them as they meet up before the class.

If . . .

"So how did you find this place?" Jim asked, taking off his coat. Gemma sat down at the table and then answered, "Back in my college days, a few friends and I used to come down here to sit on the big sofas and study. I've been coming back for years now. Anytime I want somewhere quiet to sit, then this is where I head."

"I can't believe it's only a couple of blocks away from where I work and I never even knew it existed," Jim said. A waitress approached with a notebook. "Hi, Gem, what can I get you and your friend this evening?" Gemma quickly ordered. "I'm afraid we haven't got long tonight, so can I just have an iced tea and the chef's Caesar salad?"

"Sounds good. The same, but with a regular coffee, please," said Jim. "With cream, but no sugar." The waitress left with their order. "So how'd you get my home e-mail address?"

"Aha! A bit of light detective work," Gemma said, smiling. "No, in all honesty it was easy. You know the e-mail that Ken sent about him not being available for the first half of today's lesson?"

"Yep," said Jim.

"He forgot to BCC the group, so everyone's address was on it," said Gemma. "It wasn't too hard to figure out your name from the list . . . Mr. Exley, I presume?"

Jim laughed. "Well, you've certainly got me there, Detective . . .?"

"Windham," Gemma replied.

"Well, Miss Windham, are we really here to study?" asked Jim. At that moment, the waitress appeared with their drinks. "Your food will be about 10 minutes. Gimme a call if you need anything in the meantime," she said.

"Thanks," responded Gemma. She paused for the waitress to leave, and then continued. "Yes, my intentions are pure. We've got to look over Ken's notes on conditions ready for the second half of the class tonight, so I thought we might as well put our brains together on it. Many hands make light work and all." Jim stirred his coffee. "I don't know if that analogy quite fits, but anyway . . ." He took a sip. "I have to admit that I haven't read his notes yet, though. I skimmed them when the e-mail came in, but I've been a bit busy lately."

"Just as well that I printed two copies then," said Gemma with a smile. She reached behind her and pulled the paper from her bag. "Here you go," she said, handing Jim a copy of Ken's notes. "So have you read them?" Jim asked. "Not really, much the same as you—I just skimmed them," she replied. Jim looked at the heading:

Conditionals

"I know the general theory behind them," Jim said. "I remember it from my BASIC days."

"Ah yes, the child prodigy programmer," said Gemma.

Jim almost spilled his coffee as he laughed. "I don't know if I'd quite go that far. It was mostly just typing in listings from old magazines, and even then they were usually games or graphics programs. Once a geek, always a geek, I suppose."

"Well, Mr. Geek, as long as you can recall enough to explain these conditionals to me then I'm happy," said Gemma.

"If that's all I'm worth, then I suppose I'd better get it right. How much do you know from skimming the notes?" asked Jim.

"Assume that I know nothing—start from the beginning," Gemma replied.

"Okay, a **conditional** is a programming structure used for decision making. So, for example, the simplest conditional is known as an **`if` statement**, and the logic basically goes, 'If a certain condition is satisfied, then do something.' For instance, '*If* my coffee is black, then I add milk.' '*If* it's the end of the month, then I get paid.'"

"*If* you just got paid, then you can pick up the bill?" asked Gemma.

"You see, you've got it already," said Jim.

"So what happens if the condition isn't satisfied?" asked Gemma.

"Then you'd better have some money in your purse, or we're in trouble," Jim replied.

"No, silly. What happens in the program? Does it just continue?" asked Gemma.

"Yeah, if the `if` is the only condition that you have, then the program will just carry on whether or not the condition was satisfied. If you want something to happen when the condition isn't satisfied, then you need a . . . hang on a minute." Jim checked through the notes before saying, "Yep, it all looks pretty similar. You have an **`else`** section paired with the `if` that says what will happen if the condition isn't satisfied. It's kind of like an anti-`if`. Just as the `if` will only play if the condition is satisfied, the `else` will only run if it isn't."

"*If* the bill comes, then you'll pay it, *else* you'll be washing dishes for a week?" asked Gemma.

"Something like that. Although I'm not sure I like the way this discussion is going," said Jim.

Gemma ignored him. "So this is kind of like the events that we looked at last week?"

"I guess in some respects it is," Jim said. "The `if` is the trigger waiting to be set off, and when its condition is fulfilled, then it fires off its code as surely as an `onRelease` handler that's been clicked will. Strangely enough, I never thought of them as events before, but I guess you're right, they're internal events."

"So how do we write them?" asked Gemma.

"On a VIC-20 or in Flash?" Jim asked. Gemma glared at him. "Gemma, I have no idea. I'm as new to this Flash thing as you are. I know how they work in theory, but I haven't a clue how to put that into practice. We'll just have to turn to the word of Ken." They both shuffled the notes and started reading. "We could really do with testing these out on a computer," said Jim. "It would be good to see how the conditions work together in Flash, and there are some structures here that I've never seen before."

"Your wish is my command," said Gemma, reaching into her bag and pulling out a laptop computer. "Regular little James Bond, aren't you?" joked Jim. "I told you," said Gemma, "I'm here to work. And if you spill any of that coffee on my laptop you're a dead man."

"All right, all right," said Jim, surreptitiously pulling his coffee cup closer to him. "Now then," said Gemma, "how do we do this `if` thing?"

"Before we can do that, there are a couple of other paragraphs of notes to get through. First up, **Booleans**," said Jim.

"Boole-whats?" asked Gemma.

"Booleans. Apparently they're named after some mathematician named George Boole," Jim replied.

"Does that help me understand what they are?" asked Gemma.

"No," replied Jim, "but I thought you might appreciate some history."

"Okay, okay, George Boole is the founding father of all Boole-things. Got it, carry on," said Gemma.

"A Boolean is a special type of variable that has only two states: true or false," Jim started.

"I presume it's true seeing as how you're reading it straight from the notes," Gemma said.

Jim chuckled. "No, no, the two states are true and false, I wasn't testing you."

"Ah, I see. Sorry. I think I can picture how this will work with the `if` statements, then. It will just be something like 'If hunger is true, then eat.' It's kind of like a switched focus from the normal `if`—rather than saying 'If I am hungry,' you say 'If hunger is true.'"

"Yeah, I think you've got it there," Jim said.

"Wow, Booleans dusted and we haven't even finished our drinks! Not bad," said Gemma, with a satisfied smile.

"I don't think we've quite finished them yet," warned Jim. "Ken's written at the bottom: 'If we have time, we'll look into using implicit Booleans later in the course.'"

"What are implicit Booleans?" asked Gemma.

"Beats me—I've never heard of them before," Jim replied.

"Okay, then we'll cross that can of worms when we open it. As far as I'm concerned, Booleans are done for today. What's next?" asked Gemma.

Comparison and logical operators

"Looks like code," said Jim. "You'd better start up Flash."

"Okay," said Gemma, opening up Flash on her laptop. "So what code are we looking at?"

"You remember we had the numerical operators before?" asked Jim.

"Yep," Gemma affirmed.

"Well, these are called **comparison operators**," said Jim. "Basically, they qualify the `if` statement. For example, take the statement 'If the cup equals half empty,' the equals there is the comparison operator. You can also have things like 'less than or equal to,' 'greater than,' and so on. Comparison operators can also be combined by using **logical operators**. Did you ever do any electronics at school?"

"I vaguely remember doing some, yes," Gemma responded.

"Do you remember the logic gates?" asked Jim. "AND, OR, NOT, NOR, NAND, XOR, and all those weird things?"

"Nope, you rapidly lost me there," Gemma said.

"It doesn't really matter," said Jim, "all you need to know is that those gates controlled the flow of electricity through the circuit, and it's the same with these operators: they can control the flow of a program. By combining the operators, you can make some complicated conditions, like if the temperature of my coffee is less than boiling, and it's also greater than cold, then I'll drink it, but if it crosses either of those extremes, then I'll leave it where it is. Let's take a look at the first example Ken's given. Are you okay to type as I read it out?"

"Certainly am," said Gemma, pressing the F9 key to open the Actions panel in Flash. "I'm hoping this will make it clearer than your crazy explanations."

"Why thank you," said Jim. "Okay, we're starting with an `if` statement. Type 'If space open bracket . . . ."

"It's gone blue!" exclaimed Gemma.

"What has?" asked Jim.

"If," said Gemma.

"Well, I guess that means you spelled it right. We're off to a good start," Jim responded. Gemma poked her tongue out at Jim. "There's a code hint too," she said. "It's telling me to put the condition between the brackets and then to use those squiggly things."

"Braces?" asked Jim.

"They're the ones, look," said Gemma.

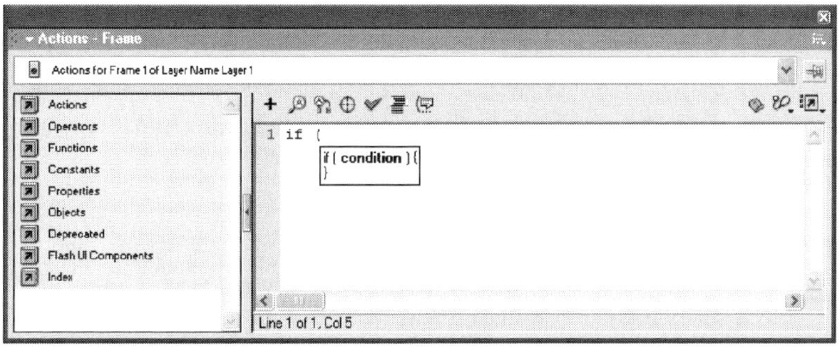

"Cool, that's just what Ken says to do," said Jim. "Right, now we have to give it a condition. Put, 'coffee = cold'. Actually, hang on a minute, it looks like there might be two sets of equals there. It's hard to tell from this printout."

Jim read on a bit further. "Yep, here it is. There's a big NB box-out saying to remember to use double equals instead of single equals. It says here, 'A single equals is an assignment operator, so that would make the `if` statement pointless by automatically setting the variable to the value that you were checking it against. The double equals is a comparison operator and is used for comparing values in a condition.'"

"Oh, I see," said Gemma. "If we only use a single equals, then we're setting the coffee to be cold as soon as Flash comes across it. I'm going to think of it as double for emphasis. We're checking to see if the coffee *really* is cold, so we need to have a double equals in there to make sure."

"That's certainly a novel interpretation," Jim laughed, "but if it helps you to remember, then who am I to argue?"

"Exactly!" Gemma replied, correcting her typing. "Do I close the brackets now?" Jim nodded.

```
if ( coffee == cold )
```

"And then what?" she asked.

Jim replied, "Then we have the braces that contain the code that we want to run if the condition is true. Kind of like events, as you said before. So in this case it will be 'timeToGetANewCupOfCoffee = true'."

"Is that a hint?" asked Gemma.

"Well, it might be nice to have another cup," Jim replied.

"In that case then, I'll have another iced tea," said Gemma. "It's best to go up to the bar and order. In the meantime, I'll try making something with an `if` statement." Jim smiled and then got up and left for the bar.

When he returned, he saw a couple of circles on Gemma's screen. "What have you got so far, then?" Jim asked, passing Gemma's drink over to her. "Okay, so far I've created two movie clips, which are just a blue and a pink circle," said Gemma. "The blue one has the instance name `blue`, and you can probably guess what the instance name of the pink one is. I was thinking about last week's lesson, so I've written a simple callback to move each of them. The blue one moves along the x-axis, and the pink one goes along the y-axis. Here's the code that I've attached to the first frame of my movie. You came back at the right time, actually—I just ran into a slight quandary."

```
blue.onEnterFrame = function() {
    this._x += 2;
};
pink.onEnterFrame = function() {
    this._y += 2;
};

```

Line 7 of 7, Col 1

"Okay, shoot," said Jim.

"What I've got at the moment works fine, but it doesn't take long for the circles to move off the screen. I was planning on having them somehow bounce off the edge of the screen, but then I realized that I have absolutely no idea how to do that," said Gemma.

"Yes, you do. We did it in last week's class," Jim responded.

"We didn't cover screen boundaries in last week's class, did we?" asked Gemma.

"No, but we did cover coordinates," said Jim. "We know the size of the screen, because we define it when we create the Flash file, so we know what coordinates the screen edges will have. We can then just tell it to go back the other way when it reaches those coordinates."

"Of course! Nice bit of lateral thinking there, Sherlock," said Gemma. "Okay, let me have a go at the `if` statement. Sit back and drink your coffee, and I'll give you a shout if I get stuck." Gemma smiled, and Jim leaned back in his chair and sipped at his coffee obediently. Within minutes Gemma said, "Okay, help."

"That didn't take long," Jim laughed. "Don't laugh," said Gemma, "I can't get it to work at all. This is what I have so far:"

```
blue.onEnterFrame = function() {
    this._x += 2;
    if (this._x == 400) {
        this._x -= 2;
    }
};
```


"The movie's actually 600 pixels wide, but when that didn't work, I thought that it might be doing something that I couldn't see at the edge of the screen, so I brought it in a bit, but it still does nothing," explained Gemma.

"Try putting a `trace` action in there to see if it's ever getting into the `if`. Just something to say 'hello' so that we know if it's working or not," said Jim.

"Okay, to see if it's ever getting into `if`, we'll need to put the `trace` inside the curly brackets after the `if` statement. That's right, isn't it?" Jim nodded, and Gemma typed away:

```
blue.onEnterFrame = function() {
    this._x += 2;
    if (this._x == 400) {
        trace ("hello")
        this._x -= 2;
    }
};
```

She then tested the movie, but the `trace` never appeared. "I've got it," said Jim, "it's because you're adding 2 to the x position every time, and that's making it miss 400. Try setting it to 1." Gemma tried it, and they watched with bated breath as the circle move across the screen. Their salads appeared in the middle of the circle's journey. "It's a bit slower than last time," said Gemma.

Finally, the circle left the edge of the screen, but still without any sign of an Output window. Jim looked puzzled. "Check the initial x position of the circle on the screen," he said to Gemma. "It's 122.5," she told him, and realization swept across her face as she said it. "It starts at .5 and adds 1 every time, so it's never going to be exactly 400. I'll change it now."

```
blue.onEnterFrame = function() {
    this._x += 1;
    if (this._x == 400.5) {
        trace ("hello")
        this._x -= 2;
    }
};
```

“There must be an easier way than this,” said Jim, “I’ll read further into the notes.”

“Whoa!” exclaimed Gemma. “That worked, but it’s making my eyes go funny.” Jim looked over and had to agree, the circle was just wobbling back and forth and throwing a string of hellos to the Output window. Gemma closed the window and said, “Phew, that’s better. There’s obviously something fairly wrong with the code.”

“Yes and no,” replied Jim. “At least we know that the `if` statement is working now. I found something in the notes that will help too. Ken’s given us a list of the other comparison operators that we can use:

```
==    Exactly equal to
>     Greater than
<     Less than
>=    Greater than or equal to
<=    Less than or equal to
```

“He’s also given the logical operators that we can use to compound conditions:

```
&&    AND
||    OR
!     NOT
```

“The Not operator can be combined with the comparison operators to negate them. For example, `!=` means that we can test to see if something is not equal to another value.

“I think we should try using the ‘greater than or equal to’ operator in our script instead of the double equals. That way, we can guarantee that whenever the circle crosses that point it will trigger the condition.”

“Okay,” said Gemma, “I’ll change that to both circles now. Right, here’s the code with those changes:

```
blue.onEnterFrame = function() {
    this._x += 2;
    if (this._x>=400) {
        this._x -= 2;
    }
};
pink.onEnterFrame = function() {
    this._y += 2;
    if (this._y>=250) {
        this._y -= 2;
    }
};
```


"Will this make any difference in the wiggling and jiggling?"

"I don't think so," replied Jim, "but it might be worth running it just to make sure it does what we're expecting it to." Gemma tested the file, and sure enough, the circles moved to their boundaries and stuck there. "Okay then, brainiac, how do we reverse the direction?" she asked.

"I've been thinking about that," said Jim. "First of all, I think Ken would tell us to use variables for the amount that we're moving the circles by. That way, if we need to change the speed then we'll only have to change one value."

"I think I agree with Ken's recommendation," said Gemma. "I'll initialize them at the beginning of the code. How's this?"

```
blue.power = 2;
pink.power = 2;
blue.onEnterFrame = function() {
    this._x += this.power;
    if (this._x>=400) {
        this._x -= this.power;
    }
};
pink.onEnterFrame = function() {
    this._y += this.power;
    if (this._y>=250) {
        this._y -= this.power;
    }
};
```

"Looks perfect to me," said Jim. "And I've got an idea for the reversal too."

"Go on," prompted Gemma.

"You probably won't care to know this," said Jim, "but I use numbers a lot in my job. Now, one thing that I know is that to reverse a number you can just multiply it by -1. This works if the original number is positive or negative, and it will simply change the number to its opposite."

"Okay, I follow that, but I'm not entirely sure how it helps us," said Gemma.

"I think that if we always add power to the position, and just multiply it by -1 when we hit a boundary, then it should bounce back off it," Jim responded. "For instance, on the x-axis, it will add positive power as it moves right, but then when it hits the boundary, power will be flipped and it will begin adding negative power to its position. Adding a negative is the same as just subtracting, so the circle will start moving back left. Do you follow?"

"Kind of," said Gemma, pushing the laptop over to Jim. "Show me." Jim tinkered with the computer while Gemma ate and then passed it back over. "Try that," he said. Gemma looked at the changes that Jim had made to the code:

```
blue.power = 2;
pink.power = 2;
blue.onEnterFrame = function() {
    this._x += this.power;
    if (this._x>=400) {
        this.power *= -1;
    }
};
pink.onEnterFrame = function() {
    this._y += this.power;
    if (this._y>=250) {
        this.power *= -1;
    }
};
```

"Does it work?" she asked. "Don't know yet, I thought you'd like to have the first go," Jim replied. Gemma ran the movie. "Nope, there are about four errors in the Output window."

"You're joking," said Jim.

"Yeah, I am," Gemma said with a smile, "it works perfectly. Now we just need to make them bounce back the other way when they hit the opposite side of the screen."

"That shouldn't be too bad," said Jim, "we only need another set of `if` statements to check when they reach the other side, and then just reverse it again. You should be able to just copy and paste the last `if` and then simply modify the condition. It wants to be if it's less than or equal to 50, or something like that."

"Or . . ." said Gemma.

"Or what?" asked Jim.

"Or . . . OR," said Gemma in a strange voice. "Or what?" asked Jim again. "You're beginning to scare me now."

"Come on, Jim, I thought you would have been up on your geeky programmer in-jokes!" said Gemma.

"You've completely lost me now," replied Jim.

"We could use an OR operator in there, couldn't we? If the result of the `if` is the same no matter if we hit one side or the other, then we only need to check for one or the other. That way we'll only need one `if`," said Gemma.

"Ah, I follow you now. You're right, that was a pretty geeky in-joke," said Jim.

"I'll do it now. What was the sign for OR? It was that weird double-line thing, wasn't it?" asked Gemma.

"Yeah, I think it's called a pipe," said Jim.

"Really?" asked Gemma.

"I think so," replied Jim.

"I don't suppose you know where it is on the keyboard, do you?" asked Gemma.

"That all depends on the keyboard," said Jim. "It's usually on the far-left side on a PC (by the Z key) or by the RETURN key on a Mac. Also, make sure you use the solid bar—there's also a bar with a break in the middle that looks fairly similar."

"Okay, got it. How does this look?" asked Gemma.

```
blue.power = 2;
pink.power = 2;
blue.onEnterFrame = function() {
     this._x += this.power;
     if (this._x>=400 || this._x<=50) {
          this.power *= -1;
     }
};
pink.onEnterFrame = function() {
     this._y += this.power;
     if (this._y>=250 || this._y<=50) {
          this.power *= -1;
     }
};
```

"Looks good to me—give it a go," said Jim.

"I thought you might want to have the first go," said Gemma, passing the laptop over to Jim. Jim smiled and turned it so that they could both see the screen, and then he ran the program. It worked perfectly, and each circle bounced back and forth along its axis. "I think I'd call that a success," he said. Gemma checked her watch, "And just in time too—we're going to have to run if we're going to make it to the class." She took out her purse and started searching for money. "I'll get it," said Jim. "You'd better pack up the computer."

"You sure?" asked Gemma.

"Of course," said Jim. He paid for the meal, and they hurriedly made their way to class. They arrived to meet Ken coming the opposite way down the corridor with his usual coffee. "Great, you're here," Ken said, "I think that's everyone." He opened the door and ushered them in.

Back in the classroom

I let the door close behind the last students to arrive and made my way to the front of the class. "Good evening, everyone, I trust you are all well? I apologize greatly for the half class today—I had some urgent matters to attend to that I couldn't reschedule. I hope you all received the notes on conditionals, and that the information is still fresh in your minds. How did you find them? Were there any significant problems?" I asked.

Mazzy put her hand up. "I managed the if and else statements without too much trouble, but I got a little lost with switch. I wouldn't mind spending a bit of time going over them again."

"Okay," I said, "did anyone else have problems with switch?" Jim and Gemma looked at each other, shrugged their shoulders, and then both put their hands up. Joe's hand also went up. "All right then, it looks like it foxed quite a few of you, so I'll take it from the top."

Switch, case, and break

"A **switch** statement is basically the equivalent of a series of if statements," I began. "It checks one condition that can have a number of outcomes.

"For example, consider the answers in a multiple-choice question. Rather than having a series of if statements for each choice, we only need one switch statement to cover all of them. The way that switch works its magic is in its combination with case.

"The case statement does exactly what it sounds like it should: it describes what happens in a particular case. So following our multiple-choice example, the first case might describe the correct answer, and the second and third might say that the answer is wrong but give some information about their particular answer anyway. In fact, let's have a look at making a quick multiple-choice switch statement. Open Flash and start a new movie.

"The basic structure of a switch is similar to other conditional structures. We have the keyword followed by the condition in brackets and then some code to run within a pair of braces. The biggest difference with switch, though, is that only the variable whose condition is being checked is included in the brackets. All of the possible outcomes will be held in the braces. We'll be checking a variable called answer, so the initial structure looks like this:

```
switch (answer) {
}
```

"Now, as I mentioned before, we use the case keyword to describe each outcome. The structure for this is:

case condition: outcome

"So, if our multiple choice allowed the answers a, b, and c, then our first case would look like this:

```
case "a" : trace("Correct");
```

"Basically, this is the same as having

```
if(answer == "a"){
    trace("Correct");
}
```

"But rather than having to have an `else` and then another `if` statement for the next outcome, we only need to have another `case`, like so:

```
case "b" : trace("Wrong");
```

"There is one other thing that we need to complete our `switch` statement. If left like that, the program would jump to the indicated case but then continue playing through the remaining cases.

"To prevent this, we need to stop the `switch` after it has completed the correct case. We do this by using the **`break`** keyword. `break` basically tells the program to finish the `switch` and continue running the rest of the program. It breaks the program out of the `switch` statement. We need to have one `break` after every `case`, and they are normally written like so:

```
case "a" :
    trace("Correct");
    break;
case "b" :
    trace("Wrong");
    break;
```

"Notice that I've separated the two halves of the `case` statement. This is a layout convention to ease visibility, as it's simpler to see each complete case. Okay, I want you all to have a go at a `switch`. Begin with a simple trace containing a multiple-choice question, and then have a case containing the answer outcomes.

"At the moment, that's all I want—just the question and the answers. I'll give you a couple of minutes to come up with something. I'll try and come up with one myself in the meantime." The students all went through a cycle of staring at the screen and then staring into the ceiling, and I racked my own brain to come up with something.

After a little while, I noticed that everyone was winding down their thinking and typing, so I asked if they were ready to move on. They replied in the affirmative. "Okay then, as an example, I'll show you what I've done so far," I said. I switched on the projector to show my screen:

```
trace("Question: Which of these does the true tarantula belong
to? a) Lycosa; b) Phaeophyceae; or c) Spirillum?");

answer = "a";

switch (answer) {
case "a" :
    trace("CORRECT! Lycosa is the genus to which the
tarantula belongs.");
    break;
case "b" :
    trace("SORRY! Phaeophyceae is actually brown seaweed.");
    break;
case "c" :
    trace("SORRY! Spirillum is a spiral-shaped bacterium.");
    break;
}
```

"Does the general structure of everyone's program look something like that?" I asked.

"Mine's in English," said Carl.

"Okay, apart from the pretentious words that I've used to try and make myself look intelligent," I said with a smile, "does everyone else's look similar?" Everybody nodded that theirs was similar. "Right, we're going to have a simple quiz. In pairs, I want you to ask your partner your question, and give him or her the three options. When your partner gives you his or her answer, you'll need to add it to the code. You do this by adding `answer =` and then inserting the appropriate letter inside quotation marks after the initial question.

"So for example, assuming someone had answered correctly, the first lines would be

```
trace("Question: Which of these does the true tarantula belong
to? a) Lycosa; b) Phaeophyceae; or c) Spirillum?");

answer = "a";
```

"When that's done, you can run your program and it should tell your partner whether he or she was right or wrong. Okay, there's an odd number of students, so someone will have to pair up with me, I'm afraid. Let me know how it goes."

The class paired up, and Joe was left with me. He asked me who the original voice of Donald Duck was, and I got the question wrong. Meanwhile, an argument was breaking out between Mazzy and Carl.

"How am I supposed to know what Curly's third 'don't' is in 'People Will Say We're In Love'?" shouted Carl. "The same way that I'm supposed to know who the original bassist of Sepultura was," countered Mazzy. "And anyway, you're more likely to have seen *Oklahoma!* than I am to have heard of Sepultura."

"I take that as a grave insult," gasped Carl. "Okay," said Mazzy, "I'll go for the stupidest one there—was it Roberto 'the cat'?"

"What, how did you know?" spluttered an indignant Carl, running his program to prove she was correct. "In that case," said Mazzy with a smile, "you have to correctly guess mine, or it just confirms the fact I'm better than you."

"No fair!" exclaimed Carl.

"A, B, or C, Carl. The choice is yours," said Mazzy.

"Is it . . . C, 'don't laugh at my jokes too much'?" asked Carl.

"I knew I'd catch you out on that one," chuckled Mazzy. "That was actually Laurey's third don't, not Curly's."

"Oh, how silly of me, I should have known," said Carl in mock disbelief.

"Okay, everyone," I cut in, "have you all finished your questions?" The students all motioned that they had. "In that case, does anybody have any questions about `switch`?" Jim raised his hand. "Yes, Jim?" I asked.

"Gemma decided that none of my answers was correct, and the real answer was actually D," Jim said. "I tried putting this in for a laugh and, as I expected, nothing happened. So I was wondering if there was an equivalent of an `else` statement for `switch`? Something to be displayed when the condition isn't fulfilled."

"Yep, there is," I answered. "There is a special keyword called **`default`** that does exactly that. This keyword is normally placed at the end of the `switch` after all of the `case` statements. It works exactly the same way as `case` does, except there is no condition." I made a few modifications to my code. "Here's an example of a `switch` statement containing a `default` option:

```
trace("Question: Which of these does the true tarantula belong
to? a) Lycosa; b) Phaeophyceae; or c) Spirillum?");

answer = "d";

switch (answer) {
case "a" :
    trace("CORRECT! Lycosa is the genus to which the
➥ tarantula belongs.");
    break;
case "b" :
    trace("SORRY! Phaeophyceae is actually brown
➥ seaweed.");
    break;
case "c" :
    trace("SORRY! Spirillum is a spiral-shaped
➥ bacterium.");
    break;
default :
    trace("Please select one of the given options only.");
}
```

"Notice that at the top of the script I've set the answer to 'd'. Flash will run through the case statements, and when it finds that none of them fit the answer that it has, it will display the default trace. This will work no matter what the answer is, even if it's a number or a Boolean—all that matters is that it's not one of the designated cases. Any more questions about conditions?

"In that case then, let's move on. We're now going to expand our programming fundamentals by learning about the other most important program structure, the loop. With this under our belts, we'll be able to really start to string together some meaningful code."

Loop structures

"Let's get straight into the case study," I said. "Can you all open a fresh window in Flash, please?" When everybody was ready, I continued, "Start by creating a new movie clip symbol called **square**, and inside it draw a—you guessed it—square. You're going to make it an exact size, so use the Property inspector to make it 50x50:

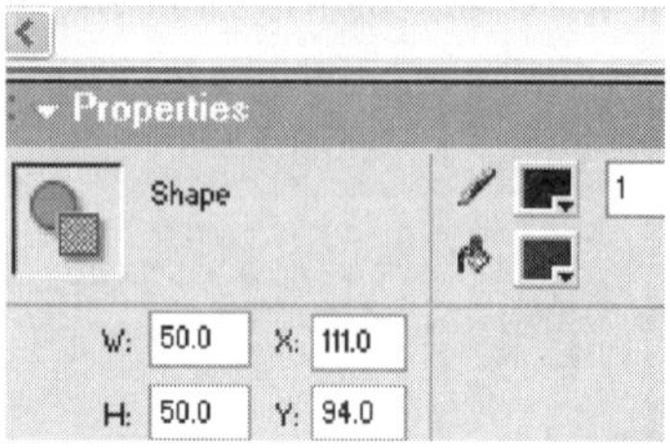

"Use the **Align** panel to center the square on the stage, and then return to the main stage and open the Library. As you did last week, you're going to give this movie clip a linkage name so that you can use code to bring it into the movie from the Library. Does everyone remember how to give a movie clip a linkage name?

"The easiest way is to right-click the symbol name in the Library and then choose **Linkage** from the menu that appears. Rather than use the default name that Flash gives you, you'll call this symbol **dummy**. The reason for this is that it will be a dummy movie clip to represent the photos that we'll be putting in the gallery.

"Now, to recap on what we did last week, let's attach a single instance of the symbol and position it at 50x50 on the stage. Give this instance the name `dummy1`, and place it on depth 1. Everyone see if you can remember how to do it, and give me a shout if you need any help."

There was a bit of head-scratching, and a couple of instances of note-checking, but I was pleased to see that everyone was soon sitting back with confident looks on their faces. "Okay," I turned the projector to display my screen, "you should all have something like this:

```
_root.attachMovie("dummy", "dummy1", 1);
dummy1._x = 50;
dummy1._y = 50;
```

"Did anyone have anything significantly different?" Mazzy spoke up, "I have to admit, I originally forgot to put the quotes around the linkage name and couldn't work out for the life of me why it wasn't working. It took a quick check of my notes to realize what I'd done wrong."

"Don't worry about it," I said. "To be perfectly honest with you, I still sometimes make that mistake. The most important thing to remember is that when attaching movie clips won't work, the linkage name is most often the cause of the problem. As long as you remember to check there first, then forgetting quotes is only a minor annoyance rather than the beginning of some serious hair loss."

"Wow, my husband must have forgotten a whole lot of quote marks in his time!" Mazzy joked. "Okay, other than that," I continued, "were there any other problems?" The class indicated that everything else had been okay. "Right, then, your next task is to make another five of them in a row, spaced exactly 17.3 pixels apart."

"What?" exclaimed Carl. "Your time starts now," I told him.

I left the class to work for about a minute, in which time a few calculators came out and much scribbling was done before I stopped them. "Okay, how far did you get?"

"I've done another two," said Carl. "I was just working on the last one," said Gemma. "If you'd only given me another 10 seconds, I would have had them all done."

"I'm impressed," I said, "but you all have to admit, it wasn't that easy, or indeed particularly fun. Luckily for us, though, computers excel at doing simple repetitive tasks like this, so we don't have to.

"Let's look at our problem and come up with our own solution to it." I turned to the board. "Okay, Joe, can you remind me what the problem that I set you was?" I wrote on the board as he spoke:

Attach 6 copies of 'dummy' on the stage
Space each one 17.3 pixels apart

"Let's refine that a bit. Mazzy, can you tell me what we need to change for each instance to fulfill these requirements?"

"Its name and its position?" Mazzy asked. "Which aspect of its position in particular are we changing?" I asked her. "Sorry, its x position," she replied. I wrote on the board:

update instance name
update x position

"Anything else?" I asked. Mazzy thought for a moment, and then Carl jumped in. "Its depth."

"Thank you, Carl, I'm sure Mazzy would have gotten there by herself," I said.

"In the end," whispered Mazzy, with a wink to Carl. I finished updating the board:

Attach 6 copies of 'dummy' on the stage
Space each one 17.3 pixels apart
update instance name
update x position
update depth

"Okay, does everyone agree that this defines our problem and tells us the steps that need to be changed for each instance to ensure we reach our solution?" I asked.

"I think it needs to be clarified a little more," said Joe. "When I was doing the exercise earlier, I wasn't sure if you wanted me to just add 17.3 pixels to the x position of each one, or if you wanted there to be a full 17.3 pixel gap visible between them."

"Good point," I said. "I didn't make that clear. I was thinking of the latter option: having a clear gap between each instance. Okay then, let's change our definition. Joe, would you like to tell me what I should have put?"

"I think we need to add 67.3 pixels to each instance's x position," Joe told me. "Hold on there, Joe, let's keep things simple for the minute. We want to add the width of the square plus 17.3 pixels. In this case you're right, it would be 67.3, but if we changed the size of the square—and don't forget, these are only dummies—then we'd have to change the code and recalculate. We can use the width property of the movie clip to avoid having to hard-code anything.

"Okay, let's change our board definition to:

Leave a visible 17.3 pixel gap between the copies

"I haven't said anything about the width there, but we'll remember it when we come to write the code. Okay, what we have here is the basis for a simple loop. We have a set of simple instructions that we want to carry out a number of times.

"The simplest loop that we can use to solve this problem is a **for** loop. It's called that because it carries out a set of instructions for a definite number of times. The other new term that we're going to come across here is a **loop counter**. A loop counter is the common name for a variable that's used to count the number of times that a loop has run. Without further ado, let's look at the code.

"Here's the basic structure of a for loop." I wrote on the board:

```
Initialize loop counter; define condition;
            \                  /
      for ( i = 0 ; i <= 10; i++ ) { ... }
                               |
Change counter by this amount and loop again
```

"You may be wondering why I've chosen such a strange name for a loop counter, but 'i' is the conventional name that most programmers use for loops," I said.

"Why's that?" asked Joe. "I'm not entirely sure," I told him. "As a guess, I'd say that it's an abbreviation of integer, but to be honest with you, I don't know. Of course, if you're not happy with using 'i,' then feel free to use a more obvious name—'counter,' for instance. It's up to you. In a second, we'll also look at defining the counter as a local variable, but for now, let's look closer at what that loop structure means.

"Okay, so we start off with the keyword `for`, and like so many things, we have the parameters in parentheses after it, and then the code that we want to run in braces after that. Note that each of the parameters in the parentheses is separated by a semicolon.

"The next thing is the initialization of the loop counter variable (the first parameter). The loop counter is the heart of the loop; it keeps track of where in the loop we are so that we know how far we've come and how far we still have to go. You can initialize the loop counter to any number that you like. You can even set it to another variable from your code.

"The next part of the loop is the condition. This is what tells the loop when to stop, and without it, the code would just—"

"Run forever, out of control?" cut in Carl.

"Well, not quite," I told him. "Flash has built-in checks to tell when an infinite loop is taking place. It will simply prompt you if you want to stop the loop."

"What does it look like?" asked Carl. "Do you really want to see it?" I inquired, and the class responded with a resounding "Yes!" "Okay, your wish is my command," I said and started typing into the computer.

"I'm writing a very simple loop exactly as I did on the board. All it's doing is tracing the current value of the loop counter. The catch is that instead of telling it to loop ten times, I'm telling it to loop a few hundred million times. Admittedly, this isn't infinite, but it's close enough to start Flash's alarm bells ringing." I finished writing the program and ran it. The class watched with bated breath. Sure enough, after a short while, an alert box popped up:

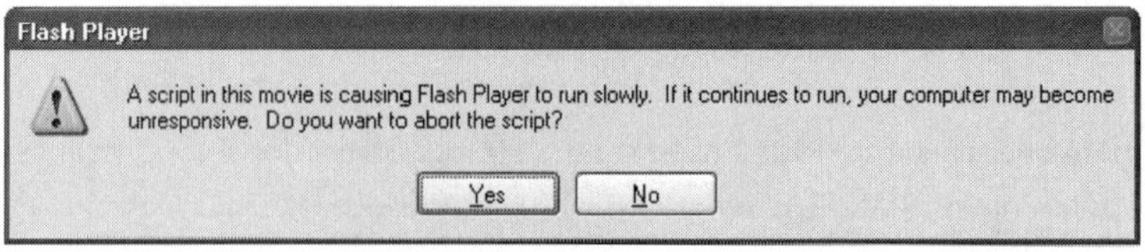

"Now, 99 times out of 100, I'd suggest that you say 'Yes' to this and allow Flash to stop running the script. The only time that you'll want to say 'No' is if you know that the script is extremely power-hungry, and you're sure that you coded it correctly. For instance, if I was carrying out an experiment and I really did want to run through something a couple of million times, then I'd say 'No.' In that case, Flash would go back to churning through the code and would probably come up with the same alert again a few more times before the loop came to an end.

"Okay, back to the loop condition. You'll notice that I have a 'less than or equals' sign in there. Hopefully, you all understood the logical operators material in the notes? Well, this means that as long as the loop counter is less than or equal to 10, then we'll continue running through the loop. Or, to put it another way, as soon as the counter is greater than 10, stop the loop.

"The last part of the loop is sometimes called the step. It defines how the counter is changed each time the loop runs. In this case, I've got `i++`, meaning that 1 will be added to the counter in each cycle of the loop. You can have any expression that you like in here to change the counter. Let's take a look at a complete loop. Here's the code for the simple loop that I've been discussing:

```
for (i=0; i<=10; i++) {
    trace(i);
}
```

"You'll notice that I've put a `trace` action in between the braces. This will simply output the current value of `i` in each cycle of the loop. If we run this, then we get:

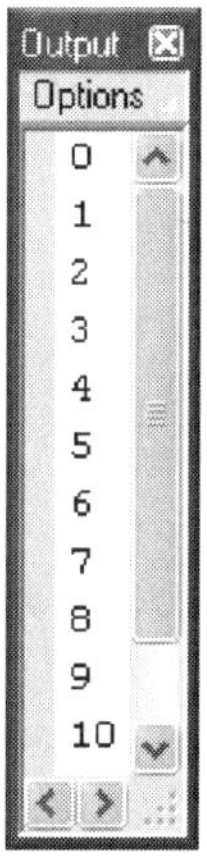

"What can we tell from this output?" I asked the class. They all looked blank. "What's the first number?" I prompted. "Zero," replied Jim. "So that must mean that . . ." I waited expectantly. "That the loop has run through once before the counter is iterated?" Gemma asked. "Precisely," I said. "In a `for` loop, the loop makes one complete cycle before the counter increment kicks in. Another behavior of `for` loops is that the condition is checked before every cycle, so if you initialized `i` as 11, then nothing would be traced to the Output window. There are also a couple of other loop types that you can use and, as you'll see, some of these act quite differently."

While and do . . . while loops

"One of the key factors of a for loop is that you initialize a counter at the beginning of the loop and then give that counter a condition. The next type, a **while** loop, takes an existing value and then applies a condition to it," I said. "Here's some example code to create a while loop similar to the earlier for loop:

```
i = 0;
while (i <= 10) {
      trace(i);
      i++;
}
```

"You can see that all of the elements of the for loop are there, but they are split onto separate lines. This may seem to make it more confusing than the compact for loop, but it also gives the loop greater flexibility. You're now free to move the increment operator around within the body of the loop, meaning that you can perform statements both before and after it's incremented.

"The partner in crime of the while loop is the **do... while** loop. Here's the structure of a do... while loop:

```
i = 0;
do {
      trace(i);
      i++;
} while (i<=10);
```

"Can anyone tell me what is so different about this loop?" I asked.

"The condition is after the body of the loop, whereas before it was at the front of the loop?" suggested Jim. "That's it," I declared. "Now can anyone tell me what this means for our loop? If we're only checking the condition at the end of the loop, then what will happen?"

"The loop will always run at least once," said Jim, his conviction growing as he spoke. "Exactly," I replied, "the do... while loop is the only loop that will give you a result when the initial condition is false.

"Right, let's look back at the case study. We decided on the changes that we need to make on each cycle of the loop, and it looks like a for loop will serve us just fine." I pointed to the list that I wrote on the board earlier:

Attach 6 copies of 'dummy' on the stage
Leave a visible 17.3 pixel gap between the copies
update instance name
update x position
update depth

"To start with, we need to set our `for` loop to run six times. Joe, can you tell me what the initial parameters of the `for` loop should be?" I asked.

"I'll give it a go. The first thing to do is initialize the counter, right? I want it to run from 1 to 6, so let's kick it off with `i = 1;`" Joe said. "All right," I told him, writing it on the board. "And what's the condition?"

"I guess we want it to run while `i` is less than or equal to 6, and then increment it by 1 every cycle," Joe responded.

"Like this?" I asked.

for (i = 1; i <= 6; i++) {

"That looks pretty good," Joe replied.

"Okay, the next thing that we need to do is create the code within the loop to duplicate and position the dummy movie clips," I said. "First of all, let's take our original duplication code and plug that into the loop." I went back to my computer and did so. "This is what we've got so far, then:

```
for (i=1; i<=6; i++) {
    _root.attachMovie("dummy", "dummy1", 1);
    dummy1._x = 50;
    dummy1._y = 50;
}
```

"By changing our attachMovie line, we can cross off three of the points on our list at once. Mazzy, can you tell me what I should change to make the line work?"

"I'll do the depth first, as that's easy," said Mazzy. "You can replace the 1 there with i." I did so. Mazzy paused in thought for a while, so I gave her a quick hint. "Remember what I said in an earlier class about how adding a number to a string will just create a longer string by simply appending the number to it?"

"So can I just say dummy plus i?" Mazzy asked.

"Yes, it's as easy as that," I said. "That will mean that on the first cycle of the loop we'll get dummy1, on the next cycle we'll have dummy2, and so on. Okay, so our completed first line looks like this:

```
_root.attachMovie("dummy", "dummy"+i, i);
```

"Let's test the movie to see what's happened so far. At the moment, it looks like we've just got two squares, but if I open the List Objects window, you should be able to see more of what's happening."

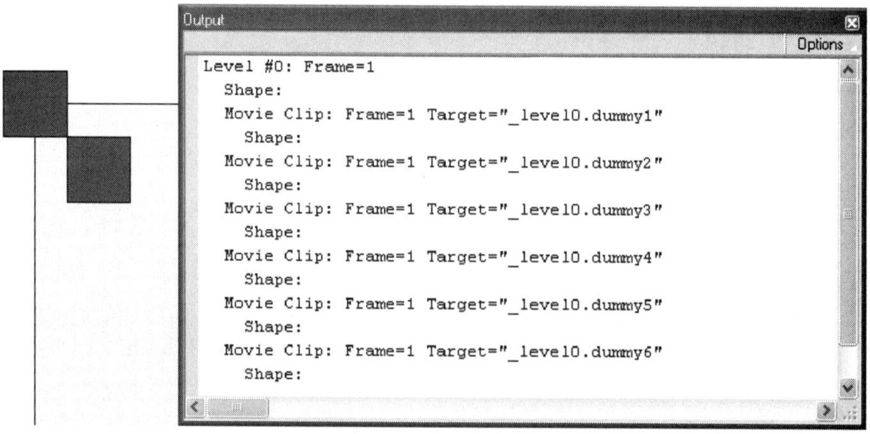

"There we go. You can clearly see there that we've successfully created our six dummy movie clips and given them all unique instance names. There is still one quandary, though. Can anyone tell me why there are two squares on the screen?"

Mazzy immediately called out, "I know, I know. It's because all of the movie clips are initially positioned at 0,0, but we still have the two lines of code in there to reposition dummy1. It means that dummy1 has been moved to the same place six times, but all of the other clips are still in their original positions." She sat back and looked pleased with herself. "Thank you, Mazzy," I said, "that is correct."

Dynamic paths

"I'm now going to let you in on a coding secret here, and it's quite a difficult piece of coding that a lot of people don't know about," I said. Carl rubbed his hands together. I continued, "You can create dynamic paths that are perfect for loops like these. The real killer is, though, that you can set a variable to hold this dynamic path. You're impressed, aren't you?" To be honest, the class looked more befuddled than impressed, but I continued regardless.

"At the moment, we've seen that dummy1 can be repositioned, but if we were to reposition dummy2, then we'd have to have unique code for that as well. Doing this for every outcome of the loop soon gets very tedious. A much better alternative to using hard-coded paths to each movie clip is simply to use a dynamic path. This is what the dynamic path to our movie clip would look like:

```
_root["dummy"+i]
```

"Notice here that I've used square brackets around the expression. This means that Flash will evaluate the expression first, and then use that as the path. So, for the first cycle it will give _root.dummy1, for the second cycle it will give _root.dummy2, and so on.

"The other important thing to note about it is that there's no dot between root and the opening square bracket. Don't worry, though, one will be automatically added when the path is evaluated. On the same lines as that missing dot, if you were to carry on the path after the expression, then there would be a dot. For example:

```
_root["dummy"+i]._x = 50;
```

"Now, rather than typing out this long path—and believe me they can get very long—every time, we can assign it to a variable instead, like so:

```
dummyName = _root["dummy"+i];
```

"Then to use this variable, we just treat it as we would if it were the full path, for example:

```
dummyName._x = 50;
```

"This is an incredibly useful asset to have in your Flash toolbox, so I urge you to remember it as best you can.

"Okay, with our dynamic paths in place, we can now alter our code to look like this:

```
for (i=1; i<=6; i++) {
        _root.attachMovie("dummy", "dummy"+i, i);
        dummyName = _root["dummy"+i];
        dummyName._x = 50;
        dummyName._y = 50;
}
```

"If you run the movie now, you'll see that all of the movie clips are being positioned in the same place. The easiest way to position them in a row is to multiply their dimensions by the current counter number. By doing this, the first clip will be placed at x position 50*1 = 50; the second will be placed at x position 50*2 = 100, and so on. The code to achieve this is as follows:

```
dummyName._x = dummyName._width * i;
```

"If you run this code now, you can see that all of the movie clips are now lined up horizontally:

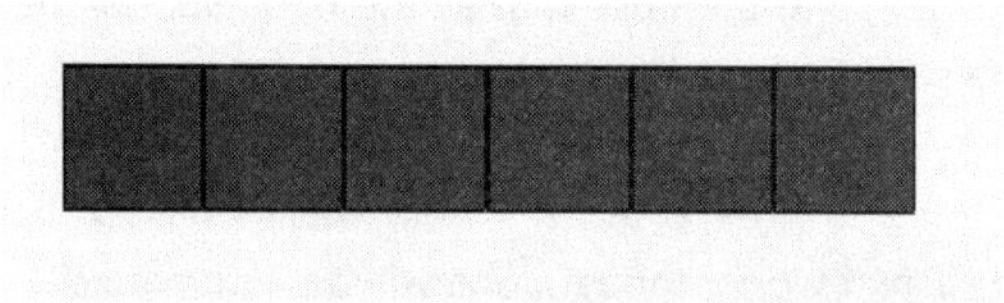

"The final thing to do, then, is insert the gap between them. You want to add this to the width before the multiplication takes place so, remembering the order of operator precedence, you'll have to put the addition in parentheses so that it is evaluated first. The finished line looks like this:

```
dummyName._x = (dummyName._width + 17.3) * i;
```

"And it gives you the desired result:

"So, to sum up, here's the complete code for that line of clips:

```
for (i=1; i<=6; i++) {
    _root.attachMovie("dummy", "dummy"+i, i);
    dummyName = _root["dummy"+i];
    dummyName._x = (dummyName._width + 17.3) * i;
    dummyName._y = 50;
}
```

"Your next task is to make another five rows of movie clips going down the screen. Your time starts now."

"Ken," Carl piped up, "is this going to be another pointless exercise for us, and in a minute you'll stop us and tell us the easy way to do it?"

"It was going to be something like that, yes," I said.

"In that case, I think I'd prefer it if we just moved straight on to the easy way if we could," said Carl.

"Really?" The class all gave me an emphatic "Yes." "All right then, in that case let's move on to look at nesting loops," I responded.

Nested loops

"You've seen how loops can be incredibly helpful for saving you time and effort when you code by automating repetitive tasks," I said. "Well, if you need to, you can also put loops within loops to double up on the time saved. If this is done wrong, then you'll find yourself hitting the infinite loop problem a lot, but done correctly, it can be a great time-saver, as you'll see.

"With a nested loop, for each cycle of the outer loop, the inner loop will run to completion. Let's have a look at the modifications that you'll need to make to the loop to nest it and create a grid. First up, you need to add in the extra loop. This time, you'll use `j` as the loop counter, but otherwise it's exactly the same:

```
for (i=1; i<=6; i++) {
    for (j=1; j<=6; j++) {
        _root.attachMovie("dummy", "dummy"+i, i);
        dummyName = _root["dummy"+i];
        dummyName._x = (dummyName._width+17.3)*i;
        dummyName._y = 50;
    }
}
```

"The first problem that you encounter is that you're using `i` in your `attachMovie` line, meaning that you're going to be trying to set whole rows of movie clips to the same name and depth. As you know, though, instance names and depths are unique, so that all you'll do if you try and create these new movie clips is overwrite the old ones that used to reside there. The same would happen if you were to use `j` as the value.

"To get around this, you need to create a new variable that will be incremented on every single cycle of the inner loop. Let's call the variable `depthNum`. You first want to initialize the variable at the beginning of the code, and then you'll increment it at the start of the inner loop like so:

```
depthNum = 0;
for (i=1; i<=6; i++) {
      for (j=1; j<=6; j++) {
            depthNum++;
            _root.attachMovie("dummy", "dummy"+i, i);
            dummyName = _root["dummy"+i];
            dummyName._x = (dummyName._width+17.3)*i;
            dummyName._y = 50;
      }
}
```

"You then want to change your `attachMovie` and `dummyName` setting lines to use this new value instead of `i`. This is simple to achieve, and leaves you with

```
_root.attachMovie("dummy", "dummy"+depthNum, depthNum);
dummyName = _root["dummy"+depthNum];
```

"Because you used a variable to hold the path, you don't need to go through and change any of the other lines. The last thing to do is to implement your columns by setting the y position of the movie clips in a similar fashion to that you used for the x position. The only differences are that you're using height instead of width and you're multiplying it by `j` rather than `i`:

```
depthNum = 0;
for (i=1; i<=6; i++) {
     for (j=1; j<=6; j++) {
          depthNum++;
          _root.attachMovie("dummy", "dummy"+depthNum,
➥ depthNum);
          dummyName = _root["dummy"+depthNum];
          dummyName._x = (dummyName._width+17.3)*i;
          dummyName._y = (dummyName._height+17.3)*j;
     }
}
```

"This gives you your final grid of movie clips, perfect for displaying thumbnails of photographs."

"It will also give you a strange optical illusion if you're not careful," Joe said, chuckling.

"Okay, that's all for today's class," I said. "Again, I must apologize for missing the first half, but hopefully that won't happen again. I'll see you again at the usual time next week, when we can actually begin to put all of this newfound knowledge to good use and start constructing our case study. See you then."

Summary

Today you learned all about how Flash makes decisions for itself as to how it should proceed. It has numerous tools at its disposal to achieve this:

- **If statements:** Depending on whether a particular condition is true or false, you can give Flash two different paths to follow.

- **Switch statements:** The bigger brother of the `if` statement, this statement is useful when there are many potential outcomes to choose among.

- **Loops:** When you're programming, often you'll need to perform repetitive tasks. Using `for` loops, `while` loops, and do...`while` loops allow you to make Flash do a lot of work with minimum effort on your part.

You also learned how to nest loops within each other to save even more time.

Class 7
Starting the Kiosk Project

Objectives

Today you'll learn about

- The properties of input text fields and dynamic text fields
- Using the TextField object in ActionScript
- Using the `swapDepths` method to move the tabs in the case study
- How to create the About and Contact pages for the case study

Introduction

"What are we going to learn today, Ken?" Carl asked. "I'm itching to get started."

"In this week's class, we'll concentrate a little on the case study," I replied. "There won't be any earth-shattering programming concepts in today's class—I'll save those for next week. Last week was fairly intense, so we'll build and recap a little on those ideas by putting them into practice. By the end of today's class, we'll have a skeleton thumbnail grid built, along with a number of other essential elements."

"I thought we covered grids in last weeks class with `for` loops," Jim said. "What more is there to do in that respect?"

"Sure, Jim, you learned all about nested loops, but the images need to be framed," I replied. Jim looked puzzled. "Do you remember that we talked about using slides as frames for each of the thumbnails?" I asked.

"Yeah, I do," Gemma laughed. "But don't expect Jim to remember—his memory is not one of his strongest assets." Gemma nudged Jim.

"I don't know what she's talking about!" Jim said, smirking. "Continue, Mr. Jokol."

"Sure, Jim," I said. "The first lesson for today is about something I covered in basic form back in the first couple of weeks: text fields."

"Is there much more to them, then?" Mazzy asked. "I'd say I'm almost an expert using them. I've used them extensively for the church website revamp. The revamp is coming along swimmingly; I'm just waiting on finishing the case study so that I can create an image gallery of all the church deacons."

"So far we've only used text fields in static, unchangeable form," I said. "Text fields can be changed using ActionScript code. This means that we can change text field information on the fly, making text fields ideal for the different fields of data for each photograph."

Text fields

"You've already seen one type of text field in action: **static** text fields," I started. "In Flash, there are two other types, each of which fills a specific role. These are dynamic and input text fields. **Input** text fields allow user entry that can be read into Flash."

"My memory can't be all that bad," said Jim. "The Input command in BASIC provided the same function. It allowed the user to type in where the cursor was set, with the entry then available as a variable. I remember my brother wrote a program once to dupe my parents. The program asked for input of their name and then filled the screen with a variety of insults about them."

"No fair!" Mazzy said. "I've been duped in a similar way using one of those JavaScript quizzes. It all starts pretty innocently, and then quickly turns sour."

Carl perked up. "Where can I see these things?" he asked, pen at the ready.

"Luckily, I can't remember, Carl," Mazzy said. Carl groaned. "But even if I could, I wouldn't tell you!"

"Although I shouldn't be telling you this, Carl," I said, "you can do the same thing in Flash. By the time you get home tonight, you'll be able to fool the rest of your family!"

"I'd better warn your mom," Mazzy joked.

"As with BASIC, the value of an input text field is retrievable as a variable or as a property of the text field," I said. "Input text fields are used for all Flash text input such as forms and, particularly relevant for Randy's site, password text fields. For added security, there's an input text setting for a password that replaces all characters with asterisks."

Gemma held her hand to cover her mouth. She whispered theatrically so that everyone could hear: "He means stars! Talking fancy like that makes him feel like the teacher."

"Thanks, Gemma!" I laughed. "If you're not careful, I'll send you to go and see the principal." Gemma concealed her laughter under the wooly neck of her sweater.

I continued, "Input text fields can be set to work in a number of different ways, from only accepting certain characters, such as numeric characters for a calculator, to limiting the maximum number of characters inputted."

"I don't suppose we'll have much use for either of those in the case study," Joe said, "but they might be of use for my own kiosk."

"True, Joe. You might also find **components** useful for your kiosk," I said. "Components are drag-and-drop prebuilt form-style objects that are created to make forms and applications easier to make in Flash. Although I'm not going to cover them in this course, you can look at the basic setup in the Components panel. Each component is documented in the Reference panel:

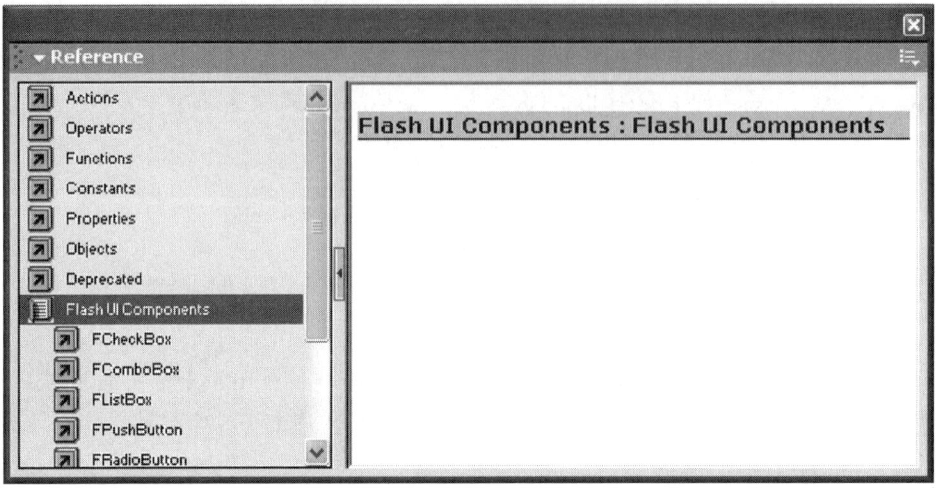

For more information on components, check out the friends of ED publication Flash MX Components Most Wanted.

"The next text field type is the **dynamic text** field, which is used for displaying values and outputting variables. Dynamic text fields can be used in Flash movies in which some information needs to be relayed back to the user. The word 'dynamic' in a Flash sense usually means that something is capable of change. If a website is dynamic, it has content that changes regularly—for example, a news website. Although I'm not going to cover truly dynamic Flash movies and websites, dynamic text fields will allow you to change content whenever or wherever required."

"What's so wrong with the Output window and the `trace` action?" Joe asked.

"Other than the fact that it's really ugly," Jim said, "I believe that the Output window is only seen in the Flash authoring environment. So only we can see it!"

"Indeed. The Output window is fine for testing, debugging, and checking variables, but it isn't seen in the final published Flash movie or outside the Flash MX program," I said. "To report something back to the user, you need to use a dynamic text field."

"How do we send something to a dynamic text field?" Gemma asked.

"You'll see how to use both input and dynamic text fields through a brief exercise in a moment, Gemma," I replied. "First, though, I'd like to talk about some properties that input and dynamic text fields have in common."

Text field properties

I asked the students to open a fresh Flash movie and to select the Text tool.

"Go ahead and click somewhere on the stage to create a text field. Then change the text field type to Input Text using the far left drop-down in the Property inspector.

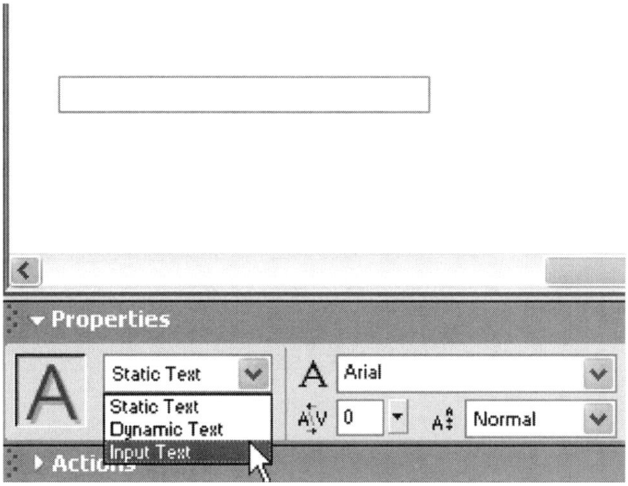

"The first thing you might notice once you've changed the type is that there is an Instance Name box. Dynamic and input text fields are both objects within Flash and thus have instance names.

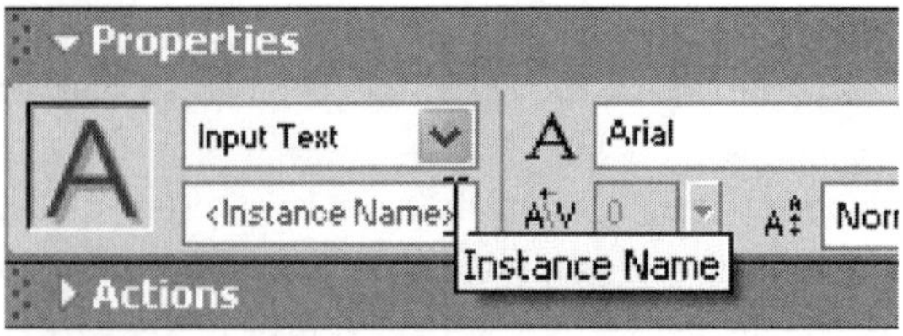

"Because they're both objects, like movie clip instances, they also have a number of properties. Some of these properties can be changed in the Property inspector but, as you'll see a little later, they can all be read and changed using ActionScript too.

"First, let's look at some of the relevant input text field properties available in the Property inspector."

Input text field properties

- Line Type: Single Line, Multiline, Multiline no wrap, and Password

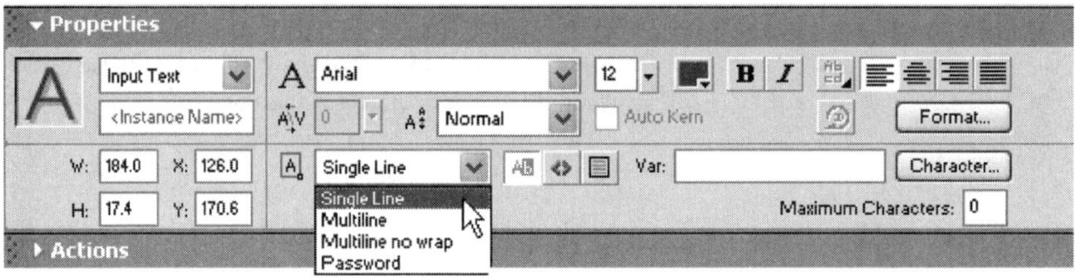

"This defines the size of the input text field," I said. "In most cases, you'd use Single or Multiline, allowing one line or many lines of input. For Randy's kiosk, we'll use the Password setting to allow him to enter his password discreetly."

"What does 'no wrap' mean?" asked Joe. "This refers to wrapping," I began, but before I could get any further, Carl started freestyling, making up a little rap about the wonders of Mondo. Jim joined in, supplying him with a verbal beat.

"Thanks, Carl," I said, "but that's rapping, and I'm talking about wrapping, with a 'w.' Wrapping is when text flows to the next line. If word wrap is set to off, then the text will only appear on the first line and will not flow to the next line.

- Maximum Characters

"This setting allows you to define a maximum number of characters for the text field. This is useful if you're limiting a field, such as a name or username, and you want the user to stay below a certain number of letters or characters."

"I hate the limit of eight numbers on my calculator," Mazzy said. "That dreaded E character foils me every time!"

"I think it's there for a reason Mazzy," I said. "If the spaces on a calculator were infinite, the calculator wouldn't be able to calculate anything—it would most likely crash every time! Limiting the number of characters in a Flash movie is usually a wise step to protect your movie from pranksters.

- Character Options

"The Character Options dialog box is called up by clicking the Character button on the far right of the Property inspector.

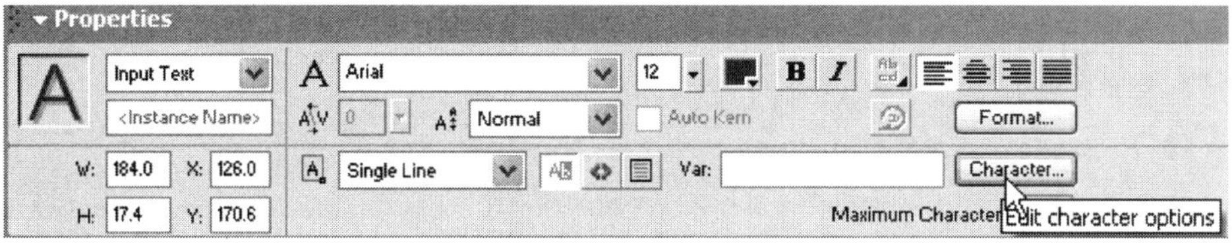

"Character Options allows you to specify the actual characters inputted into the text field," I started. "So, a Flash calculator would be constructed with an input text field with only numeric character entry allowed."

"You mean only numerals and nothing else?" Jim asked, shaking his head. "A calculator would require a decimal point and maybe even a minus character." I added the two mentioned characters.

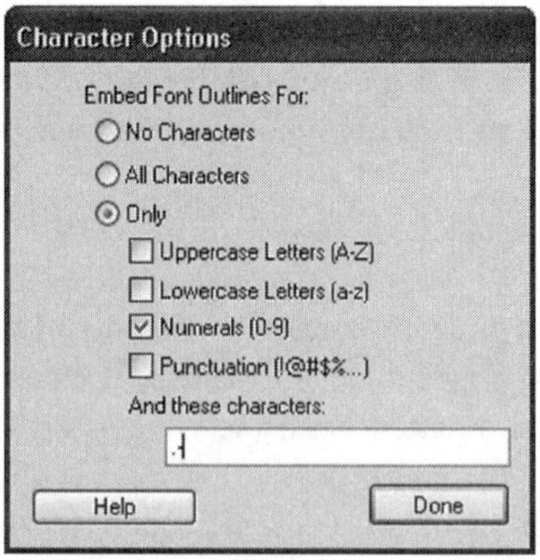

"Does this look right now?" I asked. Jim nodded. "Any extra characters can be added in the text field at the bottom of the dialog box. This is where you would add any exceptions to the rules set out above. As you can see in this dialog box, you can limit entry to all sorts of things, but you can also specify a number of options if need be.

- Show Border Around Text

"This option specifies whether the input text field has a border outline and white background. If this is switched off, your text field will be invisible! No one will be able to see it to offer any input to your movie." I invited the students to ensure that this was set to off and then test their movie. "Now try to find your input box," I challenged.

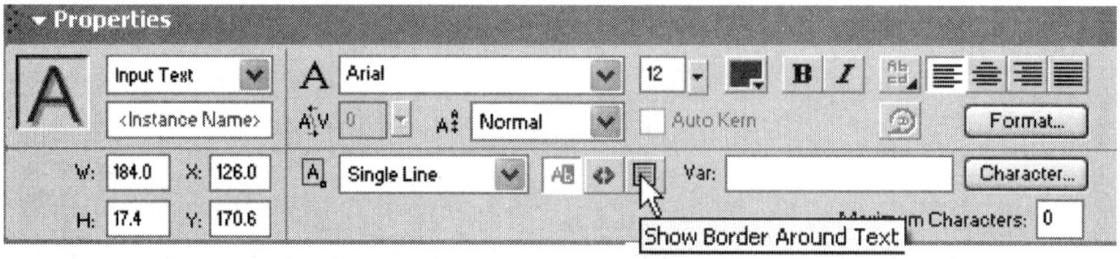

"It's impossible," Mazzy said. "Even though I have an idea where it should be, it's still really hard to find."

"I rely on the cursor changing," Gemma said. "When it changes to a text entry cursor, I know I'm in the right place. I'm with you though, Mazzy—it isn't easy at all."

"Don't panic!" I said. "This is why you have the option of switching on a background and outline. Activate this option and retest it. Also, if you change the background color of your movie to something other than white, you'll see that giving the text field a border also gives it a white background." The students all gave it a try with far more positive results.

Dynamic text field properties

I asked the students to change the field type to Dynamic Text.

- Line Type: Single Line, Multiline, Multiline no wrap

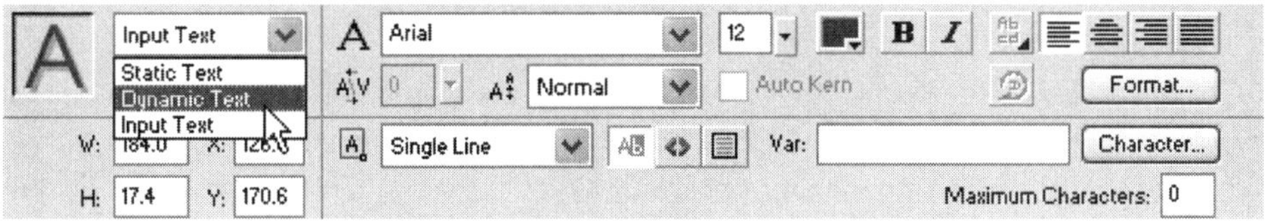

"As with input text fields, the size of dynamic text fields can be changed. The only option missing here is Password, but this is because dynamic text fields are used for output.

- Selectable

"This option defines whether the content of a dynamic text field can be selected or highlighted using the cursor. Normally, selections are made by website users, allowing them to copy and paste information. This option enables you to prevent the user from copying text."

"I guess you'd stop them from doing that if you had text you didn't want them to steal," Mazzy said. "Like prose, lyrics, or poetry, for instance. I don't think I'd prevent people from copying stuff from the church website, though. Seems a little pointless."

"You're right about why you might not want people to take your information, Mazzy," I said. "Besides that, sometimes highlighted text just looks untidy, so it's worth switching it off for that reason."

"I think Randy might like people to copy and paste his address or contact info," Gemma said. "Why prevent possible customers or press from copying it?"

"Gemma's right," Jim added. "Stopping customers from copying the information into their databases or address books is just plain dumb! Look at all the business and contacts Randy can gain from it."

"Okay, that's settled then," I said firmly. "The text fields on Randy's kiosk will be selectable.

- Render text as HTML

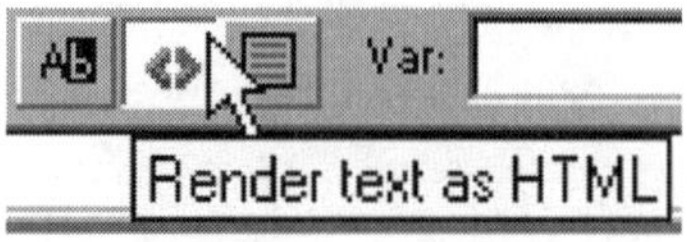

"This option specifies whether the text is displayed considering HTML markup. If this is switched on, text contained within HTML tags such as <B> for bold and <I> for italic will be rendered in such styles. The number of tags that can be read within a dynamic text field is limited to font or style-based markup, so you'd best leave image markup to normal HTML documents." I looked at Mazzy.

"Drat!" Mazzy said. "Just when I thought my skills would come in useful in Flash after all! Oh well, if anyone has any questions about HTML code, just give me a shout. There has got to be some use for hand-coding these days."

"I'll take you up on that," Gemma smiled. "I don't even know what HTML code looks like. I stick to the Design Layout mode in Dreamweaver."

Using the TextField object in ActionScript

"Besides the text field properties available in the Property inspector, there are a huge number of other properties available to manipulate through ActionScript. A full list of these is viewable through the Reference panel (**Objects > Movie > TextField**):

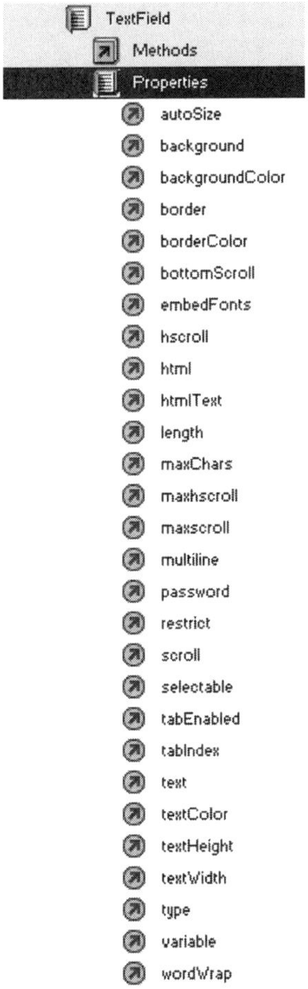

"As with other instances and objects, text fields have properties. So far you've looked at some basic properties of text fields, but I haven't covered the most important aspect for each: setting a dynamic text field and getting the input of an input text field. You might have already guessed that properties have something to do with both of these actions.

"The content of a text box is set using the `text` property:

```
myTextBox.text = "Hello!";
```

"This example will set the `myTextBox` instance to output a joyous 'Hello!' The `text` property is also used to read the value of a text box:

```
greeting = myTextBox.text;
```

"This property is relevant for both input and dynamic text fields. In fact, an input text field can be set, and a dynamic text field can be read. Both types of text fields are instances of the **TextField** type, and the main difference is that the input type allows user input, whereas the dynamic type doesn't."

"I just discovered that for myself," Jim said. "I was looking through the properties and noticed that the **type** property allows you to change the type of a text field."

"That's true, Jim," I said. "Although we might not use that many of these properties here, many of them are most relevant to text fields created with ActionScript."

"You mean we can just tell Flash to create one with some code?" Carl asked. "Why do anything on the stage?"

"The method to create a text field from scratch is `createTextField`. This method is perfectly good, but it requires five arguments! For Randy's kiosk, we'll be using a mixture of stage-created and code-created text fields. The stats part of Randy's site will most likely use `createTextField`, so I'll cover it when we come to that part of the case study.

"For now, I think it's best that you all have some experience with the two types of text fields. Seeing as we've talked about calculators, let's make a simple machine to work with two numbers and any of the operators."

Creating a calculator

1. Open a new Flash document and rename the existing layer **textfields**.

2. On the textfields layer, add two input text fields, one for each number. Give them the instance names `first` and `second`.

3. Position the two text fields respective to their instance names, `first` on the left and `second` on the right, leaving a small gap between them.

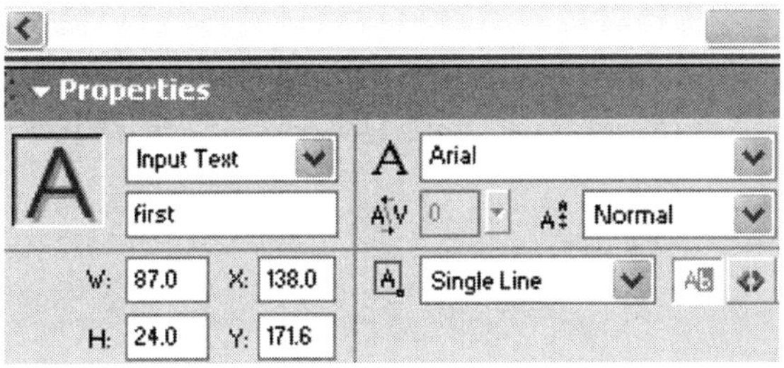

4. Select both text fields and click the **Character** button to bring up the **Character Options** dialog box. Set the boxes to receive Numerals, and enter a **.** (period/decimal point) and a **–** (hyphen/minus symbol).

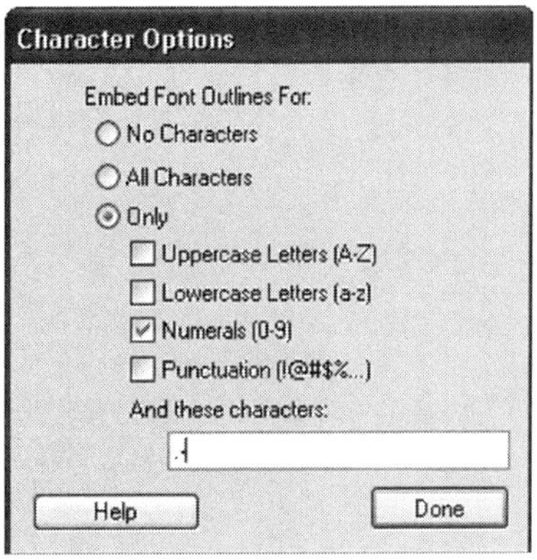

5. Ensure that **Show Border Around Text** is selected, **Render Text as HTML** is unselected, and enter **5** in the **Maximum Characters** field.

6. In the gap between the two text boxes, place another input text field, giving it the instance name `operator`.

7. Limit the number of characters of operator to **1**, switch on the **Show Border Around Text option**, and open up the **Character Options** dialog box. Set it to receive the four main mathematical operators only (plus, minus, multiply, and divide).

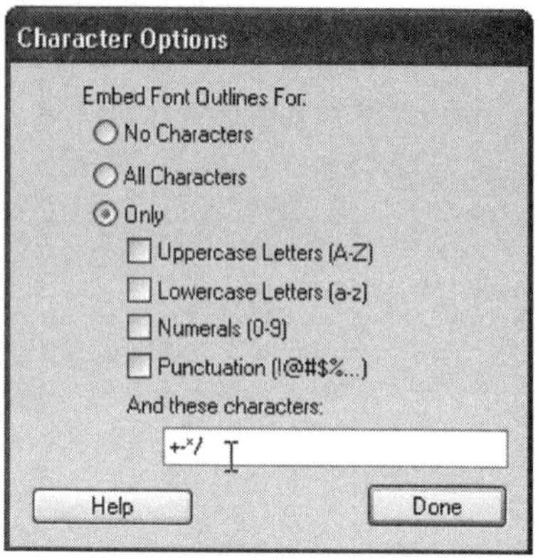

8. Alongside the second instance, add a static text field with an equals symbol.

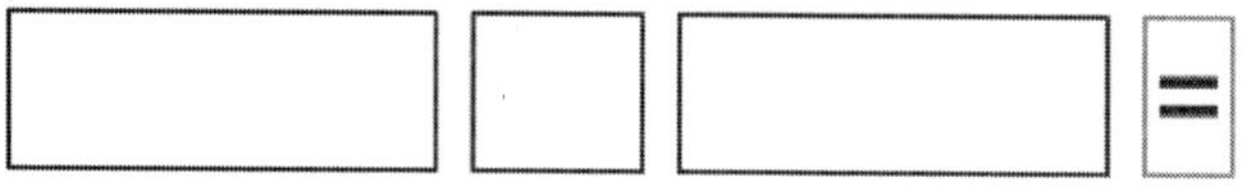

9. Alongside the equals text field, insert a new dynamic text field with the instance name of **result**.

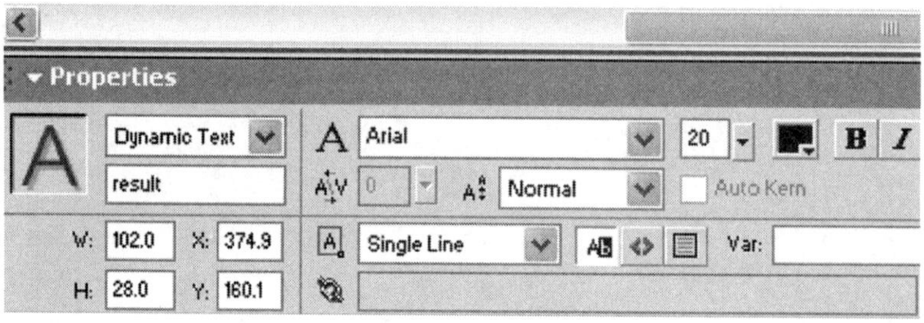

Make sure that this is unselectable and has no border.

10. Insert a new movie clip symbol called **button**, and draw a simple square button with the word "calculate" layered over it.

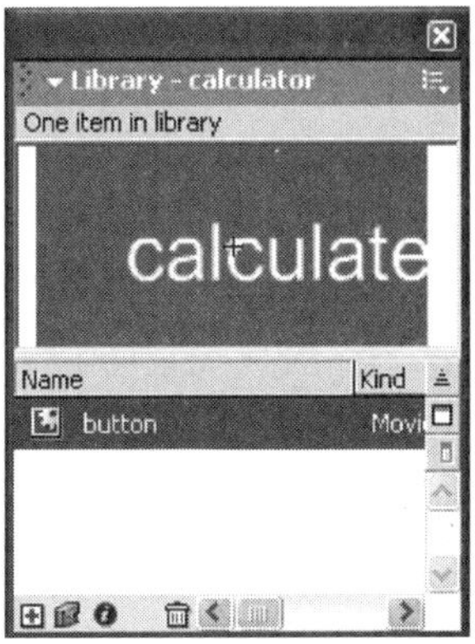

11. Drag a copy of this onto the stage and position it below the `result` instance. Give it the instance name `calculateButton`.

12. Insert a new layer called **actions**.

13. Select the keyframe on the actions layer and insert the following ActionScript code:

```
calculateButton.onRelease = function() {
    // extract values of first and second instances
    firstnumber = Number(first.text);
    secondnumber = Number(second.text);
    // conditional to get operator
    switch (operator.text) {
    case "+" :
        score = firstnumber + secondnumber;
        break;
    case "-" :
        score = firstnumber - secondnumber;
        break;
    case "*" :
        score = firstnumber * secondnumber;
        break;
    case "/" :
        score = firstnumber / secondnumber;
        break;
    default :
        operator.text = "+";
        score = firstnumber + secondnumber;
    }
    // display result
    result.text = score;
};
```

14. Test the movie, entering a number in the first box, an operator in the next, and another number in the next. Click the calculate button to work out the result.

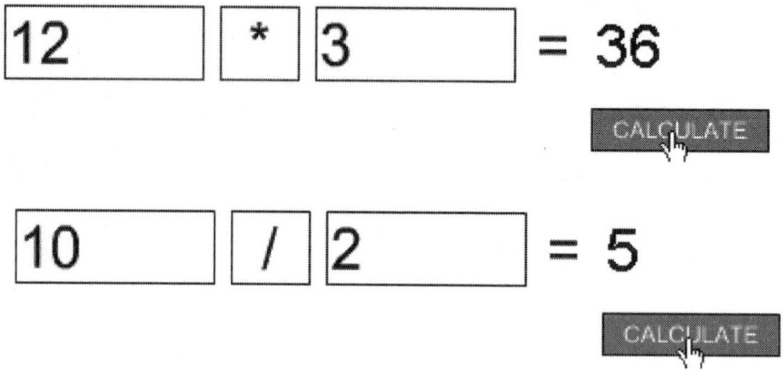

"Okay, who'd like to have a stab at explaining how all the code works to the rest of the class?" I asked.

Mazzy stood up and came to the front of the class. "I'll have a go, Ken," she said. "I'll work it out as I go along." Mazzy looked at the projection for a moment and then said, "Actually, I think I get lost on line 3."

"I'll help you with those two lines," Jim said. "I think I can see where you're coming from!" Mazzy swiftly sat down. I motioned Jim to come to the front.

"I'll do it from here, Ken," he said. "Mazzy is going to take it after these couple of lines!" Mazzy looked shocked. Jim laughed.

"I think the reason you use `Number` on lines 3 and 4 is to change the value extracted from the input text fields to numeric values. Am I right?" Jim asked. I nodded. "It seems strange how Flash doesn't explicitly show number and string variables differently. In BASIC, a string variable is indicated by a dollar symbol—`name$`, for instance. Variable names without $ symbols in BASIC are numeric variables."

"That's a very good point, Jim," I said, "and one that's well worth remembering. Even though you might have limited the character input to numeric characters, Flash is still unable to see past the input being anything other than a string. Using the `Number` function, Flash will convert the content of the input field into a numeric variable.

"If you didn't do this, 2 + 2 would equal 22 because you'd just add the string value of 2 to another 2." I wrote on the board:

```
strings              numerics

a = "2";             a = 2;
b = "2";             b = 2;
c = a + b;           c = a + b;
------------         ------------
c = "22"             c = 4
```


"A few amendments to the first set of code here will allow you to change both variables into numeric values," I said, making a few changes on the whiteboard:

```
strings into numerics

a = "2";
b = "2";
c = Number (a) + Number (b);
------------
c = 4
```

"Does everyone understand this?" I asked. The students all nodded.

"Is there any way to check if a variable is a numeric or string variable?" Joe asked.

"That was my next question," Jim said. "There must be some way of doing it. Otherwise ActionScript has way too many flaws."

"You'll be glad to know that there is a way, Jim," I said. "The `typeof` operator will return the type of any instance or object. Most important, it can distinguish between a string and number variable if you should need to." I quickly wrote some code on the board:

```
a= "2";
b= 2;
trace (typeof (a)); -------------> returns "string"
trace (typeof (b)); -------------> returns "number"
```

"Darn it! This magic marker is running out," I said, putting the pen down. "Anyway, you can see the `typeof` operator in use here. It accepts one argument: the object or variable to report on. In the two traces here, `typeof` is able to distinguish the obvious difference between them." I paused. "Where were we?"

"Mazzy was about to explain the rest of the code," Carl laughed.

"Oh yeah. Mazzy, please step up and continue," I said. "Start from the top."

Mazzy came to the front of the class again. "Okay," Mazzy took a deep breath. "On line 1, we set up the `onRelease` event for `calculateButton`. Then we begin with the event handler. On lines 3 and 4, the values of the input text fields, named `first` and `second`, are extracted out to variables using the `text` property. These values are converted into numbers using the . . . uh . . ."

Joe helped Mazzy out: "Using the `Number` function." Mazzy mouthed "Thank you" to Joe. Joe smiled.

"On line 6," Mazzy continued, "the `switch` statement is set, using the value of `operator` to determine what action to take. The `case` statements below then check to see if an add, subtract, multiply, or divide symbol was inputted.

"The code within each `case` statement acts as necessary, with the variable `score` being set to the result of the action. In the case of an add symbol, `firstnumber` and `secondnumber` are added. The following three case statements repeat this pattern with the different operator changed as necessary.

"Finally, the `result` dynamic text field is set to the value of the `score` variable," Mazzy finished and quickly sat down.

"Almost perfect, Mazzy," I said. "Well done. Just a few things you missed out, though." Mazzy laughed. "First, you didn't talk about the `break` statement. Do you all remember why these are necessary?" Most of the students nodded. "The `break` statement is used to break out of a set of conditionals when a condition is true."

"I noticed that you declined to talk about the `default` statement," Joe said. "I think you did the right thing, Mazzy. I don't really know why it's there."

"The `default` statement here is just a catch-all for all input errors," I said. "For example, the user might decline to give you an operator. Never assume that the user will always give you what you want—bad mistake! To cover all possible errors, I've set the default action as addition, so in the event that the input isn't as expected, the operator text field is set to show a plus sign (purely for cosmetic effect) and the numbers are added up and displayed.

"If you all feel pretty comfortable with text fields, we'll start working on elements of the case study." Carl cheered. Mazzy silenced him.

Building the kiosk project

"In this part of the class, we're finally getting down to working on the case study," I said. "We'll start working on it now, and from this class onward we'll add something new each class. You may remember that when we discussed the project life cycle, there were six steps in the process." I wrote the six steps on the whiteboard again to jog the students' memories:

The Project Life Cycle:

1. Accepting the Project
2. Defining the problem
3. Designing the project output
4. Breaking the problem into logical steps
5. Writing the code
6. Testing the code

"So, which stage are we up to now?" I asked.

"Let's see," said Joe, looking at the whiteboard, "accepting the project—well, we did that when we all agreed to this case study. Defining the problem—would that have been when we compiled the requirements document and asked Randy for more details?"

"That's right," I said.

"And we've already designed the project output," said Mazzy. "Gemma did that fantastic sketch of the interface."

"Thanks, Mazzy," said Gemma, "but it wasn't just me. Everyone had a hand in it."

"I have that sketch right here," I said. "Let's take a look at it so we can see what we have to create." I pulled up the design on my computer and projected it on the whiteboard:

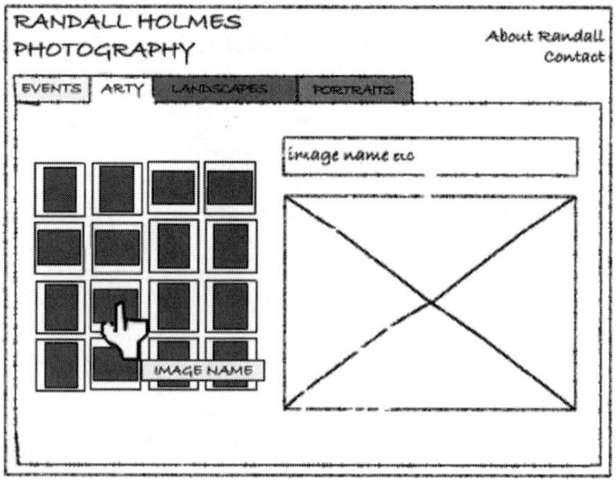

"So, here we are at stage 4: breaking the project into logical steps. Let's start with the tabs. If you recall, in a previous class we discussed the notion of using folder-like tabs as a device to change the photo category. Who would like to guess how the colored tabs might work?"

Tabs

"When a tab is selected in a real folder," Carl started, miming the motion, "the previous tab is turned over and the selected one is at the front. The only problem is that you can only see the tabs below the selected one." Carl looked puzzled. "This isn't going to work!"

"I think it's a little easier to think of them as buttons." Mazzy said. "When a button is clicked, the selected colored tab comes to the front and the previous tab goes behind it. A little like stacking."

"Or card shuffling," Joe said. "Cards are continually shuffled to the front, and then they're sent into the pack to be replaced by new cards at the front." Mazzy looked puzzled. Joe and Carl became restless.

"Don't panic!" Gemma said firmly. "I've already been here. You're all lucky that Jim and I created a prototype outside the class." Gemma pulled something out of her bag. "Ta-daa!" she announced as she showed the brightly colored object to the class.

"Gemma and I created this paper prototype to logically work out how the tabs would function," Jim said. "Gemma seems to collect colored paper!"

"Excuse the crudeness of it," Gemma said. "Jim wouldn't let me use a ruler or a scalpel."

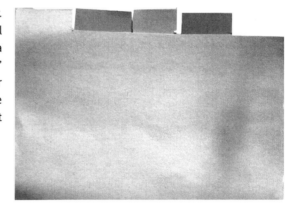

"As you can see, we have four pieces of colored paper, each with its own tab at the top," Jim started. "The tabs are present so whichever page is at the front, you're still able to see the tabs from all the other pages."

"Okay, so far you've told us everything we know about tabs," Mazzy said. "When are you going to tell us the best way to do it?"

"Well, Mazzy," Gemma said, "after a little while it just came to Jim. It's all about switching the stacking order of the paper, so that when a new color tab is selected, that sheet just comes to the front. If I select the yellow sheet, I just pull it to the front.

"The order of the other sheets of paper is irrelevant. The chosen sheet just comes to the front each time."

"That all sounds ideal," Joe said, "but can that be pulled off in Flash?"

"It can," I said, "but it's a little easier than the way Gemma and Jim came up with. The way you were both thinking might make a lot more sense after next week's class, when we'll be looking at arrays. There is, in fact, an easy way that we can use now."

"The method **swapDepths** will allow us to switch the depth of any two given objects."

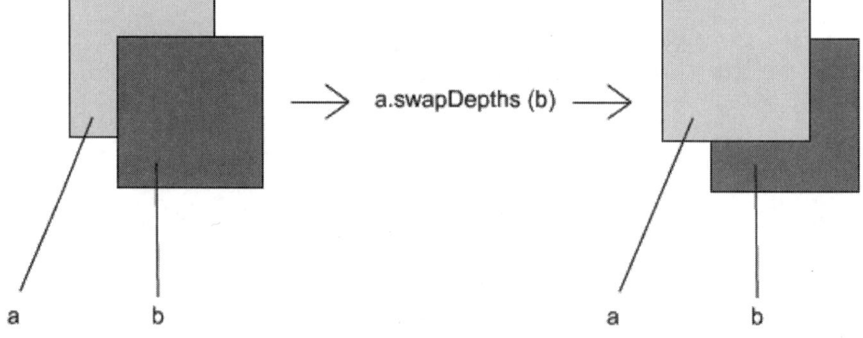

The swapDepths method

"The method `swapDepths` requires either an object to swap depth with or a numeric depth level," I said. "Although the first option might sound like the obvious one to use, the problem with it is that we'll have to store the previous highest object each time. If we use a predetermined depth, then the objects will simply compete for the highest depth each time and swap around with each other. You'll see `swapDepths` in practice in a moment. Before that, let's take a look at the tab graphics.

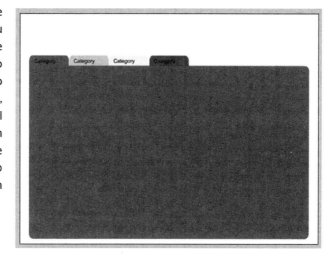

"To save you all a little time—and to keep you from from arguing—I've created the basic tab graphics. If you all want to personalize them yourselves, please feel free to do so." I asked the students to open the file `tab.fla`. "This file features all four colored tab sheets—one for each category.

"Each colored tab is constructed from the library pieces stored in the tab assets Library folder. These are the tab sheet and tab leaf.

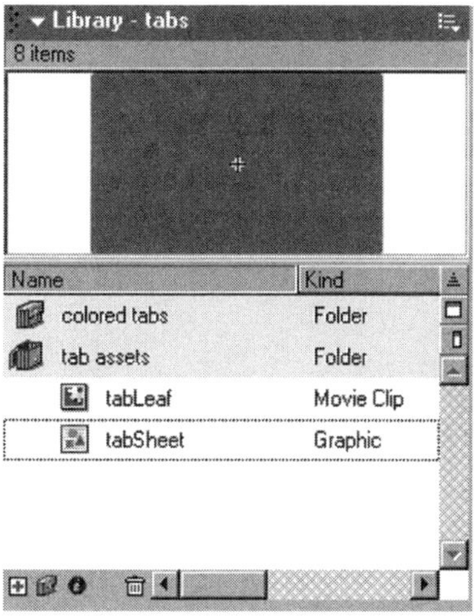

"You might have noticed already that both assets are different types of symbols. The tabSheet graphic is used purely as a cosmetic asset, but the `tabLeaf` movie clip is such because it will be used as a button to change between the sheets."

"Oh, I see, to change a category (or sheet) the leaf at the top is clicked," Joe said. "That seems to make sense."

"I'd like you all to see how a single colored tab is constructed," I said. "Double-click the red tab to edit it in place. Select the leaf at the top of the tab, making sure not to select the 'Category' text, but the leaf the text is sitting on. In the Property inspector you'll notice that it has the instance name of `tabButton`. This is the same with all the colored tabs. We'll program this button later.

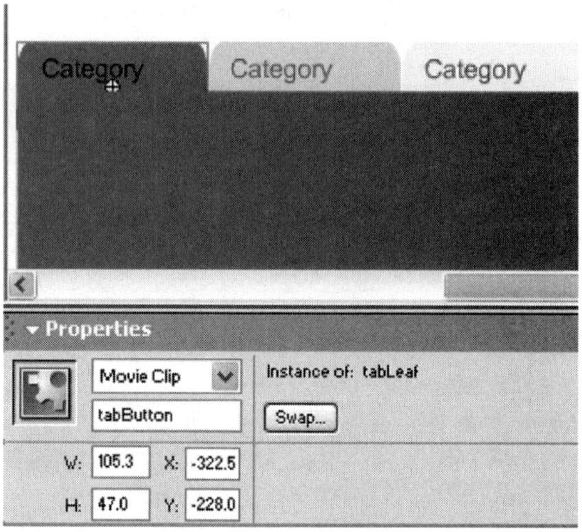

"The text layer is, unsurprisingly, where the category name should be written. All the other colored tabs were constructed from a copy of this red one. The only difference is that each is color tinted and the leaf of the tab is shifted along." I invited the students to click back to the main timeline and to double-click the yellow tab to see the same elements:

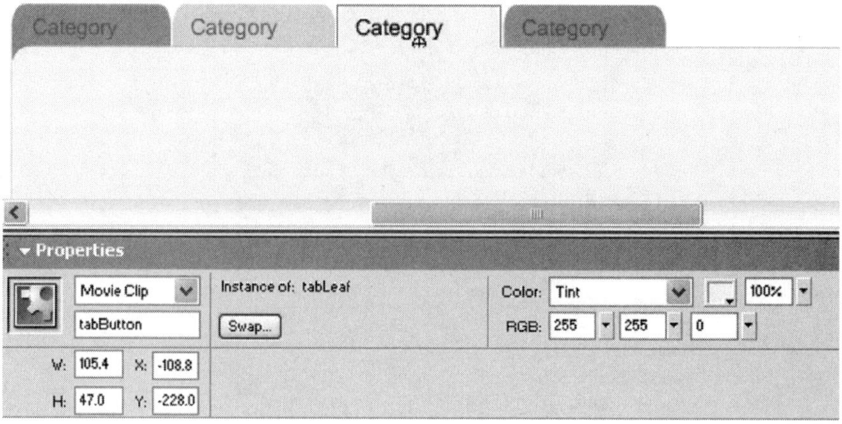

"Returning to the main timeline, each of the tabs has been given an appropriate instance name, from `redtab` through to `bluetab`. This is so we can reference the button within each of them. Let's do that now."

Moving tabs to the front

1. Ensuring you're on the main timeline of `tabs.fla`, rename the existing layer category **tabs**, and insert a new layer called **actions**.

2. Select frame 1 of the actions layer and open the Actions panel.

3. Enter the following code:

```
redtab.tabButton.onRelease = function() {
    this._parent.swapDepths(500);
};
greentab.tabButton.onRelease = function() {
    this._parent.swapDepths(500);
};
yellowtab.tabButton.onRelease = function() {
    this._parent.swapDepths(500);
};
bluetab.tabButton.onRelease = function() {
    this._parent.swapDepths(500);
};
```

To save typing all this in, you can copy the code for the green, yellow, and blue buttons from the red code and alter it slightly by changing the instance name.

4. Test the movie by clicking the tabs to alter their depths.

"Okay, let's run through the code for the red tab," I said. "You have the rather lengthy instance reference: `redtab.tabButton`. This refers to the `tabButton` within the `redtab` instance. Placing one instance within another is called nesting."

"Always the birds are getting in the way!" Carl joked.

"Referencing a nested instance is logically done by stepping through each parent or holder," I said. "You go through every instance until you arrive at the one you want to target. Say you want to fetch a bottle of milk from the fridge. You'd first need to open the fridge, and then you could get your hands on the milk. The milk is nested within the fridge." Before Carl could say anything, I silenced him. "Yes, Carl, I know the milk would go warm if it was really nested!" I wrote on the board. "Referencing the milk in this instance would look like this:"

```
fridge.milk
```

"If you weren't in the kitchen, I guess you could add that before fridge too," said Joe. "So it would be `kitchen.fridge.milk`."

"Not if you're a playboy like Ken." Mazzy said. "I bet he has a fridge in every room stocked with sparkling wine and . . . milk!" Mazzy winked at me. Joe rolled his eyes.

"That's right, Joe," I said. "I didn't put much consideration into my environment. In the case of the code here, the `tabButton` instance is nested within `redtab`. The handler code uses the nested consideration using `this._parent`. `this`, as you probably know, refers to the `tabButton` instance—the object calling the code.

"`this._parent` therefore refers to the `_parent` of `this`. Can anyone guess what that is?" I asked.

"Logically it would be `redtab`, " Jim said. "You just read backward instead of forwards. Why do we need to do this?"

"The reason you do this, Jim, is so that all of the assets within `redtab` are brought to the foreground. If you changed the code to `this.swapDepths (500);` only the button would come to the foreground." I recommended they give it a try.

"The figure 500 here is the aforementioned top depth. If you assume that nothing else in the movie will occupy this depth, it can be kept exclusively for the highest tab. However, one of the prices to pay for doing this is ensuring that everything that needs to be above the tab—that is, the thumbnail grid and the main image area—is above this."

"We can lower this figure, though, right?" Gemma asked.

"Sure. As long as the same depth is used for each of the `swapDepths` calls, it doesn't matter; the tabs will always be shifted around correctly." I paused. "Although we've finished the tabs for now, we'll need to add some code to the function blocks in a couple of weeks to actually draw the grid for that category. At the moment, the tabs are pretty cosmetic."

Working with the grid

Following on from what the class learned in the last lesson, I wanted them to start working on drawing the thumbnail grid using ActionScript.

"The thumbnail grid is possibly the most important element of Randy's kiosk, and there's a lot of work to do on it!" I said. "We can start this week on deciding the layout, size, and spacing with relation to the stage size and the main image area. So far, we know that we have four categories with 12 images in each category.

"What we don't know is how large the thumbnail images should be and also how large the main image should be. Something we do know is that both the grid and main image area should fit within the physical size of the tabs. I'd like you to add a new layer to your tabs movie and spend a few minutes playing in the space, coming up with some physical sizes. Feel free to discuss it as a group and decide on the best course. If you feel confident enough, try to design or lay down the other parts of the interface from the original sketches."

"Ken, did you forget to talk about the slide frames?" Mazzy asked.

"Thanks, Mazzy," I said. "The slides were decided upon to allow both portrait and landscape images within the same space. Because of this, they'll need to be perfect squares, measuring at least the size of the largest side. Okay?" The students began working and I left them alone for 10 minutes while I went to grab some coffee.

When I returned to the class, the students looked rather smug. "Let me guess," I said. "You've finished Randy's kiosk?"

"Not quite, Mr. Jokol," Gemma said. "But we have the layout of the interface sorted out, I think." Gemma invited me to switch the projector to her computer.

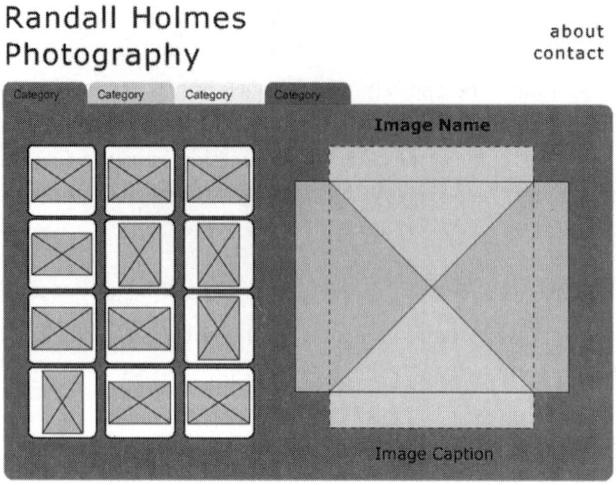

"Pretty impressive," I said. "I guess you all had a hand in this?" The students nodded.

"Even though we all had a hand in it, Gemma's fast drawing skills enabled us to put it on the computer screen in the time you were out," Joe said.

"I'm impressed that you've kept both landscape and portrait photographs in mind," I said. "I can see you've considered it for both the thumbnails and the main image area."

"No, Ken," Carl winked, "that's an origami pattern." Gemma reached over to strike Carl, who swiftly dodged her.

"In next week's class, we'll have access to Randy's photos, but for now, we'll draw the grid without photos, assuming a 3:2 size ratio—the same as Randy's photos," I said.

I asked Gemma what sizes she had used in her drawings. "I used 75x50 for the thumbnails, and 350x233 for the main image. Both are roughly in the 3:2 ratio. The slides measure in at 85 pixels square," Gemma said.

"Thanks, Gemma," I said. "These will give us some figures to work from when we create the code to draw the grid."

Drawing the grid

I asked the students to return to the tabs Flash movie. "The first thing we need to do is create the slide frame that will act as a container for the photograph thumbnails," I said.

1. Continuing with the `swapDepths_tabs.fla`, create a new movie clip symbol called **slideFrame**.

2. Within it, draw an 85 pixel square. Use a black stroke and white fill, click the Round Rectangle Radius button at the bottom of the toolbar, and change the Corner Radius to 10 to get softer corners.

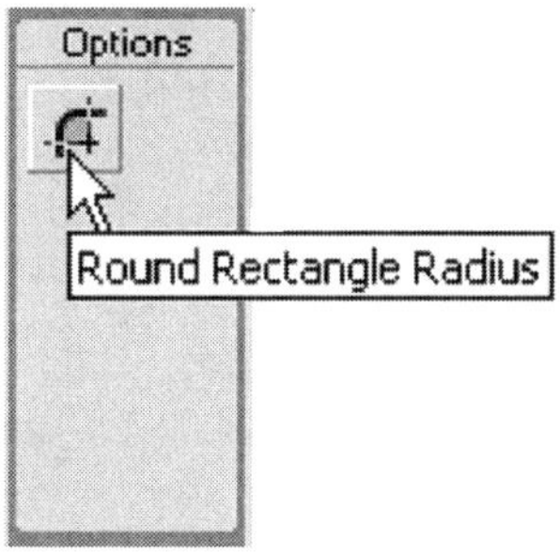

3. Once you've drawn the square, set the registration point of the movie clip to the center using the Info panel, and then center it on the stage using the Align panel.

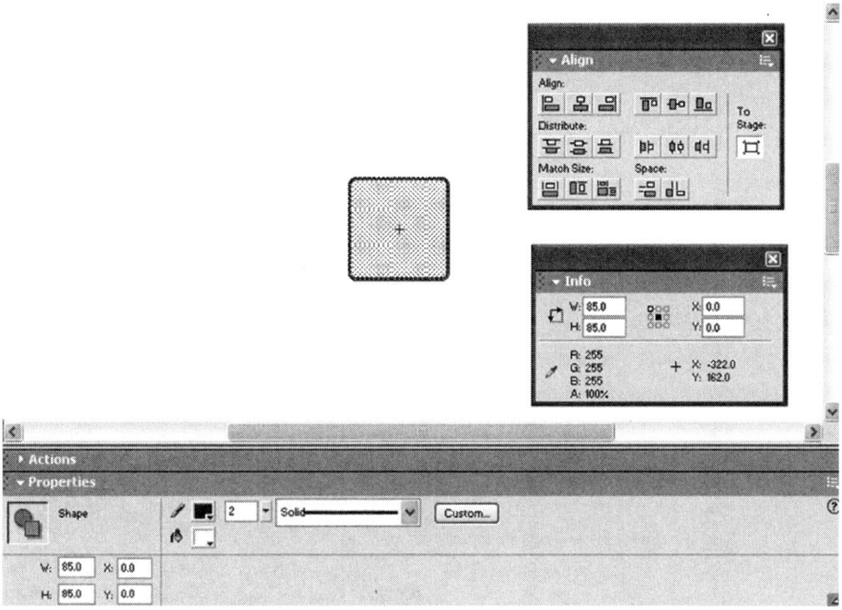

4. Give this symbol a linkage name of `slideFrame`.

5. Return to the main timeline. On frame 1 of the actions layer, add the following code:

```
bluetab.tabButton.onRelease = function() {
      this._parent.swapDepths(500);
};
// grid initialization
rows = 4;
columns = 3;
gap = 5;
startx = 98;
starty = 228;
count = 0;
//  grid drawing
for (i=0; i<rows; i++) {
      for (j=0; j<columns; j++) {
            frame = _root.attachMovie("slideFrame",
            ➥ "slideFrame"+count, count);
            frame._x = ((frame._width+gap)*j) + startx;
            frame._y = ((frame._height+gap)*i) + starty;
            count++;
      }
}
```

6. Test the movie. An empty grid should be drawn:

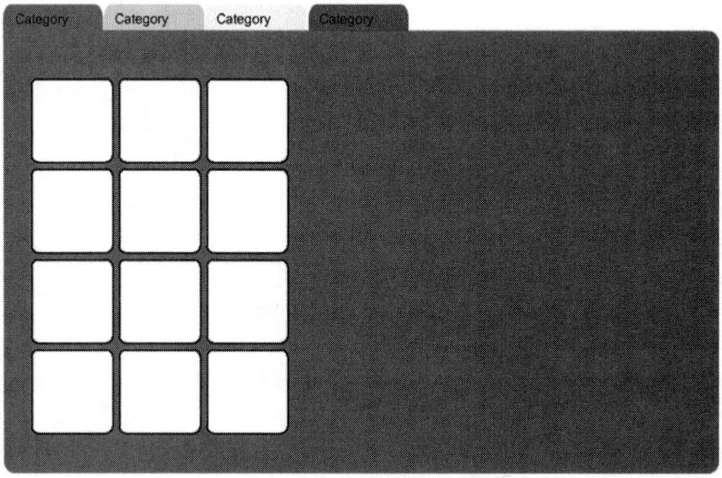

"Okay," I said, "the code here is clearly divided into two sections: the initialization, where all the variables are initialized, and the actual drawing of the grid with nested `for` loops.

"The variables `rows` and `columns` set the size of the grid. As you're probably aware, rows read horizontally and columns go vertically. These variables are used when we come to set the `for` loops.

"The `gap` variable specifies the spacing in between each slide, or the number of pixels in between each slide vertically and horizontally. `gap` is used when we position the slides.

"`startx` and `starty` set the top-left corner position of the grid. This value is added to every slide instance. This is calculated from the registration point of the slide instance—in this case, it is the center of it.

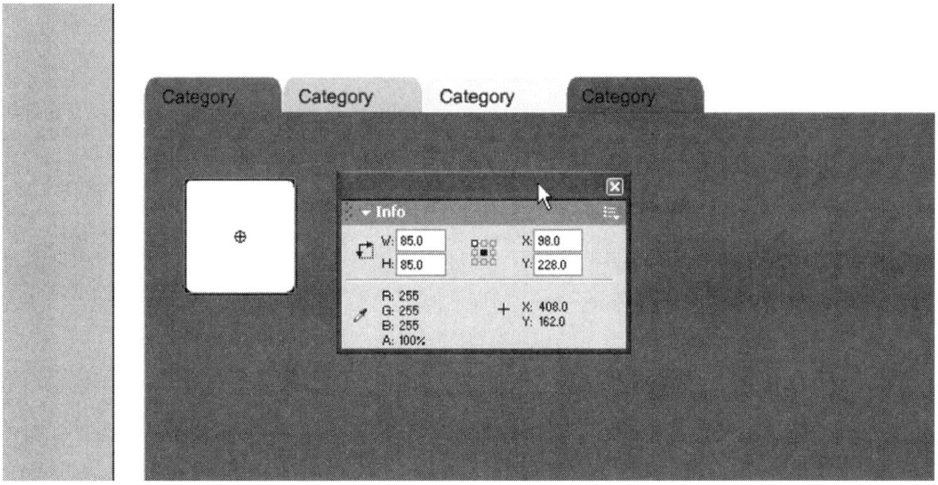

"As always, the `count` variable is used to increase the depth and naming of the instances.

"We then set up the `for` loops. As you learned in last week's class, two loops are required for grid-based drawing. Both loops run according to the value of the `rows` and `columns` variables. The way the loops are constructed ensure that the grid is drawn from top left to bottom right. Each time the columns of a row are drawn, a new row is constructed.

"Line 23 uses the `attachMovie` method to fetch an instance of the slide from the Library. As before, we declare it to a variable here so that we can refer to it using this shortcut on the next couple of lines.

"Lines 24 and 25 actually do the hard work. These lines position the new instance on the stage. The first calculation for the `_x` property is to work out the value of its `_width` property plus `gap`. This value is then multiplied by `j`. `i` represents the current column position or the counter of the inner `for` loop. The value of `startx` is then added to the current subtotal to make sure that the frame is positioned correctly within the context of the other frames.

"The `_y` property is calculated in much the same way, using the height of the frame, the outer loop counter `i`, and `starty`." I paused for a moment. "Is that clear to everyone?"

"There's one thing I don't understand," Carl started. "Why work out the `_height` and `_width` properties when they're the same?"

"Although you're right and they are the same, remember that our coding should be modular. If at any time we decide to change the physical size of the frame, just its height for example, we don't have to update the code to consider it."

"Ah, but you've made one vital mistake, Ken," Jim said. "You have one `gap` variable used for both the horizontal and vertical spacing. If we wanted to change the spacing in either direction, we would need to change the code quite a bit."

"That's a very good point, Jim. I'm glad to see that you were paying attention," I said. "If you expected me to come back with some excuse, you're wrong! Your point is wholly valid."

"That's a gold star for Jim," Gemma said. "Why doesn't anyone else ever get one?" Jim grinned.

"There's still time, Gemma," I joked. "Before we have the grid finished, I want to load in a dummy thumbnail image into each of the frames."

Filling the grid with images

1. Import the file `thumbnail.jpg` into the Library using **File > Import to Library**. This image is correctly sized for a thumbnail.

2. Create a new movie clip called **dummyPhoto**.

3. Drag a copy of `thumbnail.jpg` from the Library into the dummyPhoto movie clip. Center it.

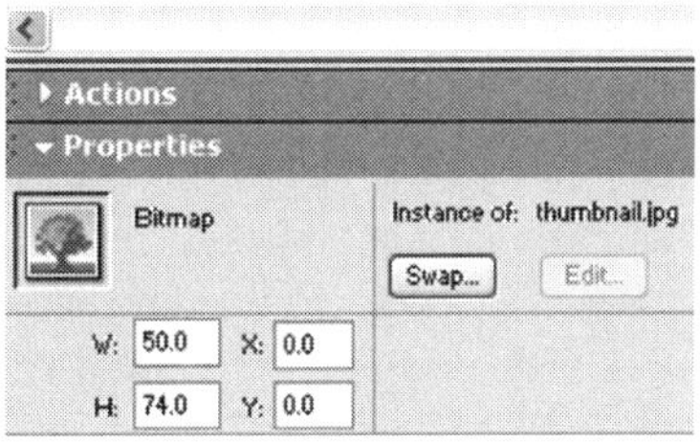

4. Return to the main timeline and open the Actions panel. Insert the following line:

```
thumb = frame.attachMovie("dummyPhoto", dummyPhoto"+count,
➥ count);
```

```
for (i=0; i<rows; i++) {
    for (j=0; j<columns; j++) {
        frame = _root.attachMovie("slideFrame", "slideFrame"+count, count);
        frame._x = ((frame._width+gap)*j)+startx;
        frame._y = ((frame._height+gap)*i)+starty;
        thumb = frame.attachMovie("dummyPhoto", "dummyPhoto"+count, count);
        count++;
    }
}
```

5. Test the movie. The frames should now be filled with a dummy image:

"As you might have noticed, the dummy thumbnails are attached within the slide frame," I said. "This is done because they both have a central registration point and are therefore matched up. We don't need to position the thumbnail image—it will automatically be positioned where the registration point is."

"You appear to have used `count` for the depth of the thumbnails," Joe said. "Shouldn't this overwrite anything previously at that depth?"

"Each level or instance has its own depth hierarchy. The thumbnails are sitting within the slide frame instance, so they won't affect anything on other levels. The slides themselves are sitting on the `_root` level. Usually it's `_root` depths that you need to be careful of."

"I've noticed one thing already," Gemma said. "When I click the tabs, the grid disappears and I can never seem to get it back."

"This is because I haven't considered the depth yet," I said. "The thumbnails and slides are at a much lower depth than the tabs, so they're being hidden by them. Don't worry too much about this for now—we'll lower the depth of the tabs in a later class.

"In next week's class, we'll be able to pull in the actual thumbnail images. In the last part of this class, I'd like to create and activate the About and Contact pages."

Making the About and Contact pages

"The best way to show the About and Contact pages is to attach either of the pages to the stage using the good old `attachMovie` method," I said. "Placement where the main image area is would be a suitable option. First, we need to create both pages, or boxes, and then we need to provide the buttons to link them."

1. Create a new movie clip called **page template**.

2. Within page template, draw a box measuring 350x355 pixels, and center it. Rename the existing layer **box**.

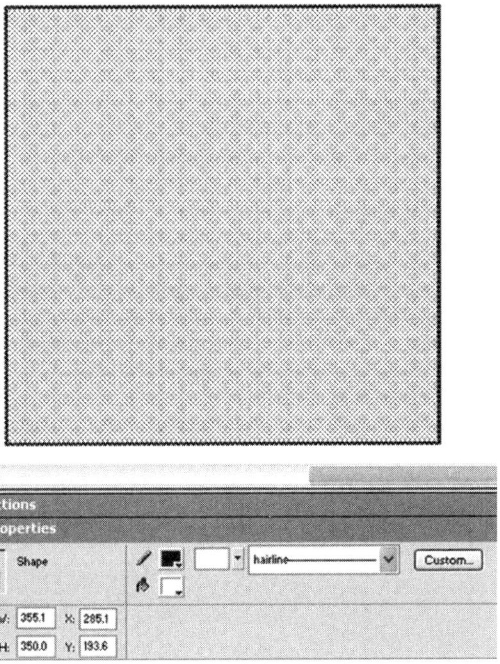

3. Insert a new layer called **text** and make sure it's stacked above the box layer. On this layer. use the Text tool to type "page title" close to the top of the box in quite a large font.

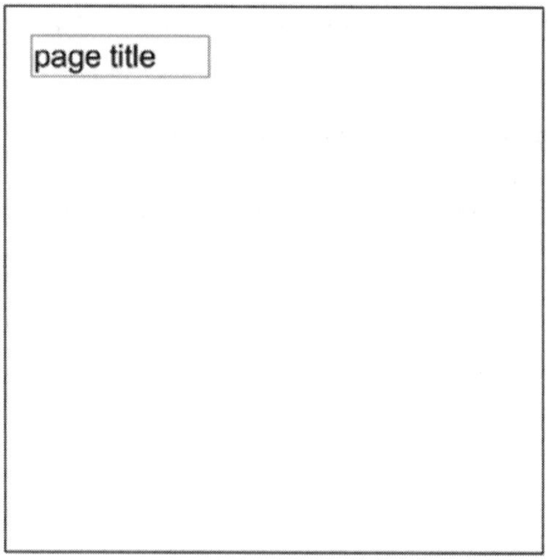

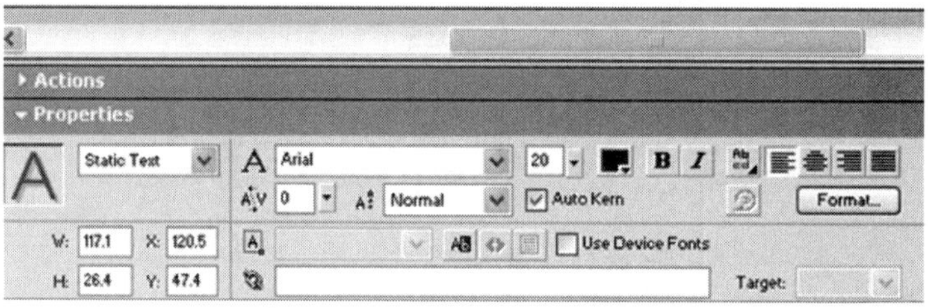

4. Below this, type "body text" in a smaller font—say size 12.

5. Ensure that Align to Stage is switched off, and align both text boxes to the left edge.

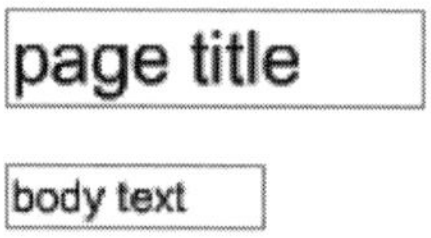

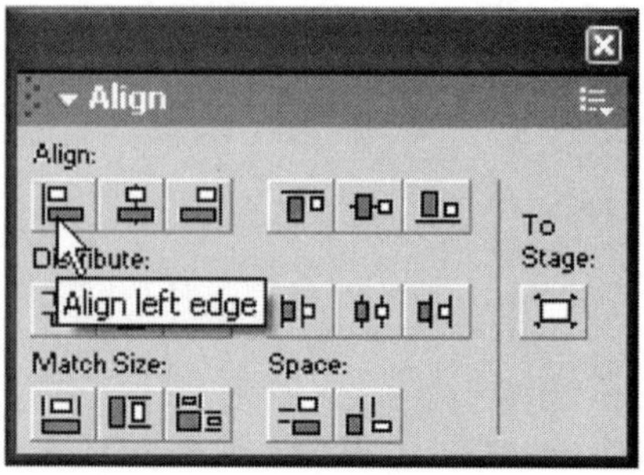

6. Right-click (CTRL-click for Mac) on the page template symbol in the Library and select **Duplicate** from the context menu.

7. Name the duplicate symbol **about page** and then double-click the about page symbol to edit it.

8. Change the page title to **About Randall Holmes**.

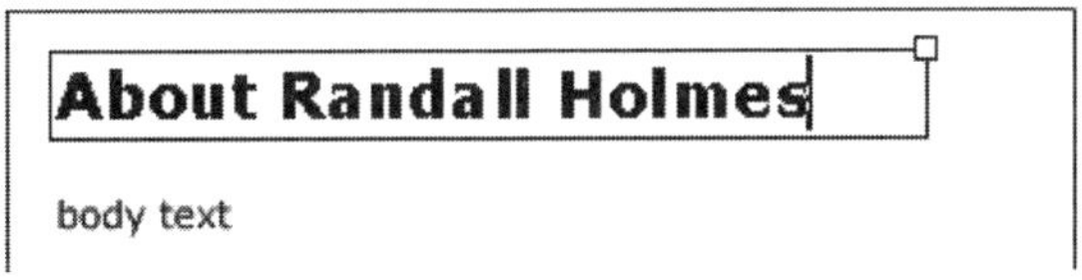

9. Give the about page symbol a linkage name of `aboutPage`.

10. Repeat the process from steps 6 through 9, calling the duplicate symbol **contact page**, using **Contact Randall** as the page title and `contactPage` for the linkage name.

11. On the main timeline, insert a new layer called **buttons** and create two simple movie clip buttons: one for about and the other for contact. Drag a copy of each onto the buttons layer and give these the instance names `aboutButton` and `contactButton`.

12. Open the main Actions panel and add the following:

```
aboutButton.onRelease = function() {
    page = _root.attachMovie("aboutPage", "aboutPage", 1000);
    page._x = 552;
    page._y = 362;
};
contactButton.onRelease = function() {
    page = _root.attachMovie("contactPage", "contactPage",
1000);
    page._x = 552;
    page._y = 362;
};
```

13. Test the movie and click the contact and about buttons.

"Is everyone clear what is happening here?" I asked.

"Just one thing puzzles me, Ken," Mazzy said. She paused for a moment. "Oh no, I think I've got it."

"What was it?" asked Carl. "I might have been thinking the same thing."

"I think I understand it now," Mazzy said. "I was going to ask about the depth initially, but once I thought about it for a moment, it made sense. Both instances are attached on the same depth because they overwrite each other. Am I right?"

I confirmed Mazzy's statement. "That's right. The Contact and About pages won't be on stage together; therefore, one can be placed over the other one. It might help for the rest of you to imagine two siblings fighting over the top bunk bed." Carl looked puzzled. "When we use `swapDepths`, there is a space for both siblings on the top and lower bunks. However, when we just set the depth level of something outright, it's as if there's only one bunk bed and only space for one brother or sister."

"I imagine the other one falls into a deep vortex?" Carl said.

"If that's how you'd like to think of it, Carl," I said. "I imagine the sibling without a bed would just leave the room and go to their own bedroom. In Flash, the newly set instance wipes out the previous instance occupying that depth level. I suppose Flash is a little meaner than kids are.

"In the next class, we'll use the same depth level to display the main image. This way, the user can still click a thumbnail when either of these pages are on display."

"That makes sense," Joe said. "It might be strange to have the thumbnails still present but not be able to click them."

"Not strange, Joe: unusable," I said. Joe smiled. "Unless anyone has any other questions, we're done for today."

"I have a question," Jim started. "Why did we create two pages that are virtually the same using static text boxes, when we could have gotten away with one movie clip and used dynamic text boxes?"

"That's another perfectly reasonable suggestion, Jim," I said. "But this time I have a concrete answer!"

"I think I know what you're going to say," Mazzy said, smiling.

"The reason is that Randy has told me that he wants his portrait on the About page. It's as simple as that," I said. Jim smiled. "This is besides the fact that the Contact page will eventually require a mailto button."

"That's enough of a reason for me," Jim said. "Although I could probably find a way around it!"

"Save it for next time," I said, switching off the projector. "Bye!"

The class emptied, accompanied by a number of "good-byes" and "byes," and one "adios."

Summary

In today's class, you started working on the case study after learning some last programming principles that will help you build it.

You learned that text fields can be static, input, or dynamic. They share similar properties. Some text field properties can be set in the Property inspector. Text fields can also be adjusted and even created using ActionScript, using the `createTextField` method.

You began working on the case study by breaking down the way that the tabs would work into logical steps. You learned about the `swapDepths` method as a way of moving a tab to the top.

In the next class, you'll be learning about arrays, you'll see how they're used to store information, and you'll use them to add images to the kiosk project.

Class 8
Arrays

Objectives

In today's class you'll learn about

- Storing information in arrays
- Making and using arrays
- Moving and sorting information in arrays
- Multidimensional arrays (or "arrays of arrays")
- Searching for information in an array
- Using arrays to put images into the gallery case study

Introduction

I entered the classroom, stopped momentarily to scrutinize the image on the back of Carl's jacket, and then launched straight into the lesson.

"Good evening, everyone. I hope you're all feeling okay, as you'll need all of your concentration for today's lesson. Today, we look at **arrays**—what they are and how they can work for us.

"We've previously talked about the need to store all of the picture information for Randy's site, but as yet we haven't discovered a suitable medium. Arrays are the pot of gold at the end of our information storage rainbow. They'll give us a structure in which we can easily store, order, and access our information."

What is an array?

"So let's define an array," I started. "The only other data storage structure that we've looked at so far is the variable, and we know that a variable is a named container. It stores one value, and we can retrieve that value by using the variable's name. An array is more like a *linked set* of variables.

"Let's take a look at an example," I said, and drew on the board:

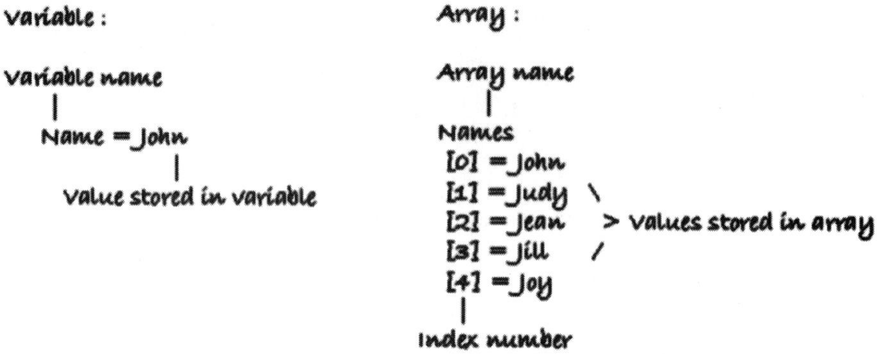

"The array itself has a name, but it can store as many values as you want it to. The different values stored within are arranged in a particular sequence and are accessed by their list number, also known as an **index**. Each entry in the list is one **element** in the array.

"The other thing to take note of here is that the index number starts counting from zero. You may come across other languages that allow you to pick your own number for the first index in an array. In Flash, though, *all* arrays are zero-based like this—all arrays that you'll be seeing in the near future begin with zero.

"If you believe it goes against nature to start lists from zero, then you can always leave the first entry in all your arrays blank and start from one. Believe me, though, in the long run it's better to get used to the idea of them starting from zero."

"Too many zeroes and ones," said Carl robotically, "brain overloading."

"Okay, point taken," I laughed. "Let's get back to something more grounded in the real world.

"Think about a Rolodex and how you use it. It's just a big collection of pieces of information. Usually, but not necessarily, those pieces are related to each other, and they're all stored sequentially in a unit that you can easily flick through to find what you want.

"An array isn't so very different, but it finds the information you want much quicker, and it makes it much easier to manipulate that information too.

"An array is an object, and just like any other object, it has methods and properties. These are what let you manipulate the information stored within the array. There are methods for adding new elements to an array, removing elements from it, sorting an array, splitting an array, and so on. You name it—there's probably a method to do it."

Joe raised his hand. "Excuse me, Ken! I see how the methods would work with an array, and I see how they're related to the movie clip methods that we saw before, but a movie clip was almost a tangible object. Its properties were physical things, such as its position and its visibility. How can something like an array have properties?"

"Is it like a cyber thing?" asked Carl. "Are arrays physical things in cyberspace, so they have properties for their position and stuff? Maybe they even have data firewall properties to defend against evil hackers!" Mazzy reached over and batted Carl on the head with a rolled-up piece of paper.

"Well, you may be getting a little carried away there, Carl," I said. "In fact, arrays have only one property. It's called `length`, and it tells you the total number of items stored in the array. But let's not get ahead of ourselves. First, let's take a look at how to construct an array in Flash."

Making arrays

I turned on the projector and opened up Flash. "Let's re-create the array that I just drew up on the board. There are a few ways of creating arrays, so let's start with the most formal. Just as you would for a variable, you assign a name to an array:

```
names = new Array();
```

"This tells Flash to create a new Array object, and to give it the title `names`. Once this is done, you can fill (or **populate**) the array with information. You do this by treating each element in the array as if it were a plain old variable, and you assign a value to it like so:

```
names[0] = "John";
names[1] = "Judy";
names[2] = "Jean";
names[3] = "Jill";
names[4] = "Joy";
```

"Notice that the index number of the array is written within square brackets. When used in this way, the square brackets are **array access operators**. Yes, yet *more* operators!

"Okay, I'd like you all to start up Flash and try creating an array and populating it with a few values." I waited for the class to do so.

"Right, then. Now you've all got your arrays, let's see how to access them. First of all, run your movie and use the Debug menu to list the variables in it. You should see something like this:

```
Output                                                    ☒
                                                  Options
  Level #0:
  Variable _level0.$version = "WIN 6,0,65,0"
  Variable _level0.names = [object #1, class 'Array'] [
      0:"John",
      1:"Judy",
      2:"Jean",
      3:"Jill",
      4:"Joy"
  ]
```

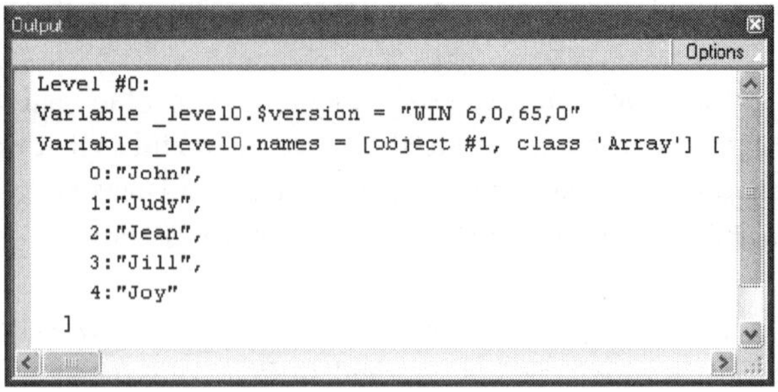

"As you can see, Flash has done as I asked: it's created an array called names and filled it with the requested data. Now, does anyone have anything different from that?"

"I don't have anything at all," said Mazzy, "just a lot of lines saying undefined." I flicked over to Mazzy's screen, and true enough, this is what I saw:

```
Output                                                    ☒
                                                  Options
  Level #0:
  Variable _level0.$version = "WIN 6,0,65,0"
  Variable _level0.flowers = [object #1, class 'Array']
      0:undefined,
      1:undefined,
      2:undefined,
      3:undefined,
      4:undefined
  ]
```

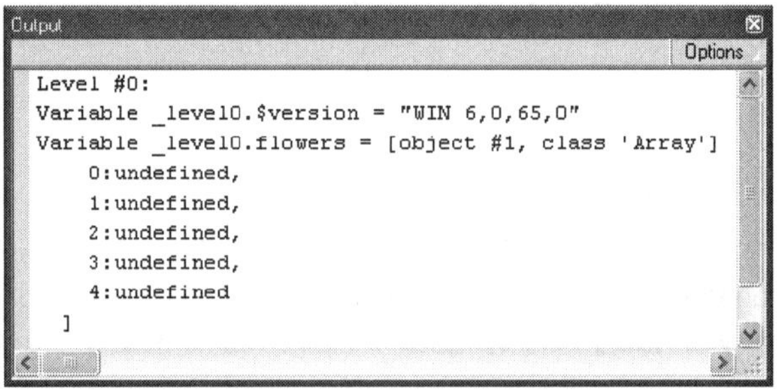

"Can you close that down and go back to the code?" I asked her. She did so, and immediately I spotted what the problem was:

```
flowers = new Array();
flowers[0] = Rose;
flowers[1] = Dahlia;
flowers[2] = Honeysuckle;
flowers[3] = Daffodil;
flowers[4] = Snapdragon;
```

"Can anyone tell me what's wrong with Mazzy's code?" I asked. Oddly enough, it was Mazzy who answered first. "Sorry, I'm being an idiot, I can see what's wrong," she said.

"Don't worry," I said, "it's a simple enough mistake to make. Can you tell the others what's wrong?"

"I forgot the quote marks to make the flower names into strings," Mazzy replied.

"And can you tell us why Flash responded in the way that it did?" I asked.

Mazzy thought for a second. "Is it because it's trying to get values from variables that don't exist? It's giving `undefined` because it can't find `Rose`, `Dahlia` and so on, so it doesn't know what values to put in the array?"

"That's exactly it," I told her. "Of course, if you had variables with those names, then it would work perfectly: Flash would track down the values being stored in those variables and copy them into the elements in the array.

"Okay, then, if no one else had any problems then we'll move on."

Looking inside arrays

"You've seen how you can use the Debug menu to look inside an array, but now I'll show you how you can use the `trace` action to get at the data. You can do this in a number of ways. First of all, you can trace the array name to get Flash to output the entire contents of the array in a comma-separated list:

```
trace (names);
```

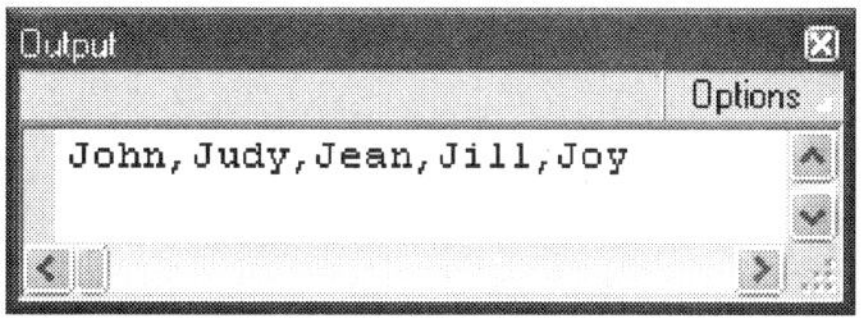

"If you want to pull out a specific element, you can put that element's index number in square brackets after the array name. Say you want to look at what is being stored inside the third element in the array. You use this:

```
trace (names[2]);
```

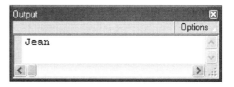

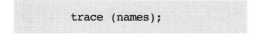

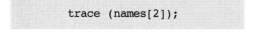

"Don't forget that arrays are zero-based—if you want to see the first element, you use `names[0]`. Likewise, `names[1]` gives you the second element, and `names[2]` gives you the third. I know it seems a little confusing at first, but you'll soon get used to it."

"I sure hope so," said Joe, "I'm cracking my nut trying to get my head round this one."

"Don't worry," I told him. "Just remember the Rolodex: an information store that's a little difficult to find your way around to begin with, but soon becomes second nature.

"Okay, while we're looking at tracing information from arrays, let's take a quick look at using that one property that we discussed earlier: `length`. Remember that you use dot notation to access properties, and finding the length is as simple as this:

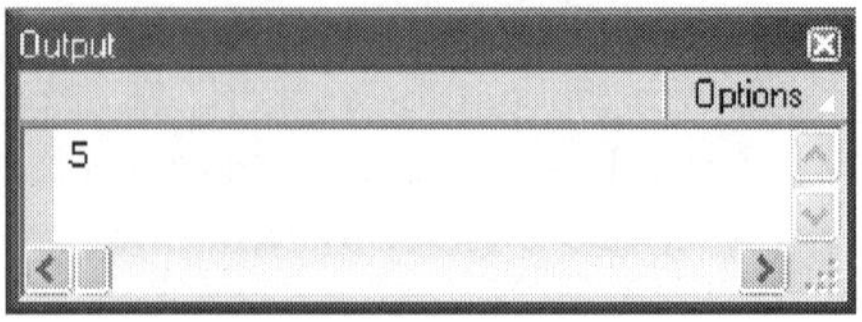


```
trace (names.length);
```

"Flash returns a single number for the total length of the array. Take note: that's the number of elements you have, *not* the last index number. Even though the last element in this array has the index number 4, there are five elements in all."

Other ways to make arrays

"Okay, let's take a look at another couple of ways in which we could create an array," I said. "The next way is to populate the array at the same time as you create it. You can do this by putting some values into the parentheses after `Array`:

```
names = new Array("John", "Judy", "Jean",  "Jill", "Joy");
```

"As you can see, this is a lot shorter. But you lose the user-friendliness of being able to immediately see which value is at which index number. They're actually just numbered sequentially from left to right, so element 0 contains 'John' and element 4 contains 'Joy' as before. If you're making a very large array, though, it won't be so obvious.

"Even if you make an array like this, there's nothing to stop you from changing or even adding elements with the first technique I covered." Jim's hand went up. "Yes, Jim?"

"Well, so far you have elements up to index 4. What happens if you leave some out and add a brand-new element at index number 9?"

"Let's give it a try, shall we?" I added another line to the code:

```
names = new Array("John", "Judy", "Jean", "Jill", "Joy");
names[9] = "Jim";

trace (names);
trace (names.length);
```

"Okay, how's that?" I asked.

"Great choice of name," said Jim. I continued, "I'm tracing the entire array and the length of the array so we should be able to see what's happening." I ran the file:

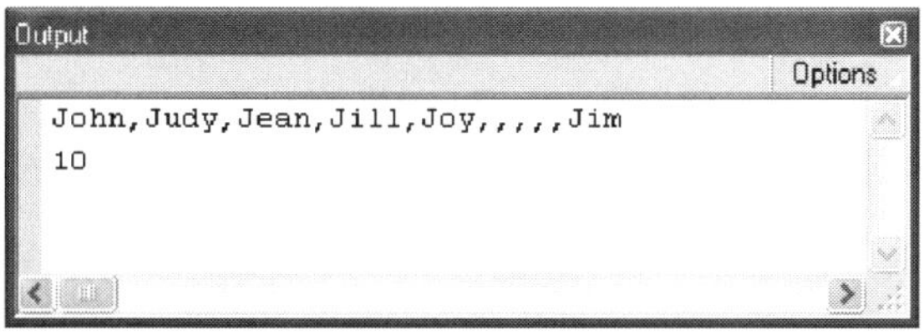

"What you can see here is that Flash has done what we asked it to and created a new element at index number 9, the tenth position in the array. To achieve this, though, it had to create four new elements between the last entry in the original array and our new one. The total length of the array, then, as you can see, is ten elements.

"The final method that we're going to look at for creating arrays is the quickest, but perhaps also the least user-friendly. Of course, it's easy if you already know what you're doing. If you don't know what you're doing, though, it can seem a tad confusing, and that's why I've left it until last. Okay, let's have a look at creating an example array using this new method:

```
names = ["John", "Judy", "Jean", "Jill", "Joy"];
```

"That's it. As you can see, there are a number of big differences from our earlier methods. The first thing is that there's no mention anywhere that what we're doing is creating a new array. That's what I meant when I said it wasn't user-friendly: we just jump straight in and create it, almost like a long variable.

"The other thing is that instead of being in parentheses, the values are contained within square brackets—as before, the brackets act as array access operators. But here, instead of letting us manipulate a single numbered element, they're setting the whole array!

"Okay, now that you've seen how to create and access an array, let's take a look at how to manipulate them using the Array object's methods."

Array methods

"First up are the methods for adding and removing elements from an array. These come in two pairs. The coolly-named **push** and **pop** are designed to add and remove elements from the *end* of an array, and the not-so-coolly-named **shift** and **unshift** do the same thing at the *beginning* of the array," I said.

Popping and pushing

"Let's take a look at pop first. It's one of the most satisfying ActionScript commands to get your head around—just think of squeezing the array until the last element pops off the end. Of course, you don't actually get to do the squeezing, but I like to imagine it all the same!

"Once pop has removed the last element, it returns the value of that element, so you can assign the value to a variable, trace it, or whatever you like. Let's see pop in action:

```
names = ["John", "Judy", "Jean", "Jill", "Joy"];
lastName = names.pop()
trace (lastName);
trace (names);
trace (names.length);
```

"Here, we pop the last element of the array into a variable called `lastName` and then `trace` that variable. We also `trace` the resulting array to see what effect the pop has had on it. Gemma, can you tell me what you expect to see in the Output window?" I asked.

"All right then," said Gemma, "the first thing is the contents of the `lastName` variable. I presume that will be 'Joy'. Next, there should be a list of all the remaining names and then the length of the array, which I think will be 4."

"Okay, let's see if you're right," I said.

```
Output                                              ☒
                                              Options
  Joy
  John,Judy,Jean,Jill
  4
```

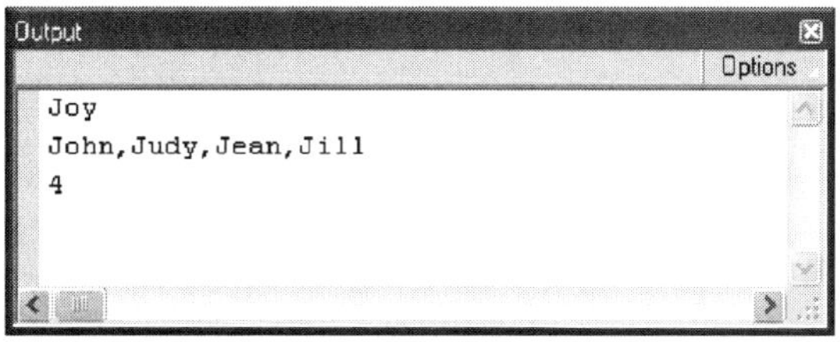

"Full marks. You see, arrays are easy," I said with a smile.

"Right, on to the counterpart of pop: push. If pop removed something from an array, then what do you expect push will do, Mazzy?" Mazzy was caught slightly off-guard. "I guess it will add something to an array?" she asked.

"Precisely. push adds elements to the end of an array," I replied. "Notice that I said *elements* there, not *element*. push can add as many elements as you like, whereas pop can only remove one element. Let's take a look at pushing a couple of elements onto the array:

```
names = ["John", "Judy", "Jean", "Jill", "Joy"];
names.push("Joseph", "Jeremy");

trace (names);
trace (names.length);
```

"The values I want to add go inside parentheses as parameters of the push method. This will simply add the two names onto the end of the array and make its length 7 elements rather than its old 5. Whereas the pop method returned the value that was popped off the end of the array, the push method returns the new *length* of the array. This is quite a handy feature, as it means that you could rewrite this code with one less line, like so:

```
names = ["John", "Judy", "Jean", "Jill", "Joy"];
trace( names.push("Joseph", "Jeremy") );

trace (names);
```

"Even though I've put the push action inside a trace command, Flash will carry it out just the same, passing the returned value straight on to the Output window."

Shifting and unshifting

"In just about every respect, these methods are exactly the same as push and pop. As I mentioned before, though, there's one big difference: they affect the elements at the beginning of an array rather than those at the end.

"Here's how to use `shift` to remove the first value from an array:

```
names = ["John", "Judy", "Jean", "Jill", "Joy"];
names.shift();
```

"Just like pop, it returns the new length of the array, which in this case will be . . .?" I queried.

"Three," came a confident response from Carl. For a moment, there was silence in the classroom. "Why do you think that, Carl?" I asked. He shifted in his seat for a few seconds and looked like he was starting to regret leaping in so quickly.

"Well, we started with five elements. Then we shifted John off the beginning, and that left us with four," Carl started.

"Okay so far," I said, nodding slowly.

"Then you count up from zero to get . . ." Carl stopped and looked around at the other students. They were all looking back at him, waiting for the end of his sentence. Once again, there was quiet.

He spoke again at last. "It's 4, isn't it. Four elements in the array, so the length is just 4."

"That's right," I said, "I couldn't have put it better myself!" The rest of the class smiled, and Carl relaxed visibly as I went on. "The index numbers start counting from zero, so *they* go up to three, but the length is still 4."

"Anyway, you seem to have `shift` figured out now—let's take a look at its partner in crime. `unshift` is the 'start of the array' equivalent of push: it adds in new elements. For example, you could use this code:

```
names = ["John", "Judy", "Jean", "Jill", "Joy"];
names.unshift("Joseph", "Jeremy");

trace (names);
trace (names.length);
```

"Type that in, test run the movie, and here's the output you get:

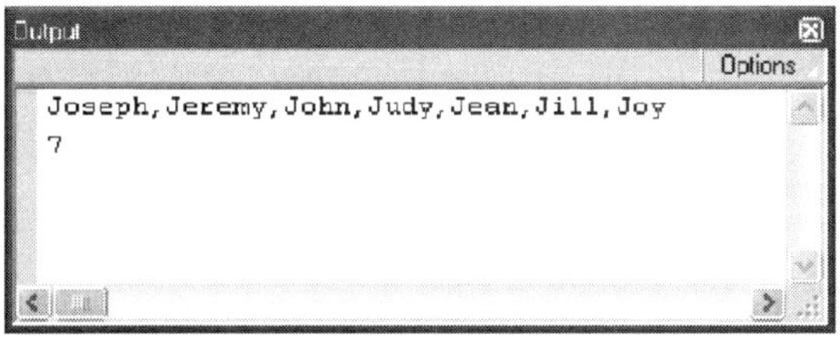

"Now you've got two new elements at the start, and all the others have moved up to make space. Okay?" There were nods all round, but Jim had a question.

"I get what we've done so far; using pop and push and shift and unshift to fool around with elements at either end of the array. But what about the elements in the middle? What if I want to change one of them?" Jim asked.

"Good question," I said. "Let's take a look at how you can do that too."

Slicing and splicing

"There are two more methods that you can use to manipulate elements in the depths of arrays: they're called **slice** and **splice**.

"Let's take a look at slice first. It doesn't behave quite as its name might suggest; it's actually more of a copy and paste, but that's not so catchy as a name! slice lets you specify a sequence of elements from an existing array and it then copies them into a brand-new array.

"Let's see what it looks like in action." I started writing on the board:

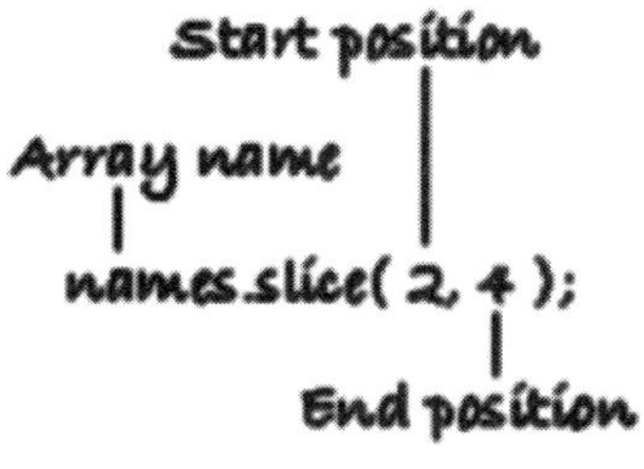

"The two parameters that you pass to the slice method represent the start and end positions of the slice you want to take. One thing to be especially wary of is that the slice you copy will include the element at the start position, but it *won't* include the element at the end position.

"In this example, you're going to slice out two elements from the middle of the `names` array. You specifically want the elements numbered 2 and 3:

```
names = ["John", "Judy", "Jean", "Jill", "Joy"];
newNames = names.slice(2, 4);

trace (names);
trace (names.length);
trace (newNames);
trace (newNames.length);
```

"Okay, what I'm doing here is creating a new array called `newNames` that will hopefully contain two elements from the middle of the old array. I'm tracing both the old and new arrays after the slice so that I can see if anything has happened to the old array.

"Let's see what happens:

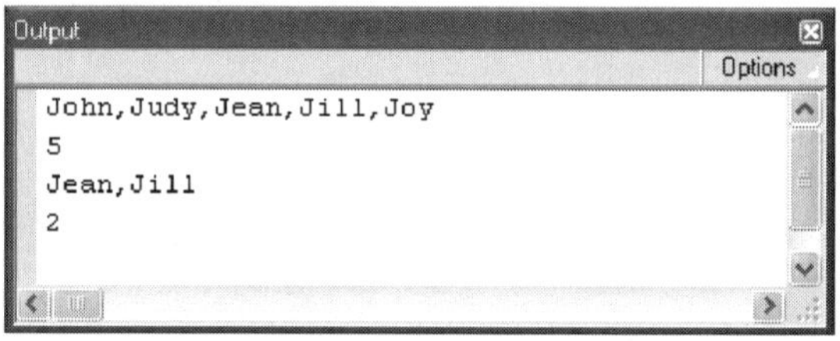

"You can clearly see here that the first array is still the same length and contains all of the original names. As expected, the new array is only two elements long and contains the third and fourth elements of the original array.

"Let's now turn to look at the other method of array middle management: `splice`. Although it's only one letter different from `slice`, `splice` is quite a different beast. It's a little more complicated, but it contains a host of different functions."

"They do say something about splice being the variety of life," quipped Jim. I rolled my eyes and continued. "Let's take a look at the anatomy of the `splice` method's first function: removing elements from an array.

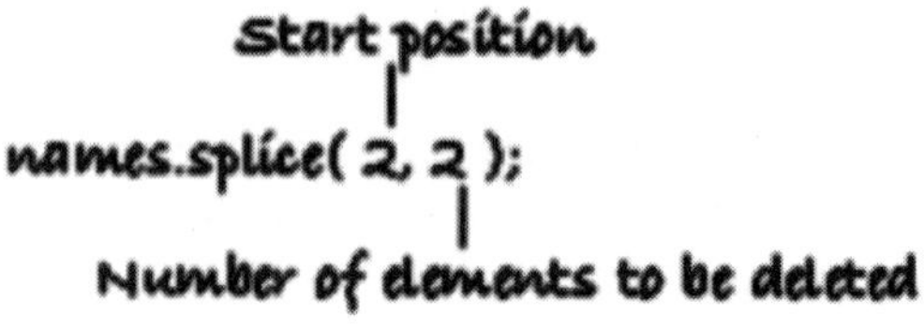

"Even though it looks quite similar to `slice`, there's a big difference. The second value *isn't* the end position, but the *number* of items to be deleted. In this case, you're deleting two elements, beginning with element number 2. If slicing was copy and paste, then this can be seen as cut and paste. Let's modify the code of the last example, and see what results:

```
names = ["John", "Judy", "Jean", "Jill", "Joy"];
newNames = names.splice(2, 2);

trace (names);
trace (names.length);
trace (newNames);
trace (newNames.length);
```


"All I've changed here is `slice` to `splice`, and the second parameter to a 2. The results are quite different, though:

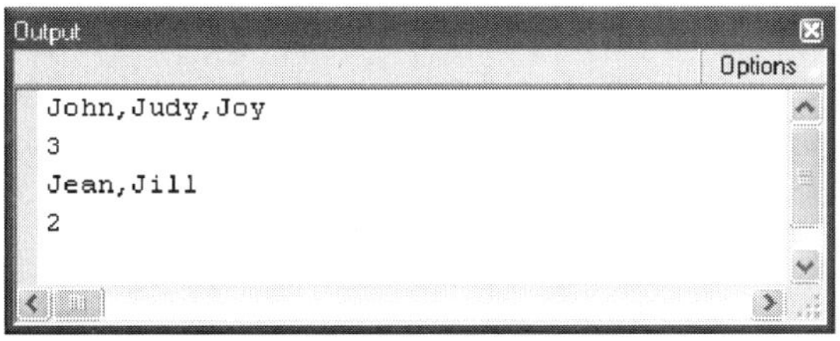

"As you can see, the third and fourth elements of the original `names` array have been removed and used to create the `newNames` array.

"That's not all `splice` can do, though. It can also add new elements into the middle of an array. To do this, you simply feed in the new element values as extra parameters like so:

```
names.splice(2, 2, "Jerry", "Jennifer");
```

"In effect, this will remove two elements from the original array and replace them with the two new elements. The new elements are always added from the start position specified in the first parameter. Bear in mind, though, you can add as many elements as you like—you aren't limited to the number that you removed.

"In the same way, you don't have to remove any elements in order to add new ones. You just need to specify 0 as the number of elements to be deleted, and Flash will insert the new values at the start position.

"Let's use our trustworthy example to see splice in action:

```
names = ["John", "Judy", "Jean", "Jill", "Joy"];
newNames = names.splice(2, 2, "Jerry", "Jennifer");

trace (names);
trace (names.length);
trace (newNames);
trace (newNames.length);
```

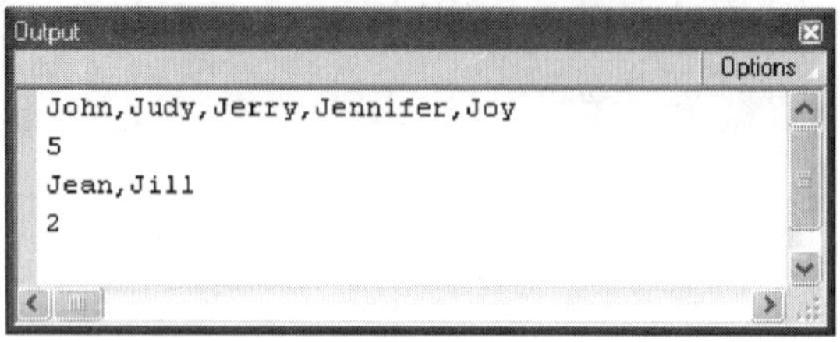

"Here we've removed two elements to form a new array, while at the same time we've replaced them in the original array with two new values. How's that for getting a whole lot of power from one small action?

"Okay, let's look at just a couple more quick array methods, and then we'll move on."

Simple sorting

"One of the things that Randy is likely to want to do with the data that we provide him with every day is to sort it into a meaningful order," I started. "Now, companies can devote thousands of dollars to finding the most efficient sorting algorithm for them, and we may look at some more complicated examples later on, but for now we can be happy with Flash's free, built-in array-sorting method. It's called, predictably enough, **sort**.

"The sort method sorts an array in ascending order, starting with the lowest value and moving up to the highest. You can also use it to sort strings into alphabetical order. For example:

```
names = ["John", "Judy", "Jean", "Jill", "Joy"];
ages = [85, 12, 54, 73, 28];
names.sort();
ages.sort();
trace (names);
trace (ages);
```

"Here I have two arrays: one of strings and one of numbers. I'm simply sorting both arrays and then tracing them to the Output window:

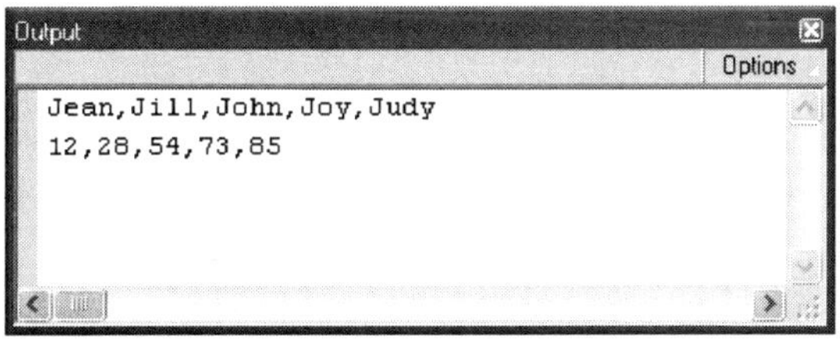

"I now have two arrays sorted into perfect order: one alphabetical and the other numerical.

"Another simple but useful array method is **reverse**. This does exactly what it says on the package: it reverses the order of elements in an array. You can combine this with sort to get the elements sorted in reverse order like so:

```
names = ["John", "Judy", "Jean", "Jill", "Joy"];
ages = [85, 12, 54, 73, 28];
names.sort();
ages.sort();
names.reverse();
ages.reverse();
trace (names);
trace (ages);
```

"Logically, this should give you two arrays whose elements are sorted in reverse order, from highest to lowest:

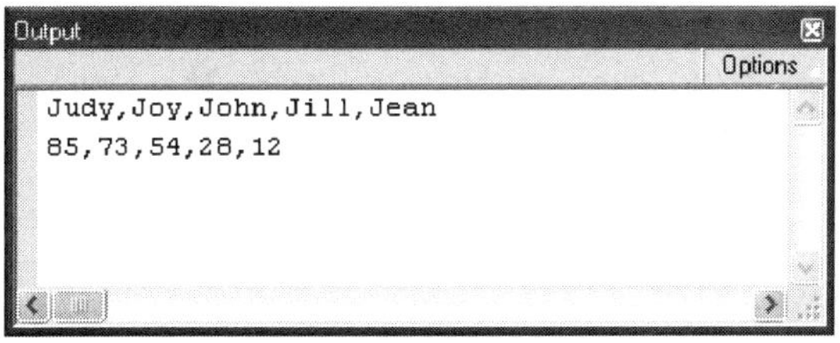

"Lo and behold, that's precisely what it does!

"That's all for simple array manipulation, but we're not quite done with arrays yet."

Multidimensional arrays

"Do you remember how you extended the power of loops by nesting them within one another?" I began. "Well, the same thing is possible with arrays. Instead of storing a single value within an array element, you can store a whole other array in there. This is known as a **multidimensional array**.

"Okay, it sounds intimidating, but it really isn't. Just think of it as a filing cabinet. The filing cabinet has a number of drawers, and each drawer holds several documents. You get to a particular document by specifying two pieces of information: which drawer it is in and where it is within that drawer.

"Let's take a look at an example. To make it easier to read, I'll combine two of the techniques that you saw earlier for creating arrays. First, you create your master array:

```
music = new Array();
```

"Next, you define each element of this array as a new array, like so:

```
music[0] = ["classical","Schubert","Mozart","Bach"];
music[1] = ["pop","Minogue","Timberlake","Spears"];
music[2] = ["musical", "Rogers","Hammerstein", "Gilbert"];
music[3] = ["alt", "Coyne", "Wagner", "Oldham"];
```

"And that's all there is to it. If you run this file and then view the **List Variables** output, here's what you'll see:

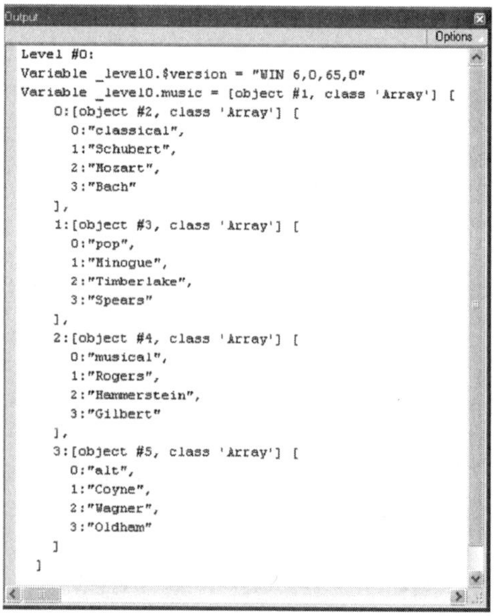

"You can clearly see that Flash has done as you asked and created your arrays. The next thing you need to know is how you can access your arrays using ActionScript. As before, let's use trace to extract a value from one of the arrays.

"To access a value in a multidimensional array, you need to give Flash two pieces of information: the index number of the main array in which the subarray resides and the index number of the particular element in that subarray that holds the value you're looking for.

```
Output                                                   ☒
                                                    Options
Level #0:
Variable _level0.$version = "WIN 6,0,65,0"
Variable _level0.music = [object #1, class 'Array'] [
    0:[object #2, class 'Array'] [
        0:"classical",
        1:"Schubert",
        2:"Mozart",
        3:"Bach"
    ],
    1:[object #3, class 'Array'] [
        0:"pop",
        1:"Minogue",
        2:"Timberlake",
        3:"Spears"
    ],
    2:[object #4, class 'Array'] [
        0:"musical",
        1:"Rogers",
        2:"Hammerstein",
        3:"Gilbert"
    ],
    3:[object #5, class 'Array'] [
        0:"alt",
        1:"Coyne",
        2:"Wagner",
        3:"Oldham"
    ]
]
```

"So, for example, let's access Mr. Rogers. His name is stored inside the third element of the main array. That means index number 2, so you start with this:

```
trace( music[2]
```

"Now you need to give Flash the index number of the subarray. Rogers is the second element in the array, so the number you want is 1. You add this in by simply placing it in square brackets immediately after the index number of the main array. Okay, so it's easier if I just show you:

```
trace( music[2][1] );
```

"If you now run this code, you get the result you expected:

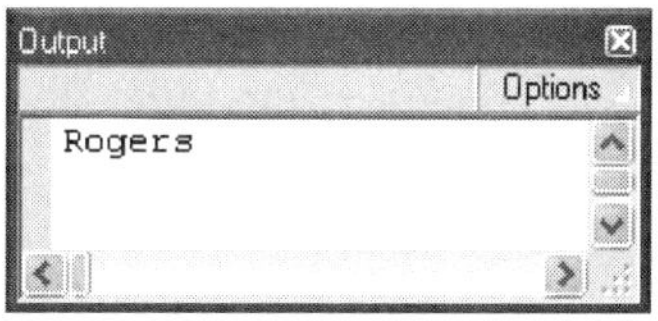

"I don't know whether you realize it yet, but you've actually now learned quite a lot of code."

"No fear, Teach," said Carl, "we realize it." I smiled. "Well, now you can bring together everything that you know," I said. "You've seen how to extract a value from an array when you know its position, but how can you retrieve something when you don't know exactly where it is?"

"You mean like the other of Carl's socks in a pair?" asked Mazzy.

"Hey, I have a pair of . . ." Carl hauled first one leg into the air to display his sock, and then stopped short of lifting the other into view. "Umm . . . odd socks are the sign of a creative mind. Let's get back to the program—all this talk of socks is making me impatient."

I laughed, "Okay, Carl, your wish is my command."

Parsing arrays

"In programming, there's a special term for 'looking through the elements in an array:' we call it **parsing**. So your challenge, should you choose to accept it, is basically to *parse* your multidimensional array until you find the element with a particular value.

"Okay, now I want you all to work together as a team and try and come up with a way of finding a value, let's say 'Gilbert,' from within the array. I'm not expecting you to program the solution into Flash; I just want you to tell me the general process that you should follow in order to find your value. I'll be on hand to give you any assistance you need. All right, go."

"Okay, everyone, huddle," called out Carl, and there was a mass scraping of chairs as people moved over to gather around Carl's screen. "Right," said Gemma, "the value that we're looking for is stored inside the third subarray, so we need some way of getting inside there to look for it."

"Hold on a minute," said Jim, "Flash doesn't know which array the value is stored in, so we've got to step back and start from the very beginning."

"You're right," said Gemma. "So how do we step through the main array and look at each subarray?"

"A loop!" said Carl and Mazzy in unison. "I said it first," said Carl. "Okay, okay," Gemma intervened, "so we use a loop to check through the main array. But how do we know which of the other arrays contains the value? We need to know which of the subarrays contains the value before we can check the main array for it, but we need to check the main array before we can search the subarray for the value. It's a catch-22."

"I think we're going about it all wrong," said Jim. "To find the value, we need to check through every single element in every subarray until we get a match. I think a nested loop might do the trick. The outer loop can check through each element in the main array, and then the inner loop can check through each element in the subarrays."

"I think you're on to something there, lad," said Joe. "Then we can just put a simple `if` statement inside the inner `for` loop to check if the value stored there is the one we're looking for or not."

"Okay," said Mazzy, furiously writing on her pad, "how's this?"

```
for (main music array){
for(elements in sub array) {
 if (value=="Gilbert") {
  trace("Ha! Found it.");
  }
 }
}
```

"I reckon that's about right," said Joe. "Let's show Ken." The students unhuddled, and Mazzy approached me with a page torn from her pad.

"Here's our answer," she said.

I studied the piece and gave the class my congratulations. "That's pretty good," I said. "The theory's all there, so let's try converting it into code.

"First of all, we're going to store the value we're looking for as a variable. This will make it easier to find and change when we want to search for something else:

```
search = "Gilbert";
```


"Now we're ready for the first loop. We know that arrays are zero-based, so we'll start by initializing our loop counter to zero. Carl, when do we want the loop counter to stop?"

"When it gets to 3," Carl replied.

"Why 3?" I asked.

"Because that's the end of the array," Carl said.

"Is there another way to find out the end of the array without hard-coding it?" I asked.

"Ah, I see," said Carl, "use the `length` property."

"That's right," I told him. "The reason I keep going on about *not* hard-coding values wherever possible is that it makes your code more flexible. If we hard-coded the length, then we'd have to change it as soon as we wanted to run the same code on a different array. By letting Flash find the length of the array for itself, we make sure that the code as it stands will work with any array.

"Okay, that's our condition sorted out, and we know that we want to increment the counter in steps of one, so our first line of code is this:

```
for (i=0; i<music.length; i++) {
```

"Notice that I've used less than (<) here rather than less than or equal to (<=). This is again because of the zero-based nature of arrays. The array has four elements, but the last element in the array is number 3. This means that we can stop the search at the loop as soon as it's finished 3 because there aren't any more elements in the array.

"Next, we need to initialize our second for loop. We'll use j as a loop counter for this one. Again, we'll start the counter at zero, but this time the condition will be a little different. We need to find the length of the current subarray. How do we know which array we're in?"

"Because we're keeping track of it with i, the previous loop counter," called out Jim.

"Exactly," I confirmed, "and we can use our loop counter variable as the index number for the array. So, the first couple of lines should look like this:

```
for (i=0; i<music.length; i++) {
    for (j=0; j<music[i].length; j++) {
```

"Does everyone follow what we've done so far? Our first loop is running for the entire length of the music array; for each cycle of that, the inner loop runs through each element in the subarray.

"Anyway, that's the main loop engine done. Now all we need to do is put in our actual check to see if we've found the correct value.

"To do this, we'll need to tell Flash where we are in the array right now and then what we want it to check against. To put it in slightly futuristic terms, we're testing the jth element of the ith array to see if it's the same as our search variable.

"In programming-speak, that all looks like this:

```
if (music[i][j] == search) {
```

"Remember how we saw that to access a multidimensional array we had to use the index number of the main array in square brackets followed by the index number of the subarray? That's all we're doing here, checking the current element against the search variable.

"Okay, we're almost done. The next thing to do is send a meaningful message to the Output window to make sure we've achieved what we set out to do. We use a slightly complicated trace action to give us some detailed information:

```
        trace(search+ " found at music[" +i+ "][" +j+ "]");
```

"All we've really done here is trace the variable we were originally searching for and then give the array position we found it at, modeled in the style of an array index.

"There's one last thing that we want to do before we test the loop. We want to terminate the search as soon as we've found the correct result. This will save a lot of time in a large array. Remember that we used break to get out of switch statements in an earlier class? Well, there's a similar thing we can do here. We can add a simple **return** action to stop the loop and return Flash to the main program. Of course, this only works if we know there's just one occurrence of the value that we're looking for in the array; if not, then we could just let it run and it would give us every occurrence of the value in the array.

"Okay, without any more fuss, the final code for our array and search engine looks like this:

```
music = new Array();
music[0] = ["classical","Schubert","Mozart","Bach"];
music[1] = ["pop","Minogue","Timberlake","Spears"];
music[2] = ["musical","Rogers","Hammerstein","Gilbert"];
music[3] = ["alt", "Coyne", "Wagner", "Oldham"];

search = "Gilbert";
for (i=0; i<music.length; i++) {
    for (j=0; j<music[i].length; j++) {
        if (music[i][j] == search) {
            trace(search+
➥              " found at music[" +i+ "][" +j+ "]");
            return;
        }
    }
}
```

"Now's the time of judgment." I ran the file:

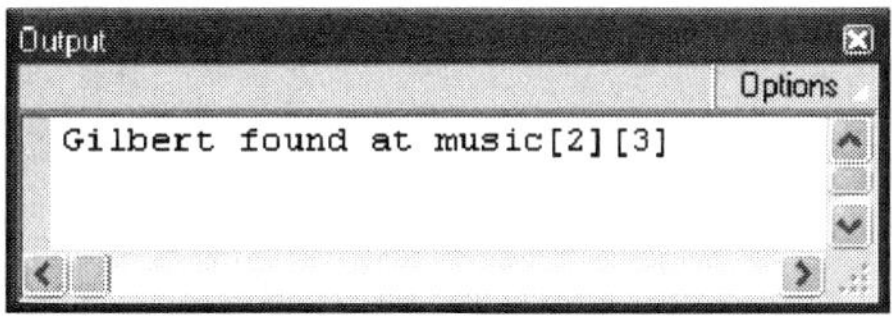

"All that code for one little line," said Mazzy.

"Yeah, but it's the *right* line," countered Carl. "Thanks for the backup," I told him.

"Now that our search engine's in place, we can search for any value, and if it's in there, Flash will find it.

"Okay, arrays play a large part in our case study, because all of the photos and their details will be stored in a set of multidimensional arrays. Before we head straight back into the code, though, let's take a look at bringing the pictures into Flash."

Importing images

"Randy supplied me with a set of images earlier in the week," I said, "and I used Photoshop Elements to resize them all to the correct dimensions that we'll be using."

"Can you show us how to do that?" Jim asked. "It's not really programming," I replied. "I'd find it helpful too," chimed in Mazzy. "Okay, does anyone have any objections to quickly going into Photoshop and seeing how to resize a photo?" The students all said that they didn't.

I started up Photoshop Elements on my computer. "Okay," I said, "here's one of Randy's pictures:

"As you can see, it's an image of some footprints on a beach. All of the images that Randy provided me with are at a ratio of 1:1.5—that is, if the short side was 1 unit long, then the long side would be 1.5 units long, and so on. The agreed sizes for thumbnails and full images using this ratio was 75x50 pixels for thumbnails and 350x233 pixels for the full images, with a resolution of 96 dpi.

"Now, the images that Randy gave me were at different sizes and resolutions—for example, the footprints image was at 1675x1115 pixels and 1200 dpi. Because I was doing a heap of images, and I was performing the same process on all of them, I decided to let Photoshop do the hard work for me. First of all, I opened up the **Batch** window:

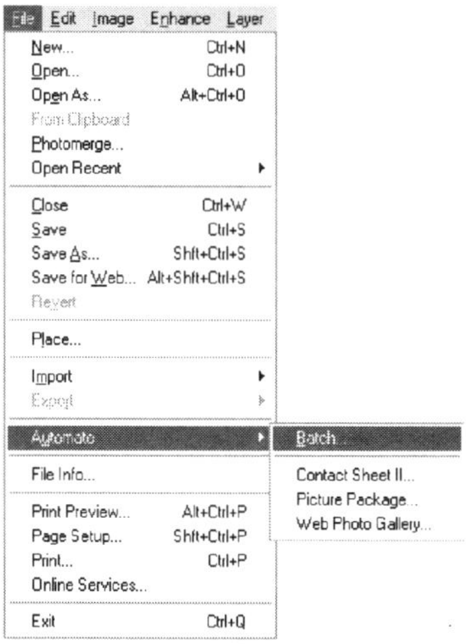

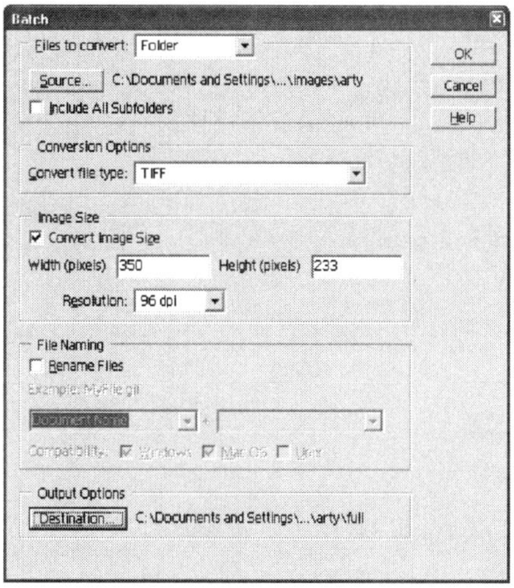

"I chose source and destination folders for my images, and set the dimensions and resolution that I wanted all of the pictures to end up at. I also chose to keep the images as TIFF files so that they would still hold as much detail as possible. When you're bringing pictures into Flash, it's better to bring them in at as high a quality as possible and let Flash do all the compression for you.

"After giving Photoshop the required information, I simply clicked **OK** and it went away and resized the images for me, as simple as that.

"Now that the images are the right size, you can try importing them into Flash. I took the liberty of copying the images onto your desktops before class. You'll find a folder called `images` there that contains all of the thumbnails and full pictures. Gemma, I'm afraid I didn't have time to copy them onto everyone's computer, so you'll have to borrow this CD. You'll find the images in a folder called `CaseStudy\Images`.

"In Flash, you want to bring the images into the Library, and if you check in the **File** menu, you should find an option that looks like it will do the trick:

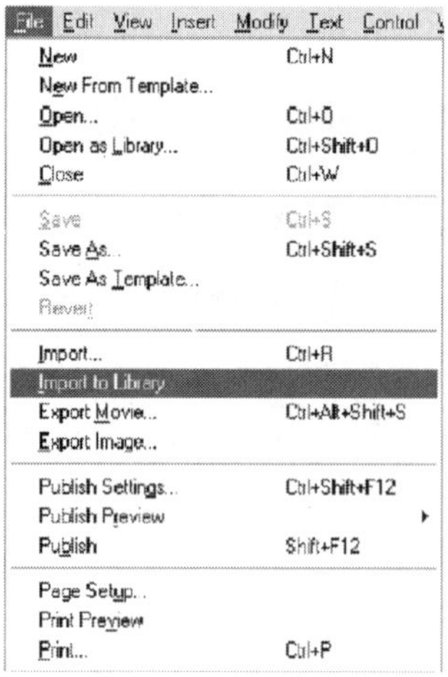

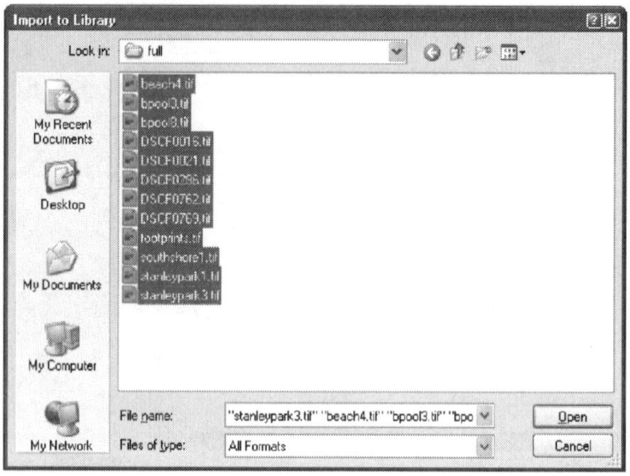

"In the **Import to Library** window, navigate your way to the images folder on your desktop. From there, go to `arty\full` and highlight all the files there. If you don't see anything, make sure that Flash is set to look for **All Formats**. Once that's done, click the **Open** button.

"The next thing that you'll be greeted with is an error message from Flash:

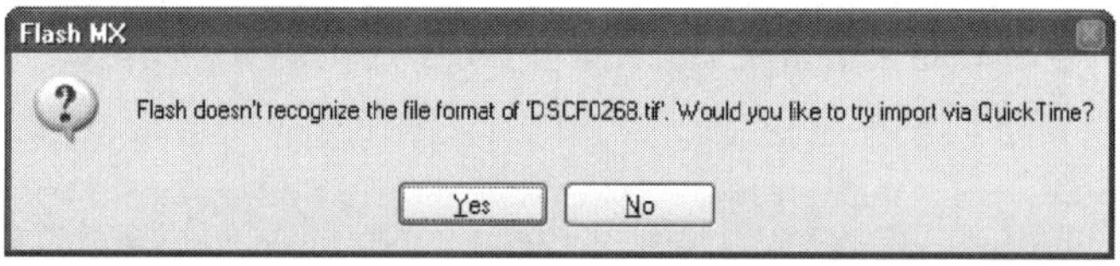

"Don't worry, this isn't as bad as it might sound. Flash doesn't have built-in support for certain file types, but as long as you have QuickTime installed, it can use that to open up the files. Click **Yes** to this box, and Flash will open the file for you. You'll find that you might have to do this for every file, but it doesn't take too long.

"If you don't have QuickTime on hand, you can always go back to Photoshop and perform another batch-to-convert operation on all the picture files to turn them into JPEGs. This isn't ideal, as it means the images lose quality even before they're brought into Flash, but it's better than no pictures at all."

"I wish there was a Yes to All button," said Carl. "This isn't much fun at all."

"Don't worry," I told him. "There are only 12 pictures, so it won't take long. Once you've finished that, open the Library and you should be able to see all of your pictures stored inside:

"You can order them by creating folders in the Library to keep them in. Mine are in a folder called `images\arty\full\`.

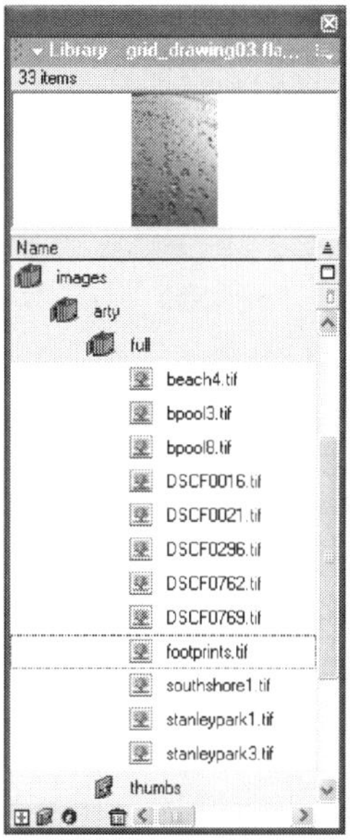

"Okay, now that you have the images in Flash, let's see what Flash can do with them. Drag a copy of the footprints photo onto the stage, and zoom in on a part of it. You'll see that the image looks quite smooth. Now go back into the Library and right-click the `footprints.tif` image there. From here, click **Properties**.

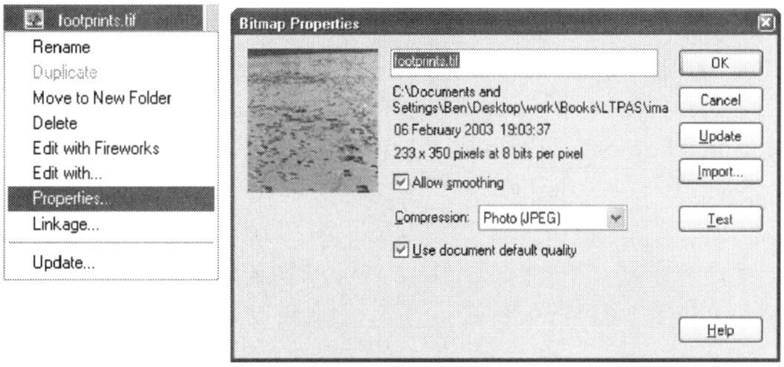

"This will open the **Bitmap Properties** window and allow you to change the way that Flash compresses the image. Remember when we defined bitmaps back in the first lesson? As far as we're concerned, it's an image made up of pixels, as opposed to a vector image that's made up of mathematical descriptions. To see the amount of difference that Flash can make, uncheck the **Allow smoothing** box and click **OK**. You should see your image change quite considerably:

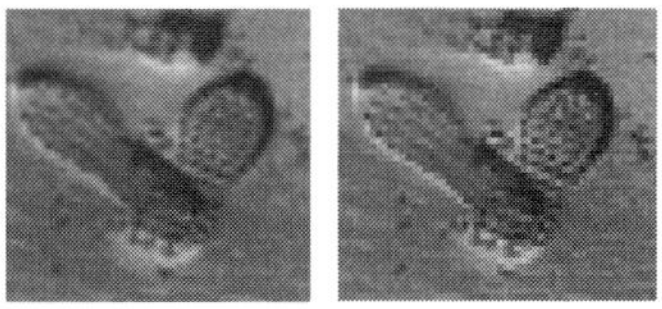

"Okay, go back to the properties and check the smoothing box again. Underneath the box, you'll see a setting to control the compression. Note that it's currently set to JPEG compression and follows the document default quality. The other option in the drop-down box is to use PNG compression, which maintains the original quality of the image but doesn't save much file size. Leave it at JPEG for now so you can control the compression.

"Going back to the compression properties, what's this 'document default quality' all about? You didn't set that. The default image compression quality is stored in the **Publish Settings** window, which you can find in the **File** menu:

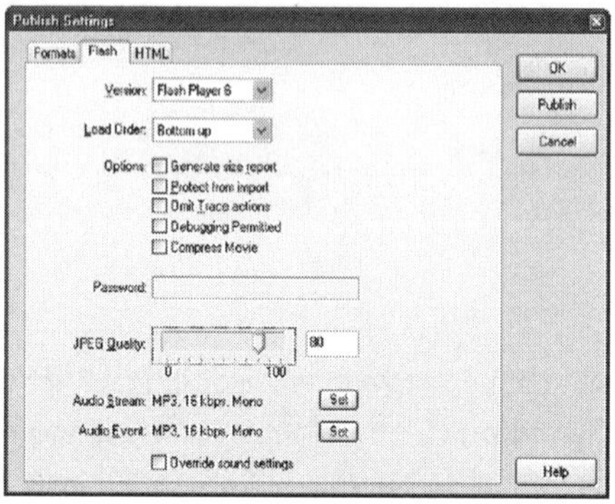

"Toward the bottom of this window, you'll see a **JPEG Quality** setting that works on a percentage. The best quality is 100% but the biggest file size, and 0% is the worst quality but the smallest file size. If you were creating an image gallery for the Web, you'd have to bear in mind the download time for your files. You'd probably make the **Quality** setting quite low, because you'd want to keep the files as small as possible.

"Fortunately, we're working on a kiosk, so we can either set the **Quality** value quite high or use the lossless PNG compression method that we saw in the **Bitmap Properties** window.

"One tip is to set this to a medium value, and then look through each of your images in turn and individually tweak any that particularly need it. To tweak an individual image, you need to go back into the **Bitmap Properties** window and uncheck the **Use Document Default Quality** box. This will open up another option that allows you to set the quality of just that image."

Building the case study

"Okay, let's create a simple image array and see if we can make the images appear in our case study," I said. "First of all, you need to import the thumbnail images for this set, so go back into the **Import to Library** window and bring in the images from the `thumbs` directory. You might also want to create a `thumbs` folder in the Library and put these in there to keep things tidy.

"Right, who can tell me how we're going to store all the of the data that goes with the images?"

"In an array!" called back the students in unison.

"That's right," I said with a smile, "to be more precise, in a set of multidimensional arrays. Each category is a multidimensional array, with each element holding an array of the data for one picture. Mazzy, can you remind me what information we needed for each picture?"

"Yep," she replied, "an index number, a simple description for the tooltip, and a longer, more detailed description."

"Thanks," I said, "we also want to add to that the linkage name for the thumbnail and the full-size images for each picture. Okay, so the array will look something like this." I wrote on the board:

Array = [indexNum, thumbName, fullName, tooltipText, fullText]

"Bearing that in mind, let's take a look at coding it. You've already seen how to create a multidimensional array, so you'll take exactly the same approach to creating the image arrays. Call the first one `art`, and just leave double quotes as placeholders for now:

```
art = new Array();
art[0] = ["", "", "", "", ""];
```

"Okay, type those lines in at the beginning of the case study code, and then copy and paste the second line another 11 times. Once that's done, you'll need to renumber the array index so that it runs from 0 to 11 rather than all being 0." I waited until everyone was ready.

"Next, let's populate just the first element in the array, and then it should be easy to go through and fill in the rest. So, let's fill in the blanks. Randy has his own index numbers for each of the images, but we'll just number them sequentially for now, beginning with '000.'

"For the thumbnail name and full name, I thought we could use a simple two-letter code for each. The first letter of the code is the first letter of the category name; so for art it would be 'a,' and the second letter would be 't' for thumbnail, and 'f' for full picture. Following these two letters we'll have the number of that picture's position in the array. So, for example, the first thumbnail in the `art` array will be 'at00,' The next will be 'at01', and so on.

"You can make up your own text for the last two fields for now. Randy has agreed to fill all of these details in, so we just need to give him the structure to do it in. Your finished first line should look something like this:

```
art[0] = ["000", "at00", "af00", "Footprints",
➥                              "Footprints on a beach"];
```

"You now need to give the thumbnail photo a linkage name. If you remember, last week you achieved this by creating a dummy photo holder for your image. You can do exactly the same thing today; in fact, you can even use exactly the same holder that you did before. Find the dummy photo holder in the Library, right-click it, and select **Duplicate**:

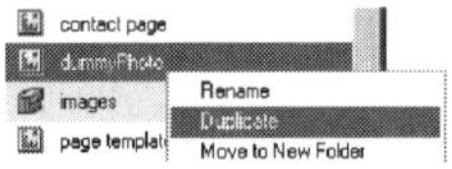

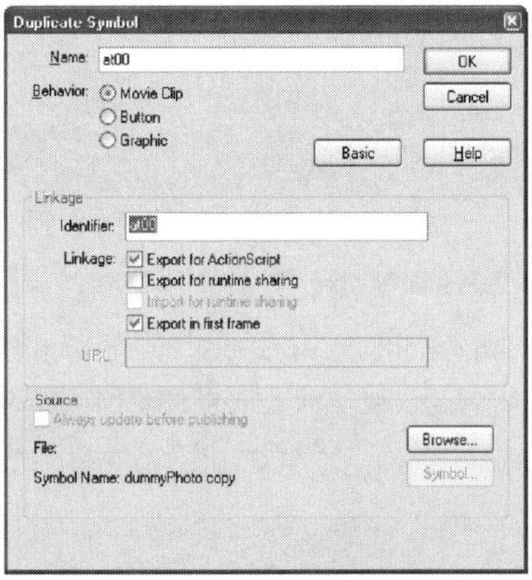

"This will open the **Duplicate Symbol** window. In this window you can give the symbol a new name, in this case 'at00,' and you can also choose to give the symbol a linkage name by checking the **Export for ActionScript** box. Flash will give a default name as 'at00,' the same as the symbol name, and luckily this is exactly what you want. Click **OK** and you should see a new symbol appear in the Library.

"You'll probably also notice that the new symbol still has the same image in it. Don't fret, though, help is only a couple of clicks away. Open the symbol and then right-click the image on the stage and select **Swap Bitmap** from the menu that appears:

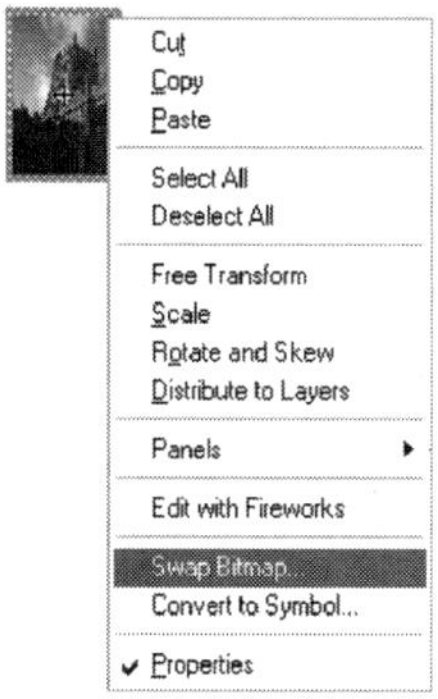

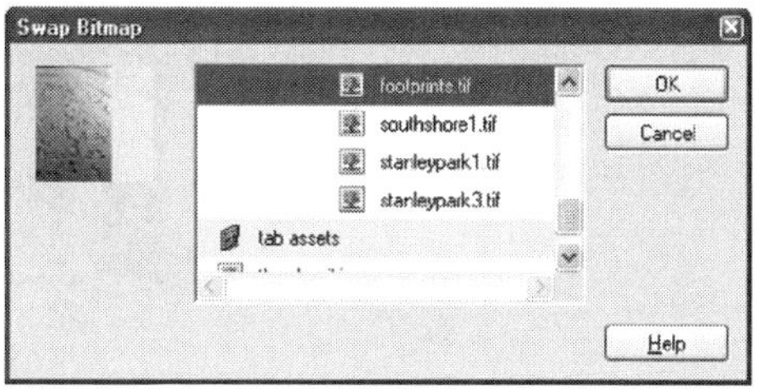

"This will open the **Swap Bitmap** menu, which allows you to do just that: swap the bitmap. Navigate to the image that you want—I'm using footprints—and then click **OK**. Flash will do the rest for you and swap the old picture for the one that you really want.

"Okay, you've created the array, and you have the image ready. Now all you need to do is make some alterations to your existing grid code to display the image from the array rather than straight from a given file name.

"The line that you want to change is the one that attaches the dummy photo. At the moment, it looks like this:

```
thumb = frame.attachMovie("dummyPhoto",
➥                          "dummyPhoto"+count, count);
```

"All you need to do is replace both those dummy photo names with references to your array. The part of the array you want to access is the bit that names the thumbnail, and you know that this is always the second element in your arrays. The only part that changes is which element of the main array you're looking at. Fortunately, you already have its index number defined in the count variable, so the information you want can be called up with this:

```
art[count][1]
```

"You then need to insert this into the attachMovie line, replacing both occurrences of dummyPhoto, and you're done:

```
        thumb = frame.attachMovie(art[count][1],
                                  art[count][1]+count, count);
```

"You can now run the movie, and if all goes well, you should see your image in the first position:

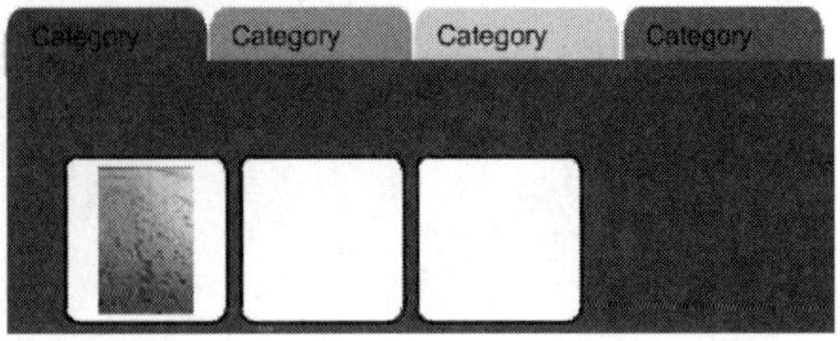

"Okay, that's all for today. If you want, you can go through and populate the rest of the array with pictures. Don't worry if you don't have time, though, as next week I'll supply you with a ready-made file with all of the pictures in it. See you all next week!"

Summary

In today's class, you learned how arrays can be used to store lots of separate pieces of information in a single place. Not only does the array link together several variablelike elements, but it also lists them in a particular order. You learned that each array has a name, and that each element in the array has a number, its index, which counts up the list from zero.

You looked at three different ways to create an array:

- `names = new Array();`
- `names = new Array("John", "Judy", "Jean", "Jill", "Joy");`
- `names = ["John", "Judy", "Jean", "Jill", "Joy"];`

You also saw how array access operators `[]` can be used to read and write individual elements:

- `names[0] = "John";`
- `trace(names[2]);`

You examined some important methods of the Array object that let you add, remove, and reorder an array's elements:

- `pop` and `push` for removing and adding elements at the end of an array
- `shift` and `unshift` for removing and adding elements at the start of an array
- `slice` and `splice` for copying and cutting elements from the middle of an array and pasting them into a new one

You looked at storing multidimensional arrays, a set of arrays stored as elements within another array, which let you store even more information. You saw how to parse a multidimensional array, looking for an element that contained a particular value, and saw the use of another in the gallery case study to access information about the images you're importing.

In the next class, you're going to learn about functions and how they help you produce ecologically friendly, recyclable code that can be used over and over.

Class 9
Functions

Objectives

In today's class, you'll learn about

- Breaking down tasks with functions
- Using functions with parameters
- Returning values from functions
- Adding functions to the case study

Introduction

"In today's class, we're going to look into functions," I started. "You've already used them to deal with events, but now you're going to see where else they can be useful. As I'm sure you remember from a few weeks back, functions are essentially self-contained chunks of code. They're useful when you have a lot of repetitive tasks in a program. With functions, you can write a piece of code once and call it up whenever it's required.

"Looking at functions in relation to variables might help. You know that variables are really just containers for data. Well, functions are containers for actions that are run on demand. They don't run automatically; rather, they wait until they're called for.

"There's no absolute limit to the amount of code you can put inside functions, but they tend to be most useful when they focus on doing one specific thing. Whenever your program has to tackle a task, you can think about how it might be broken down into subtasks. Then you can put each subtask into its own function.

"Think about a simple task like making a sandwich. It's not particularly complicated, but it's still made up of several subtasks: getting bread out of the cupboard, getting a knife, buttering the bread, choosing a filling, pressing the slices of bread together. Each subtask is an individual process, but they all add up to form the 'sandwich making' task.

"Now these subtasks aren't just useful for making sandwiches—they can be used for other things too. For example, getting bread out of the cupboard is a vital step in the task of making toast, or even feeding ducks."

"All this talk about food is making me hungry," said Carl, holding his stomach. "Lucky ducks!"

Using functions

"To use a function in a Flash movie, you need to do two things," I said. "First, you need to **declare** the function, which involves giving it a name and a block of actions to perform. You then use that name to **call** the function, and Flash runs the function's actions just as it would any others.

"Let's look at declaring a function. Imagine we're making a game in which all the baddies suddenly grow to double their size at the same time."

"There's no chance of that happening to me," said Carl. "I'm going to fade away at this rate." Mazzy patted Carl on the head.

I continued, "This growth could be done using a loop that cycles through all the baddies, doubling their `_xscale` and `_yscale` properties. The function might look something like this:

```
inflateBaddies = function () {
    for (i=0; i<baddiesCount; i++) {
        currentBaddie = _root["baddie"+i];
        currentBaddie._xscale *= 2;
        currentBaddie._yscale *= 2;
    }
};
```

"Remind you of anything?" I asked, looking around for a glimmer of recognition.

"It's just like those event handlers we did before, Teach," volunteered Carl, who I now noticed was looking rather pale. "Good, Carl," I said. "You really have been paying attention! Why don't you pop down to the canteen and grab yourself something to eat? Be quick though—I've got some really good examples coming up, and I wouldn't want you to miss them." As quick as a flash, Carl bolted.

"This function is stored in a container called `inflateBaddies`, so to run the actions inside, you simply call it like this:

```
inflateBaddies ();
```

"You can call the function at any time during the movie, and Flash will go right ahead and run all the actions inside it."

"This looks different from the functions I've seen before now," said Mazzy. "I'm sure they weren't declared like that in JavaScript."

"You're right, Mazzy," I said. "Let me rewrite the function a little, and it may look more familiar." I wrote on the board:

```
function inflateBaddies () {
    for (i=0; i<baddiesCount; i++) {
        currentBaddie = _root["baddie"+i];
        currentBaddie._xscale *= 2;
        currentBaddie._yscale *= 2;
    }
};
```

"Yeah, that's it," she said. "That's the way I've done it before. Can I use this type in ActionScript?"

"You can," I said. "In fact, until quite recently, this was the *only* way you could declare functions in Flash. The other way is actually a new technique that was introduced with Flash MX—its technical name is **callback**."

"So what's the point in doing it the other way?" Mazzy asked.

"Well, apart from the fact that it lets you write event handler functions, there are lots of advanced techniques that are much easier to tackle if your functions are defined with callbacks," I said. "I won't go into any more detail, but trust me, it will make your lives easier in the long run if you've learned it that way to begin with. That said, a lot of people still use the second form, so it pays to be aware of both. Ultimately, it's up to you which version you use, and I certainly won't penalize you for using one over the other.

"One important thing to note about callback functions is that you can only call them *after* they've been declared. Otherwise, Flash won't know about the function and won't understand what you've asked it to do. This is one thing the old-style functions *aren't* limited by—you can declare and call those in whatever order you like."

Carl returned to class grasping a sandwich and sat back down.

"That was quick!" exclaimed Joe.

"I didn't have to use all the commands Ken mentioned earlier," said Carl. "I just used the `getSnackFromMachine` function!"

"I hope you thought about all the subtasks involved, Carl," I said. "You might find the `getMoneyFromWallet` function to be useful for all sorts of things."

"I don't get much of a chance to call that function," Carl said. "I usually have to clean my mom's car to be able to declare it." The other students laughed.

"Carl appears to have highlighted the need to pick good names for functions," I said. "As with variables, try to keep your function names . . . well, *functional*. Remember that you might have to return to some code at a later date and it will make the job easier if your functions have sensible, self-explanatory names.

"Okay, class, crank up Flash and we'll create our first function. In this movie we're going to show how Carl's hunger is satisfied by eating healthy apples!"

Eating apples

1. Open a new Flash movie.

2. Type the following code on frame 1 of the existing layer:

```
1  // initialize variables
2  numberOfApples = 3;
3  satisfaction = 0;
4  // function declaration
5  eatAnApple = function () {
6      numberOfApples--;
7      satisfaction++;
8  };
9  // call function
10 eatAnApple();
11 // report status!
12 trace("Carl has a satisfaction level of "+satisfaction);
13 trace("There are "+numberOfApples+" apples left in the bowl");
```

3. Press CTRL+ENTER to test the movie.

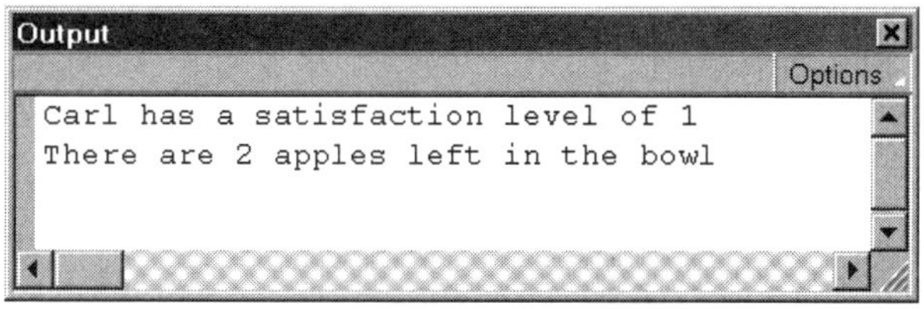

"Very amusing," said Carl.

"Thanks, Carl," I replied. "And thanks to the rest of you for refraining from making jokes about how Carl likes them apples!" I paused. "Let's look at the code.

"As usual, we start by initializing some variables: `numberOfApples` will represent the number of apples in the basket, and `satisfaction` will represent Carl's satisfaction level. If we forget that Carl just wolfed that sandwich, we'll imagine that this is set to zero—he was pretty hungry after all!

"Lines 5 through 8 declare the function `eatAnApple`. The actions in this function will reduce the quantity of apples by 1 and raise Carl's satisfaction level by 1. If you remember from previous classes, - - and ++ are shorthand for saying 'decrement by 1' and 'increment by 1.'

"Line 10 calls the function `eatAnApple`, and all the actions within it are run at this point. Lines 12 and 13 then report on Carl's status and the stock in the fruit bowl."

"What if I want to eat two apples instead of one?" Carl said, rubbing his stomach heartily.

"Using the function in its current state," I said, "you'd need to call the function twice:

```
/// initialize variables
numberOfApples = 3;
satisfaction = 0;
// function declaration
eatAnApple = function () {
    numberOfApples--;
    satisfaction++;
};
// call function
eatAnApple();
eatAnApple();
// report status!
trace("Carl has a satisfaction level of "+satisfaction);
trace("There are "+numberOfApples+" apples left in the bowl");
```

"Here's the result this would give you:

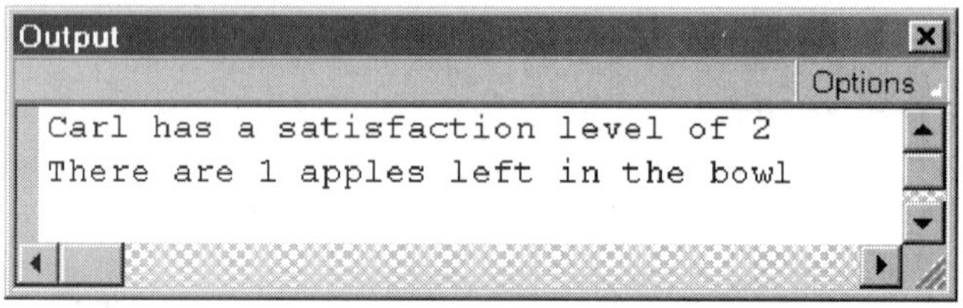
Output
Options
Carl has a satisfaction level of 2
There are 1 apples left in the bowl

"Now, if you overlook the obvious grammatical error in the window here, you can see that Carl has eaten two apples, thereby improving his satisfaction level and reducing the number of apples in the bowl.

"Even though we have the result we wanted, this isn't the most efficient way to use our function. Calling it multiple times to repeat the same action may not be too much of an issue in this case, but that's because we're only calling it twice. What if we had 20 apples? What if we had 20,000?"

"What about putting it inside a loop?" asked Gemma.

"That's certainly one way we could do it, but there's actually a much better way," I said.

Functions with parameters

"We've already seen some methods, `attachMovie` for example, that require arguments to tell them what exactly to do. Functions can also use arguments for greater flexibility. In the last version of Carl's apple-munching code, Carl eats a single apple each time simply because the function is hard-coded to only do that.

"However, if we change the function a little to require a parameter, we can tell Carl how many apples to eat when we call the function. The revised function code will look like this:

```
eatApples = function (numberToEat) {
    var numberToEat;
    numberOfApples -= numberToEat;
    satisfaction += numberToEat;
};
```

"We now have a variable called `numberToEat` in the brackets after function—this is a function **parameter**. When the function is called, whatever argument value we specify in the brackets will be stored in the parameter variable `numberToEat`."

"I'm confused—one minute something is an argument, and then it's a parameter," Joe said. "Which is which?"

"That's a very common question, Joe," I said. "The parameter is a variable, and it only ever exists *inside* the function declaration, like `numberToEat` here. Parameters are local to functions and don't exist outside of them, so until we call this function, `numberToEat` will have absolutely no value.

"The argument is simply a value that we specify when we call the function. Let's see how a function call might now look:

```
eatApples (3);
```

"When Flash sees this, it takes the argument value, 3 in this case, and stores it inside the parameter `numberToEat`, making it available to all the function code.

"The keyword `var` tells Flash that we only want to use the `numberToEat` variable within the function. Once the function ends, its value is cleared and it isn't available to the rest of the code. Although this might sound bizarre, this means that the parameter is simply there to do its thing within the function before disappearing. This also means that you can have different functions using the same parameter names because they don't coexist and can't clash.

"There is one explicit way to retain a value from a function: using the return action."

Returning values from a function

"Besides using functions to run a bunch of code, you can also use them to calculate and return values," I said. "For example, say you want to calculate the amount of tax you have to pay every year. Your salary would be passed as an argument and the function would do the entire calculation for you. The amount of tax would be returned.

"In many programming languages, this is the only real use for functions. Functions are often required to return a value exclusively. Do you all remember the Number function?" The students nodded. "The Number function accepts a string variable as an argument and returns a numeric value.

```
myNumberVariable = Number (myStringVariable);
```

"The value of myStringVariable here is specified as the argument for the Number function. myNumberVariable is then set to the numeric value returned from the function."

"Would calculating the square root of a number be a function, then?" Jim asked. "The required number that you want to know the square root of would be sent as the argument."

"That's right, Jim," I replied. "Flash MX has a built-in square root action that does that task. This action will be based on a function with all the relevant math calculations. "Let's perform a quick exercise to create our very own useful function.

"Very often I fly to the UK on business trips, and luckily I have my very own pocket currency converter. Let's see how we might program it in Flash. The function and call might look like this:

```
convertSterlingToDollars = function (sterlingAmount) {
     exchangeRate = 1.5;
     var sterlingAmount;
     dollarAmount = sterlingAmount*exchangeRate;
     return dollarAmount;
}

theCashInMyWallet = convertSterlingToDollars (20);
```

"Let's see how we can use it in Flash."

Exchanging currency

1. Open a new Flash movie, insert two extra layers, and name the three layers **actions**, **convert button**, and **text fields**.

2. On the text fields layer, add two text fields, one static and one input.

3. Put a £ symbol in the static text field.

4. Place the input text field alongside it, give it the instance name of `currencyIn`, and select the show border option.

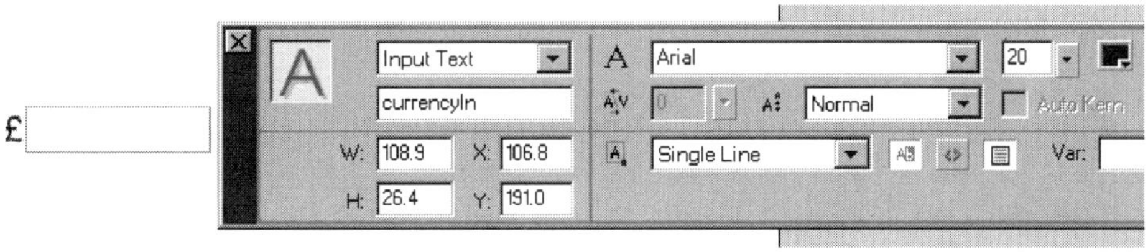

5. Limit the characters of `currencyIn` to numerals and the period character (.).

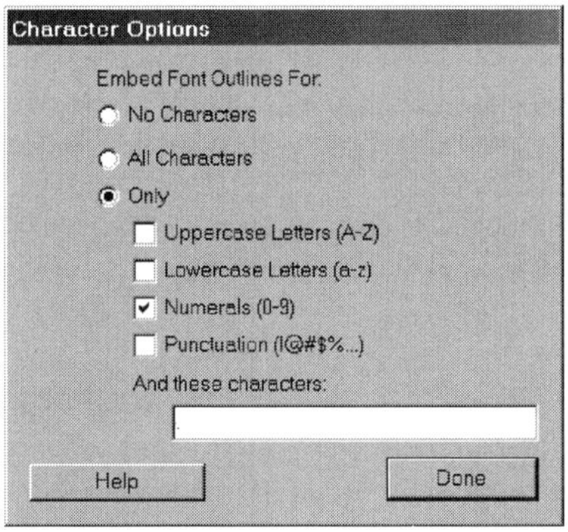

6. Add a static text field containing a dollar symbol (with no border and not selectable) and a dynamic text field.

7. Give the dynamic text field the instance name `currencyOut`. Place it a short distance from the other text fields.

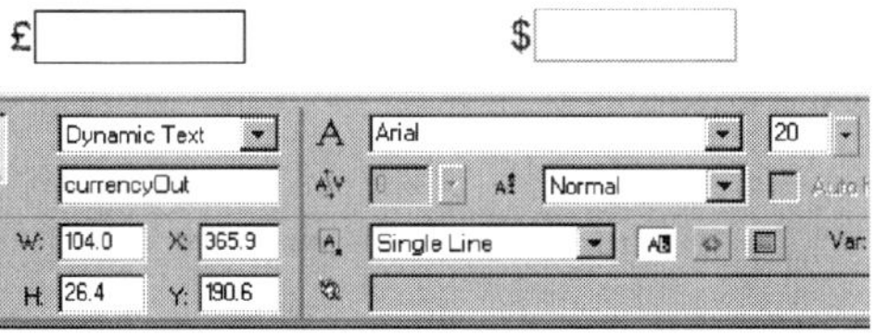

8. Create a new movie clip called **convert button**. Draw a rectangular button with the text **CONVERT**. Drag an instance of it onto the convert button layer. Give it the instance name `convertButton`.

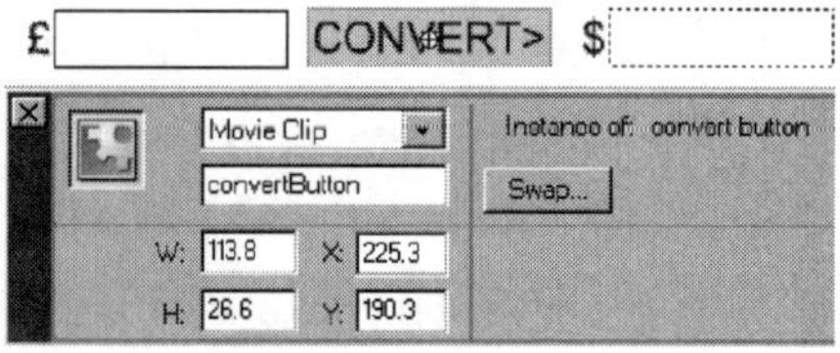

9. Add the following actions to the keyframe on the **actions** layer.

```
1 convertSterlingToDollars = function (sterlingAmount) {
2     exchangeRate = 1.5;
3     var sterlingAmount;
4     dollarAmount = Number(sterlingAmount)*exchangeRate;
5     return dollarAmount;
6 };
7 convertButton.onRelease = function() {
8     currencyOut.text = convertSterlingToDollars(currencyIn.text);
9 };
```

10. Test the movie. Enter a value in the input box and click the CONVERT button to calculate the equivalent value in dollars.

"Okay, let's go through what is happening here," I started. "The sterling value of the `currencyIn` input field is being translated into dollars and outputted into the `currencyOut` text field. All the calculation is done via the lengthily named function `convertSterlingToDollars`.

"This function uses a single parameter, `sterlingAmount`, that contains the cash value of British pounds, which we want to be converted into good old greenbacks. Before the actual calculation, we define `exchangeRate`, using it to store the conversion rate of sterling to dollars.

"On line 3, `sterlingAmount`—the parameter variable—is defined as a local variable, making it exclusive to this function. The next line does all the good, hard mathematics: declaring a new variable called `dollarAmount` and making it equal to the converted value. The `Number` function is used here to ensure that the input from the text box is in numeric form. Finally, we return the value of `dollarAmount`, so that when the function is called, this is the value it will equate to.

"Lines 7 and 8 set up the event and handler for the CONVERT button. On line 8, the dynamic text field `currencyOut` is set to receive the value returned from the function call. The argument passed to the function is the text entered into the input text field `currencyIn`. Does everyone understand?"

"Sure," said Gemma, "though I can't see why you would type all that function in, just to perform such a small operation."

"I can see where you're coming from, Gemma," said Jim. "In the long run, though, this function will save you a lot of unnecessary coding clutter. Even though this Flash movie only performs one function, imagine the benefit this function would have for larger movies in which the sterling-to-dollar conversion happened more and more. If you didn't functionalize this, you'd need to write out the formula each time you required it."

"I can see the benefits from that point of view," said Joe. "I have a different question, Ken." I nodded. "I know you're using a flat exchange rate, but what if the exchange rate changes or I want to convert another international currency to dollars? I often import a lot of my goods from China and Europe. Would I need a function for every currency?"

"Excellent question, Joe," I said. "You're absolutely right to say this function doesn't have much room for reuse: all the values in it are hard-coded. But functions aren't limited to using one parameter; they can have as many as we need.

"With this in mind, this function can be updated to accept both the international currency value—as with the sterling value before—and the exchange rate. Let's rewire things a little."

Multiple parameters

"Our recoded function requires two parameters: the foreign cash value and exchange rate. We might as well change its name too. Here's the brand-new function:

```
convertForeignToDollars = function (foreignAmount,
➥                                    exchangeRate) {
    var foreignAmount;
    var exchangeRate;
    dollarAmount = foreignAmount * exchangeRate;
    return dollarAmount;
};

theCashInMyWallet = convertForeignToDollars (20, 1.5);

trace (theCashInMyWallet);
```

"Open a new Flash movie and try this out," I said. "Feel free to also play with the arguments sent to the function.

"Multiple parameters for functions are separated by a comma. As with a single parameter, it's usually best to define all parameters as local variables using the `var` keyword. Multiple parameters can be applied to all sorts of functions, not simply functions that return a value.

"Now that we've exhausted the concept of functions, let's update our case study with the additional capabilities that functions provide us with."

Case study

"For the rest of today's class, we'll expand the coding of our case study using functions for certain actions. The actions that can be functionalized so far include

- Grid drawing/changing categories
- Main image loading/picture information
- Tooltips

"We'll run through all these now, and by the end of today we'll have our front-end 90% functional."

Image preparations

"Open the file `case_study01.fla`, whose Library holds all of Randy's photographic images and contains the corresponding information in arrays.

"In the Library, you'll find that each photo is represented at full size and in thumbnail form. The folder **image holders** contains four subfolders, one for each category, and each of these contains two more subfolders: **full mcs** and **thumbs mcs**.

"As you can probably guess, **full mcs** contains the full-size photos measuring 350x233, and **thumbs mcs** has the thumbnail versions at 75x50.

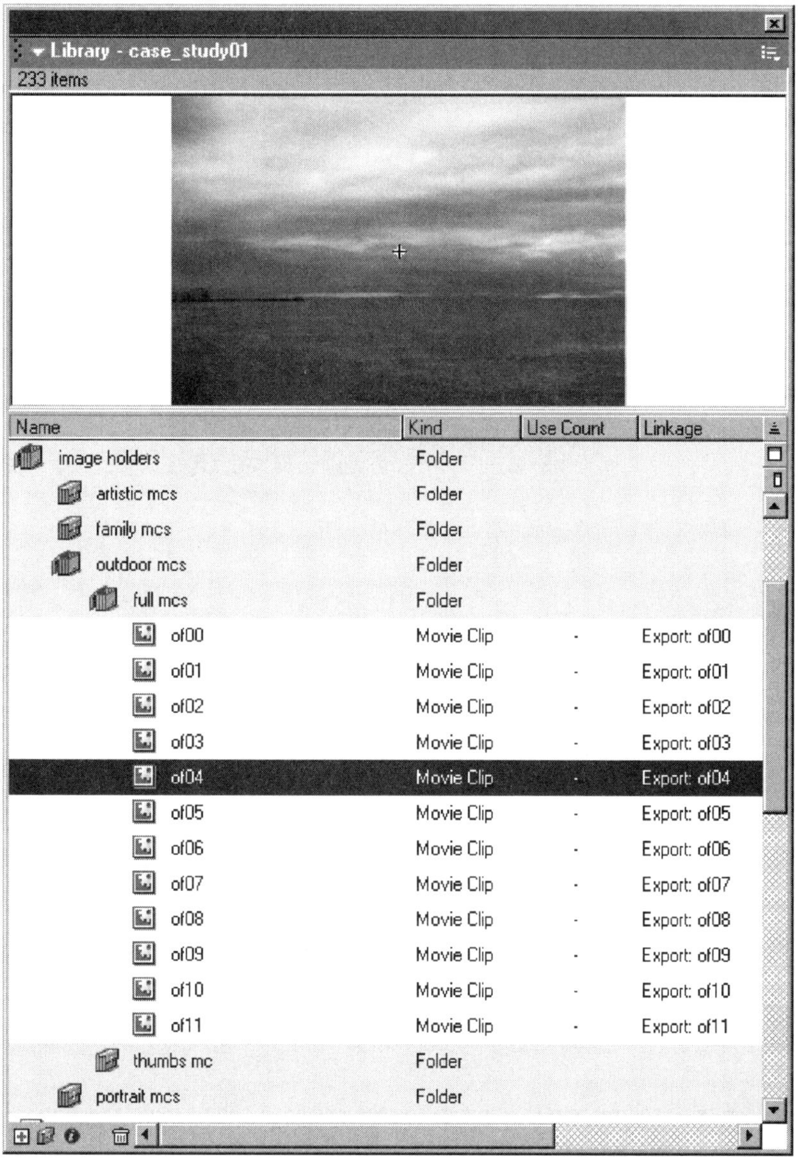

"Each of the photo movie clips has a central registration point and a linkage name identical to the symbol name. The linkage and symbol names are constructed of two letters and a zero-based number. The letters are the first letter of the category name, and either 'f' for full-size or 't' for thumbnail.

"These linkage names are stored in the arrays. As you might remember from the last class, the information for each of the photos is stored in a multidimensional array. The data for the portraits category looks like this:

```
portraits = new Array ();
portraits[0] = ["013", "pt00", "pf00",
➥          "Untitled (2001)", "Study of a body."];
portraits[1] = ["014", "pt01", "pf01",
➥          "Beth", "Life Study with Beth."];
portraits[2] = ["015", "pt02", "pf02",
➥          "Look Closer", "Study of an eye."];
portraits[3] = ["016", "pt03", "pf03",
➥          "Gabi", "Turn on, tune in, drop out."];
portraits[4] = ["017", "pt04", "pf04",
➥          "Stretch", "Gabi in relaxed pose."];
portraits[5] = ["018", "pt05", "pf05",
➥          "Jasper", "Close-up of Jasper."];
portraits[6] = ["019", "pt06", "pf06",
➥          "Rachel", "Head shot of Rachel."];
portraits[7] = ["020", "pt07", "pf07",
➥          "Rachel II", "Rachel shoe gazes."];
portraits[8] = ["021", "pt08", "pf08",
➥          "Katy", "B&W photograph of Katy."];
portraits[9] = ["022", "pt09", "pf09",
➥          "Amsterdam", "Katy in red coat."];
portraits[10] = ["023", "pt10", "pf10",
➥          "Rebecca", "Close-up of Becky."];
portraits[11] = ["024", "pt11", "pf11",
➥          "David", "Portrait of David."];
```

"Each subarray has five elements: a unique index number, a thumbnail linkage reference, the linkage name of the full-size image, the photo name (which is also used for the tooltip rollover), and a description of the photograph.

"First, we're going to make a few changes to the previous grid drawing code, and we're going to use one of these array elements: the thumbnail linkage reference."

The drawGrid function

"Now that you have knowledge of functions, you can go ahead and program the category tabs, redrawing the grid for the new category selection," I continued. "The only parameter required in the function, therefore, is the newly selected category. Our previous grid drawing code after the initialization looked like this:

```
count = 0;

for (i=0; i<rows; i++) {
     for (j=0; j<columns; j++) {
          frame = _root.attachMovie("slideFrame",
➥                                  "slideFrame"+count, count);
          frame._x = ((frame._width+gap)*j)+startx;
          frame._y = ((frame._height+gap)*i)+starty;
          //
          thumb = frame.attachMovie(artistic[count][1],
➥                             artistic[count][1]+count, count);
          count++;
     }
}
```

"Working this into a function really isn't that difficult, because most of the code doesn't need changing at all. The main change to be made is to the line where the thumbnail is attached. This line is currently calling an instance from the artistic category array, whereas this is where the thumbnail linkage names should be called. Let's make the relevant changes now."

Redrawing the grid

1. If you haven't done so already, open the movie `case_study01.fla`.

2. Select the keyframe on the actions layer and open the Actions panel.

3. Locate the grid drawing code in its entirety (it should be around line 71):

```
// grid initialization
rows = 4;
columns = 3;
gap = 5;
startx = 98;
starty = 228;
count = 0;
for (i=0; i<rows; i++) {
    for (j=0; j<columns; j++) {
        frame = _root.attachMovie("slideFrame",
➥                                  "slideFrame"+count, count);
        frame._x = ((frame._width+gap)*j)+startx;
        frame._y = ((frame._height+gap)*i)+starty;
        //
        thumb = frame.attachMovie(artistic[count][1],
➥                           artistic[count][1]+count, count);
        count++;
    }
}
```

4. Rewrite the code as follows:

```
// grid initialization
rows = 4;
columns = 3;
gap = 5;
startx = 98;
starty = 228;
// grid drawing function
drawGrid = function (category) {
    var category;
    count = 0;
    for (i=0; i<rows; i++) {
        for (j=0; j<columns; j++) {
            frame = _root.attachMovie("slideFrame",
➥                              "slideFrame"+count, count+10);
            frame._x = ((frame._width+gap)*j)+startx;
            frame._y = ((frame._height+gap)*i)+starty;
            //
```

```
                    thumb = frame.attachMovie(category[count][1],
➥                           category[count][1]+count, count);
                    count++;
               }
          }
     };
```

5. Below this code, add the following function call:

```
drawGrid (artistic);
```

6. Test the movie. A grid for the artistic category will be drawn, but as yet the category tabs will still not work.

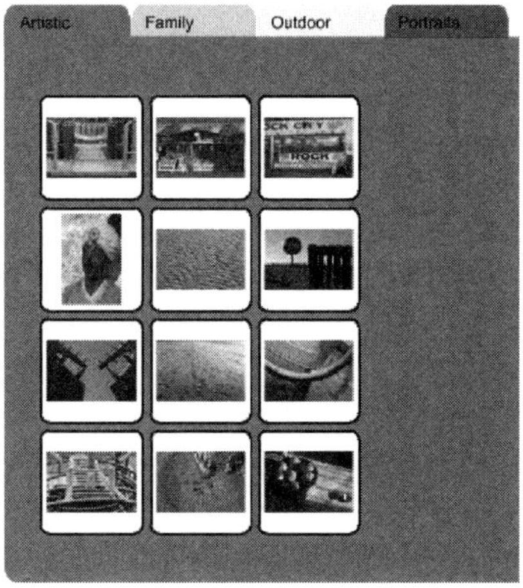

7. Locate the tab code, which looks like this (line 59):

```
redtab.tabButton.onRelease = function() {
     this._parent.swapDepths(500);
};
greentab.tabButton.onRelease = function() {
     this._parent.swapDepths(500);
};
yellowtab.tabButton.onRelease = function() {
     this._parent.swapDepths(500);
};
bluetab.tabButton.onRelease = function() {
     this._parent.swapDepths(500);
};
```

8. Update this section of code to look like the following:

```
redtab.tabButton.onRelease = function() {
    this._parent.swapDepths(1);
    drawGrid (artistic);
};
greentab.tabButton.onRelease = function() {
    this._parent.swapDepths(1);
    drawGrid (family);
};
yellowtab.tabButton.onRelease = function() {
    this._parent.swapDepths(1);
    drawGrid (outdoor);
};
bluetab.tabButton.onRelease = function() {
    this._parent.swapDepths(1);
    drawGrid (portraits);
};
```

9. Test the movie again. This time, changing a category will redraw the appropriate grid.

"Okay, we've done a few things here that need to be covered," I said. "First, we changed the grid drawing code a little to create a function.

"We did this so that the function can be called at different times in the movie, rather than just at the start of it. By passing the newly selected photo category to the function, we can specify which array of data to use to draw the grid. The array to use is passed in to the category parameter. On this line:

```
thumb = frame.attachMovie(category[count][1],
➥                        category[count][1]+count, count);
```

"the category parameter is referenced in multidimensional array format. `count` here represents the photo number, from 0 to 11, and the following `1` in brackets fetches the thumbnail linkage name from that photograph's record. Remember that arrays are zero-based, therefore `1` here is the second array element.

"If we assume that `category` is set to outdoor and `count` is 3, a reading of `category [count][1]` would give us the following:

```
outdoor[3] = ["028", "ot03", "of03", "Swirls",
➥             "Trails and shapes drawn in the sand."];
```

"You might also notice that count is included within the function and is away from the other initialization variables. Whereas the rest of these variables are constants—they won't change—count needs to be reset every time the function is called. This is because each new grid will replace the depths of the previous one and overwrite it."

"Why has the depth of each new slideFrame increased?" asked Joe.

"Isn't it so the grid is always at a higher depth than the tabs?" suggested Jim. "This would explain why we lowered the swapDepths level for each of the buttons to 1."

"That's a perfect answer, Jim," I said. "By using count+10, we ensure that the lowest slideFrame instance is never less than 10. If we limit the tabs to a depth of 1, this means that they can never go above any of the grid elements. Remember that we don't need to increase the depth of the thumbnails because they're contained within the slideFrame instances hierarchy.

"The only remaining thing to cover is how each of the tab buttons calls the function with a different category. As you might have guessed from running the movie, the tabs in order represent artistic, family, outdoor, and portraits. Each button therefore calls the function, passing its own particular category as the argument. This then creates the illusion of the different tabs changing the image category."

Programming events for the thumbnails

"However, before I get you too excited, we still have thumbnails that don't do anything," I said. "All of the promised features for them, such as clicking to show the full-size image and a tooltip rollover, haven't even been started yet. In this part of the class, we'll program the events for the thumbnails as we talked about many weeks ago.

"First, let's remind ourselves of the events for each thumbnail." I wrote the events on the board:

```
thumbnail.onRollover {
    show tooltip;
}
thumbnail.onRollout {
    hide tooltip;
}
thumbnail.onRelease {
    show fullsize photo;
    show photo information;
}
```

"How much of this are we going to do in today's class?" Carl asked.

"All of it," I said. Carl gulped. "Don't be scared—we've covered all the relevant concepts already. Now we just need to get down to doing the hard work. We'll start by programming the tooltips."

Tooltips

"As we discussed in previous classes, the tooltips will appear on thumbnail rollover and disappear on rollout. The information displayed within the tooltips will be the image name—the fourth element of the array.

```
outdoor[3] = ["028", "ot03", "of03", "Swirls",
➥              "Trails and shapes drawn in the sand."];
```

"The magic of the tooltips comes down to an attached movie clip containing a dynamic text field. When a thumbnail is rolled over, the tooltip movie clip is attached and positioned according to the mouse, and the dynamic text field within it is set."

Creating tooltips

1. With the previous movie still open, create a new movie clip symbol called **tooltip**.

2. Within the new movie clip, create a dynamic text field with the instance name `tooltipText`. Switch **Show Border Around Text** on, switch **Selectable** off, and **Center Justify** it. Ensure your text field is placed just below the center of the stage.

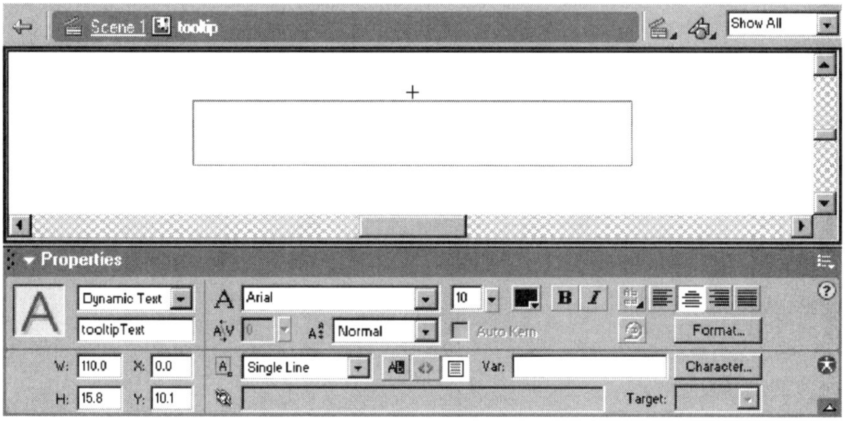

Also make sure that the font size is fairly small and the font color is black.

3. Now open the Linkage dialog box for **tooltip** and give it an Identifier of `libraryTooltip`.

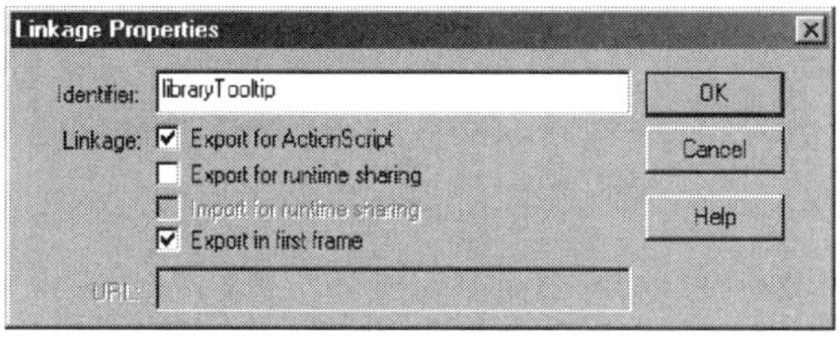

4. On the main timeline, open the Actions panel for the actions layer. Before any of the grid code (line 58), type the following:

```
// tooltips function
registerTooltip = function(photoCategory, photoCount){
    var photoCategory;
    var photoCount;
    this.onRollOver = function(){
        tooltip = _root.attachMovie("libraryTooltip",
➥                                 "libraryTooltip", 2000);
        tooltip.tooltipText.text =
➥                             photoCategory[photoCount][3];
```

```
            tooltip.tooltipText.backgroundColor = "0xFFFF00";
            tooltip.tooltipText._width =
➥                   tooltip.tooltipText.textWidth+(10);
            tooltip._x = _root._xmouse+(10);
            tooltip._y = _root._ymouse+(10);
        };
        this.onRollOut = function() {
            removeMovieClip (tooltip);
        };
    };
```

5. Locate the grid code (line 97) and add the following new line as follows:

```
    drawGrid = function (category) {
        var category;
        count = 0;
        for (i=0; i<rows; i++) {
            for (j=0; j<columns; j++) {
                frame = _root.attachMovie("slideFrame",
➥                             "slideFrame"+count, count+10);
                frame._x = ((frame._width+gap)*j)+startx;
                frame._y = ((frame._height+gap)*i)+starty;
                //
                thumb = frame.attachMovie(category[count][1],
➥                                  "thumbnail"+count, count);
              registerTooltip.apply (thumb,[category,count]);
                count++;
            }
        }
    };
```

6. Now test the movie. Run your cursor over and off any of the thumbnails in the grid.

"There's a lot more code in this function than you're normally used to seeing, so let's run through it in small chunks," I said.

"First, there's the function declaration. The two parameters here correspond to values in the `drawGrid` function. If you remove the word 'photo' from the start of either of them, you'll probably guess which variables they match up with.

"The next couple of lines set `photoCategory` and `photoCount` as local variables. The next line sets up the `onRollOver` event for `this`. Although we don't have a handle on what `this` is just now, it refers to the most current thumbnail. I'll talk more about this in a moment.

"The event handler code does a number of vital things. First, a copy of the tooltip movie clip is attached to the `_root` timeline and is set at a depth of 2000."

"Here we go again with the high depths!" Mazzy said. "What made you choose 2000 this time?"

"I know it's the very highest depth on the _root depth hierarchy," I said. "If all these different depths are troubling you, Mazzy, feel free to write the used depths down. In larger projects than this, with many objects requiring their own airspace, it's definitely worth keeping a note or planning out your depth hierarchy beforehand."

"It's a little like air-traffic control," Gemma said. "It feels like everything is going for the highest level."

"You can all rest easy from now on," I said. "This is the highest level I'm going to reach in this case study. If you see me going higher, please try to flag me down at 35,000 feet.

"Now, where was I?" I pondered. "Oh yeah, the next line of code might look familiar to you. This sets the dynamic text field within the newly attached instance to output a value pulled from the multidimensional array.

```
tooltip.tooltipText.text =
➥                        photoCategory[photoCount][3];
```

"First, photoCategory is used to reference the current image category array. Next, photoCount reads the current image number. Finally, 3 references the name field of the array: the fourth array element. For example, if photoCategory is artistic and photoCount is set to 5, then we'd be looking at this field:

```
artistic[5] = ["006", "at05", "af05",
➥                      "Disco on the Beachfront",
➥                      "A giant mirror ball on the shore."];
```

"This is very similar to how we fetch the thumbnail linkage name," Mazzy said. "The most difficult thing to remember is what the number in the last set of brackets represents."

"Just open the code and take a look at the arrays, Mazzy," I replied, "and remember that arrays start counting from zero! You can't really go wrong then." Mazzy nodded. "The next line of code uses the backgroundColor property of text fields to change it to a yellow color."

"Aha, you've used the hex value of yellow," Mazzy said. "I can tell you what color a hex value translates to like that." Mazzy snapped her fingers.

Before Carl had a chance to take her up on that offer, I continued. "The next line of code sets the `_width` of the text field to a little larger than the `textWidth` property. Although this might sound confusing, without it the text field wouldn't be large enough to accommodate all of the text lengths. The `_width` and `textWidth` properties are very different, with the former representing the physical width of the text field and `textWidth` equal to the physical length of the actual text."

"I get it," Jim said. "You're making the text box as wide as the actual text. Adding 10 pixels to it will make it a comfortable fit, I presume."

"Correct, Jim," I said. "Remember also that we set the dynamic text field to be center justified, so the extra space is shared to the sides of the text field.

"The last two lines of code here position the tooltip using the `_xmouse` and `_ymouse` properties. These properties represent the cursor's x and y screen coordinates and are useful when programming games or interactive movies. When used with `_root`, the coordinates are read from the top left of the stage. Ten pixels are added to both these values to position the tooltip a little away from the cursor." I drew on the board to illustrate. "This will prevent the tooltip from being obscured by the mouse cursor.

"The last bit of code in this function sets up the `onRollOut` event and its handler. The handler here uses the `removeMovieClip` method to delete the tooltip instance. This then concludes all the code for the function—we've now set up both the rollover and rollout events for each of the thumbnails.

"The last remaining bit of code to cover is that which calls the function. This line was added to the `drawGrid` function:

```
registerTooltip.apply (thumb, [category,count]);
```

"This function call is a little different from any we've done before, because the `apply` method is used. The benefit of using it is that the assigned instance—`thumb` here—becomes `this` throughout the running of the function. In the tooltip function, `this` is used for both events, making each of the thumbnails into buttons with rollover and rollout code.

"With apply, the arguments are passed to the tooltips function in square brackets. The required parameters for apply look like this:

```
function.apply (instance to become 'this',
➥                    [arguments to pass to function, …]);
```

> *The call method works in a very similar way to the apply method. Both are located in the reference panel* ***Objects > Core > Functions > Methods****.*

"Now that we've got our tooltips working, we can go ahead and program the remaining event for the thumbnails: the main image viewing.

"The last event for the thumbnails is an onRelease event. When the user clicks a thumbnail, the full size version of the image is displayed on the right side of the screen. As with each of the thumbnails, the full-size linkage name is called from the multidimensional array. Let's take a look at how this is done."

Displaying the full-size image and image information

1. Return to the keyframe where the code has been written so far and add the following function after the registerTooltip function (at about line 74):

```
showLargePhoto = function (photoCategory, photoCount){
    this.onRelease = function() {
        fullsize = _root.attachMovie(
➥                  photoCategory[photoCount][2],
➥                  photoCategory[photoCount][2], 1000);
        fullsize._x = 550;
        fullsize._y = 360;
    };
};
```

2. Add the following line of code to the drawGrid function where shown:

```
drawGrid = function (category) {
    var category;
    count = 0;
    for (i=0; i<rows; i++) {
        for (j=0; j<columns; j++) {
            frame = _root.attachMovie("slideFrame",
➥                  "slideFrame"+count, count+10);
            frame._x = ((frame._width+gap)*j)+startx;
            frame._y = ((frame._height+gap)*i)+starty;
            //
            thumb = frame.attachMovie(
➥                      category[count][1],
➥                      "thumbnail"+count, count);
            registerTooltip.apply(thumb,
➥                              [category, count]);
            showLargePhoto.apply(thumb,
➥                              [category, count]);
            count++;
        }
    }
};
```


3. Test the movie and the main image will be displayed when you click a thumbnail.

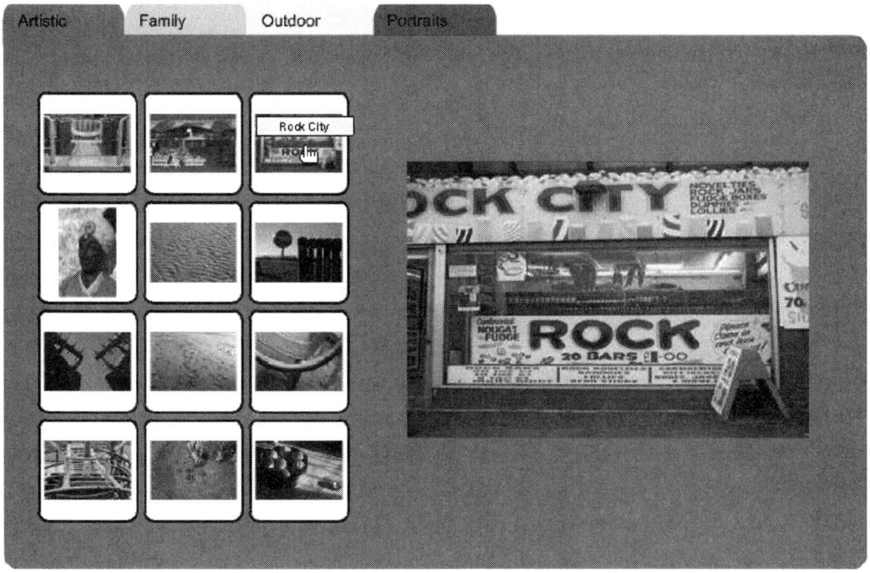

The next thing to do is to add the dynamic text fields to display the image name and the image description.

4. Create a new movie clip symbol called **name textbox** and insert a dynamic text field that is 350x20 pixels in size. Give it the instance name `nameText`, center justify it, and set the font size to 14. Use the Info panel to make sure its registration point is central, and zero its x and y settings.

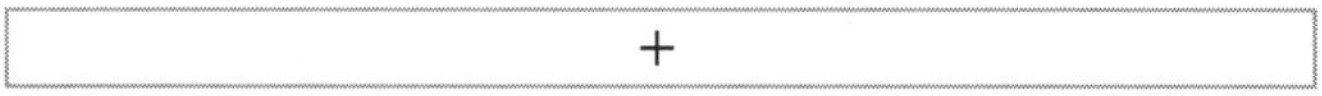

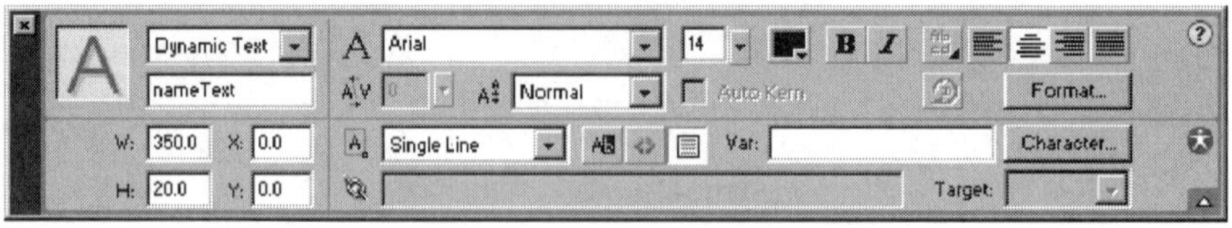

5. Position an instance of name textbox on the stage in the main timeline at an x position of 550 and a y position of 160. Give it the instance name `name`.

6. Create another new movie clip symbol called **description textbox**. As with the last symbol, insert a dynamic text field with an instance name of `descriptionText`. Give it the same properties but a height of 50 and change its type to **Multiline**. Center its registration point and zero its x and y position.

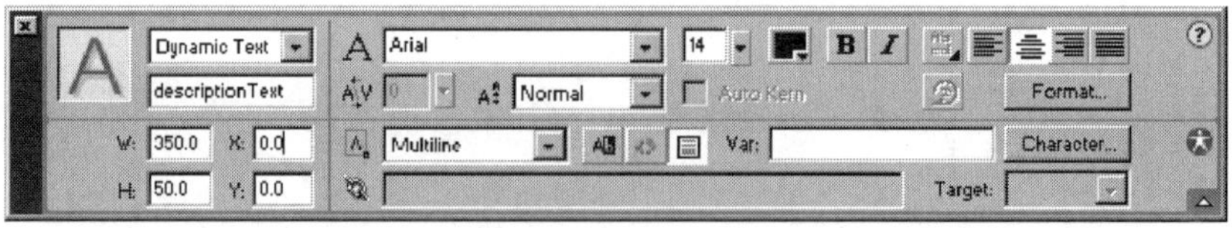

7. Position an instance of description textbox on the main stage at an x position of 550 and a y position of 560. Give it the instance name `description`.

8. Add the following code to the `showLargePhoto` function (line 79):

```
showLargePhoto = function (photoCategory, photoCount){
    this.onRelease = function() {
        fullsize = _root.attachMovie(
➥                photoCategory[photoCount][2],
➥                photoCategory[photoCount][2], 1000);
        fullsize._x = 550;
        fullsize._y = 360;
        _root.name.nameText.text = "#"
➥                  + photoCategory[photoCount][0]+" "
➥                  + photoCategory[photoCount][3];
        _root.description.descriptionText.text =
➥                  photoCategory[photoCount][4];
    };
};
```


9. Now add the following two lines at the bottom of all the code:

```
_root.name.swapDepths (2);
_root.description.swapDepths (3);
```

10. Add the following code where shown (about line 124):

```
clearTextBoxes = function () {
    _root.name.nameText.text  = "";
    _root.description.descriptionText.text = "";
}
aboutButton.onRelease = function() {
    page = _root.attachMovie("aboutPage",
➥                          "aboutPage", 1000);
    page._x = 552;
    page._y = 362;
    clearTextBoxes();
};
contactButton.onRelease = function() {
    page = _root.attachMovie("contactPage",
➥                          "contactPage", 1000);
    page._x = 552;
    page._y = 362;
    clearTextBoxes();
};
```

11. Test the movie:

#35 Florence
A view of the beautiful city of Florence.

"Okay, let's start by looking at the `showLargePhoto` function," I said. "The general purpose of this is to give an `onRelease` event to each of the thumbnails. As with the tooltip function, this requires two parameters, `photoCategory` and `photoCount`. These are used on the third line of code to fetch and attach the full-size image linkage name. The depth 1000 is used here to coordinate with the depth of the About and Contact pages. The last two lines of the function then position the image in the correct place.

"As before, the line added to the `drawGrid` function uses the `apply` method to call the function. The function and this line alone are enough to display the full-size image. The rest of the code and actions that we followed activate the text fields to display the image information.

"After we set up the text box movie clips, a couple of lines are added to the `showLargePhoto` function to send the relevant information from the arrays to the text fields. The line setting the `nameText` text field might look a little complicated, but it just uses two bits of data: the index number stored as element 0 of the array and the photo name or element 3. A hyphen character separates these elements.

"The descriptionText text field fetches and shows the description from the array, stored as the last element or 4."

"Why did we change the depth of the two text field instances?" asked Joe.

"Objects placed on the stage have depths below 0, so by adding these swapDepths actions, we make sure that these instances are above the tabs. Simple enough, really," I said.

"Why do we declare a new function at the end?" asked Mazzy.

"The clearTextBoxes function is just used to clear the nameText and descriptionText boxes. This is necessary when either the About or Contact pages are called up; otherwise, the text fields would still be visible onscreen. The function simply sets both fields to empty strings. A function call to this is placed in both the About and Contact button event code. Remove one of these function calls and try the movie."

"I think it's all coming together," Gemma said. "We've really shifted along this week."

"I've noticed one thing that we appear to have overlooked," Carl said. "When I click an image to display it, and then change to another category, the image from the last category sticks. It doesn't feel right."

"I've noticed that too," Jim agreed. "Can we make a change somewhere, Ken?"

"Yes we can," I said. "The most logical and immediate option seems to be to set a default image for each category. That way, when the user changes category, he or she sees the default image of the new category."

"How about a random image selection?" suggested Carl.

"Whichever way we choose, it will have to wait until next week, I'm afraid," I said. "We've quickly run out of time for today. You're all free to go, class. I'll see you all next week."

Summary

In this lesson, you learned about functions. You discovered that functions, like variables, act as containers for things you're likely to want to use more than once; in this case, functions act as containers for code. You learned how functions can help you to organize your programs, breaking each task down into smaller subtasks and reusing sets of commands whenever you need to.

You saw two different ways to declare a function:

- `callbackFunction = function() { commands in here };`
- `function oldStyleFunction() { commands in here };`

and one way to call a function:

- `functionName();`

You learned that callback functions must always be declared *before* they can be called.

Next, you looked at declaring functions that use parameters to help customize what they do:

- Parameters are variables that can be used inside the body of a function.
- Arguments are values that can be specified when you call a function.
- The values provided as arguments are passed to the function parameters and can then be used by the function code to determine what it should do.

You also saw how to return values from functions, and you spent some time adding some function-based features to the case study.

In the next lesson, you'll concentrate on the statistics report page for Randy's website, and you'll learn (among other things) how to detect keystrokes and collect data on the site.

Class 10
The Statistics Report

Objectives

In today's class, you'll cover

- Using keyboard listeners, which enable Flash to detect keyboard input and deal with it accordingly
- Adding a login box to the kiosk project case study
- Creating a statistics page to keep track of how many times each photo has been looked at
- Sorting the statistics so they're presented in the most useful way

Introduction

I welcomed the students to the class. "We're getting closer," I told them. "The end is in sight now, but we've still got a lot to learn. All I ask is that you keep your concentration levels up to carry you through these last few lessons.

"We've got our arrays in place and our images working, and that's almost our entire customer front-end done. Today, we'll be focusing the majority of our attention on building the statistics report page for Randy and covering his side of the operation. Can anyone remember how we said that Randy would access the statistics report?" I asked.

"Using the keyboard to enter a password," said Mazzy.

"That's correct," I responded. "So far, we've used the mouse for all of our interaction, but it's time to find out how to get the keyboard to respond to our touch."

Keyboard listeners

"The keyboard is different from the mouse in one important way: the mouse interacts with objects on the stage, but the keyboard does not," I started. "The way that we can get around this in Flash is to use **listeners**. A listener is an object that listens for something, whether a key press, a text entry, or a selection.

"In our case study we need Flash to listen for a key press. Once it detects the key press, then it behaves much like a button would, and we can give it actions through an `on...` action.

"Let's look at what we want to do. When we detect a key press, we want to bring up a login box that Randy can type a password into. We'll then check this password, and if it's right then we'll go through to the statistics screen. If the password is wrong, then we'll simply close the login box and go back to waiting for a key press.

"Okay, looking back at that structure, we can immediately see that waiting for a key press occurs twice, and we learned last week what to do with code that we'll be using more than once . . .?"

"Put it in a function!" the class responded in unison.

"Ah, you're thinking like programmers now," I said, smiling. "Open the case study that you saved last week and scroll to the bottom of the code."

I waited for the students to open the file before continuing. "First things first, create a new function called `loginListener`:

```
loginListener = function () {
```

"As I mentioned earlier, the listener is an `Object`, so before you can use it, you need to create a new instance of it. You do this by simply defining it as a new object, like so:

```
login = new Object();
```

"Note that you haven't defined this as a listener anywhere yet. What you're using here is the confusingly named **`Object` object**. To put it simply, the `Object` object is just a blank object template. You create your object using this template, and then you register it as a keyboard listener later.

"This sounds a little backward, but it will all become clear when you see it in action. The advantage of creating your listeners this way is that because they're all registered with Flash when they're created, whenever a key is pressed, Flash can set off all of the key listeners at once.

"Just as you used an `onRelease` event handler to check for a button press, you'll use an `onKeyUp` event to listen for a key press. You do this in exactly the same way as you did for your button callbacks, like so:

```
login.onKeyUp = function() {
```

"For the time being, you'll just put a `trace` action in there to make sure it works, so complete your callback like this:

```
login.onKeyUp = function() {
    trace("Key press detected.");
};
```

"Next, you have to register your object as a listener. You do this using a method of the **`Key`** object. The method speaks for itself and is written like this:

```
Key.addListener(login);
```

"Finally, you just need to finish off the function with a closing brace and—"

"It doesn't work!" exclaimed Carl.

"What doesn't work, Carl?" I asked.

"I'm pressing keys left, right, and center, but it's not doing anything," said Carl.

"What's not doing anything?" I asked.

"The function, what else would it be?" asked Carl, growing slightly irate.

"And how do you make a function work, Carl?" I asked.

"By calling it, of course . . . Ah," Carl said.

"That's right, Carl, if you'd let me finish my sentence, the last thing that you need to do is call the function," I said. "The completed code should look like this:

```
loginListener = function () {
    login = new Object();
    login.onKeyUp = function() {
        trace("Key press detected.");
    };
    Key.addListener(login);
};
loginListener();
```

"Now if you run the code, you—"

"It works now. Sorry about disturbing you earlier, Ken, it's running beautifully now," interrupted Carl.

"Think nothing of it, Carl," I said. "Where was I? Oh yes—now if you run the code, you should be able to see the result of your hard work. When you press any key, you should see this in the Output window:

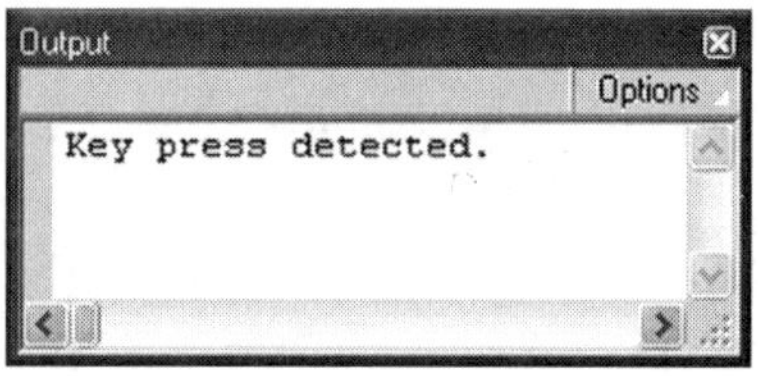

"Okay, that's the initial coding done. Now you need to create a login box that you can attach when a key is pressed."

Creating a login box

1. The login box will just contain a space for entering the password, so create a new movie clip symbol and call it **pword**.

2. While you're there, click the **Advanced** button, and you'll see that this brings up some more options. Check the **Export for ActionScript** box as well to give it the linkage name `pword` so that you can attach it with your key press.

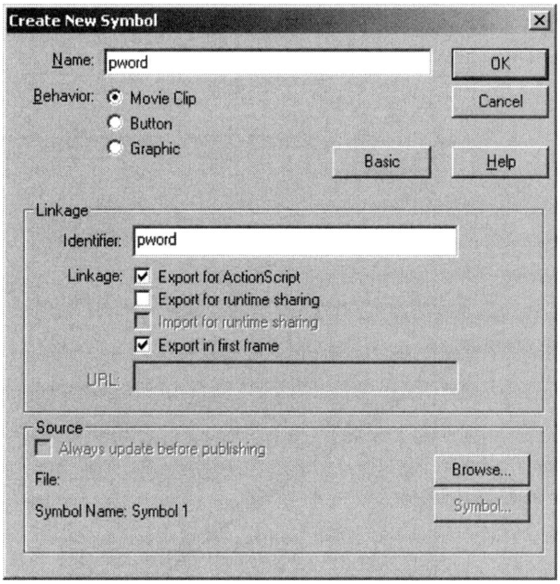

3. The first things that you need for your box are a simple rectangle for a background and a static text field that simply says something like "Please Enter Password":

10

4. Make sure that you center the box on the screen with the Align panel, and then position the text appropriately. Keep it in the top half of the box, as you'll be putting the password entry field in the bottom half.

5. Flash comes with a built-in password option for text fields that will make everything that's typed into them show as asterisks. To take advantage of this feature, you first need to create an input text field below your static text:

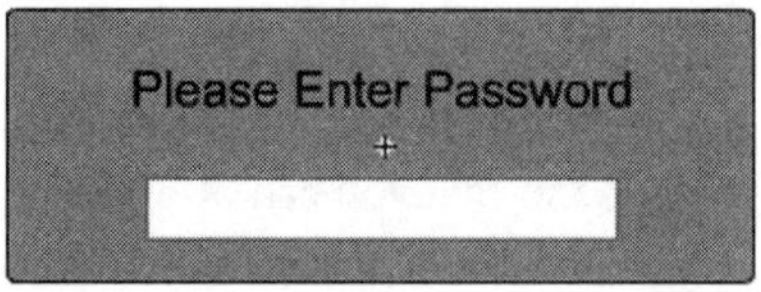

6. Use the Property inspector to show a border around the text, and then change the **Line Type** box to set the text field as a password.

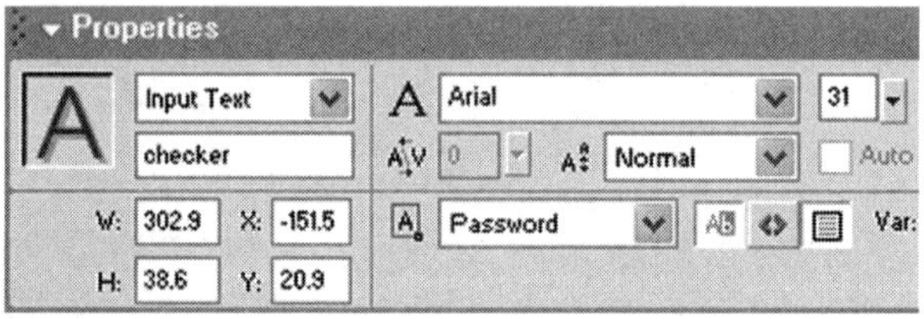

7. You also want to give the text field an instance name so that you can check what's written in it. Give it the name `checker`.

8. You're now ready to add the login box into your code. You just need to attach it, give it a high enough depth to ensure it's at the top, and then position it in the middle of the screen.

```
loginListener = function () {
    login = new Object();
    login.onKeyUp = function() {
        _root.attachMovie("pword", "pword", 9999);
        pword._x = 400;
        pword._y = 300;
    };
    Key.addListener(login);
};
loginListener();
```

9. If you now run the program, you should see the login box appear when you press a key. You can then click in the text field and type in your password. Play around with it and tell me what you find.

The students finished typing and ran their programs, but their looks of anticipation soon turned to confusion.

"I don't understand . . ."

"Why won't it . . .?"

"Stupid machine!"

I called out over their consternation, "Mazzy, can you tell me what's happening?"

"Certainly," Mazzy replied, "the login box is appearing but it won't let me type anything. Actually, that's not quite true, I see a brief flash of an asterisk, but then it's gone and I need to click in the box again. This just goes on ad nauseam."

"Okay," I said, "you've actually given quite a good description there. You mentioned seeing an asterisk flash and then having to click the box again before you can type. What does that tell you? Any ideas, Joe?"

"It feels like the box is being reset whenever I press a key," said Joe.

"Okay, Joe, stop there. I think you just identified the problem," I said. Joe looked puzzled for a moment, but then a realization hit him. "I see what you're getting at—the listener is still listening, so whenever a key is pressed, a new login box is attached."

"You're right, Joe" I said. "With this in mind, " I continued, "it follows that you need to turn off your listener. You do this by using another self-explanatory method of the `Key` object:

```
Key.removeListener(login);
```

10. Put this method inside your onKeyUp event so that as soon as a key press is detected, Flash stops listening and you're free to type a password. Try it now if you like. Your code should look like this now.

```
loginListener = function () {
     login = new Object();
     login.onKeyUp = function() {
          _root.attachMovie("pword", "pword", 9999);
          pword._x = 400;
          pword._y = 300;
          Key.removeListener(login);
     };
     Key.addListener(login);
};
loginListener();
```

When the students had finished testing their programs, I continued. "Now that you're free to type what you like, you need some way of telling Flash that you've finished typing and that you're ready for it to check the password you've entered.

"You could do this with a button that the user could click to indicate that he or she has finished, but I think it's more natural for people to press ENTER when they've finished typing something. You already know how to listen for any key, but you don't yet know how to check to see which key it was. I think it's time for another function.

11. Call this one enterListener, and put it straight after the loginListener function. The way that you check for a key is to look at every key that's pressed and see if that was the right one. Your function, then, starts very similarly to the last one:

```
enterListener = function () {
enterCheck = new Object();
enterCheck.onKeyUp = function() {
```

"You create a new function, then create a new object that you'll use as a listener, and begin its onKeyUp event. This is where you start to see a difference. You need to test if a pressed key was the ENTER key. Jim, what's the best way to check a condition in Flash?"

"With an if statement," he replied instantly. "That's correct," I continued. "Okay, has anybody heard of **ASCII** before?"

"ActionScript Code Is Impossible?" suggested Carl.

"Not quite," I smiled. "It actually stands for American Standard Code for Information Interchange, but that's not really important for us. What is important is to know that each character you can produce on a keyboard—well, almost all of them, technically it's only the first 127—has its own unique ASCII value.

"It's important to remember that ASCII values are for specific characters, and this means that there is a different value for a capital letter or a regular letter. Here are a few ASCII values for an example." I wrote on the board:

k = 107

K = 75

6 = 54

"Flash has another way of detecting which key is pressed, though: it can use **key codes**. The difference between the two is that key codes report back which *key* has been pressed, and ASCII values report on which *character* has been produced."

I could see a few furrowed brows around the class, so I explained further.

"Although this may initially sound like they'd be the same, they're not. For one thing, most keys can produce more than one character."

Pointing at the codes I'd just written on the whiteboard, I continued, "Look at the codes here for a lowercase k and an uppercase K. As you can see, the ASCII codes for uppercase letters are different from those for lowercase letters. With key codes, these values are the same because you use the same key to produce both characters. Another difference comes with different keyboard layouts."

"Like the difference between Mac and PC keyboards?" asked Gemma. "It sometimes takes me ages to find the right key on these bizarre PC devices."

"You're right, Gemma" I laughed. "But enough of the Mac snobbery—I don't want a war to break out! Anyway, the problem isn't just to do with which platform you're using. Laptop keyboards are often different from full-size keyboards, and the same goes for keyboards in different languages. You know, they sometimes have 'bizarre' layouts, too." I winked at Gemma and she laughed.

"To help you get through this minefield, you'll find a useful table in the ActionScript Dictionary that loads with Flash MX. Go to **Help > ActionScript Dictionary** to open it."

> *There are many online lists of ASCII codes, including* `www.gh-gold.co.uk/asciicodes.asp`.

"That's a relief," muttered Mazzy, loud enough to make everyone chuckle.

"Luckily for us all, Mazzy," I said, "we don't need to know these values by heart or carry a key code chart around with us in our wallets. Flash has an easier way of checking for the most common keys—instead of a value, we can just specify which key it is in English.

"For example, to check for the ENTER key, we'd look for `Key.ENTER`, to check for the SPACEBAR we'd look for `Key.SPACE`, and so on. I've also included a list of these on your handout. It's worth remembering, though, that you can use these only in place of key codes, so if you want to use ASCII values, then you'll just have to carry that chart around with you.

12. The way to report which key has been pressed is to use another method of the `Key` object. To report the ASCII value, you use `Key.getAscii()`, and to report the key code, you use `Key.getCode()`. You'll be using the latter because you're using the word rather than the value. Your `if` condition, then, will look something like this:

```
if (Key.getCode() == Key.ENTER) {
```

13. Finish off the function with a trace action so you can see if everything's working. Don't forget to add the listener at the end of the function like this:

```
enterListener = function () {
    enterCheck = new Object();
    enterCheck.onKeyUp = function() {
        if (Key.getCode() == Key.ENTER) {
            trace("Enter key pressed.");
        }
    };
    Key.addListener(enterCheck);
};
```

14. You'll also need to put a call to this function into the `loginListener` script:

```
loginListener = function () {
```

```
        login = new Object();
        login.onKeyUp = function() {
            _root.attachMovie("pword", "pword", 9999);
            pword._x = 400;
            pword._y = 300;
            Key.removeListener(login);
            enterListener();
        };
        Key.addListener(login);
    };
```

15. You should now be able to run the program, bring up the login box, enter a password, and then press ENTER to tell Flash that the password is ready to be checked.

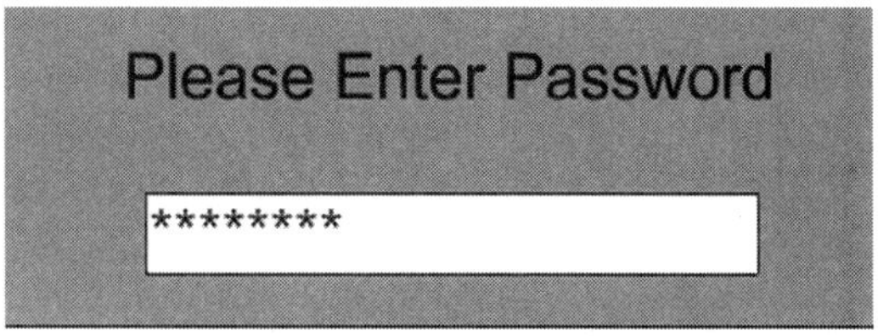

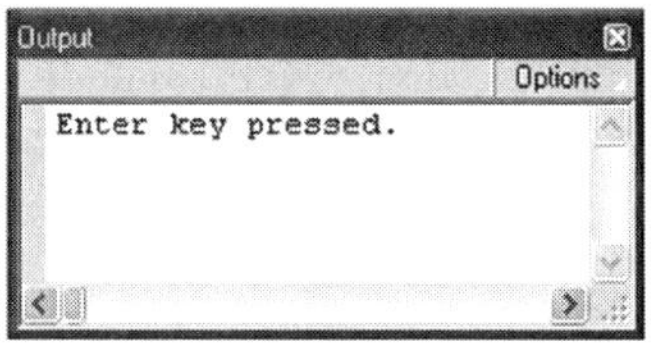

"Okay, you've successfully got the key checks working, so the next thing that you need to do is check the password. You gave your text field an instance name, so you can easily check what has been typed in it by using its `text` property. Again, you only need a simple `if` condition to check for this. For the time being, you'll just use an arbitrary password, and you can change it for Randy later. Mazzy, can you think of anything that might be appropriate?"

"Well, I know that his favorite food is cheese," Mazzy said, "but I'm not sure which cheese is his favorite . . . maybe a piece of old Monterey Jack? He's always telling me about this place called Murray's on Bleecker Street that he goes to get weird, and often moldy, cheeses from." "Okay, okay," I laughed, "that's enough information. We'll just go for 'cheese' for now, shall we?"

16. Put a quick `trace` in there to make sure that your code is working, and while you're there, you may as well add a `trace` to tell you if the password that you've entered is incorrect too. Don't forget that once you've used a `trace` and you're satisfied that it's working, then you can remove it to stop being interrupted by the Output window flashing up when you're testing your movies.

```
if (Key.getCode() == Key.ENTER) {
    if (_root.pword.checker.text == "cheese") {
        trace("Password is correct.");
    } else {
        trace("Password is incorrect.");
    }
}
```

"Your code should look like this now:

```
Key.addListener(enterCheck);
loginListener = function () {
    login = new Object();
    login.onKeyUp = function() {
        _root.attachMovie("pword", "pword", 9999);
        pword._x = 400;
        pword._y = 300;
        Key.removeListener(login);
        enterListener();
    };
    Key.addListener(login);
};
loginListener();
//
enterListener = function () {
    enterCheck = new Object();
    enterCheck.onKeyUp = function() {
if (Key.getCode() == Key.ENTER) {
    if (_root.pword.checker.text == "cheese") {
        trace("Password is correct.");
    } else {
        trace("Password is incorrect.");
    }
}
}
Key.addListener(enterCheck);
};
```

"Run that to make sure that you're happy, and then we'll continue with the code.

17. The next thing that you need to do is tell Flash what to do after a password has been entered. If the password is correct, then you want to close the login box and stop the listener. You then want to run your next function to bring up your stats screen. To remove a movie clip, you just use the `removeMovieClip` method, and you've recently looked at how to stop a listener. You don't yet know what the name of your function will be, so for the time being just put a comment in there. This means that the code, if the password is correct, is as follows:

```
if (_root.pword.checker.text == "cheese") {
    _root.pword.removeMovieClip();
    Key.removeListener(enterCheck);
    // PUT NAME OF STATISTICS FUNCTION HERE
}
```

18. You'll do a similar thing if the password is incorrect, but instead of running the statistics function, you'll just restart the login listener, and the process will begin again. Continue typing after the last piece of code.


```
else {
    _root.pword.removeMovieClip();
    Key.removeListener(enterCheck);
    loginListener();
}
```

19. Add this code to your program, and give it a try to see if it all works as planned. You should be able to go on putting the wrong password in as often as you like, but the program will come to a stop as soon as you enter the correct password.

Creating the statistics screen

"The next thing you need to do is create your statistics screen. The basic background for this will just be a large rectangle—make it 800x600 so it covers the whole screen, and include a title to tell you which page you're on.

1. Create a new movie clip called **statReport**, and choose to give it the same linkage name.

2. Draw a rectangle, use the Property inspector to set it to the correct size, and then create a static text field in the top left to hold the title "Statistics Report". You should have something like this:

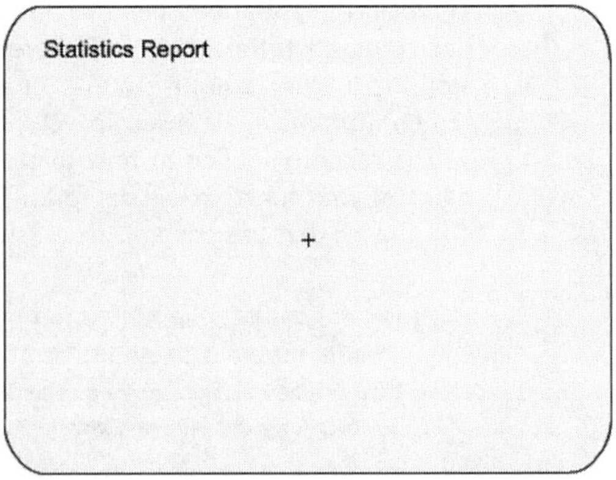

"Okay, that's enough graphics for the time being. Now let's take a look back at the code and see about attaching the report clip.

3. Create a new function called `runStats`. To start off with, you just want to attach the movie clip to the stage and position it. You've done this many times already, so I won't go into it in detail again. The code will look like this:

```
runStats = function () {
    _root.attachMovie("statReport", "statReport", 7000);
    _root.statReport._x = 400;
    _root.statReport._y = 300;
};
```

4. Remember how earlier you left a comment to mark where you'd call your function from in the `enterListener` code? Well, now it's time to go back and replace that comment with a simple `runStats();`function call, like so:

```
if (Key.getCode() == Key.ENTER) {
    if (_root.pword.checker.text == "cheese") {
        _root.pword.removeMovieClip();
        Key.removeListener(enterCheck);
        runStats();
    }
```

5. If you run the code and enter the correct password now, you should see the statistics report screen. Stay there a minute, though, and move your mouse over the screen. You might be surprised to see that every now and then, the cursor changes to a hand, and then back to an arrow, even though there's nothing on the screen:

"Can anyone guess what's happening here?" I asked. "Think about the positions where the cursor changes."

"Is it somehow picking up on our earlier buttons?" Gemma asked. "The cursor seems to change in the same places that they're underneath it."

"That's right," I said, "even though you've placed the new movie clip over the top of the buttons, they're still being picked up by Flash. You'll have to hide them so that Flash can no longer pick them up. You can do this using the movie clip property, **`visible`**. `Visible` is normally set to `true`, but you can set it to `false` to make the movie clip invisible. You want to do this to a number of movie clips, so the neatest way would be to create a new function to hold the code. Let's call it `hideMainButtons`.

6. Basically, all this function wants to do is run through the buttons on the stage and set their visibility to false. For the tabs and the About and Contact buttons, it would look like this:

```
hideMainButtons = function () {
    _root.redtab.tabButton._visible = false;
    _root.bluetab.tabButton._visible = false;
    _root.yellowtab.tabButton._visible = false;
    _root.greentab.tabButton._visible = false;
    _root.aboutButton._visible = false;
    _root.contactButton._visible = false;
};
```

"The last things that you need to hide are the individual thumbnail buttons that are on the stage. You'll do these a little differently, though. You've already written a `drawGrid` function that sets up all of the thumbnails, so instead of hiding them with this function, you'll remove them from the stage, and they can be reapplied by just calling the `drawGrid` function later. You do this with a simple loop.

7. You've already created variables for the number of rows and columns, so you can simply multiply those to find the total number of thumbnail frames on the stage. You then just need to run the loop for that many cycles and remove all of the pictures. The loop looks something like this:

```
for (i=0; i<(rows*columns); i++) {
     _root["slideFrame"+i].removeMovieClip();
}
```

8. You've kept the dynamic naming within square brackets as you saw earlier, meaning that Flash will create the name in the brackets first, and then run the `removeMovieClip` method on that name. Put this loop inside the `hideMainButtons` function, and put a call to the function inside the `runStats` function like so:

```
runStats = function () {
     _root.attachMovie("statReport", "statReport", 7000);
     _root.statReport._x = 400;
     _root.statReport._y = 300;
     _root.hideMainButtons();
};
```

9. Now run the movie, and you should see that the problem with the mouse cursor changing has now disappeared.

"Of course, now that you've hidden the buttons, you'll need to put them back again once Randy's finished with the statistics report. Even though you won't actually be using the function right now, you may as well make it because it's so similar to our function to hide the buttons.

10. Create a new function beneath the last one, and call it `showMainButtons`. All of the main button-hiding code is the same, except that you're setting `visibility` to `true` rather than `false`. The other change is that instead of a loop for the thumbnails, you just need to call your `drawGrid` function like so:

```
showMainButtons = function () {
     _root.redtab.tabButton._visible = true;
     _root.bluetab.tabButton._visible = true;
     _root.yellowtab.tabButton._visible = true;
     _root.greentab.tabButton._visible = true;
     _root.aboutButton._visible = true;
     _root.contactButton._visible = true;
     drawGrid(artistic);
};
```

"You'll be calling this function later on when you've finished with the statistics screen, so for the time being, just leave it here."

Creating the hitArray

"Let's have another think about what kind of statistics we should be providing for Randy," I said. "Mazzy, can you remind me what we said that we'd supply Randy with?"

"Certainly, Ken, just give me a second to find it in my notes," Mazzy replied. "Ah, here we are, it was the number of times each picture had been accessed, the index number for the pictures, their title, and the category that they belong to. We also wanted to be able to order the list by any of the fields except the name."

"Thank you very much," I said. "Okay, what we'll do is make a note of every time that a thumbnail is clicked and add its details into a new array. We can then simply use this array to give us all of our statistics. Let's look back at our code and see where we can fit this new functionality. At the moment, we're not storing any information with our thumbnails, so let's make a change to them so that we can easily find out what we need to know when they're clicked.

"This code is found in the `drawGrid` function, and at the moment, the relevant part of the code looks like this:

```
thumb = frame.attachMovie(category[count][1],
➥ "thumbnail"+count, 1);
registerTooltip.apply(thumb, [category, count]);
showLargePhoto.apply(thumb, [category, count]);
```

"You're going to generate some new variables on each thumbnail as it's created. You'll use these variables to store the index number, title, and category of each image so that you can easily access it when you need it. You'll add these three variables after the `attachMovie` line. The title of the image is the tooltip caption, so you'll name your three variables `index`, `capName`, and `cat`.

1. You're already using your image arrays in the `drawGrid` function, so you can just use the same calls to get your information for the variables. You can check back to your image arrays to make sure that you get the right elements here:

```
drawGrid = function (category, catName) {
     var category;
     count = 0;
     for (i=0; i<rows; i++) {
          for (j=0; j<columns; j++) {
               frame = _root.attachMovie("slideFrame",
➥ "slideFrame"+count, count+10);
               frame._x = ((frame._width+gap)*j)+startx;
               frame._y = ((frame._height+gap)*i)+starty;
               //
               thumb = frame.attachMovie(category[count][1],
➥ "thumbnail"+count, 1);
               thumb.index = category[count][0];
               thumb.capName = category[count][3];
               thumb.cat = catName;
```

"Add a simple trace action for each of these like this, so you can check if they're working."

```
trace(thumb.index);
trace(thumb.capName);
trace(thumb.cat);
```

"Whoa!" said Carl. "Where'd all that stuff come from? There's tons of text here."

"Can you tell me exactly what you see?" I asked.

"Yep, the index number and the title seem to have come out okay, but the category's all over the place," said Carl. "It looks like it contains the whole of the category array rather than just the name of the category."

"That's pretty close," I said. "Can you tell me why you think it's done that?"

"Yeah, I think I know," Carl told me. "Is it because Flash is treating the variable as a link to the array instead of just using the title of it?"

"That's it," I said. "The way that you're going to get around this is to create another variable to store the category name. You'll do this back before the name has been linked to the array, when you call the drawGrid function. Let's look at the first time you call the function:

```
drawGrid(artistic);
```

2. Add another parameter here and pass the same category title as a string and as the category name. So, you'll change the line to look like this:

```
drawGrid(artistic, "artistic");
```

3. You also need to change this for all of the other times that you call the `drawGrid` function. Those times are once for each of the category buttons and once in the `showMainButtons` function that you recently created.

4. Next, you need to change the `drawGrid` function itself to make use of your new parameter. Change the function definition line to this:

```
drawGrid = function (category, catName) {
```

5. `catName` is your new string parameter that holds the category name. You just need to change the variable setting now to use this value instead:

```
thumb.cat = catName;
```


"Okay, once you've done that, try the `trace` again and tell me what you get."

"That's done it," said Jim. "It's working now—all of the variables hold the right values."

"Excellent," I replied. "You might as well remove the `traces` now that they've served their purpose. Okay, what's next? We said that we wanted to add these values to an array whenever a button is clicked. Can anyone tell me where we've already got an `onRelease` event for the thumbnails?"

"I remember," said Jim, "it was in our function to show the large photo. We attached the new photo whenever a thumbnail was clicked." "Right," I said, "let's take a look at that and see what you can do.

6. Right after the callback definition, you'll add a function call. Now, you haven't created the function yet, but you know that it will be checking an array, so call it `checkArray` now and then use the same name when you come to create it in a second.

"You want to pass all of the variables that you've just assigned to each thumbnail to your new function. What do you use to reference values that are on the movie clip that the function is being run from?"

"THIS!" said the students in unison.

7. "That's correct, so your function call will be written like so:"

```
_root.checkArray(this.index, this.capName, this.cat);
```

"Youre simply calling the function that you're about to create and then passing it the values that you've added to each thumbnail."

"Wow," said Carl, "passing values to functions that we haven't created yet. It's future-code!" The class laughed at his comment. "Quite," I replied. "There's no point testing the code yet, because what you've written won't have any visible effect. To do that, you'll have to go ahead and create your `checkArray` function. Let's do that now.

"You'll be creating a new array for this function, so put it immediately underneath your image arrays for the sake of consistency. Before you start coding, you'll want to identify what you're trying to do in this function.

"You need to create a new array to hold the information for all of the thumbnails that have been clicked. You've already got most of the information—the image title, index number, and category—but you still need to store one more thing: the amount of times that the picture has been clicked.

"Okay, as well as storing the number of hits, you need to think of some logic for how you create your array. Jim, can you have a think and let me know what you come up with?"

"All right, Ken," Jim said. "Let's see, we're creating an array from scratch, and we're adding elements to that array for every picture that is clicked. I guess we'll need to have some kind of check in there to see if the picture is already in the array; otherwise, we'd just end up with the same thing loads of times."

"Good," I said, "go on. What do we do if the picture is already in the array?"

"You said we'd be storing a `hits` variable, didn't you?" Jim asked. "In that case, we'd just add one to the `hits` variable of that picture in the array rather than adding a new element containing that picture."

"Not bad at all," I commended him. "Can you sum that up to give us our basic logic structure?"

"Okay," Jim replied, "how about this? If the picture that's just been clicked is already in the array, then add one to its `hits` variable. If it's not there, then add it as a new array element." "That seems pretty sound to me," I said, "hopefully the rest of you followed that?" The students nodded that they had.

8. The first thing that you need to do is create your new array. It's an array to store hits, so call it `hitArray`. The initialization line looks like this:

```
hitArray = new Array();
```


9. You're now ready to create your function. You already know the name of it and which parameters you'll be passing to it, so the first line should be easy:

```
function checkArray(index, capName, cat) {
```

"The next line is a little more complicated, though, as you'll be using a semi-new concept: a **flag**. Rather than being a new ActionScript command, a flag is just a programming term. A flag is a variable, usually a Boolean, that's used to check a state.

"For example, in this function you'll be using a flag to let you know whether a picture already exists in the array or not. Another example might be the state of a spaceship in a game. The flag, `alive` = `true`, might be present for most of the game, but if an asteroid hits, then the state changes and all of the other checks (such as if it's the end of the game) that you're looking out for the flag will suddenly spring into action. As I said before, though, all it is really is a Boolean variable.

10. Call your flag `newHit` to indicate that it stores if the hit is new or preexisting. Also, initially set it to be true, and then run a check to see if it should in fact be false. So, your next line is this:

```
_root.newHit = true;
```

11. The next thing that you have to do is loop through your array and check if it already contains the image that has been clicked. You can do this by simply checking whether the index number of the current picture already exists in the array. You're using the index number here because you know it will always be unique, whereas I presume that there's a possibility that two pictures may have the same name by mistake. The first line of the `for` loop is as follows:

```
for (i=0; i<hitArray.length; i++) {
```

"As you did before, you're using the `length` property of the array to allow you to dynamically parse all of the way through it, no matter how long it is.

"Next, you need to define the order of the data for each element of the array so that you'll know where the index number is so that you can check if it's there or not. You'll store your data in the following order." I wrote on the board:

Hits; Index Number; Category; Caption Name/Title

"So the value that you want to check against will be at position 1 in each of the elements in the array.

12. You can then begin to write your `if` statement for the index checking:

```
if (hitArray[i][1] == index) {
```

"Here, you're checking each element of the array to see if its `index` value stored in position 1 is the same as the current `index` value of the picture that has just been passed to the function.

13. If it's the same, then you want to add one to the `hits` value of the relevant `hitArray` element:

```
hitArray[i][0]++;
```

"You know that the `hits` value is at position 0, because that's what we just discussed 10 seconds ago," I said, smiling.

14. Before you finish the loop, though, there's one more thing you need to do: you need to set the newHit flag to false to indicate that this isn't a new element. Finally, you can return from the loop, as there's no need to keep cycling through it if you've already found the index number that you're looking for:

```
_root.newHit = false;
return;
```

"With that done, your loop is finished. Here's the total code to make sure you have everything right:

```
for (i=0; i<hitArray.length; i++) {
    if (hitArray[i][1] == index) {
        hitArray[i][0]++;
        _root.newHit = false;
        return;
    }
}
```


"Okay, the next thing that you need is a condition to check your flag and to add a new element if newHit is true. This if condition itself is fairly simple, but to add another element, you'll have to use an array method that we discussed a couple of weeks ago. Can anyone remember the name of the method to add an element to an array?"

"Push and pop," sang Carl.

"And which of those adds an element to the array?" I asked.

"Err . . . push?" Carl responded.

"That's right," I said. "Optionally, you could also use the unshift method, as you'll be sorting the array anyway so it doesn't really matter where you place the new element. Personally, though, I prefer the sound of push. So, Joe, can you tell me what we should be pushing into the array?"

"Well, the three variables that we've brought with us to the function, and I guess the number of hits too," said Joe.

"And how many hits should you add?" I asked.

"One?" said Joe, uncertainly. "That's right," I said, "this is the first time that the image has been clicked, so you need to initialize it with one hit.

15. The code for the condition, then, looks like this:

```
function checkArray(index, capName, cat) {
    _root.newHit = true;
    for (i=0; i<hitArray.length; i++) {
        if (hitArray[i][1] == index) {
            hitArray[i][0]++;
            _root.newHit = false;
            return;
        }
    }
    if (_root.newHit == true) {
        hitArray.push([1, index, cat, capName]);
    }
```

"You don't need to keep track of where you are in the array, because push will just automatically add the new element to the end, no matter where that is. You just need a final closing brace, and your checkArray function is done.

16. Let's test the array now and see if it's filling up properly. The best place to do this at the moment is in the runStats function. Go back and add a trace action to the end of the function:

```
runStats = function () {
    _root.attachMovie("statReport", "statReport", 7000);
    _root.statReport._x = 400;
    _root.statReport._y = 300;
    _root.hideMainButtons();
    trace(hitArray);
};
```

"Now run the movie and click a few thumbnails. When you're done, press a key to bring up the login box, type in the correct password, and press ENTER. Hopefully, you should now see a long string of values telling you the number of hits, and the index number, category, and name of every thumbnail that you clicked. Success! That's all of the data done and dusted.

"What next? Well, you now have an array filling up with new data, so you need somewhere to display that data, and you need to create a way to sort it."

Adding the text fields

"Okay, back to making assets for the report. The next thing we need is somewhere to actually display the report. We'll use two text fields for this," I said.

"Any reason why we're using two, Ken?" asked Carl.

"Yes," I replied. "Looking at our thumbnails, there are a possible 48 separate entries that can be in the array. 48 lines is actually quite a lot to have in one long list, so I decided to split it into two lists of 24 lines each.

1. The easiest way to ensure that a text field is the right length is simply to start with it one line deep, but at the correct width, and then press ENTER the required number of times. Once you've done that for one text field, you can just copy and paste the field to create the second one.

2. Make each one a dynamic text field, and ensure that you have the **Show Border Around Text** button clicked.

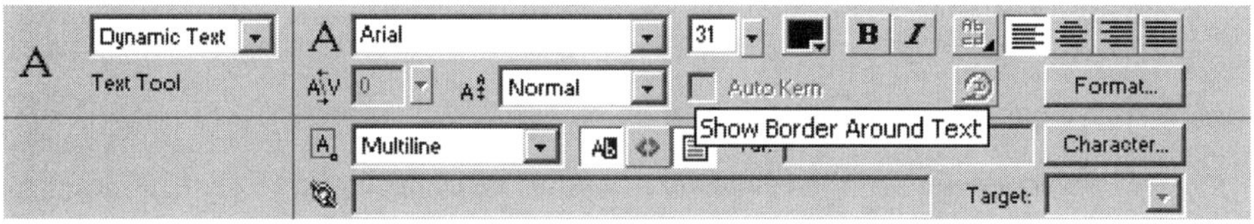

"You should end up with something like this:

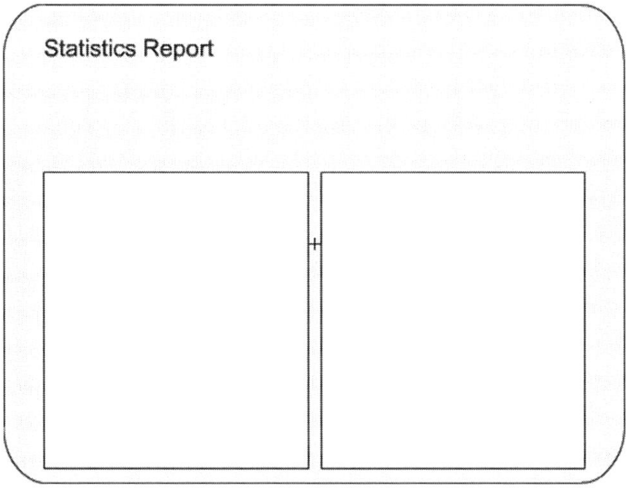

3. Next, you need to give each text field an instance name so that you can access them. Give the first the name `results`, and give the second the name `resultsOver`. This second one will hold the overspill of results that don't fit into the first box.

"You can now write a function to transfer your results from the `hitArray` into your text fields. Let's call this function `getStats`."

The getStats function

"The purpose of this function is simply to retrieve the statistics from the array of hits, and then display them in a readable fashion in the text field. You'll create it at the bottom of your code, and you'll call it from the `runStats` function.

4. Somewhat paradoxically, the first thing that you'll be doing is making sure that there's nothing in the text fields. You do this by setting the `text` property of each of the fields to an empty string:

```
getStats = function () {
    _root.statReport.results.text = "";
    _root.statReport.resultsOver.text = "";
```

"This is necessary because of the technique that you'll be using to display the data, you'll be adding the data to the field rather than writing it over the top of what's already there.

"You've already seen how to trace and display strings, but so far you haven't seen how to format them—they've always been sent straight to the screen. This formatting is done by using escape sequences."

"Wow, like when James Bond gets away from the laser table?" asked Carl.

"A little like that," I said, "but not quite as exciting. An escape sequence is used to tell Flash that you want to insert a special character into a string. For example, you know that you use quotation marks to denote the start and end of a string, but have any of you ever wondered how you would get Flash to display quotation marks? Try it now if you like—just a simple `trace`."

The students all tried it and soon found that it was impossible. All except for Carl, that is, who worked himself into a frenzied infinite quote loop. "Help!" he cried, "someone break me out or I'll be stuck here forever." Mazzy obliged with a friendly cuff around the ear.

"Thanks," said Carl, "my head was starting to spin there. You're right, Ken, it's mighty hard to trace a quotation mark. They're darned elusive things."

"They are that, Carl," I agreed. "The solution to our little mystery is to precede the quote mark with an escape character, and the escape character in Flash is a backslash (\)." I wrote some common escape sequences on the board:

\" = Double quotation mark
\' = Single quotation mark
\t = Tab
\n = New line
\r = Carriage return
\b = Backspace
\\ = Backslash

"Try the `trace` now using the escape sequence for the quotation mark, and you should finally see what you were looking for."

5. Okay, with that knowledge under your belt, you can finally see how to legibly format the statistics. You can insert tabs between the values and then put a new line after each element. By putting this into a loop, you can run through all of the elements and add each one to the text field to make one long list:

```
for (i=0; i<hitArray.length; i++) {
    _root.statReport.results.text += "\t" +
➥ hitArray[i][0] + "\t" + hitArray[i][1] + "\t\t" +
➥ hitArray[i][2] + "\t\t" + hitArray[i][3] + "\n";
}
```

"The code looks a little odd because your escape sequences are all contained within quotes with nothing else in them, but that's just the way it goes. You'll notice that I've put some tabs in some odd places and sometimes doubled up on them. This is because when I tested the program earlier, some of the fields needed to have a bit more space between them to make them legible.

6. Remember that you included two text fields, one to flow over into the other? Well, you can easily make that happen by putting in a simple condition to put the first 24 elements into the first box, and then use the same display line, but pointing to the second text field, to display the remaining elements in the `resultsOver` text field. The completed function then looks like this:

```
getStats = function () {
    _root.statReport.results.text = "";
    _root.statReport.resultsOver.text = "";
    for (i=0; i<hitArray.length; i++) {
        if (i<24) {
            _root.statReport.results.text += "\t" +
➥ hitArray[i][0] + "\t" + hitArray[i][1] + "\t\t" +
➥ hitArray[i][2] + "\t\t" + hitArray[i][3] + "\n";
        } else {
            _root.statReport.resultsOver.text += "\t" +
➥ hitArray[i][0] + "\t" + hitArray[i][1] + "\t\t" +
➥ hitArray[i][2] + "\t\t" + hitArray[i][3] + "\n";
        }
    }
};
```

7. You now just need to call the function from within the `runStats` function, like so:

```
runStats = function () {
    _root.attachMovie("statReport", "statReport", 7000);
    _root.statReport._x = 400;
    _root.statReport._y = 300;
    _root.hideMainButtons();
    getStats();
};
```

"Then you can test it, and hopefully see the data display in action. Try clicking more than 24 unique images to test the overflow condition. If you don't want to have to click 24 images, then you can always temporarily change the condition to a smaller number—say 2. If all went according to plan, you should see something like this:

Statistics Report

1	001	artistic	karl
1	002	artistic	Blackpool Rock
1	003	artistic	Rock City
1	004	artistic	katy
1	005	artistic	Ripples
1	006	artistic	Disco on the Beachfront
1	009	artistic	Curve
1	008	artistic	Footprints
1	007	artistic	Prickly
1	010	artistic	Skeletal
1	011	artistic	**
1	012	artistic	x
1	061	family	Charlie
1	062	family	Charlie
1	063	family	nia
1	065	family	ben
1	064	family	katy
1	025	outdoor	Rocks
1	026	outdoor	Dunes
1	027	outdoor	North Cerney
1	030	outdoor	Donkey Rides a Pound
1	029	outdoor	Stormy Skies
1	028	outdoor	Swirls
1	031	outdoor	Distance

1	032	outdoor	Blazing Pier
1	033	outdoor	Fishing Village
1	036	outdoor	Forest of Light
1	035	outdoor	Florence
1	034	outdoor	Sistine Chapel

8. At the moment, although you know what each column represents, it would probably be more helpful to have some labels at the top of each text field. You can add simple static text fields to the top of each results field. A good way to make sure that the headings are above the right columns is to type in a dummy entry into the results field and then delete it when you have the layout right. You only need to create one text field, and then you can copy and paste it into position for the second field:

Hits	Index	Category	Image name
4	005	artistic	Ripples
1	012	artistic	x
5	010	artistic	Skeletal
2	007	artistic	Prickly

Hits	Index	Category	Image name
1	017	portraits	ben
1	016	portraits	katy
1	013	portraits	karl
1	021	portraits	x

"Now the display is finished. The next thing that you need to look into is how to sort the data you've assembled."

Data sorting

"You've already seen that the `Array` object has a `sort` method, but so far you've only seen how it can sort the first values in the array. You can do more with sorting, though, and you're going to have to if you want to get Randy's statistics in order.

"Before you get to the nitty-gritty of sorting, though, you need some way of letting Flash know what order you want to sort the statistics in. You want to be able to sort by hits, index, and category. You could easily sort by name, too, but there doesn't really seem to be much point in being able to view the statistics in alphabetical name order.

"The other thing that you want to be able to specify when sorting is the direction of the sort. You want to be able to sort the pictures either highest to lowest, or lowest to highest, for ease of reference. This is quite a simple thing to do, though, as you've already encountered an `Array` method that will serve this purpose. Any ideas what it might be?"

"Just to flip the order that the array's in?" asked Jim.

"Yep, just that," I replied.

"In that case, I guess we could just reverse it," Jim said.

"That's right, we can use the `reverse` method that we looked at earlier to change the direction of the sorted order.

"Okay, so we've got two sets of options that we want to present to Randy. We could do this with a number of buttons, but it seems more natural to have them in two drop-down menus. That way, Randy knows that he can change both menus but also that he can only have one selection from each menu."

Components

"Rather than having to create drop-down menus from scratch, those kind folks at Macromedia have included a set of prebuilt interface components that ship with Flash. If you'd ever noticed that panel on the right side and wondered what it was for, now's the time to find out:

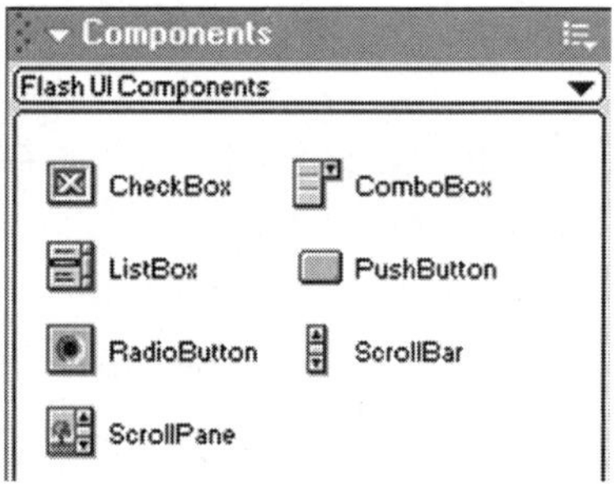

"As you can see, the components that come with Flash are often-used interface elements, such as scrollbars and check boxes. Macromedia has released more components to perform other functions, and these can be found on the Macromedia website.

"Other Flash users have also created their own components, and you can find some handy things with a quick search on the Web. Back to our case study: we're looking for a drop-down menu that, at first glance, doesn't seem to be there, but is stored under the title **ComboBox**.

"To use a component, we just need to drag it out of the panel and onto the stage. The component comes with all of its own graphics and functionality built in, and we just need to fill in the values that we want to use with it. We could do this by clicking the component on the stage and using the Property inspector to change the values:

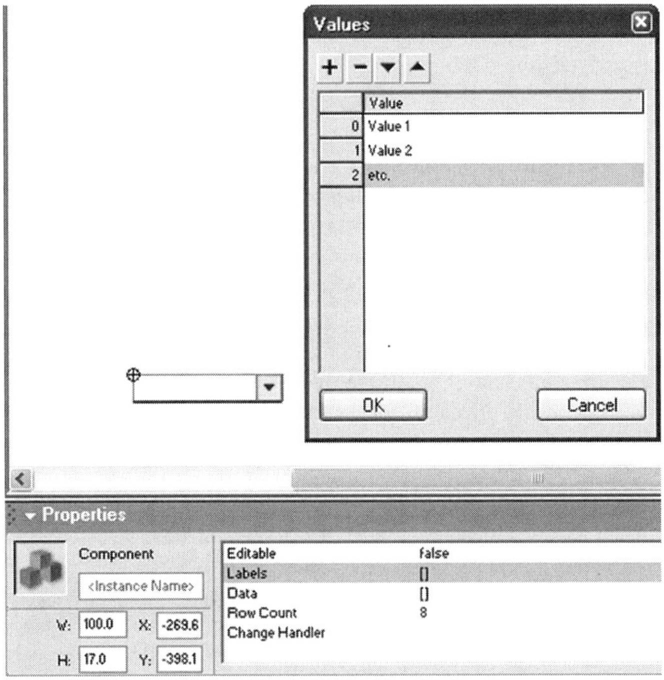

"Being the gluttons for punishment that I know you are, we'll be doing it the hard way and filling in the values using code."

"Do we have to?" groaned Carl. "Can't we just do things the easy way for a change?"

I laughed, "I'm sorry Carl, I promise I'm not doing this to punish you. I want you to learn how to use components dynamically, and to do that we have to attach them from the Library and populate them using ActionScript. Anyway, I promise it's not that hard, I was only pulling your leg about that.

1. The easiest way to get a component into the Library is to drag it onto the stage and then delete it. The component will be gone from the stage, but it will still exist in the Library. You'll find it in a folder called "Flash UI Components." Inside that folder, you'll find the pieces that make up the component split into two folders, one that you can go into and alter to personalize the component, and another that contains important elements that you shouldn't tamper with unless you know what you're doing. You can see that the creators have made this obvious for you:

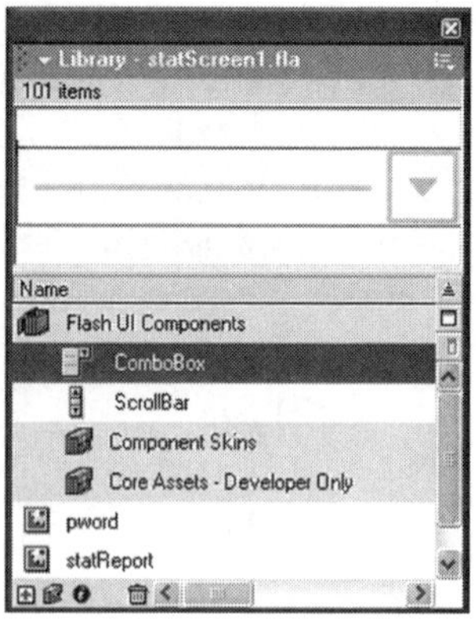

2. While you're in the Library, right-click the ComboBox symbol and look at its linkage name. You'll see that it already has one, `FComboBoxSymbol`. This is a little unwieldy, but you can use it to attach a new combo box onto your stats symbol.

3. Another thing that you can do while you're looking at the combo box symbols is drag a couple of them out of the Components panel and onto the stage. You can use these to get an idea for the position that you want to put them in, make a note of the coordinates, and then delete them from the stage again. I lined mine up with the inside edges of the text fields, putting them at coordinates: -107,-140 and 9,-140.

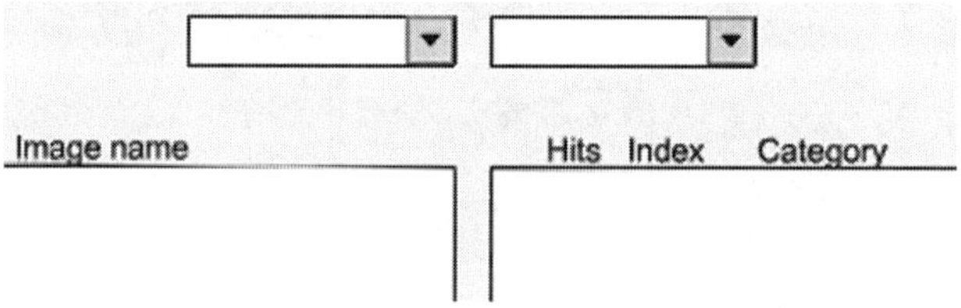

"Okay, now that you know what you want to do with your drop-down menus, you can write the code for them.

4. Just as you did with getStats, you'll write this function and then call it from inside the runStats function. You'll call this function addMenus because it adds the drop-down menus to the screen. The first thing to do is attach the menus from the Library and into the statistics report. You'll code the menus one at a time: first the sort menu, and then the direction menu. You know what the linkage name of the component is, so you can use that and name your new instance sortMenu:

```
addMenus = function () {
    _root.statReport.attachMovie("FComboBoxSymbol",
➥ "sortMenu", 5000);
```

5. Next, you need to position the menu on the screen. You made a note of the coordinates earlier, so the next couple of lines are relatively simple:

```
_root.statReport.sortMenu._x = -107;
_root.statReport.sortMenu._y = -140;
```


6. Then add the options to the drop-down menu. You do this using a method of the component called addItem. The items that you want to add are hits, index number, and category:

```
_root.statReport.sortMenu.addItem("Hits");
_root.statReport.sortMenu.addItem("Index Number");
_root.statReport.sortMenu.addItem("Category");
```

7. You now want to tell Flash what to do when you select an option. You do this with another method of the component. You have to write a function to handle the option changing and then tell Flash that this is the function that you want to use with this menu. You'll write that function in a second, but for now you'll use Carl's patented future-code again and use the name of the function before you've written it. The name of the function will be reSort.

"The method that you use to tell Flash the function name is called setChangeHandler. The change handler is the function that handles changes to the menu. Simple, really.

8. The other thing that you need to tell Flash is where this function is located, and in this case it will be on the root timeline. With all of this information on hand, you're ready to use the method:

```
_root.statReport.sortMenu.setChangeHandler("reSort", _root);
```

"Note that the name of the change handler function is written in quotation marks. Even though you haven't written the change handler, you can still test the function now to see if the menu appears in the right place.

9. Add the finishing brace to the function, and then call it from within `runStats`. You should be able to see the menu and click it to reveal the options:

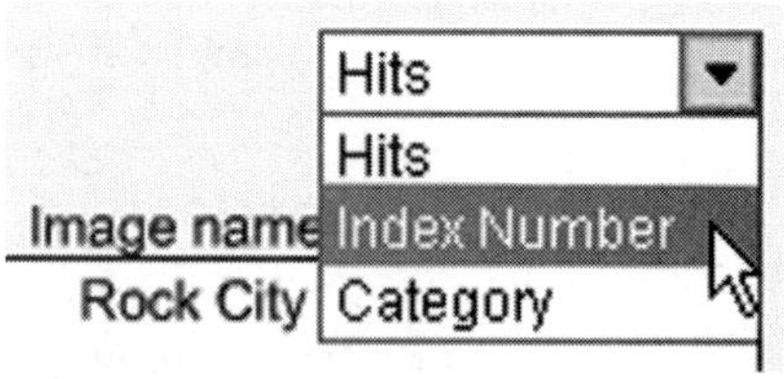

10. Adding the second menu is a much simpler task now, because the code is almost the same as for the first. The only things that need changing are the instance name—this one's called `dirMenu`—the depth, the position, and the menu items—in this case we want "High – Low" and "Low – High". The change handler is the same for both components:

```
_root.statReport.attachMovie("FComboBoxSymbol", "dirMenu",
➥ 5001);
_root.statReport.dirMenu._x = 9;
_root.statReport.dirMenu._y = -140;
_root.statReport.dirMenu.addItem("High - Low");
_root.statReport.dirMenu.addItem("Low - High");
_root.statReport.dirMenu.setChangeHandler("reSort", _root);
```

"Here's a complete listing of the `addMenus` function:

```
addMenus = function () {
    _root.statReport.attachMovie("FComboBoxSymbol",
➥ "sortMenu", 5000);
    _root.statReport.sortMenu._x = -106.9;
    _root.statReport.sortMenu._y = -140;
    _root.statReport.sortMenu.addItem("Hits");
    _root.statReport.sortMenu.addItem("Index Number");
    _root.statReport.sortMenu.addItem("Category");
    _root.statReport.sortMenu.setChangeHandler("reSort",
➥ _root);

      _root.statReport.attachMovie("FComboBoxSymbol",
➥ "dirMenu", 5001);
    _root.statReport.dirMenu._x = 8.7;
    _root.statReport.dirMenu._y = -140;
```

```
            _root.statReport.dirMenu.addItem("High - Low");
            _root.statReport.dirMenu.addItem("Low - High");
            _root.statReport.dirMenu.setChangeHandler("reSort",
   ➥ _root);
   };
```

"If you test the movie again now, you should see both of your menus positioned correctly and containing the correct values:

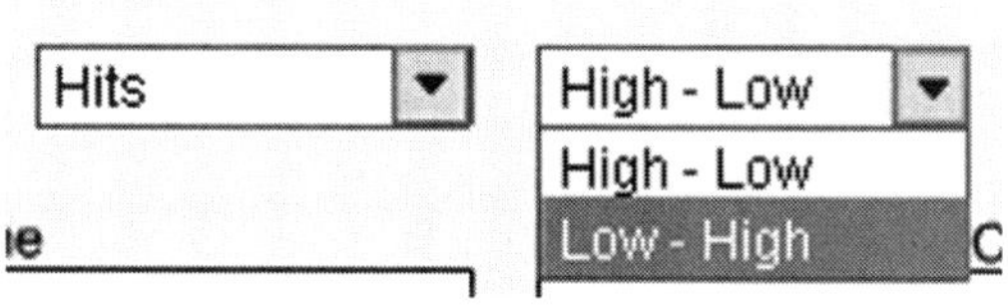

"Okay, we're really getting there now. We're ready for our last major piece of coding of the day: the sorting function."

The reSort function

"As I briefly mentioned before, when we looked at the `sort` method of the `Array` object, we only saw a glimpse of what it could do," I started. "It's now time to take a deeper look.

"The `sort` method can take an optional parameter if desired, and this parameter can be the name of a function that Flash can use to sort the data by. In the same way that you saw components had a method to specify a function to tell them how to handle changes, the `sort` method can take a function that tells it how to handle the sort.

"You need three different sort options to sort by for each of the three different menu items. I know it was a long time ago, but can anyone tell me what structure you need to use for a condition with multiple outcomes?"

"It was the switch and case thing, wasn't it?" suggested Jim.

"That's the one," I said. "You'll need to set the switch to react to the current menu item.

1. You use another component method to find out what the currently selected item is. There's something peculiar about this method, though, because you specify a property with it. Each menu item can contain a label and a value. You've only used labels, but the method will still return both, so you need to specify which it is that you want to look for. The final switch line looks like this:

```
   reSort = function () {
        switch (_root.statReport.sortMenu.getSelectedItem().label)
   {
```

"There aren't many times in Flash when you'll see code written like that, so it's worth remembering it. This will return the label of the menu item that has been clicked.

2. You can then use these values for each of your case statements:

```
case "Hits" :
```

"Okay, now it's time to write the sort function. It's not actually as difficult as it sounds, because all of the sorting code is already contained within the sort method. All your function needs to do is tell Flash what you're sorting by and how you want it to be sorted.

"All sort functions take two parameters: A and B. These represent the two values that Flash is currently checking against each other during its sort. All sort functions also return a standard value: -1 if A should appear before B in the sequence, 1 if A should appear after B in the sequence, and 0 if both A and B are equal.

"The function then just needs to contain a number of if statements to check those conditions and to return the desired value. In the function, A represents the current element of the array, so for example it might be hitArray[3]. This means that to get a particular value within that element, you need to have something like a[1], which would be the second value in the current element. You know enough to write your first sort function now.

3. There will be one sort function for each case, so write it directly after the colon of the case statement:

```
case "Hits" :
    hitSort = function (a, b) {
        if (a[0]<b[0]) {
            return -1;
        } else if (a[0]>b[0]) {
            return 1;
        } else {
            return 0;
        }
    };
```

"All you've done here is written a series of checks to compare the hits values of two elements in the array. Depending on how they compare, you return a different value back to the sort method, which uses these values to properly sort the array.

4. After this, you need to call the function with the sort method:

```
_root.hitArray.sort(hitSort);
```

5. And finally, you just need to break out of the switch once you're done. The completed case statement looks like this:

```
case "Hits" :
     hitSort = function (a, b) {
          if (a[0]<b[0]) {
               return -1;
          } else if (a[0]>b[0]) {
               return 1;
          } else {
               return 0;
          }
     };
     _root.hitArray.sort(hitSort);
     break;
```


6. The remaining two case statements are very similar to this one. All that you're changing is the case, the function name, the value in the array element that you're comparing, and the function call. The final two case statements are written like this:

```
case "Index Number" :
     indexSort = function (a, b) {
          if (a[1]<b[1]) {
               return -1;
          } else if (a[1]>b[1]) {
               return 1;
          } else {
               return 0;
          }
     };
     _root.hitArray.sort(indexSort);
     break;

case "Category" :
catSort = function (a, b) {
          if (a[2]<b[2]) {
               return -1;
```

```
            } else if (a[2]>b[2]) {
                return 1;
            } else {
                return 0;
            }
        };
        _root.hitArray.sort(catSort);
        break;
```

7. You then need to add a final brace to finish the switch.

"The second menu is a lot simpler. As I said before, all that you need to do here is check to see which direction you want the array to run in, and then reverse it if necessary.

8. Arrays are normally sorted from low to high, so you need to see if the menu has been set to "High – Low". If it has, then you reverse the array:

```
if (_root.statReport.dirMenu.getSelectedItem().label ==
➥ "High - Low") {
    _root.hitArray.reverse();
}
```

9. All of the array code is done now. The last thing that you want to do is refill your text fields with the newly sorted array. You can do this by simply calling the `getStats` function and then closing the `resort` function with a brace.

"Here's the `reSort` function in full:

```
reSort = function () {
    switch (_root.statReport.sortMenu.getSelectedItem().label)
{
    case "Hits" :
        hitSort = function (a, b) { if (a[0]<b[0]) {return
➥ -1;} else if (a[0]>b[0]) {return 1;} else {return 0;}};
        _root.hitArray.sort(hitSort);
        break;
    case "Index Number" :
        indexSort = function (a, b) { if (a[1]<b[1])
➥ {return -1;} else if (a[1]>b[1]) {return 1;} else
➥ {return 0;}};
        _root.hitArray.sort(indexSort);
        break;
```

```
        case "Category" :
            catSort = function (a, b) { if (a[2]<b[2]) {return
➥ -1;} else if (a[2]>b[2]) {return 1;} else {return 0;}};
            _root.hitArray.sort(catSort);
            break;
        }
        if (_root.statReport.dirMenu.getSelectedItem().label
➥ == "High - Low") {
            _root.hitArray.reverse();
        }
        getStats();
    };
```

"You wrote a function call into your code earlier, so you should be able to go ahead and test the code now. Each of the drop-down menus should correctly sort the array:

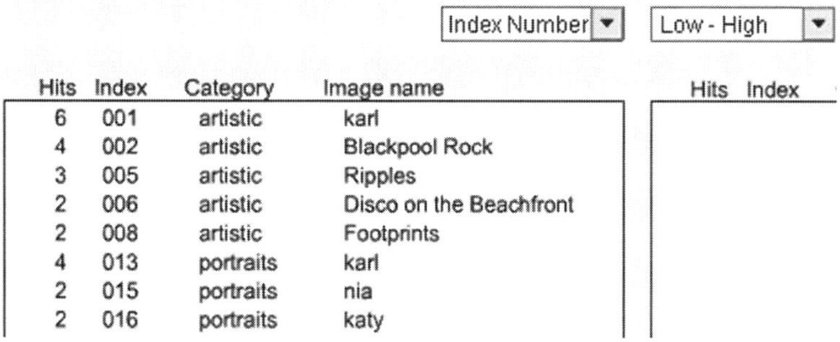

Index Number
Low - High
Hits Index Category Image name
6 001 artistic karl
4 002 artistic Blackpool Rock
3 005 artistic Ripples
2 006 artistic Disco on the Beachfront
2 008 artistic Footprints
4 013 portraits karl
2 015 portraits nia
2 016 portraits katy
Hits Index

"Okay, celebrations are due for that, but you may also have noticed a small grumble. Although the array can be sorted by the drop-down menus, when you first open up the statistics report it shows the array in its unordered state. It would be good to sort the array when it's first displayed so that it's immediately useful for Randy.

10. This is easy enough to do by just calling the resort function from the `runStats` function. This function is getting full now, so let's take a look at the code it contains to make sure we're all in the same place:

```
runStats = function () {
    _root.attachMovie("statReport", "statReport", 7000);
    _root.statReport._x = 400;
    _root.statReport._y = 300;
    _root.hideMainButtons();
    addMenus();
```

```
        reSort();
        getStats();
    };
```

"Wow, we're almost finished. There are just a few simple pieces of extra functionality that we can add to the statistics screen for Randy. The first of these is an Exit button to quit the statistics and return to the main movie. We'll also add a button to print the screen so Randy can keep a record of any interesting statistics and a button to clear the hit array so that once Randy has finished analyzing the information he can reset it for another run."

The final buttons

"The buttons will all have a fairly standard appearance. They're all just rectangles with a static text field proclaiming their use on them.

1. Each button is a separate movie clip, with the instance names exitButton, printButton, and clearButton. I've placed them in the top-left corner of the statistics report:

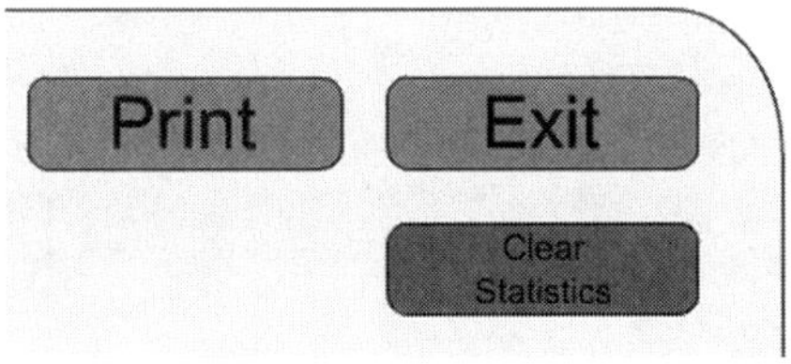

"You'll put the callbacks for the buttons within a function, and, as you have done so many times now, you'll call it from the runStats function. Call the new function activateButtons.

"The Exit button needs to close the statistics report, restart the main buttons on the stage, and set up the login listener again.

2. These three things are all pretty easy to code using the functions that you've already created:

```
activateButtons = function () {
    _root.statReport.exitButton.onRelease = function() {
        _root.statReport.removeMovieClip();
        _root.showMainButtons();
        loginListener();
    };
```

3. The Clear button is also pretty simple. All that it needs to do is reset the hit array and then clear the text fields. To reset the array, you can just define it as new again:

```
_root.statReport.clearButton.onRelease = function() {
    _root.hitArray = new Array();
    _root.statReport.results.text = "";
    _root.statReport.resultsOver.text = "";
};
```

"The last of the buttons is the only one that contains any new processes. You haven't yet encountered printing in Flash, but it's pretty simple. There's an action in Flash specifically for printing called, quite predictably, `print`. The `print` action takes two arguments: the first is the movie clip that you want to print, and the second is the print area. The print area options can be used to tell Flash to print different frames in the movie, but because this movie consists of only one frame, we only need to use one option, `bmovie`."

"We're printing B-movies?" asked Mazzy in mock shock.

"I knew that joke was coming," I said, "but I have to admit, I didn't expect it from you. In this case, the 'b' in `bmovie` stands for bounding box, and 'movie' tells it that we want to print the whole movie.

4. Both of these arguments need to be in quotes, so the button code looks like this:

```
_root.statReport.printButton.onRelease = function() {
    print("_root.statScreen", "bmovie");
};
```

"This will bring up the default print dialog box for the operating system and will print out the full statistics screen.

"That's it! All you need to do now is add the closing brace to the function, and then add a function call to `runStats`. The case study is now very nearly complete, so play around with it and see what you think. All of the computers are linked up to the network printer at the back of the classroom, so feel free to test out the printing as well.

"It's been a long class today, but you've achieved a lot in it. Next week, we'll tidy up a few loose ends in the case study, but until then, bask in the glory of your code and I'll see you all in 7 days' time."

Summary

Today you added a statistics page to the kiosk. In doing so, you learned about the following:

- Enabling Flash movies to handle input from the keyboard. You do this through keyboard listeners, which are continually ready to detect key presses.

- Using keyboard listeners to enable login functionality through a password.

- Storing information about the number of times Randy's thumbnails were accessed in an array and then displaying this information onscreen.

- Sorting through this information to enable it to be displayed in the most useful way.

In the next class, you'll add the remaining features that the case study requires, such as giving it dual kiosk/CD functionality.

Class 11
Finishing the Kiosk Project

Objectives

In this class, you'll learn

- How to create a time delay for the tooltips using the `setInterval` action
- How to display an image from a certain category and display a random image
- How to customize the Contact page
- How to work with stand-alone projector files
- How to add kiosk and CD functionality
- How to publish the Flash movie and the projectors

Introduction

In this class, the students will complete the case study, finishing up all the outstanding coding and finalizing graphic elements.

“Hello everyone,” I said. “In today’s class, we’ll finish the case study.” Carl gave a whoop. “As far as I can see, we have a number of outstanding elements. Who’d like to go through them with the class?”

Gemma raised her hand. “For one, an image needs to load when the user changes category,” she said.

“We still need to add Randy’s details on the About and Contact pages,” Mazzy said. “The Contact page also needs a mailto link directly to Randy, and the About page needs an image of him.” I nodded.

“The tooltips,” Jim said firmly. Gemma looked at him with puzzlement. “The tooltips need to appear with timing. At the moment, they pop up instantly.” Jim moved his mouse and looked at his screen. “I’d say a half-second delay is about right.”

“What is he talking about?” Joe asked. “I don’t remember any of this. The tooltips are finished, aren’t they?”

“Jim is right,” I said. “Many weeks ago we agreed that the tooltips should only appear after a little time has passed. Tooltips are delayed in most applications you’ll use.” Jim motioned Joe to look over to his screen and showed him something.

“Oh yeah,” Joe said. “There’s a little bit of time that passes before they appear. I guess you could call it a delay.”

“Anything else?” I asked. I was met with shaking heads. “Besides generally tidying up the graphical elements, the last thing that I think we need to add is a Quit button for the CD version. Although you haven’t seen a Flash movie run full-screen yet, when they do, they have no menus or interface elements, and unless the user knows to press the Escape key, he or she will need a Quit button to get out of it. Remember, we’ve got to make sure our kiosk is as usable as possible and won’t confuse the person looking at the photos; otherwise the user will just walk away.”

"I guess we overlooked that," Carl said. "I might leave a Quit button off my band's Flash movies. That way, the users will have to listen and learn to like . . ." Carl's voice deepened cinematically, ". . . THE SOUND OF MONDO."

"Scary," Jim said. "I wish I could say that the 'sound of Mondo' sounds enticing, but it doesn't." Mazzy and Joe laughed.

"Okay class, we'll begin with the tooltips," I said.

Timed events

"So far we've only seen one time-based event," I said. "Who remembers what that was?" I was met with blank, staring faces. "The time-based event that we learned about a few weeks ago was `onEnterFrame`."

"Oh yeah!" Jim exclaimed. "I remember now. `onEnterFrame` is the event that happens every frame."

"Yes, that's right, Jim," I replied. "In Flash 5, `onEnterFrame` was the only way of regularly running an event every so often; therefore, it was used widely by developers.

"However, the problem with `onEnterFrame` is that it's affected by the frame rate. If a Flash movie stage gets pretty busy with vector shapes and instances, the movie tends to slow down considerably, affecting the frame rate. An `onEnterFrame` then might go from running 12 times a second in a 12 fps Flash movie to half or even a quarter of that speed.

"This is where the **`setInterval`** action introduced in Flash MX comes in. The `setInterval` action is configured to run after the passage of time as opposed to frames. This makes it a whole lot more reliable—because time never changes! Besides this, it also allows us to work with time a little easier than `onEnterFrame`, making it ideal for our tooltips delay. Let's see how it is used."

Seeing setInterval in action

1. Open a new Flash movie.

2. On the existing layer, select the keyframe and open the Actions panel. Type the following code:

```
count = 10;

hideOrSeek = setInterval(function () {
    if (count == 0) {
        trace("Ready or not, I'm coming to get you!");
        clearInterval(hideOrSeek);
    } else {
        trace(count);
    }
    count--;
}, 1000);
```

3. Test the movie.

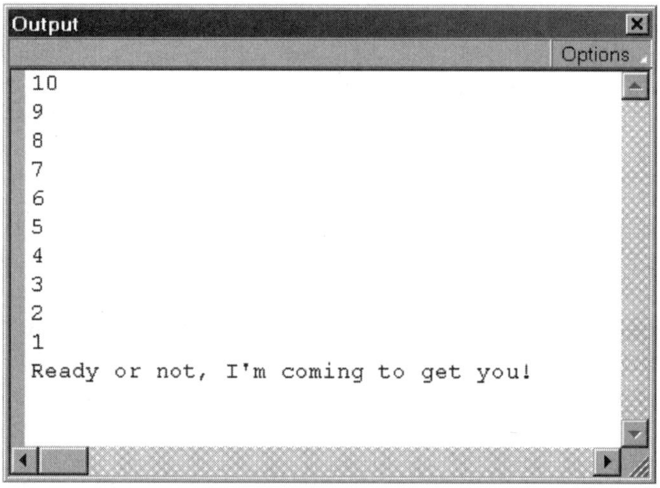

Carl whispered to Gemma, "And I'm wearing my fright mask!" Gemma shrieked. Carl and the rest of the students laughed.

"That was harsh!" Jim said. "It was very funny, though."

"I'll get you for that, Carl," Gemma said, smirking.

"Leave any 'getting' until after class," I started, "and let's take a look at the code. The premise of this Flash movie is to count down from 10 to 1 second by second, and then shout 'Boo!'

"Line 1 here sets a `count` variable to equal 10—pretty straightforward. On Line 3 the `setInterval` event is set up. If you then skip to line 11, you'll see the tail end of the `setInterval` action. A `setInterval` action consists of two parameters:

- What you should do when the time has passed (the event handler)
- The amount of time that needs to pass (measured in milliseconds)

"A more simplistic `setInterval` action, then, might look like this:

```
myInterval = setInterval( function(){ do this; }, 1000 );
```


"This code sets up a `setInterval` to run every 1,000 milliseconds, the equivalent of 1 second. Every time a second passes, the code within the function brackets is performed. If you reformat the code to the way you're used to seeing ActionScript syntax, it would look like this:

```
myInterval = setInterval( function(){
        do this;
}, 1000 );
```

"The very same thing has been done for the `setInterval` in the hide-and-seek movie, except there's a lot more of it!

"As with the code I just showed you, this code also runs every second—see line 11 for this. The handler code within the function brackets does a number of rather simple things. First, it checks to see if `count` is equal to zero. If `count` isn't equal to it, you trace its current value, which gives the illusion of counting down . . . .

"If count is zero, then the counting ends with a 'Ready or not..' trace. Next, on line 6, you use clearInterval to remove the setInterval event. Because you've used the event as much as required, you can simply delete it so that it doesn't run any more and waste any processing power in the process.

"You have the ability to set up as many intervals as you require in a Flash movie. It's good practice, as I've done, to reference a setInterval when you create one. This way, you can easily delete it with a clearInterval action. Otherwise, you'll be stuck with a setInterval that you can't get rid of!

"The last thing that happens within the handler code is to decrement count, ready for the next time the handler runs," I said. "Now that you've seen how setInterval works traditionally, who'd like to guess how you'd change the registerToolTip function?"

"That's easy," Jim said. "We have both rollover and rollout events for each thumbnail. So, if we insert a setInterval event within the rollover handler to show the tooltip after a short delay, we can cancel it on rollout."

"That's about right, Jim," I said. I asked the class to open their newest case study movie.

Delaying the tooltip

1. Open class11_start.fla and open the Actions panel on the actions layer.

2. Insert the following new code into the registerTooltip function:

```
registerTooltip = function (photoCategory, photoCount) {
     var photoCategory;
     var photoCount;
     this.onRollOver = function() {
          tooltipDelay = setInterval(function () {
               tooltip = _root.attachMovie("libraryToolTip",
➥ "libraryToolTip", 2000);
               tooltip.tooltipText.text =
➥ photoCategory[photoCount][3];
               tooltip.tooltipText.backgroundColor = "0xFFFF00";
               tooltip.tooltipText._width =
➥ tooltip.tooltipText.textWidth+(10);
               tooltip._x = _root._xmouse+(10);
               tooltip._y = _root._ymouse+(10);
          }, 750);
     };
```

```
        this.onRollOut = function() {
            clearInterval (tooltipDelay);
            removeMovieClip(tooltip);
        }
    };
```

3. Test the movie and hold the cursor over a thumbnail for a short length of time. There should be a slight delay before the tooltip appears.

4. Leave the Flash movie open, as you'll be adding to it shortly.

"I was right," Jim said. "There's not much to this, is there?"

"Your estimation was correct, Jim," I said. "As you can see, all of the rollover event is placed within the `setInterval` code. When the first 750 milliseconds—three quarters of a second—pass, the tooltip appears. Every three quarters of a second after that, the position of the tooltip is updated, until the cursor rolls off the thumbnail and the tooltip is removed, and the `clearInterval` action is called to cancel the `setInterval` event."

"Why did you use three quarters of a second and not a second or half a second?" Gemma asked.

"It's just the timing I chose after testing," I replied. "It felt right and was responsive enough." I paused. "Now that you've seen the `setInterval` action in use, and you've used it where necessary in the case study, we're ready to move on. Before we do, however, I recommend that you look up the `setInterval` action in the Reference panel, because it can be used a number of different ways."

"What's next?" Carl asked.

Displaying an image on category change

"Let's move swiftly on to the image changing for each category," I said. "Did we decide on a random image selection or a set image?"

"I think a random image," Joe said. "Otherwise, it's very easy for the interface to appear stagnant."

"I agree with Joe," Mazzy said. "People want to see something new, even if it isn't actually new at all! It's just the illusion of it."

"Does anyone totally disagree?" I asked.

"I'm not sure," Jim said. "I'd like to feel it in use first. I don't imagine there will be much of a change to the code, will there?"

"No major changes, Jim," I said. "Just one line of code. Let's try it with a random selection and see how it runs. There won't be anything major that we haven't covered before in this new code, but we'll dissect the code afterward just to refresh things that we've learned."

Displaying a random image

1. In the Actions panel, add the following code after the `showLargePhoto` function:

```
selectCategoryImage = function (category) {
    rnd = Math.ceil(Math.random()*12)-1;
    fullsize = _root.attachMovie(category[rnd][2],
➥ category[rnd][2], 1000);
    fullsize._x = 550;
    fullsize._y = 360;
    _root.name.nameText.text = "#"+category[rnd][0]
➥ +" "+category[rnd][3];
    _root.description.descriptionText.text = category[rnd][4];
};
```

2. Now change the code for the category tabs. Add the new lines where shown:

```
redtab.tabButton.onRelease = function() {
     this._parent.swapDepths(1);
     selectCategoryImage (artistic);
     drawGrid(artistic, "artistic");
};
greentab.tabButton.onRelease = function() {
     this._parent.swapDepths(1);
     selectCategoryImage (family);
     drawGrid(family, "family");
};
yellowtab.tabButton.onRelease = function() {
     this._parent.swapDepths(1);
     selectCategoryImage (outdoor);
     drawGrid(outdoor, "outdoor");
};
bluetab.tabButton.onRelease = function() {
     this._parent.swapDepths(1);
     selectCategoryImage (portraits);
     drawGrid(portraits, "portraits");
};
```


3. Add this code to the very end of the script:

```
selectCategoryImage (artistic);
```

4. Now test the movie. Each time you click a category tab, a new random image for that category is displayed.

"This new function is almost the same as the code to display an image on thumbnail click. The main difference with this function is that a random number is created to choose a random image from the array.

"Generating a random number isn't as clean as you might think. As you can see here, there are lots of brackets and a little more code than you might expect. Let's start with the inner brackets. First, `Math.random` creates a random figure between 0 and 0.99999. This figure is multiplied by 12 to get a number from 0 to 11.999."

"What? Why do we have to go through all this work?" Jim asked. "Isn't there a random function like the one in BASIC?"

"Although this is a little more long-winded, Jim, it does the same thing," I said. "This line produces a random integer from 0 to 11 using the most compliant current script. `Math.ceil` is used to round the figure produced in the brackets up to the nearest whole number. Because the number produced from this will be from 1 to 12, we subtract 1 from it—remember, the array starts from 0.

"The `rnd` variable is then used to specify which image and data to pull out of the multidimensional array.

"This function is then called from each of the tab buttons as required, meaning that a random image is loaded each time any of the category tabs is clicked. The last bit of code we added initializes the interface, loading an image at start-up.

"Does that seem clear?" I asked, and to my delight the whole class nodded.

"As Mazzy has reminded us, we still need to finish off the About and Contact pages. We first created this movie clip in Class 7, but we still need to add Randy's details and a mailto button to the Contact page, so let's do that now."

"Sorry to interrupt, Ken, but what's a 'mailto' button?" asked Joe.

"A mailto is a simple e-mail link that will trigger the default e-mail package to open and create a new message to the mailto recipient," I replied

"Sounds like something people could probably do themselves!" Carl said.

"That's true, Carl, but a mailto saves the user a few valuable key presses, and it also makes getting in contact a little more accessible," I said.

"You have to face the fact that some people are just plain lazy," said Joe, and everyone laughed.

Customizing the Contact page

1. Open the Contact page movie clip.

2. On the **text** layer, use the Text tool to create a static text field and type in the following text, using Verdana font at 12 point font size:

Contact Randall
Please feel free to send any questions or comments to Randy at:
Randall Holmes,
221 Jefferson Avenue,
Nobinky,
SL 63614
USA
Tel: 800-800-8000
Email : randall@rhphotostudios.inc

3. Create a new layer beneath the text layer and call it **button**.

4. Draw a light-colored square on this layer. Convert this into a movie clip symbol called **mailto button** and give it the instance name `mailtoButton`.

Contact Randall
Please feel free to send any questions or comments to Randy at:
Randall Holmes,
221 Jefferson Avenue,
Nobinky,
SL 63614
USA
Tel: 800-800-8000
Email : randall@rhphotostudios.inc

5. Now add the following code to the `contactButton` callback:

```
contactButton.onRelease = function() {
    page = _root.attachMovie("contactPage", "contactPage",
➥ 1000);
    page._x = 552;
    page._y = 362;
    page.mailtoButton.onRelease = function () {
        getURL ("mailto:randall@rhphotostudios.inc");
    }
    clearTextBoxes();
};
```

"The action used to call the mailto is `getURL`. This action is the Flash equivalent of calling an HTML hyperlink. In scenarios in which you want to link to another website or web page, the URL location would be passed to `getURL` in the following manner:

```
getURL ("http://www.google.com");
```

"With this action, the Google main page would be loaded into the current browser window."

"Do we need to add those 'http://' bits?" Joe asked. "I never have to type them into my browser."

“Yes!” Gemma and Mazzy said firmly in unison. “If you don’t,” Mazzy continued, “the browser won’t know how to handle your request, and it will throw up a horrible error. Hardly professional!”

“It’s one of the first things I learned,” Gemma said. “I guess everyone tries to avoid typing full addresses to start with. I sure did. You’ll get used to typing them in, Joe!” Joe sighed.

“You sure will,” I laughed. I continued, “As with HTML anchors, the target browser window for the `getURL` action can be specified as part of the call. A link to Google in a new browser window looks like this:

```
getURL ("http://www.google.com", "_blank");
```

“For those of you who don’t already know, a `_blank` target opens a fresh browser window. The URL specified is then loaded into this fresh window. This is useful if you’re linking to external websites but want to retain the user at your own site. If no target is specified, the current browser window is assumed. For the `mailto` call, no target is required.

“It’s quite important to know that even though `getURL` is primarily used for hyperlinks, it can perform other functions, just like `mailto`. Even though you might not have much use for knowing this now, `getURL` is also used to call JavaScript functions and commands. Is everyone clear on this?”

The students nodded. “What about the About page?” Jim asked. “I thought we were going to add the photo of Randy to it.”

“Ironically, Randy has yet to choose a photo that he would actually like to use for this page,” I replied. “He might be in the studio with his assistant photographing a new portrait as we speak! He’s promised to get this to me in a few days, so I’ll update this page and bring in the finished file to next week’s class. Don’t worry, Jim, we have a few more things to do today.”

Working with projector files

“When Flash files are traditionally published, an SWF file is produced,” I started. “This SWF file is then embedded within an HTML document and displayed on the Web for viewing in a browser.

"Projector files are stand-alone Flash files that usually run full-screen. By 'stand-alone,' I mean that they don't require the user to have the Flash plug-in or any version of Flash to run them, because the Flash player is embedded in the file. Each Flash projector is its own executable EXE on Windows and is an application on the Mac.

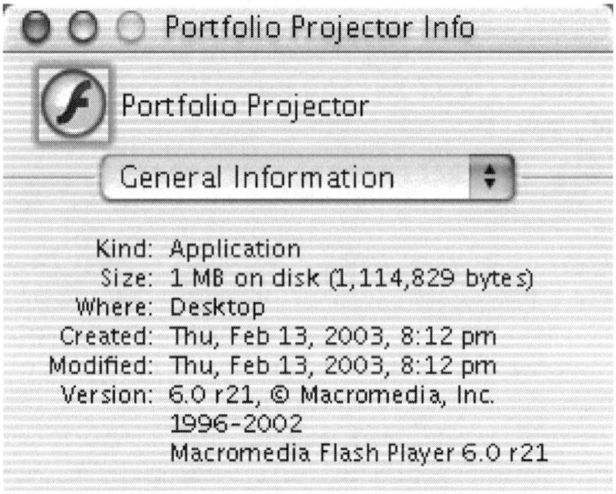

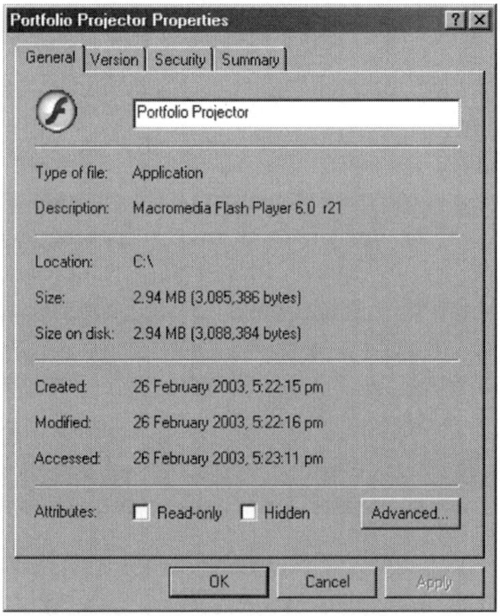

"Projector files also have the added option of being to able to run full-screen and without any interface restrictions. This gives a presentation a professional feel, and it's a far more immersive environment for the user without all the screen clutter."

"Will I have ever seen any Flash projectors?" Mazzy said. "I'm finding it hard to visualize them."

"You might have already experienced a Flash projector file on an enhanced music CD, Mazzy." Mazzy nodded. "Most of them have a few music videos that you can watch, along with a gallery of photos. The first thing that each of these CD presentations does is whisk you away from your desktop and operating system and place you in their full-screen world."

"For this reason, I imagine that projector files are cross-platform-friendly," Jim said. "If there are no operating system elements, I mean."

"They are, Jim, as long as you remember to publish a projector file for both Mac and Windows!" I replied. "The absence of screen clutter once a full-screen projector is launched makes it impossible to tell what the underlying operating system is.

"Randy's kiosk and CD presentations will be presented as a full-screen projector file to intentionally draw the user's attention to the photographs and nothing else."

Joe said, "A full-screen projector sounds like a movie experience in the movie theater. Because the screen is so big, the volume is so loud, and you're seated in the dark, it's hard to think about anything else. In comparison, watching a movie on VCR is just an inferior experience—the kids are fighting, the wife is making noise in the kitchen, and cars are roaring by outside!"

"Sounds like my house!" Carl said. "Without the wife, of course . . . ."

"Okay, so now that we know that we're going to work with full-screen projectors, does anyone remember anything about the two different versions of the Flash movie?" I asked.

"Sure. There's a CD and a kiosk version," Gemma said. "For the kiosk version, we don't require the About and Contact buttons . . . ."

"The CD version doesn't require the stats login," Mazzy added. "I imagine we'd leave the Quit button off the kiosk version too, otherwise people would be able to quit the projector."

"You've both highlighted all the things that we need to change," I said. "I'll write them on the board so we can all see them clearly." I wrote some notes on the board:

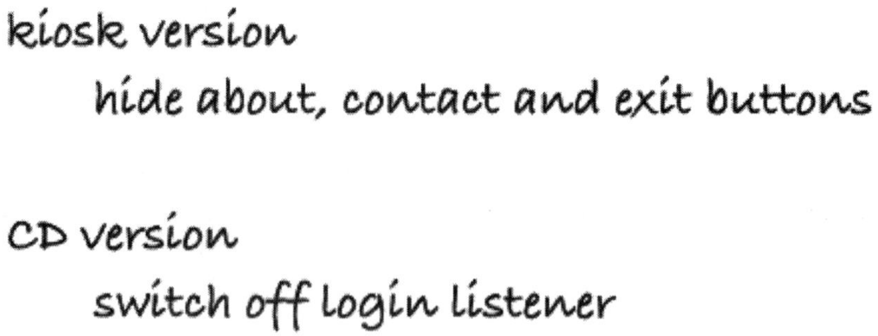

kiosk version
hide about, contact and exit buttons
CD version
switch off login listener

"Let's make some amendments to the code for each version."

Preparing code for two different presentation versions

"Making two versions of our code isn't too difficult because most of the considerations necessary were made in the last class. In particular, the functions `showCDButtons`, `hideCDButtons`, and `loginListener` are relevant for the two different presentation versions. Let's recap what each does:

```
showCDButtons = function () {
     _root.aboutButton._visible = true;
     _root.contactButton._visible = true;
};
```

"This function reveals the About and Contact buttons. Remember that these are required for the CD version.

```
hideCDButtons = function () {
     _root.aboutButton._visible = false;
     _root.contactButton._visible = false;
};
```

"This function hides the About and Contact buttons from view. It therefore needs to be called for the kiosk version.

"The `loginListener` function sets up the key detection event to access the stats screen. Once it's called, the keyboard detects a key press."

Adding kiosk functionality

1. Insert this code within the `initButtons` function:

```
if (isKiosk == false) {
    showCDButtons ();
} else {
    hideCDButtons();
}
if (isKiosk == true) {
    loginListener();
}
```

2. Now add the following lines in the `hideMainButtons` function:

```
hideMainButtons = function () {
    _root.redtab.tabButton._visible = false;
    _root.bluetab.tabButton._visible = false;
    _root.yellowtab.tabButton._visible = false;
    _root.greentab.tabButton._visible = false;
    if (isKiosk == false) {
        showCDbuttons();
    } else {
        hideCDButtons();
    }
    for (i=0; i<(rows*columns); i++) {
        _root["slideFrame"+i].removeMovieClip();
    }
};
```

11

3. Repeat the same for the showMainButtons function:

```
showMainButtons = function () {
    _root.redtab.tabButton._visible = true;
    _root.bluetab.tabButton._visible = true;
    _root.yellowtab.tabButton._visible = true;
    _root.greentab.tabButton._visible = true;
    drawGrid(artistic, "artistic");
    if (isKiosk == false) {
        showCDButtons();
    } else {
        hideCDButtons();
    }
};
```

4. Add this line of code where shown near the very end of the code:

```
isKiosk = true;
initButtons();
```

5. Test the movie.

"Okay, the first thing you might notice is that the About and Contact buttons have disappeared from the screen," I said. "This is because we've set up a flag variable called isKiosk that informs Flash if the presentation should run in kiosk or CD mode. In this case, isKiosk is set to true, and therefore runs as a kiosk presentation, hiding the About and Contact buttons. The actual calculations come down to simple if...else conditionals.

"If isKiosk is changed to false, then the key listener login won't be called, but the buttons will reappear.

"The actions added at steps 2 and 3 make the buttons disappear and reappear following login or logout from the stats screen."

"I'm surprised that it's all so easy," Joe said. "Changing one variable can change the presentation from one type to another."

"That's the power programming gives you, Joe," I said. "Every element can be switched on or off with one simple instruction. Now let's add the final button: the Quit button."

FSCommands

"Alongside the standard fare of Flash methods and actions, there is one action that doesn't really fit in with the others: `fscommand`. `fscommand` allows communication from a Flash movie to the Flash player or other technologies," I said. "If it sounds a little bizarre, that's because it is. `fscommand` has been around since version 3 of Flash and could do with a little updating!

"Although I'm not going to go into too much detail here, there are a few reasons why we have to use the `fscommand`. Most important, `fscommand` allows us to specify whether a movie should play full-screen. It also allows us to exit the projector file. Both these actions are exclusively available to `fscommand`, so if you're making a projector file, you'll have to work with them some time.

> *For more information on FSCommands specific to projectors, go to* www.macromedia.com/support/flash/ts/documents/fscommand_projectors.htm.

"Let's start with the Quit button," I said.

Adding CD functionality

1. Create a new movie clip symbol called **quit button**. Draw a basic rectangle and give it the text **quit**.

2. Drag a copy of this symbol onto the stage and give it an instance name of quitButton.

3. Open the Actions panel and add the following code to the initButtons function:

```
quitButton.onRelease = function() {
    fscommand("quit", true);
};
```

4. Now change the hideCDButtons function:

```
hideCDButtons = function () {
    _root.aboutButton._visible = false;
    _root.contactButton._visible = false;
    _root.quitButton._visible = false;
};
```

5. Add the following line to the showCDButtons function:

```
showCDButtons = function () {
    _root.aboutButton._visible = true;
    _root.contactButton._visible = true;
    _root.quitButton._visible = true;
};
```

6. Change the `isKiosk` variable to false:

```
isKiosk = false;
```

7. Publish the movie and open the SWF file from your desktop. It should open in the Flash player application.

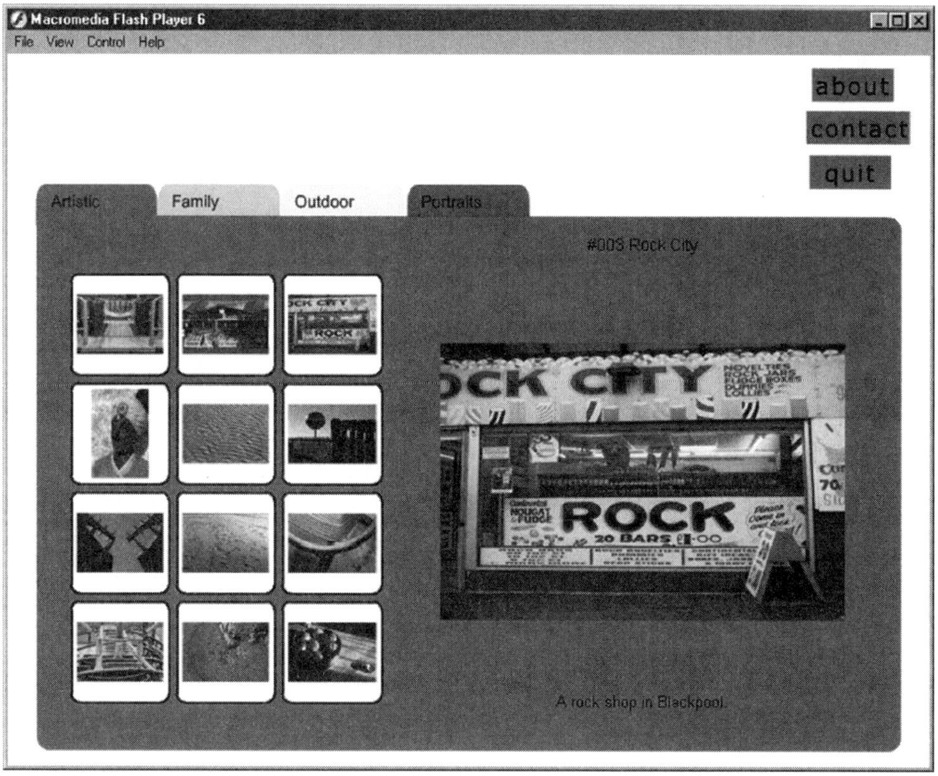

8. Click the quit button to close the Flash movie.

"Okay, there isn't much to really go over here because you're hopefully all savvy with events by now!" I said. "This code enables a Quit button with the `fscommand` action `quit`. Most `fscommands` are called like this."

"It looks more like a property than an action," Jim said. "Then again, I suppose it is a property—of whether the movie is running or not."

"I suppose you're right, Jim, but there's no telling with `fscommands`!" I said. "They're clearly necessary for certain situations, so if you must use them, use them. The next two commands are more like properties as you're used to seeing them." I asked the students to add the following to the end of the code:

```
fscommand("allowscale", false);
fscommand("fullscreen", true);
```

"As I mentioned a little while ago, the `fullscreen` property specifies if a Flash movie covers the screen," I said. "The `allowscale` property is necessary to prevent the Flash movie from scaling to fit the maximum screen space. If you don't set this to false, users who have their resolution set to higher than 800x600 will see a resized and distorted version of your Flash movie."

"I thought vectors scaled perfectly," Mazzy said.

"Vectors do, but bitmap images don't," Carl said. "Randy's photos are JPEGS, so they're bitmap images. Rescaled JPEGs tend to show blocky textures. It's pretty ugly and is best prevented!"

"Go ahead and publish the movie and open it from your desktop as before," I said. The students were occupied for a moment. "This time the presentation is dramatically different because it is the center of focus. Do any of you have your displays set to higher than 800x600?" I asked. Gemma and Jim nodded. "Why not comment out the allowscale action and republish the movie?

```
// fscommand("allowscale", false);
fscommand("fullscreen", true);
```

"I'd like you all to see how it looks when it is scaled, so you can tell the difference between a scaled and a nonscaled movie."

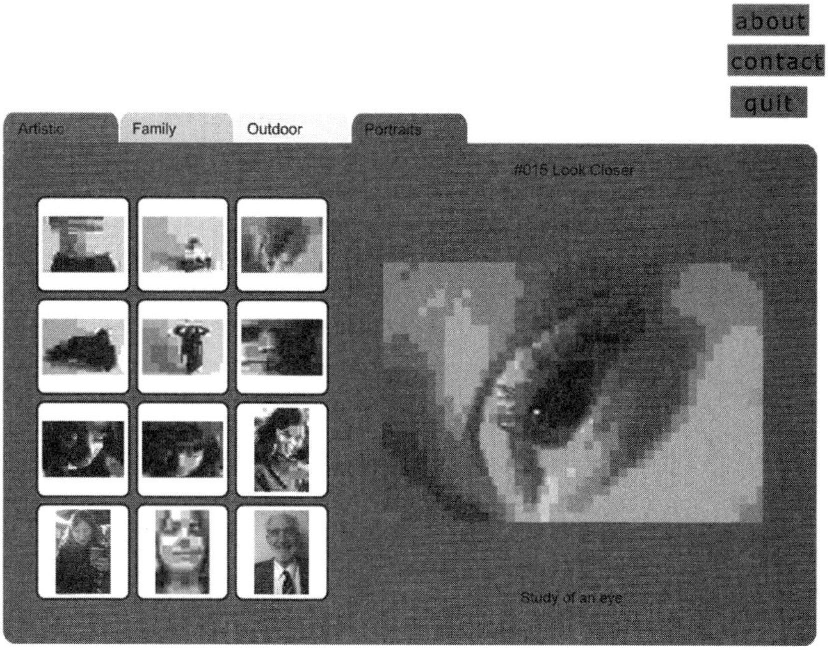

"There's that texture I was talking about," Carl said. "Doesn't make Randy's pictures look good, does it?"

"Are we satisfied with our two presentation modes?" I asked. "Is there anything else that needs implementing?"

"There is one thing, Ken," Mazzy started. "If the Quit button is hidden in kiosk mode, how does Randy quit the projector at the end of the day?"

"There are a few ways, Mazzy," I said, "most of which can be done with the keyboard. The projector file can be quit just like any other application using the ESCAPE key or the standard quit keyboard shortcut, which is CTRL/CMD+Q.

"Alternatively, pressing CTRL+F will toggle the full-screen mode and will allow Randy to return to his desktop with the movie still running. The movie can then be quit from the file menu or toggled back into full-screen mode."

"I think it needs a Quit button, all the same," Mazzy said. "Do you mind if I go ahead and place one on the stats screen?"

"Go ahead and do it if you think it's necessary, Mazzy," I said. "Use the `fscommand` quit action, and remember to place the button within the stats movie clip." Mazzy began working on it. "While Mazzy is working on that, the rest of us can look at the final step of production: publishing the file."

Publishing the Flash movie

"Now that the Flash movie is 99% complete, it's probably a good time to learn about finally publishing it as a projector file," I began.

"I'd like to learn about publishing for the Web," Mazzy said. "The updated church website is almost finished, and I need to put it online!"

"Okay Mazzy, I'll cover web publishing here too. First, I'd like you all to open the **Publish Settings** dialog box from the **File** menu. This dialog box has all the required options for publishing to a multitude of formats, but the most commonly used formats are Flash, HTML, and the two projector formats:

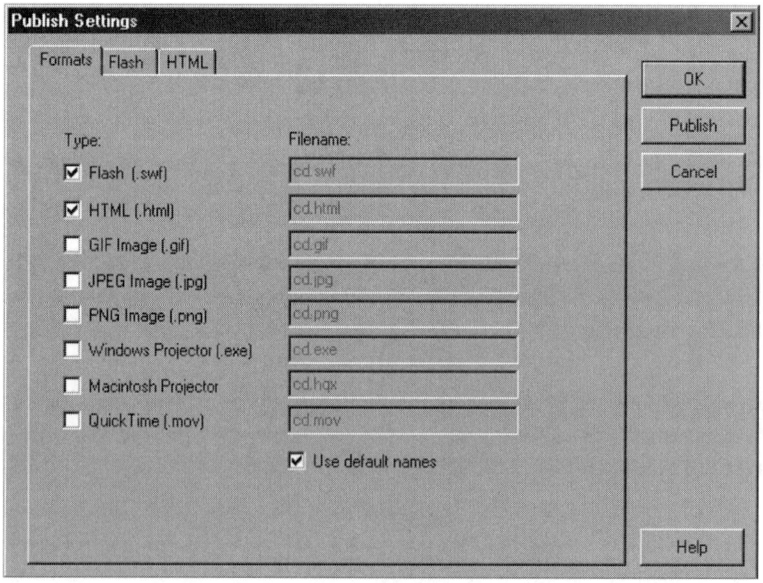

"The first screen allows you to specify which formats to publish to. Most of the options, when ticked, will show a tab with options specific to that file format." I turned to Mazzy. "When publishing for the Web, you only require two formats to be ticked: Flash and HTML. Having both of these ticked will produce an HTML file with the Flash file embedded within it." I asked the students to select the **Flash** tab:

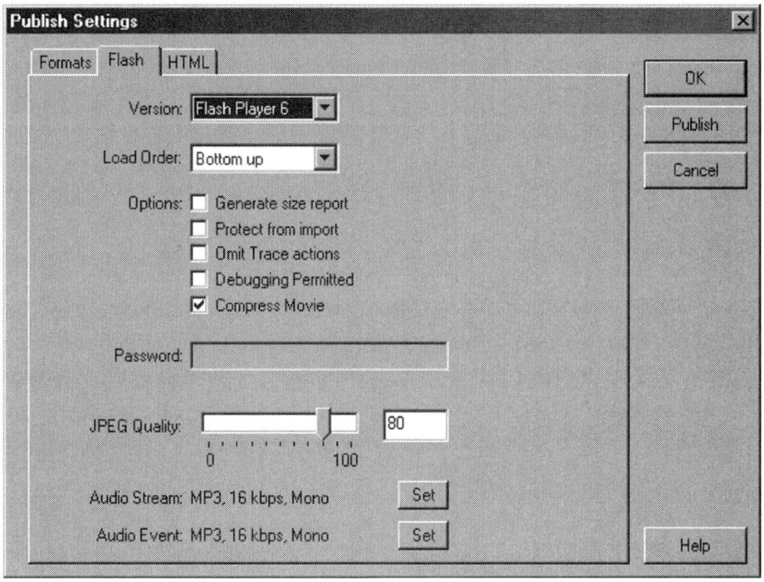

"The various options here will affect the published state of the Flash movie. At the moment, we can see the default settings, which are suitable for most published projects. One thing to note is the **JPEG Quality** setting, which affects the exported quality of JPEG images. As we talked about in a previous class, 80% will produce a good visual quality but an inflated file size. You'll need to change this, depending on the particular project involved.

"The **HTML** tab has options pertaining to embedding the Flash movie, from the page alignment to the movie size. As with the last tab, the default settings will be fine for most projects. You always have the option, of course, of changing your HTML code at a later date." I asked the students to click **Publish**.

"Now open the published HTML file in a browser. As you can see, the SWF file is displayed because it is embedded—or called—from the HTML page." I asked the students to view the HTML code of the page using **View > Source** or **Page Source**.

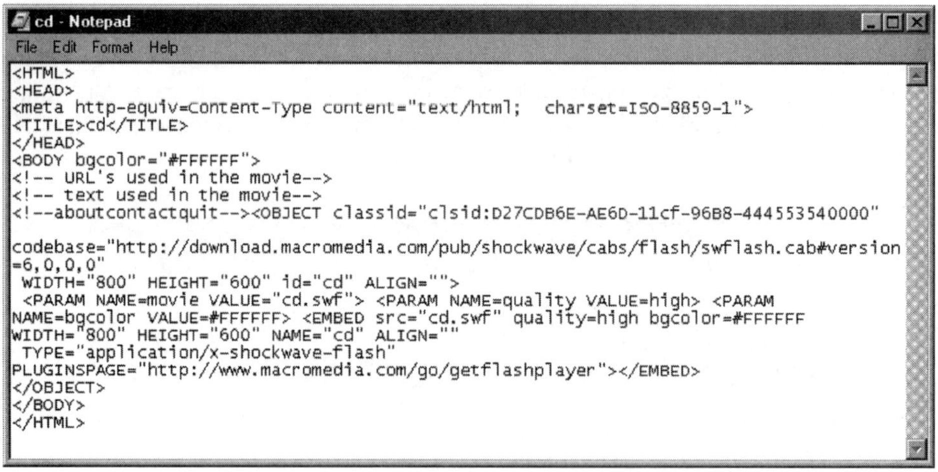


```
<HTML>
<HEAD>
<meta http-equiv=Content-Type content="text/html;  charset=ISO-8859-1">
<TITLE>cd</TITLE>
</HEAD>
<BODY bgcolor="#FFFFFF">
<!-- URL's used in the movie-->
<!-- text used in the movie-->
<!--aboutcontactquit--><OBJECT classid="clsid:D27CDB6E-AE6D-11cf-96B8-444553540000"

codebase="http://download.macromedia.com/pub/shockwave/cabs/flash/swflash.cab#version
=6,0,0,0"
 WIDTH="800" HEIGHT="600" id="cd" ALIGN="">
 <PARAM NAME=movie VALUE="cd.swf"> <PARAM NAME=quality VALUE=high> <PARAM
NAME=bgcolor VALUE=#FFFFFF> <EMBED src="cd.swf" quality=high bgcolor=#FFFFFF
WIDTH="800" HEIGHT="600" NAME="cd" ALIGN=""
 TYPE="application/x-shockwave-flash"
PLUGINSPAGE="http://www.macromedia.com/go/getflashplayer"></EMBED>
</OBJECT>
</BODY>
</HTML>
```

"Some of you might recognize this as HTML markup. If not, don't worry, because this just shows you that Flash has produced this code for you, and you haven't had to do anything by hand. You can go ahead and edit the layout of this page by hand using a text editor or using an HTML layout program such as Dreamweaver. Putting this website on the Web is now a case of FTPing both the HTML and SWF files to your web space."

"What did he just say?" Carl asked.

"Don't worry, Carl," Mazzy said. "I can show you how to do it."

"When you want to put your website on the Internet," continued Mazzy, "the files need to be uploaded. Uploading is the process of transferring files from your computer to another computer. The other computer is usually referred to as a 'server'."

"How are servers different if they're just computers?" asked Carl.

"Besides servers being slightly more powerful," said Mazzy, "files stored on servers are publicly available over the Internet. All of the websites on the Internet are stored on many, many servers, each of which allows access to its files. Without servers, there would be no Internet to speak of."

"I think that's a tangent," Mazzy said. "What Ken was going to say is that files are uploaded via a program called an FTP client." Carl opened his mouth to speak, but Mazzy continued nonetheless. "FTP stands for File Transfer Protocol, but that's not too important. Uploading files is usually referred to as FTPing."

"Aha. Now I think I understand. Where do I get this FTP client program?" Carl asked.

"There are quite a number available, Carl," I said. "Try CuteFTP for the PC or Fetch for the Mac. Both of these are FTP clients and function in a very similar way. However, you'll need a web space first . . . it's probably best to leave that step to you.

> *You can check out CuteFTP for Windows at* www.cuteftp.com *or Fetch for Mac at* www.fetchsoftworks.com. *For a free alternative, do a search on "FTP Clients" at* www.Google.com.

"Is there anything else you want to know about publishing Flash for the Web, Mazzy?" I asked.

"I don't think so, Ken," Mazzy said. "As long as I'm aware that I need both the HTML and Flash files uploaded, I should be able to figure the rest of it out from there."

"One last thing, though, Mazzy," I said. "As you might have guessed from the locale of both files, by default both of them need to be in the same folder. If you change the HTML file, though, you can change this." I paused. "Now we'll look at publishing the projector files."

Publishing the projector files

"As we briefly dicussed earlier, projector files run as stand-alone applications or executables. On a PC, this will usually be an EXE file, whereas Mac users will be accustomed to seeing application files without any visible extensions. Unlike the Director application, one copy of Flash running on either platform is able to publish projector files for both operating systems.

"Open the Publish Settings again, and tick only the Windows and Macintosh Projector boxes. The first thing you'll notice is that there aren't any tabs for them. This is simply because a projector is a projector! Projector files have little or no image compression, and as you learned earlier with the `fscommands`, any full-screen or scaling capabilities have been set up by you in the code.

"Before you go ahead and click Publish, I'd like to point out one thing. You see where it says Macintosh Projector here, notice the extension `.hqx` in the parentheses?" Most of the students nodded. "As I said earlier, Mac applications and projectors don't have any extensions. The extension you see here is a compressed format of the Mac projector. The reason for doing this relates to the PC's necessity for file extensions, so to undo this you'll need to decompress the file on a Mac before you can use it."

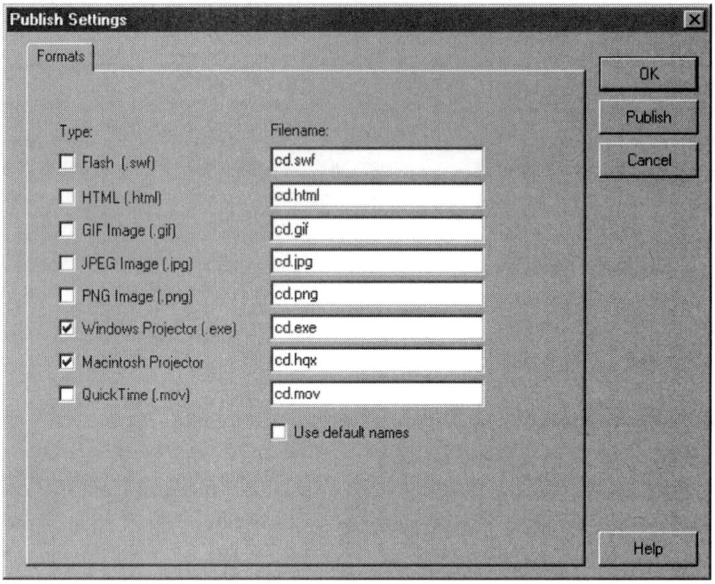

"It's also true that only Macs can write dual-format CDs," Gemma said. "If any of you want to create a Mac- and PC-format CD, you'll need to burn it on a Mac. The simple reason for this is that PCs can't support Mac formatting."

"This is where a Mac-user friend is helpful," I said, providing the rest of the students with a nudge toward Gemma. "I've already arranged for Gemma to burn the final CDs for Randy on her Mac at home.

"Okay, now go ahead and click Publish." The students all clicked together. "This will now produce both projector files wherever you have the FLA saved on your hard drive. Go ahead and open the version relevant to you and give it a try. These projectors work absolutely independently of the FLA, SWF, or any of the image files."

"You mean I can send this by e-mail to show my family?" Carl asked.

"Sure, Carl," I replied. "You can send the file in projector form, and assuming you've got the recipient's operating system right, the recipient will be able to run it. However, don't forget that the file is pretty hefty in size, so your relatives might not thank you for clogging up their inboxes. Projector files are larger than SWF files because the plug-in is contained within the projector file.

"Okay, that's about it for publishing," I said. "Gemma, will you be okay to finish the Flash file graphically and produce the CDs for us?"

"Sure," Gemma said. "Jim has offered to help me out this weekend. I'll bring the finished files into the class next week."

"Before we're able to tie up the project, though, there are a few things we need to do to the code to make it easier for us to maintain, should we need to," I said.

Coding conventions

"So far throughout the course, you've been adding code to the Flash file without really giving much thought as to where you're putting it," I started. "You've seen some obvious pieces of program flow—for example, a function must be defined before it can be called, but everything else has been placed rather arbitrarily.

"In fact, you've been putting them in a specific order, but you may not have noticed."

"I saw that certain things were grouped together," Mazzy spoke up. "The arrays were all in one place and the functions in another."

"That's right," I said, "one of the coding conventions is to keep similar or related code in the same place. This helps when you're trying to find something specific in the code, or there's a bug that needs to be cleared up. If you know the general thing that you're looking for—that is, a function, an array, or whatever—then you can narrow down your search to a specific area, rather than having to check through your entire code.

"Another convention is the order in which you structure your code. You've used a common order, starting by declaring your arrays, then following that with your functions, and finally your initialization information that sets the program running. Another thing that you also may not have realized is that you followed another Flash programming convention by keeping all of your code on the same frame.

"Why should you use these conventions? Well, code is rarely perfect forever, and conventions make it easier not only for you to maintain your code, but also for other people to maintain it. After all, it's likely that if you ever go into programming professionally, you'll seldom be the only person to work on your code. Years after you've moved on from the company, your code could still be in use, so it's good practice to make your code as easily maintainable as possible.

"This leads to another convention: commenting. It's good practice to include as many comments as required to allow other people—and yourself too, depending on how good your memory is—to easily get acquainted with the program and quickly pick up what it does and how it does it.

"Also, a convention that you haven't yet followed, but you can remedy that now, is to include a standard set of commented information at the beginning of every file you write. This information includes such things as your name, the date that the program was created, and the version number of the program. Let's add some information to the start of your file now:

```
/*     Program Name: Randall Holmes Photo Gallery
 *     Programmer: Ken Jokol
 *     Created: 03/03/03
 *     Version: 1.0
 */
```

"You'd put any copyright notices pertaining to the file in here as well. Although this information isn't as essential for everyday use as it is in a commercial programming environment, it's still good practice to add it, and you'll find it comes in handy when you next get around to updating the file.

"Other conventions include more general things, such as spacing out your code and not having more than one instruction per line. These kinds of conventions are more essential in other programming languages than Flash, though, as Flash has the handy autoformat button that can take care of all of your code formatting for you. It's worth bearing in mind, though, that the autoformat button is not infallible. Do you remember the case statements in your sort functions? You broke out the code within these onto separate lines for increased readability like so:

```
case "Hits" :
    hitSort = function (a, b) {
        if (a[0]<b[0]) {
            return -1;
        } else if (a[0]>b[0]) {
            return 1;
        } else {
            return 0;
        }
    };
```

"If you autoformat them in Flash, though, they get compressed onto one line, making them difficult to read, like this:

```
hitSort = function (a, b) { if (a[0]<b[0]) {return -1;} else
➥ if (a[0]>b[0]) {return 1;} else {return 0;}};
```

"Although it feels like a hassle sometimes going through and correcting Flash's autoformatting, it's well worth it for the trouble it will save you when you're trawling through your code trying to find a bug. Although 11 weeks ago, both of those would have looked as readable as each other to you, hopefully you can now see what a huge difference readable code makes to a programmer.

"Another case when autoformatting can make things less readable is regarding blank lines. When you're writing code, you'll find that you quite often put in blank lines to separate blocks of code. These separations can be incredibly helpful in making your code readable, but they disappear when the code is autoformatted. An easy way to keep your program broken into blocks is to use empty comment lines to separate sections.

"We encountered another example of code readability back when we looked at the order of operator precedence. Although these

X = a*b+7*4/c-56;
X = (a*b) + ((7*4)/c) - 56;

"may give the same answer, the second one is easier to follow. Use parentheses to tidy up expressions whenever you can.

"Yet another programming convention that you can follow is in naming. We've already discussed some aspects of Flash naming conventions, but here's a list of pointers." I then wrote on the board:

*Always use unique names.

*Always use meaningful names rather than abstract or over-simplified references that you'll quickly forget.

*Use a mix of lower- and uppercase letters to split names into words, for example, myArray, or mainMenuButton.

*You may find it helpful to add suffixes to your names, for example - thing_mc for a movieclip, thing_btn for a button, thing_array for an array, and so on.

"We also encountered a coding convention when we looked at loops. We saw then that the name given to the loop counter variable was usually '`i`', and for a nested loop it was followed by '`j`'.

"That's about all of the common conventions that spring to mind right now, but you may encounter more, or create some of your own, along your programming journey. Of course, nothing will happen to you if you don't follow these conventions (unless they're enforced by your employer), but by following them you'll find that not only is the code easier for you to read, but also it's easier for other people to read, and that's always a good thing.

"To save you all the hard work, I'm going to take all these rules into consideration and I'm going to make sure that the code is clear, well structured, and commented. You're all free to go." The students got up and left. Gemma and Jim came over to me.

"Will you send me the newly structured code via e-mail, Ken?" Gemma asked.

"Sure," I replied. "I'll get the code and photo of Randy to you before this weekend, so you can work your magic on it. Thanks to you both for doing this."

"No problem," they said, smiling at each other blissfully.

Summary

In this lesson, you've made some final adjustments to the kiosk project, starting with using the `setInterval` action to create a time delay for the tooltips. You learned the following:

- The `setInterval` action is a timed event configured to run after a certain amount of time has passed. It isn't dependent on frame rate and is therefore more reliable.
- A `setInterval` action consists of two parameters:
    - What you should do when the time has passed (the event handler)
    - The amount of time that needs to pass (measured in milliseconds)
- A `setInterval` action can be deleted using the `clearInterval` action. For the case study, the `setInterval` event was placed inside the rollover handler, so as to set a 750 milliseconds delay before showing the tooltip. The `clearInterval` action was placed after the rollout handler so that as the cursor rolls off the image the `setInterval` action is cleared.

You then discovered how to display an image from a certain category and display a random image using `Math.random`:

```
Math.ceil(Math.random()*12)-1;
```

Next, you customized the Contact page by adding a mailto button. You used the `getURL` action to call the mailto, using the following format:

```
getURL ("mailto:randall@rhphotostudios.inc");
```

You learned about preparing your code for two different presentation formats by ensuring that the appropriate buttons would be displayed for each format.

- You used the `showCDButtons` and `hideCDButtons` functions to either display or hide the About and Contact buttons.

- You used a simple `if...else` command to check to see whether the flag variable `isKiosk` is set to true.

The lesson finished by looking at some basic coding conventions, including the following:

- Keeping related code together.

- Following a common order. Your code started with declaring the arrays, followed by the functions and then the initialization information.

- Keeping all the code on the same frame of a Flash movie.

- Commenting the code so that it can be easily understood years later or by other users.

- Adding commented information to the beginning of every file, including programmer name, date, program version, and any copyright information.

- Spacing code out so that it is readable and follows the order of precedence.

The next lesson is the final one. You'll customize the case study by looking at using sound and video in Flash, and you'll learn about optimizing Flash files for the Internet. It will also be time to say good-bye to the students.

Class 12
Modifying the Case Study

Objectives

In the final class of the course, the students will focus on altering the kiosk project so that each can derive personal benefit from it. They'll be looking at

- How Flash deals with sound
- Loading in MP3s dynamically
- Using video in Flash
- Optimizing Flash for the Web

The class will finish off by looking at a few extra things Flash can do, such as draw just by using ActionScript and tell the time.

The end of the road

Today was the last day of the course, and I arrived early to copy a few surprise files onto the students' computers. It had seemed like a long 12 weeks, and I felt that the students deserved to have a bit of a rest and a reward after all of the hard work that they'd put in.

The students arrived on time and in jovial spirits, with Carl trying to balance a pencil on Joe's hat without him noticing and Mazzy trying to keep from laughing as she was talking to Joe. I waited for them all to sit down and then began. "Good evening to you all, and welcome to your last 'Learn Programming' lesson. As you all know, we finished up the coding of the case study last week, and Jim and Gemma informed me that the graphical overhaul is done too, so you might be wondering what is left to do today."

“Can we go home early then, Ken?” suggested Carl.

“I'm afraid not,” I said, smiling, “you don't think I'd let you off that easy, do you? There's still plenty for us to do today. Do you remember back in the first couple of weeks when we first discussed taking on this project, that you all gave me reasons for why you felt that the gallery would be helpful to each of you personally? Well, today I thought we'd spend a bit of time going over those reasons, and expanding on them all.

“We'll be covering such things as optimizing the gallery for the Web, and adding sounds and videos, and we'll possibly also look into adding some more dynamic elements to it. I figure that should take up at least the first half of the class, and in the second half, I've got a few surprises for you, one of which is a mystery guest.

“Okay, let's start by taking a look at the case study. Gemma, Jim, would you like to take the stage and let us know how you performed your miracle makeover?” Jim and Gemma exchanged a glance and then scraped back their chairs and made their way to the front of the class. In the meantime, I made my way to the back to watch.

The cosmetically enhanced case study

“Is it okay to use the projector on your computer?” Gemma asked.

“Sure, no problem,” I replied. “Just flick the switch at the back to turn it on, and then just say 'yes' to the box that appears on screen. It should work fine from then on.” Gemma thanked me and went about setting up the projector. Meanwhile, Jim walked forward and started to speak.

“Okay, first of all, I want to point out that this was 99% Gemma's work—all I did was sit in the background and click a few buttons to burn the CD at the end.”

“Liar!” called out Gemma from behind the monitor.

“Whatever she says,” continued Jim, “I hope you enjoy it. We had a good laugh redesigning certain aspects of it, and I hope that some of that fun carries across into the work. Are we ready yet, Gemma?” he asked, turning to her with a mock whisper. “The crowd is dying on me.”

"It's the CD you burned that's taking all the time," she said. "I'm afraid I can't help you. Flash has loaded now, I'm just going to publish it and then we're off. Okay, we're ready, introduce us quick."

"Ladies and gentlemen, welcome to the world premiere of Randy's Photo Gallery version 1.2. Carl, drumroll please, if you'd be so kind." Carl beat out a pounding rhythm on the table with a couple of pencils. "That's not quite the paradiddle I was after, but it's good enough." Just then, Gemma flicked on the projector and revealed the design to the class:

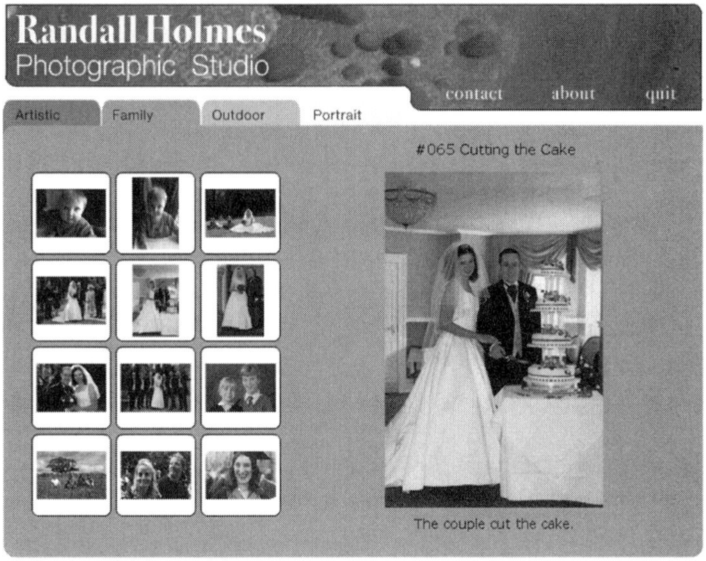

"Cool!" Carl exclaimed. "I'm glad you toned down the primary colors!"

"I think this deserves a round of applause from all of you," I said. The students erupted in a racket of claps and whoops. "Talk us through what you did," I said to Gemma and Jim.

"Ask Gemma what *she* did," Jim said. "Tell the good people why and what you did, Gemma."

"Wimp!" Gemma said, poking her tongue out at him. "We didn't really change that much, believe it or not. I suppose the main addition is the header bar at the top of the interface. We felt that it needed something to frame the page. The lip on the right side fills the chasm between this and the tabs, and it also serves as the ideal place for the CD buttons."

"The decision to use a photograph seemed obvious," said Jim, "but deciding on the image to use was quite difficult. Originally, we intended to use a more textural image," Jim nodded at Gemma, who rolled over an image from the grid, "but in the end this seemed to lack a focus."

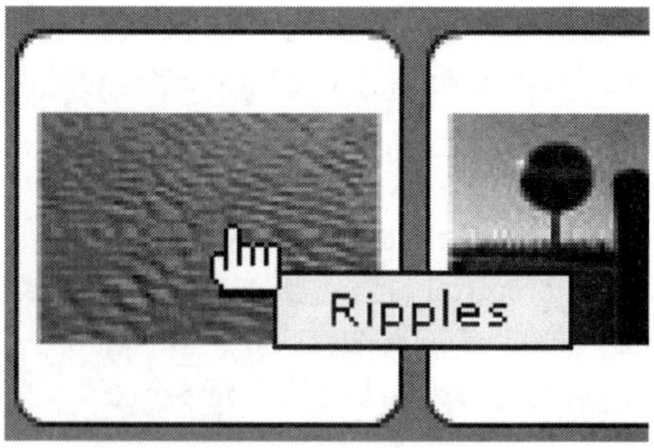

Gemma said, "The image that we chose is successful because it has detail but it isn't so detailed that it draws the user's attention from the most important element of the interface: the thumbnail grid."

"Once we had decided on this photograph," Jim started, "we decided to pick colors from it for the tabs. As Carl pointed out, the tabs were a little garish in primary colors, so we decided to tone them down a little. The new colors are quite soft, and I think they further emphasize the thumbnails." Jim looked at Gemma. "What else, Gemma?"

"All the other details are minimal changes," Gemma said, "like font changes and so on. Little tasks like reducing the outline stroke size of the slide frames also improved the general appearance."

"I think you're both being incredibly modest about your achievements," I said. "All the minor touches, like the different font for Randy's name, really make a difference."

"Gemma taught me a valuable lesson about sticking with two fonts," Jim said. "Usually, I think I go crazy with all the fonts on my system. We used the same two fonts throughout—even on the About and Contact pages. Gemma said that it added to the gestal . . .uh . . . gestas . . ."

"Gestalt!" Gemma said. "This basically means unity of form. Sticking to color schemes, fonts, shapes, and similar assets gives the whole a unified feel—this is gestalt." Gemma clicked the About button. "As you can see here, I used the same fonts as elsewhere—on the tabs, the logo, and so on. It's not clever to use loads of fonts, Jim!"

About Randall Holmes
The Randall Holmes photographic studio acts both as a gallery for selling Randy's own prints, and as a studio for client work. Randy's current line-up includes, but is not limited to:
- Portraits – both studio and natural.
- Weddings
- Company photos
- Landscape prints
- Artistic prints

"I love the photo," Mazzy said. "I know that Randy is a really keen surfer!"

"I suppose that might be why so many of his photos are taken on the beach," Joe said. "When he's not surfing, he's checking how big the waves are!"

Jim laughed. "On that note, we're done with our small presentation," he said.

"Are there any questions?" Gemma asked. "What do you all think of it?"

"I love it," Mazzy said, "but it's not us who it was made for—just wait until Randy gets here."

"Well done to you both," I started, "you've done a sterling job. The rest of you should remember, though, that we all had a part in this from the very first class. Gemma and Jim have just saved the rest of us a lot of time with all the finishing touches."

"Oh, so that's why you asked us to do it!" Gemma exclaimed. "You were all too busy living it up or something."

I coughed theatrically. "Ahem . . . on that note. Let's move on, shall we?"

The individual case studies

"It's hard to follow that fantastic presentation, but I guess I'll just have to," I said. "The next item on today's agenda is to look into modifying the case study for each of your personal gain and hopefully to benefit the rest of the class with an expansion of their Flash knowledge."

Carl: Sound in Flash

"We'll begin with Carl. If you remember, I managed to coerce Carl into getting excited about this project by hinting at the possibilities of putting his band on the Web, including a jukebox of the band's songs. Unfortunately, we don't have any of Carl's songs to use, but we can put in placeholders anyway."

"Actually, Ken," said Carl, "funny you should say that. I put some MP3s of the band onto our website just the other day. They're only HTML links at the moment, but it would be cool to put up a Flash site for them. We can download a couple to use. Wow! You'll get to hear the wonder that is Mondo."

"Oh, Lord save us," pleaded Mazzy, setting the class off laughing.

"Okay, then," I began, "Carl, can you start downloading a couple of songs onto your desktop, and I'll start preparing the file. For the time being, you'll just create a simple FLA with a few basic buttons in it, just to give you an idea of what you can do. Start a new movie and create a movie clip to be used for each of the buttons—just a simple rectangle will do, and you'll color it later. Drag six instances of this button onto the stage, three on one side and three on the other.

"Carl, do you have any preferences for a color scheme?" I asked.

"Black and yellow," said Carl, closing his eyes. "Mondo is the colors of the wasp."

"Whatever you say," I told Carl with a smile, "black and yellow it is. Anything else?"

"Nope, just black and yellow. I could draw the sign of Mondo on it too, if you'd like," Carl said.

"That's all right, Carl," I responded. "I think we'll just stick with the color scheme now.

"In Flash, sound is treated as an object, so you create it just like you would any other object, using the keyword new. You'll call this sound `currentTrack`, so open up the Actions panel and start typing:

```
currentTrack = new Sound();
```

"How are those songs coming along, Carl?"

"Almost there," Carl said. "Where do you want me to put them when they're done?"

"I made a folder on the network earlier called `Mondo MP3 Files`," I replied. "If you just drag them in there, then I'll be able to find them."

"Okay, will do. I'll give you a shout when they're done," said Carl.

"While we're waiting for the music to download, we can start on the buttons," I said. "Create a static text field over each of the buttons and name them 'play', 'pause', and 'stop' on one side, and 'song1', 'song2', and 'song3' on the other. Give them the instance names `playButton`, `pauseButton`, `stopButton`, `song1button`, `song2button`, and `song3button`.

"You all know how to code callbacks by now, so you'll just create basic empty callbacks and then fill them when you have your sounds. The code for them will look like this:"

```
song1button.onRelease = function() {
};
song2button.onRelease = function() {
};
song3button.onRelease = function() {
};
playButton.onRelease = function() {
};
pauseButton.onRelease = function() {
};
stopButton.onRelease = function() {
};
```

"Okay," said Carl, "they're there."

"Thanks, Carl, I'll get them now," I said. "Bringing sounds into Flash is much the same as bringing in images, like you did for the gallery. You use the **Import to Library** option from Flash's File menu and then navigate to the sounds that you want. Flash can import four standard computer sound formats: MP3, WAV, AIF, and AU. The most common ones you'll probably be using are MP3 and WAV. As with images, it's often better to bring sounds into Flash at as high a quality as possible, and then do all the compression in Flash."

"Mine are all MP3s," said Carl, "sorry about that."

"No problem, we'll still be able to see the settings. You can find all of the compression settings for sounds in the Library by the same process as you did for images: right-click the sound and select **Properties**.

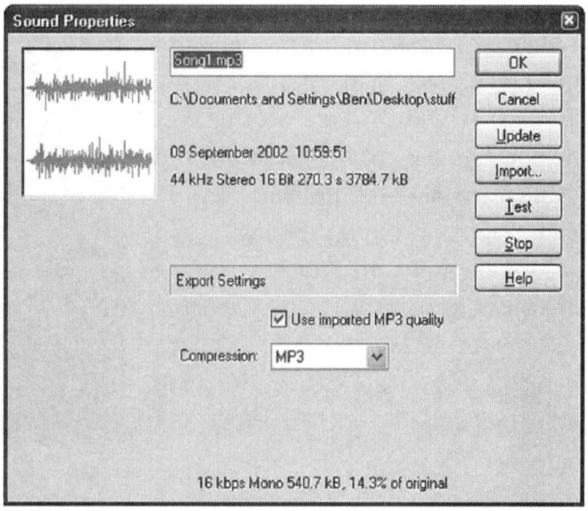

"Because the sound was already in MP3 format, you can see that Flash has automatically chosen to use the quality settings that the track was originally compressed with. If you want to change those settings, though, you can just uncheck the **Use imported MP3 quality** box to reveal the other options:

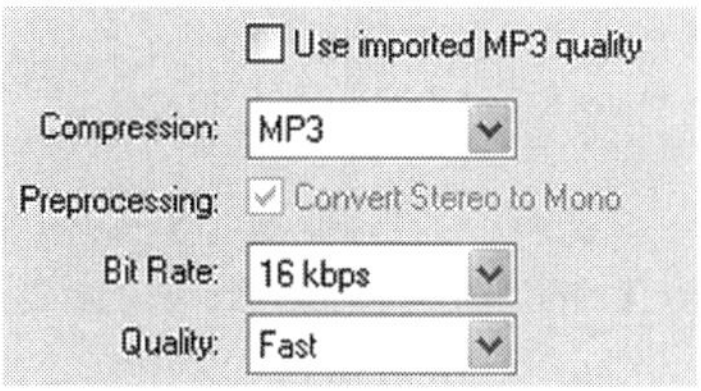

"In here, you can change the **Bit Rate** and the **Quality**. Basically, the rule goes that the higher the bit rate, the higher the sound quality, but the larger the file size. You can also use the drop-down menu to select another compression type if you like. Handily, Flash gives you a size report at the bottom of the screen so you can see how the compression fares against the original:

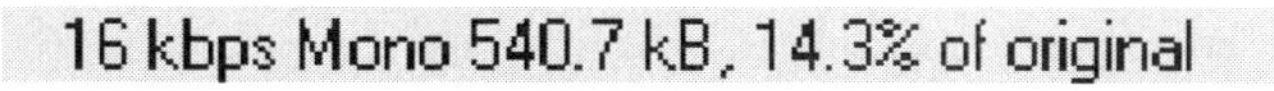

"Flash gives both a file size and a percentage comparing it to the original for ease of reference. To test the results of the new compression options, you can click the **Test** button and Flash will play the sound. It's important that you do always test the sound, as different compression settings can make huge differences to the sound quality.

"You'll also see that there's a Default option in the menu. Just as for images, you can set a default sound compression option in the Flash Publish Settings box and tell all of your sounds to use the same compression. As with images, though, it's better to tweak sounds individually to ensure that you get the best quality and file size that you can.

"Okay, now you have some sounds in Flash to play with, you can start to look at the `Sound` object in more detail. Let's start off by coding the song selection buttons. All of these buttons are pretty much the same, so we'll just look at one then use the same technique for the other two.

"You want to attach a sound from the Library to your `currentTrack` sound object. Just like attaching a movie, if you want to call a sound from the Library, then you need to give it a linkage name first. For the sake of simplicity, let's give them the names `song1`, `song2`, and `song3`. Sounds are given linkage names in the same way as movies, by right-clicking them in the Library and selecting **Linkage.**

"That's the first part of the definition taken care of. The next thing that you need to do is use the linkage name to attach your sound. You do this, as you might have guessed, by using a method of the Sound object. If you browse through the methods in the Actions panel, then you'll see one called attachSound, which looks perfect. You just need to tell Flash which sound to attach and where to attach it to:

```
currentTrack.attachSound("song1");
```

"Notice that the linkage name of the sound is in quote marks. That's basically all of the code that you need for these buttons, and it's an easy job of replicating it for the other two. The only thing that you need to change is the linkage name, as you'll be attaching the sounds over the top of each other on the same object. The complete code for the three song selection buttons then is as follows:

```
song1button.onRelease = function() {
    currentTrack.attachSound("song1");
};
song2button.onRelease = function() {
    currentTrack.attachSound("song2");
};
song3button.onRelease = function() {
    currentTrack.attachSound("song3");
};
```

"Okay, let's turn to the track control buttons. First, the Play button.

"The Play button is the easiest of the three to write code for. All that you need to do is tell the current track to start playing, and there's a method of the Sound object that does exactly that. The code looks like this:

```
playButton.onRelease = function() {
    currentTrack.start();
};
```

"If you simply use the start method like this, then Flash will start the sound playing from the beginning. You should now be able to test the movie and hear the sound playing. The only problem is that you haven't yet coded a Stop button, so you may find yourself listening to Mondo forever."

"Rock!" said Carl.

"Luckily for us," I continued, "the Stop button won't take long to code at all. Just as there's a simple and obvious command to make the sound start, there's another one to make it stop. The code for the Stop button is

```
stopButton.onRelease = function() {
    currentTrack.stop();
};
```

"Spoilsports," said Carl, "all of you."

"Sorry, Carl," I responded. "I promise we'll have a good listen to the tracks. Okay, now that you have the Play and Stop buttons working, take a listen and see if the buttons work." I published the movie and prepared to click a button. "Any preferences for which song you want first, Carl?"

"Nope, just start from one, and work your way down," said Carl.

"I won't need earplugs, will I?" asked Mazzy.

"Don't worry," I told her, "I won't be playing it too loud." Carl looked daggers at me. "What I mean, Carl, is that I shouldn't put it up too loud for fear of distortion through these tiny speakers."

"You're right, the sound quality probably won't be too hot coming through the PC speakers," said Carl, "but it should be okay. If anyone wants, I can get them some CDs of us playing. I recorded one of our gigs recently, and I've got a couple of practices on disc as well." Nobody jumped at the opportunity. "Oh well, wait until you hear it and then see if you change your mind. Okay, Ken, hit it." I did as Carl asked, and started the first track playing. Carl talked us through the tracks, and at the end Mazzy started off a round of applause that Carl basked in.

"Okay, the Stop and Play buttons are working on a basic level, so now let's see if we can get the Pause functionality to work. This button is different from all of the others, because it has two separate functionalities on the same button: pausing and unpausing. Pausing and unpausing are basically the same as stopping and starting, but with the important difference that you want to restart from where you paused the track, rather than from the beginning again.

"Flash doesn't have specific pause functionality built in, so to do this, you need to keep track of how far into the song you are when you stop it, and then start it playing again from that point. Luckily, Flash does allow you to do this quite easily. You can tell where you are in a track by making use of a property of the `Sound` object, `position`. Another thing that you need to do is keep track of whether or not the track is currently paused. Can anyone remember the name of the thing you used to keep track of something's state?"

"Was it a flag?" asked Mazzy.

"That's the one," I said. "You need to set a flag containing a Boolean value to tell you which state you're currently in.

"Okay, let's call the flag `paused` and first check to see if the button hasn't already been pressed:

```
pauseButton.onRelease = function() {
     if (paused != true) {
```

"There are three things you need to do when you pause the track. Can anyone tell me what they are?"

"Record the position of where we are?" asked Carl.

"Stop the sound playing," said Joe.

"And . . .?" I asked, when it didn't look like the third answer was forthcoming.

"Oh, and change the state flag, of course," said Gemma.

"Good, then let's do those three things," I said. "Storing the position is the only one that you haven't seen yet, but it's quite simple:

```
          soundPosition = currentTrack.position;
          currentTrack.stop();
          paused = true;
     }
```

"Okay, the track is stopped and the position is recorded. Now you just need to tell Flash what to do when the button is clicked again. There are only two possible states for `paused` and you've already coded one, so you can just use an `else` here for the other.

"All that you want to do here is start the sound playing again at the correct point where you stopped it before and then reset your state flag. It just so happens that you can pass a parameter with the `start` method to tell Flash exactly where in the track you want to start playing from.

"Problem solved? Well, not quite. You see, there's a small discrepancy between the value that the `position` property returns and the value that the `start` method takes. `position` is stored in milliseconds, and `start` takes a value in seconds. As long as you're aware of this, though, it's an easy problem to get around. You just need to divide `position` by 1,000 to change it into seconds. The code for the second half of the Pause button looks like this:

```
    else {
        currentTrack.start(soundPosition/1000);
        paused = false;
    }
```

"You can now test the movie and see if the Pause button works." I did so, and merrily paused and unpaused the music. While it was paused, Carl put a challenge to the class, "I bet you can't tell what the mystery musical instrument in the first track is. I'll give you a clue: it's something that you might find in the kitchen." Intrigued, I played the first track once more, and then again with the volume turned up a little more. I said, "Well, you've got me stumped, Carl. Does anyone else have any ideas?"

"Can you give us another clue?" asked Jim. "Can you tell us where in the track we can hear this mystery instrument?"

"It's the kind of bongo sound that you can hear," said Carl, looking a little smug. I played the track through again, but nobody had any feasible ideas of what it could be. "I'm playing on the bottom of a tube of potato chips," said Carl with a grin. I played it through again, and sure enough, we could tell what the sound was now that we knew what to listen for. "Very creative, Carl," said Mazzy, "and do you know what? I don't mind listening to that track either. Maybe children should be told to play with their food after all!"

"Now that you have the basic functionality of the buttons working, let's take a look a little further into what you've done," I said. "You may just find that your code isn't as bulletproof as you'd hoped. Let's start with the Play button.

"If I click Play, then you hear the sound start as you'd expect it to, but listen to what happens if I click it again." I did so, and the students were surprised to hear another copy of the tune starting up while the other one was still playing.

"Cool, it's like a virtual mixing desk!" said Carl.

"I guess you could see it like that," I said, "but you may also see it as an annoyance. Flash has the capability to play eight sounds at once, so every time you click the Play button, it thinks that you want it to start up another sound playing at the same time. If what you actually want to do is play only one sound at a time, then you'd have to alter the Play button code to first stop the current sound and then start the new sound playing.

"Another problem is the Pause button. If you click Pause to stop a track, then change tracks and click Pause again, the new track will start playing from the old track's paused position. You can get around this by adding some code to each of the track selection buttons to set `paused` to false whenever they're clicked.

"Hopefully, you'll find that when you come up against problems like this, you'll know enough to be able to think around the problem and come up with a simple solution.

"We won't look any deeper into the `Sound` object for now, but if you do, you'll find volume and pan controls."

"This is all excellent, Ken, thanks," said Carl. "Seeing as you are open to questions, I wonder if I could ask you about something else." I nodded. "I was hoping to set up a Mondo playlist on the Web. I've heard that there are specialist programs to do this, but I'd like to stream in some choice Mondo cuts."

"Like web radio, you mean?" I asked. Carl nodded.

"What is streaming?" Joe asked.

"I had a feeling one of you would ask that," I said. "Streaming is where content is played as soon as it's loaded, so in terms of a song, once a section is loaded it's immediately played. Then while that portion is playing, the next portion is being loaded in. There's a lot more to streaming than this, but from a Flash point of view, this is really all you need to know.

"In the last exercise, all three MP3 files are stored in the Library and are just called from there when required. In a streaming situation, the MP3 files are loaded into Flash when required, and as a portion is loaded in, it's played. If you'd like, Carl, we can make Radio Mondo right now."

"That'd be ace," Carl said. "Finally, the masses with modems can rock in a Mondo style."

Dynamically loading MP3 files

"I'd like you all to open a new Flash movie," I said. "Even though you'd probably like to customize this yourself, Carl, I'll quickly create a background in the assumed Mondo style of the wasp." I drew a couple of rectangles on the stage and added a static text box:

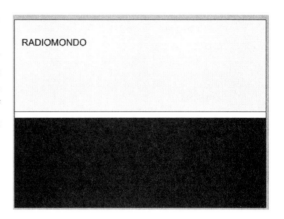

"In the bottom half, add a multiline dynamic text box with the instance name `radioText` and yellow text. This text box will display the current track that's playing.

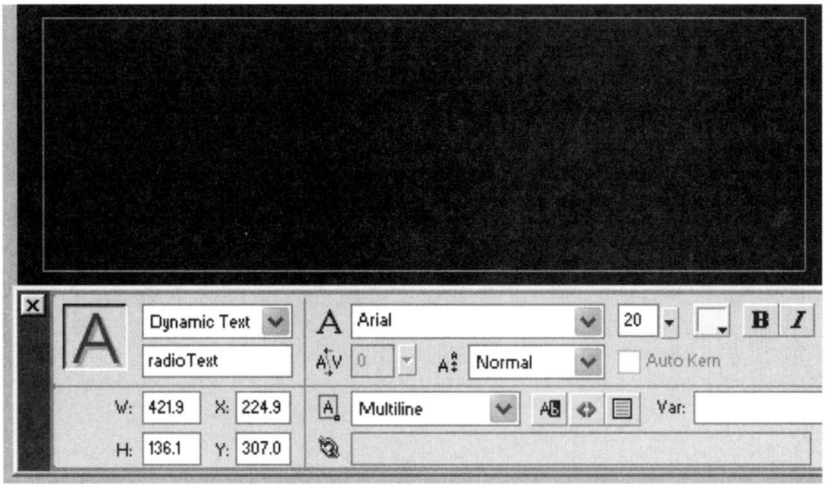

"Now you can go straight to the coding. On a new layer called **actions**, start by adding the following code:

```
songs = new Array();
songs[0] = new Array("hendridge_faulkner.mp3", "Hendridge
➥ Faulkner");
songs[1] = new Array("one_way.mp3", "One Way...");
songs[2] = new Array("no_forgiveness.mp3", "No Forgiveness");
```

"This code sets up the songs array, which stores information for each track, including the file name and the text to display. The file name field will be used to load in the MP3 file from your hard drive or the server. For this example, assume that the Flash file and MP3s are in the same folder. Now add the following code:

```
loadSong = function () {
    currentSong.onSoundComplete = function() {
        if (count<songs.length-1) {
            count++;
        } else {
            count = 0;
        }
        currentSong.loadSound(songs[count][0], true);
        radioText.text = "Radio Mondo is currently streaming
➥ the track \n'"+songs[count][1]+"' by Mondo";
        loadSong();
    };
};
// initialize
count = 0;
currentSong = new Sound();
radioText.text = "RadioMondo is currently streaming the track
➥ \n'"+songs[count][1]+"' by Mondo";
currentSong.loadSound(songs[count][0], true);
loadSong();
```

"So what's happening here? Well, first, let's look at the initialization code. Here, count is used to store the currently playing track—this is zero-based to work according to the array. Then a new sound object is set up as currentSong. This object is used to load in all the MP3 files.

"The next line sets the dynamic text box to display the name of the track. Remember that `\n` represents a new line. The name of the track is extracted from the second field of the multidimensional array.

"The next line of code is all-important because it actually does the MP3 loading from the current directory. The true argument here specifies whether the sound should stream. If this is set to false, the sound will need to have fully loaded before playing.

"One important thing to point out about streaming sounds is that they can't be manipulated or stored. Streaming works on the basis that a file is loaded in and the information is immediately lost. So if you wish to manipulate the previous exercise and have Play, Pause, or Fast Forward buttons, you'll need to load in unstreamed sounds and set the argument to `false`.

"The `loadSound` method will only load in MP3 files and will rely on their current compressed format and file size, so if your MP3 is pretty large, your audience will have to wait a little longer for it to load in, resulting in the track starting and stopping.

"The final line calls the `loadSong` function:

```
loadSong = function () {
    currentSong.onSoundComplete = function() {
        if (count<songs.length-1) {
            count++;
        } else {
            count = 0;
        }
        currentSong.loadSound(songs[count][0], true);
        radioText.text = "Radio Mondo is currently
➥ streaming the track \n'"+songs[count][1]+"' by Mondo";
        loadSong();
    };
};
```

"The `loadSong` function is used to check if the currently playing track has ended using the `onSoundComplete` event. Once the track has ended, the next track is loaded and played. Before this, though, the value of `count` is checked against the length of the array to determine whether to run on to the next track and increment `count` or to set `count` back to zero."

"This is to loop the tracks, right?" Jim asked.

"That's right, Jim," I said. "This loops all the tracks in the array endlessly. It checks against the value of the array rather than a variable so that Carl can insert new tracks into the array whenever he feels like it.

"Whatever happens in the conditionals, a new song is played, and the text field is set. `loadSong` is recalled here to repeat the process over and over. Run the movie and have a listen."

As before, the class was subjected to the sound of Mondo. "Believe me, Carl, it will loop over and over!" I said. Carl stopped the movie.

"Does it always start on the same track?" Carl asked. I nodded. "I guess I could set `count` to a random value to start with to surprise Mondo fans. This is ace—thanks, Ken."

"Let's stick with the multimedia theme, but switch disciplines from sound to filmmaking," I said.

Jim: Video in Flash

"Jim, I said at the start that we'd take a look at getting videos to run in Flash for you, so that you can put some of your films up on the Web. Controlling video with Flash is fairly simple, as you'll see, but first of all, you need to bring the video into Flash.

"To begin with, you can turn to our old friend **Import to Library** and find the video files that you want to use. As with the other imported file types you've seen, it's best to start with the highest quality video possible and then let Flash do the compression for you. After you find them, though, you'll be greeted by a screen that you haven't seen before: the **Import Video Settings** window.

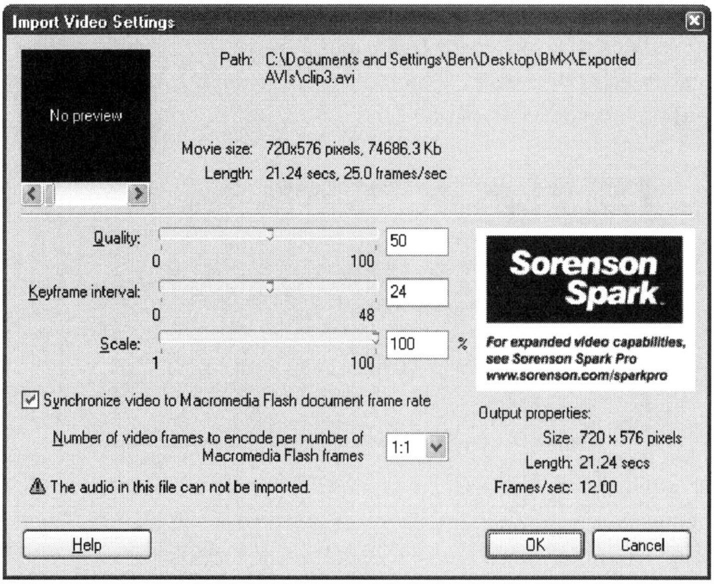

"This window gives you some basic information about the movie that you're importing, and it also allows you to set some important factors. The **Quality** slider is fairly self-explanatory, and it controls the compression of the video: at a higher setting, you get better quality but higher file size, and the opposite at the lower settings.

12

"The **Keyframe Interval** is another quality setting, but this time with the opposite effect of the Quality slider. The lower this setting, the better the quality but the higher the file size, and the opposite for a higher setting. **Scale** simply controls the scale of the imported clip. If you only want to import it at half the size of the original, then you set Scale to 50%.

"The **Synchronize** check box allows you to tell Flash whether or not it should try and keep the video frame rate and the Flash movie frame rate in sync with each other. Slower machines may stutter when they try to run video, and Flash will try to account for this if the box is checked.

"The drop-down box for specifying the number of video frames to encode compared to Flash frames is another option for reducing the size of the video file. For example, setting this to 1:2 will only encode every other video frame. Each video frame, though, would last for two Flash frames, meaning that the video would be the same length, but it would be at a lower quality. As with the other import quality settings, it's best to experiment with all of these to find the ones that give you the best trade-off between file size and quality.

"Once the video is in Flash, you can begin to code with it. Just like you did with the pictures, though, the first thing that you'll do is create an empty movie clip and store the video within it. Create a movie clip called `vidClip`, and then drag your video from the Library onto the stage. You'll see a prompt box appear:

"Flash normally displays the entire length of a video on the stage so that you can cue through it using the timeline as you would for any other Flash movie. To do this, though, it needs to increase the length of the timeline to be that of the video clip. Respond 'yes' to this, and the video will be displayed in your timeline. If you respond 'no' to this, then Flash will only play the amount of video that can fit in the current timeline.

"Drag a copy of vidClip onto the main stage and give it the instance name `vidClip`. You'll use similar buttons to those you used to control the sound, but this time you'll have four of them: `playButton`, `stopButton`, `fwdButton`, and `revButton`. The Pause button has been done away with and replaced by a Fast Forward and a Rewind button:

"Video in a Flash movie clip is controlled in exactly the same way as a normal movie clip, so you can use the same methods to control it. Start with the Play and Stop buttons. These have almost exactly the same code as for the sound examples, except that they point to a different clip, and you use `play` instead of `start` to get the clip going:

```
playButton.onRelease = function() {
    vidClip.play();
};
stopButton.onRelease = function() {
    vidClip.stop();
};
```

"You can now test these buttons to see if they work." I ran the movie, and the video started playing. I used the Stop button to pause it and the Start button to set it off again. "There are a couple of things that you may have noticed there," I began. "First of all, the video started playing as soon as I started the movie. If this isn't what you want, then it can be averted with a simple `stop` action at the start of the code.

"The other thing to notice is that the Stop button had a pauselike effect anyway. Whereas with sounds, stopping sent the playhead back to the start, with videos it just stops where it is and can then be restarted with a simple `play` action.

"Okay, now let's look at the other two buttons. When you click the buttons, you want Flash to move the video, let's say five frames, in either direction. Both of these buttons are very similar, so let's just look at the Fast Forward button and then copy it with slight amendments for the Rewind button. Because the video is based on simple Flash frame commands, you can just tell it to go to five frames ahead and start playing from there.

"From your requirements, you can easily pull out the method that you want to use: `gotoAndPlay`. The only thing is that you don't yet know how to get the current frame of the video. Luckily, a quick glance through the movie clip properties will reveal a perfect candidate. The code for the Fast Forward button then is as follows:

```
fwdButton.onRelease = function() {
    vidClip.gotoAndPlay(vidClip._currentframe + 5);
};
```

"The Rewind button is almost identical, but you're going backward from the current frame rather than forward from it:

```
revButton.onRelease = function() {
    vidClip.gotoAndPlay(vidClip._currentframe - 5);
};
```

"If you now play the movie, you'll be able to see the buttons in action. You can easily move forward and backward by clicking the relevant buttons. Of course, you can tailor these to suit your whim. If you don't like the video playing after you've skipped forward, then just change the `gotoAndPlays` to `gotoAndStops`, or if you can't see enough of a difference with that amount of movement, then just alter the number that you're adding or subtracting to move that number of frames."

"So can I put a few of my movies on there and switch between them in the same way that we did with Carl's songs?" asked Jim.

"Yes, that should be easy enough to do," I said. "The difference is that the sounds were loaded into one object, whereas the movies are in individual clips. To get around this with code, you can just use a variable name to store a reference path to the video holder, and then use the buttons to change this variable.

"Of course, the other thing to bear in mind when using video is that files can get very big very quickly."

Gemma: Web considerations

"Okay, Gemma, what would you like to talk about?" I asked.

"As much as I love Randy's projector, I must admit that the actual file size of it bothers me," Gemma said. "I've been working on picking work for my portfolio, and I'd like to put it on the Web, but there's no way that I can expect users to wait for a huge file to load."

"Right, Gemma," I said. "I totally understand your worries about this. No one can expect a user to wait for files that are very large! However, there are a number of ways that you can change the Flash file to make it easy on everyone's bandwidth.

"First, you can start with a higher level of JPEG compression. As you saw a couple of weeks ago, increasing the level of JPEG compression can significantly lower the file size of photographic images.

"If I were to put Randy's presentation on the Web, I'd be a little stricter with the compression. I say 'a little' because Randy's craft is photography, and if you increased the compression to a level where it was clearly visible, the quality of the photos would be reduced so much that it might not show Randy's skills in the best . . . ahem . . . light.

"It all depends on what you're displaying in the first instance. In your case, Gemma, you might be able to use a little more compression if the focus of the work isn't on the photography aspect. It's a balance between quality and the patience of your audience! Still, this isn't the only solution. There's a much better one.

"The stronger candidate is to load content or images on demand. As you all already know, in the current movie, all the full-size images are placed in the Library and are included in the size of the projector file. In Flash MX, the ability to load JPEGs on demand was introduced. This is very much like loading in MP3s on the fly, as you saw earlier in class.

"Have you all seen standard image galleries on the Web?" I asked. Some of the students looked puzzled. "Most HTML image galleries are made up of a set of thumbnails that load in a full-size image when clicked."

"Sounds just like Randy's kiosk!" Joe said.

"I think I know what you're talking about," Mazzy said. "In HTML, the full-size images are loaded only when required. I suppose most of these work in HTML framesets." I opened a web page to illustrate.

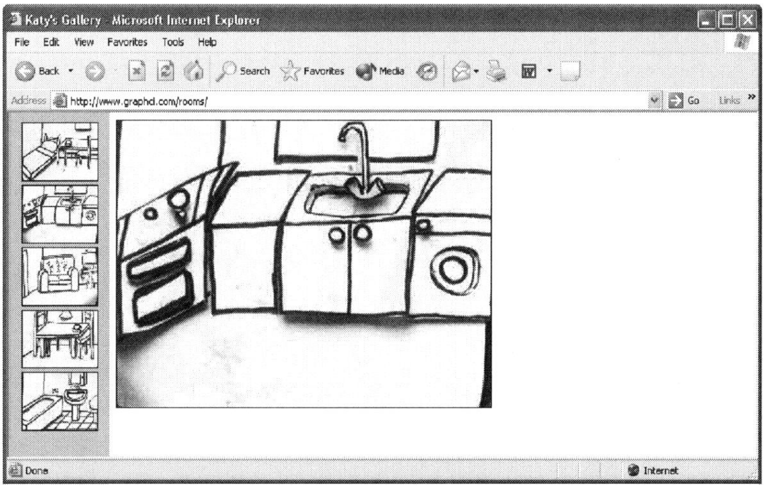

"Thanks, Ken," Mazzy said. "On this web page, for example, the thumbnail images on the sidebar are clicked to load in a full-size image in the right area. The full-size images are only loaded when the user clicks the thumbnail."

"The loading of the image isn't instantaneous," I started, "but it allows the user to choose what he or she wants to view, and therefore which images to load in. Using this method, only the main interface and perhaps the thumbnail images need to be loaded in on start-up."

"The simple answer with Flash, then, is to load in the full-size JPEGs when the user requests them?" Jim asked. "How do we do this? I thought everything had to be in the Library."

"The `loadMovie` method allows you to load in JPEG images from the server," I said. "These images are loaded into movie clip instances, so they can be manipulated just like any other instance on the stage. Let me show you how."

Using the loadMovie method to load images

1. Open a new Flash movie. Locate the folder `loadMovie exercise` and save it in this folder. This folder contains the required full-size image files.

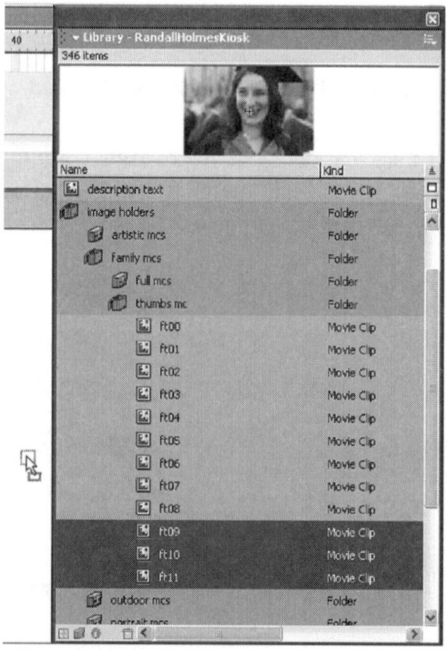

2. Use **File > Open as Library** and select one of the finished case study files.

3. Drag instances of the movie clips ft09, ft10, and ft11 onto the stage.

4. Now close the Shared Library.

5. Reposition the instances into a vertical row on the stage and give them the instance names from `buttonA` to `buttonC`.

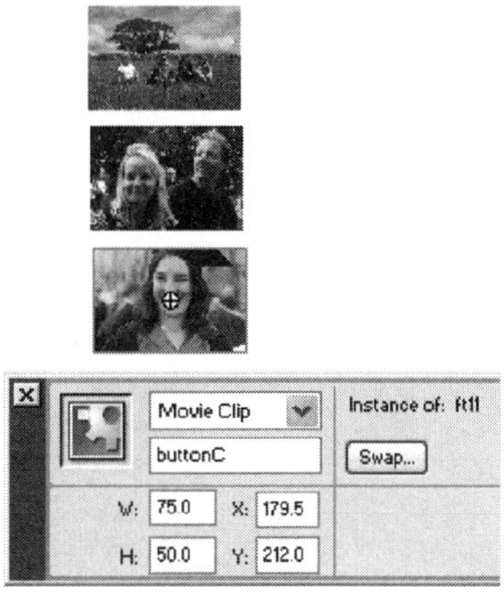

6. Now create a new movie clip called **image container**. Leave the content of the movie clip empty and drag a copy of it onto the main stage, giving it the instance name of `imageHolder`. Position it alongside the thumbnails.

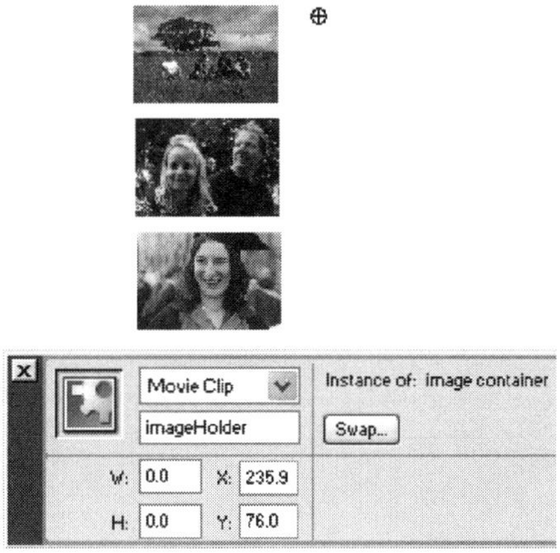

7. Now add a new layer called **actions** and open the Actions panel for it.

8. Add the following code:

```
loadJPEG = function (filename, target) {
    target.loadMovie (filename);
};
buttonA.onRelease = function () {
    loadJPEG ("family.jpg", imageHolder);
};
buttonB.onRelease = function () {
    loadJPEG ("folks.jpg", imageHolder);
};
buttonC.onRelease = function () {
    loadJPEG ("graduation.jpg", imageHolder);
};
```

9. Run the movie and click the thumbnails to load in images dynamically.

"Okay, the first thing I'd like to do is to get you to open the Library," I said. "I'd just like to show you, like a magician does, that there is nothing up my sleeves!

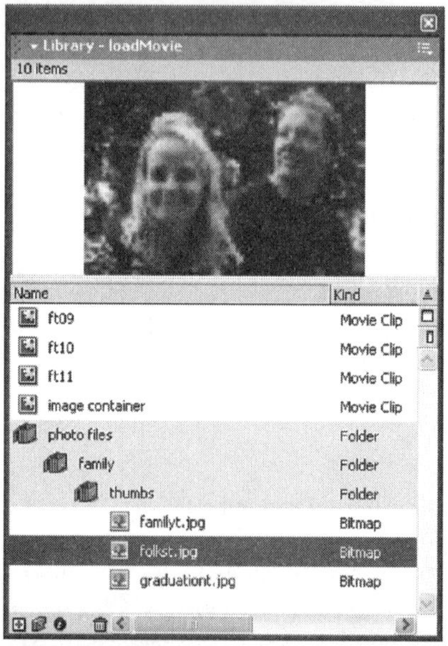

"None of the full-size images are contained in the Library—only the thumbnail JPEG files and the movie clips that use them. The folder in which I asked you to save the FLA file has the three full-size JPEGs and obviously the newly-saved Flash files."

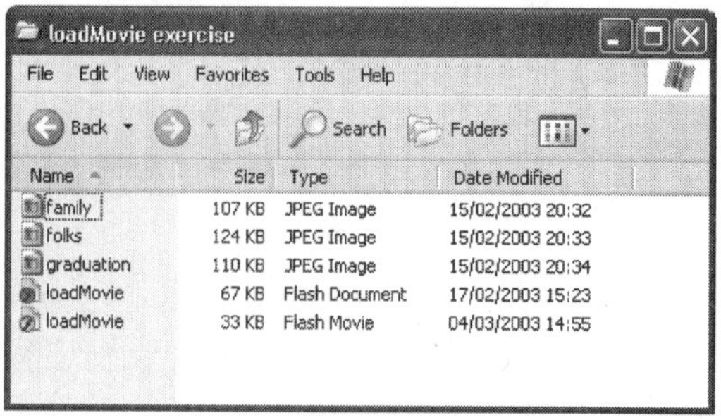

"You're a lousy magician," Carl started, "you've given away your little trick. The `loadMovie` method just loads the images into the empty instance on the stage."

"Anyone who still uses Flash 5 might think it was magic, though," I said, "so try not to spoil the fun!" I laughed. "Carl has got it right. These images are just pulled in from the folder. If you were going to make a gallery on the Web, loading each JPEG into Flash on demand would easily be the most rounded way to do it."

"Can you show us how we might change Randy's code?" Gemma asked. "I'd like to see it in context."

"Sure, Gemma." I asked the students to open the completed case study FLA.

"First, the array would need to be updated to look for the JPEG file names instead of a full-size linkage name. If you use the three images you just worked with as an example, the family array would look like this:

```
family = new Array();
family[0] = ["061", "ft00", "ff00", "Charlie", "Cheeky
➥ Charlie."];
family[1] = ["062", "ft01", "ff01", "Charlotte",
➥ "Charlotte prepares for food."];
family[2] = ["063", "ft02", "ff02", "Three Bridesmaids",
➥ "The bride chills out with the bridesmaids."];
family[3] = ["064", "ft03", "ff03", "Another Happy
➥ Couple", "The happy couple with the in-laws."];
family[4] = ["065", "ft04", "ff04", "Cutting the Cake",
➥ "The couple cut the cake."];
family[5] = ["066", "ft05", "ff05", "Leaving the Chapel",
➥ "The happy couple leave the chapel."];
family[6] = ["067", "ft06", "ff06", "Happy Days", "The sun
➥ radiates on Karl and Nia."];
family[7] = ["068", "ft07", "ff07", "Best Men", "The
➥ couple with the ushers."];
family[8] = ["069", "ft08", "ff08", "Loving Siblings",
➥ "Brother and sister in a school portrait."];
family[9] = ["070", "ft09", "family.jpg", "A Somerset
➥ Walk", "Resting on Deer Leap."];
family[10] = ["071", "ft10", "folks.jpg", "Taking a
➥ Break", "Richard and Joy take it easy."];
family[11] = ["072", "ft11", "graduation.jpg", "Graduation
➥ Day", "Katy's hard work pays off as she celebrates her
➥ graduation."];
```

12

"I've modified the array to look for the file names of the three images. Now, assuming you have an empty movie clip instance called imageHolder on the stage in the correct location, the new showLargePhoto function would only need a little changing:

```
showLargePhoto = function (photoCategory, photoCount) {
    this.onRelease = function() {
        _root.checkArray(this.index, this.capName, this.cat);
        imageHolder.loadMovie (photoCategory[photoCount][2]);
        _root.name.nameText.text =
➥ "#"+photoCategory[photoCount][0]+"
➥ "+photoCategory[photoCount][3];
        _root.description.descriptionText.text =
➥ photoCategory[photoCount][4];
    };
};
```

"Of course, I've overlooked the depth of the tabs here, so you might want to move the imageHolder instance just off the stage to see that it works. You would also have to update the selectCategoryImage function. Even though I've overlooked these things, you can begin to see how loading on the fly is beneficial—but remember this exercise loads images from the hard drive rather than over an Internet connection, so it's a little faster than it would be online."

"Thanks for covering all that, Ken," Gemma said. "I think that's a lot more beneficial and familiar to me. My current HTML portfolio loads images on demand, so I won't have to re-create or republish any of my image files!"

"Bonus!" Carl said.

The fun stuff

"Okay, then, I think you've put up with enough of my chatter for a while," I said. "It's time for a bit of light relief. I've put a few, well, I guess you'd call them 'toys,' onto your computers in a folder called extras on the main drive. These are just a few simple Flash things that I made for fun. None of them really 'do' much as such, but they'll hopefully give you a few ideas of what Flash can do and how easy it is to do it.

"I've included SWFs and FLAs, so find one or two you like and then take a look at how they were created; I think you'll be surprised by how simple they are. If there are any that you're particularly interested in, then give me a shout and I'll explain how they were made and how they work. Enjoy them." The students all delved into their hard drives and began looking through the files. I was relieved their faces begin to light up as they played.

"Ken, can we talk about `record_draw.fla`? I've been hoping to find something like this in Flash," Jim said. "Back in the days of BASIC programming, one of my favorite things was the ability to draw in BASIC code. I loved to watch colored lines randomly filling the screen!"

Drawing with ActionScript

```
x = new Array ();
y = new Array ();

_root.createEmptyMovieClip("drawHolder", 1);
drawHolder.lineStyle (2, 0x000000, 100);
maximumCount = 100;

redraw = function () {
    count = 0;
    drawHolder.moveTo (x[0], y[0]);
    ghost = attachMovie ("ghostMouse", "ghostMouse", 2);
    ghost._alpha = 20;
    _root.onEnterFrame = function () {
        status.text = "Playing... "+count;
        drawHolder.lineTo (x[count], y[count]);
        ghost._x = x[count];
        ghost._y = y[count];
     if (count < maximumCount) {
            count++;
        } else {
            _root.onEnterFrame = undefined;
            ghost._visible = false;
        }
    };
};

delayBeforeRecording = setInterval (function () {
        clearInterval (delayBeforeRecording);
        count = 0;
        _root.onEnterFrame = function () {
            status.text = "Recording... " + count;
            x[count] = _root._xmouse;
            y[count] = _root._ymouse;
            if (count == maximumCount) {
                _root.onEnterFrame = undefined;
                redraw ();
            } else {
                count++;
            }
        };
}, 3000);
```

12

"This movie first records a set number of positions of the mouse cursor, and then it redraws them for you," I started. "The actual drawing is done using the built-in Flash MX Drawing Methods. Even though it might seem like I kept these from you, Jim, it was only so that the class could learn how to program first! Knowledge of these methods isn't essential, but I must admit that they're pretty cool for drawing graphics on the fly.

"The drawing methods allow you to draw strokes and filled strokes, of any color, opacity or thickness. The full range of methods are viewable in the Reference panel under **MovieClip > Drawing Methods**."

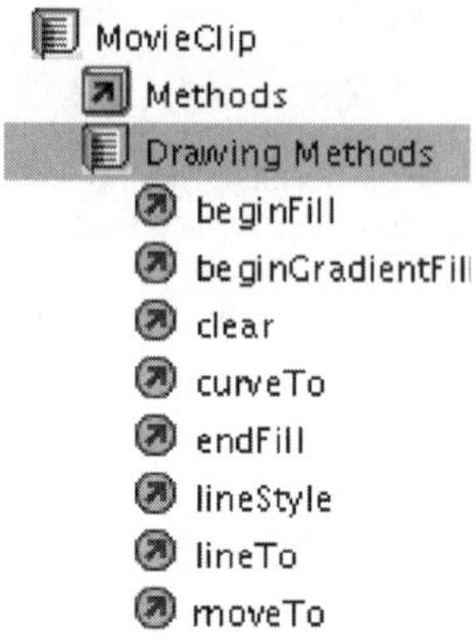

"I'm thinking that `lineTo` and `moveTo` might be familiar!" Jim said excitedly.

"You've thought right. `moveTo` and `lineTo` are the Flash MX equivalents of the BASIC `plot` and `draw`," I said. "Okay, before you explode with excitement, let's take a look at the actual processes and code.

"The first step is to record the mouse positions.

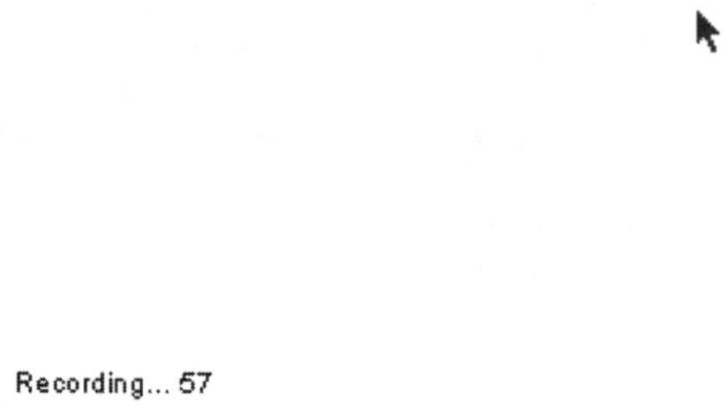

"The `_x` and `_y` positions of the mouse are stored in two arrays: `x` and `y`. The mouse position is recorded to these arrays every frame using the `onEnterFrame` event."

"Where does this happen in the code, Ken?" Jim asked.

"In the last chunk of code," I replied. "The recording is set off after a 3-second initial countdown with the interval `delayBeforeRecording`. This gives the user a chance to position his or her cursor and warm up. These two lines

```
x[count] = _root._xmouse;
y[count] = _root._ymouse;
```

are called within the `enterFrame` event code to store the mouse position. After these, an `if` statement checks to see if the value of `count`—the counting variable—is equal to the `maximumCount` variable, which stores the number of frame positions to record. If it is, then the `redraw` function is called, resulting in the invisible ghost cursor!

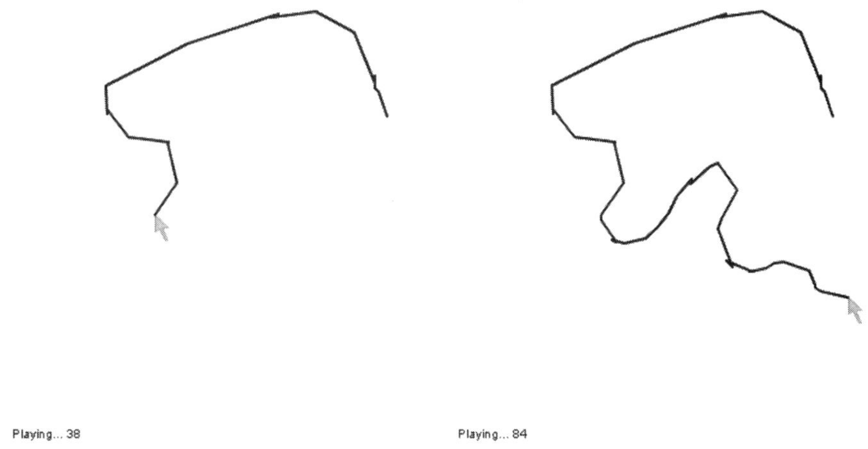

"Before I go into this function, I'd like to draw your attention to this line:

```
_root.createEmptyMovieClip("drawHolder", 1);
```

"To use the drawing methods, you need to have an empty movie clip to draw into. You could just create a blank movie clip on the stage, but you can achieve the same thing more neatly by using code.

"Flash has this ActionScript command just for creating blank movie clips, and you just need to tell it what you'd like the instance name of the clip to be and at what depth you'd like to place it. This new movie clip can be manipulated just like any other normal movie clip. Let's take a look at the line after that as well.

```
drawHolder.lineStyle (2, 0x000000, 100);
```

"The `lineStyle` method sets up the stroke type. The parameters for this method are thickness, color, and alpha. So here you have a fully opaque black pen with a thickness of 2. If you don't set the `lineStyle`, then you won't see anything you've drawn!

"Okay, now on to the `redraw` function. The first thing to point out is the `moveTo` drawing method:

```
drawHolder.moveTo (x[0], y[0]);
```

"This method here initiates the starting position to draw from, retrieving the first positions from each array. Once the pen is down, this method is used to take it off the paper and reposition it elsewhere.

"You then skip a few lines to the `enterFrame` event. This is used here to redraw frame-by-frame what was recorded. The `lineTo` method draws a line from the previous position of the pen to the new one. Remember that unless the `moveTo` function is called, the pen is one continuous stroke from one point to the next.

"The last thing in this function is the `if` statement to check whether to stop drawing or not. If you've drawn all 100 recorded positions, the `enterFrame` is canceled and the ghost pen is made fully invisible again."

"Eerie!" Jim joked. "Tell us about making fills, Ken. I've been trying to figure out the `beginFill` thing when you've been talking, but it isn't playing ball."

"Open `fill_draw.fla` to see how a fill works," I said. "In it, a stroke is drawn between four moveable points and these lines are filled.

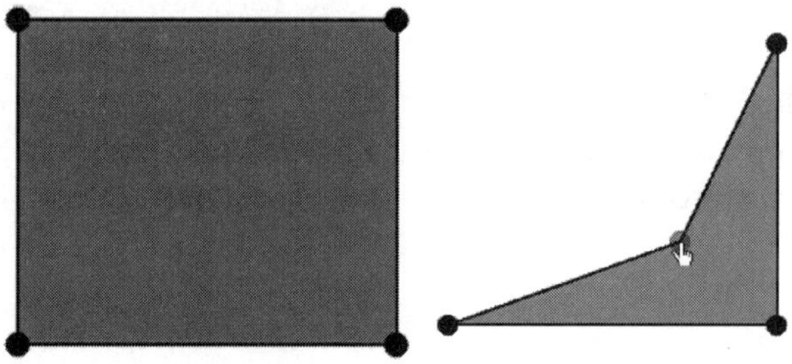

"First, you need to call the `beginFill` method, and then, when your strokes have ended, call the `endFill` method. In the situation where your stroke is an unfinished shape, Flash will finish it for you."

"Thanks, Ken, I think I can remake all my BASIC randomness now!" Jim said, and Gemma sighed.

"I'd like to talk about the clock movie please," Mazzy started. "I've always wanted to have the date and time on my website."

"How about a countdown to the next Mondo gig?" Carl asked.

Mazzy responded, "I think a countdown to the next church service would be more appropriate, don't you?"

A digital clock

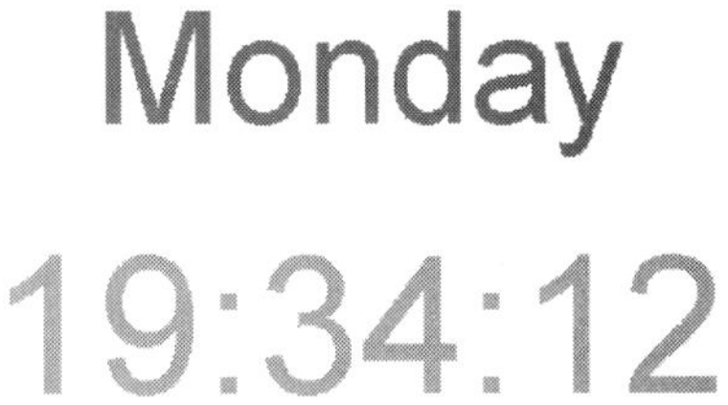


```
days = new Array ("Sunday", "Monday", "Tuesday", "Wednesday",
➥ "Thursday", "Friday", "Saturday");

checkLessThanTen = function (timeVariable) {
     if (timeVariable < 10) {
          timeVariable = “0” + timeVariable;
     }
     return timeVariable;
};

showTime = setInterval (function () {
     time = new Date ();
     hours = time.getHours ();
     minutes = checkLessThanTen (time.getMinutes ());
     seconds = checkLessThanTen (time.getSeconds ());
     now = hours + ":" + minutes + ":" + seconds;
     clockText.text = now;
     dayText.text = days[time.getDay ()];
}, 1000);
```

"As you can see from the code, there's very little to this movie," I said. "The actual hard work is already done for you with Flash's built-in Date object. Let's start by looking at the showTime setInterval code.

"The setInterval is set to run every second for obvious reasons: the clock is updated every second! Within the handler code, a new Date object is created. This object will take a snapshot of the current system date, time, and so on. This is called every second because the time is constantly changing.

"The next three variables are set up to retrieve the hours, minutes, or seconds values from the aforementioned date object using the methods getHours, getMinutes, and getSeconds. These values, however, are returned as numeric values and are therefore not prefixed with a zero character. The function checkLessThanTen is used on the latter two values to check if they're less than ten and, if so, it prefixes them with a zero character. The figure 7 for the seconds, for example, will become 07 after the function has done its magic.

"Back in the setInterval code, the variable now is set to the actual display of the clock. The colon characters are used as separators. The clockText dynamic text field is then set to display it.

"On the next line, the dayText text field is set to display the current day. The getDay method returns a value from 0—representing Sunday—to 6 for Saturday. The array at the start of the code is set up according to this, and the value from getDay is retrieved from that element of the array displaying the correct day."

"How can I get some flashing colons?" Mazzy asked.

"Drink lots of alcohol and don't eat for many days," Jim joked. "My guess is that you would use a flag variable and a simple conditional." I changed the code a little.

"This should do it," I said, displaying the code. I ran the new version (clock02.fla).

```
showTime = setInterval (function () {
    time = new Date ();
    hours = time.getHours ();
    minutes = checkLessThanTen (time.getMinutes ());
    seconds = checkLessThanTen (time.getSeconds ());
    if (flashOn) {
        now = hours + ":" + minutes + ":" + seconds;
```

```
            flashOn = false;
        } else {
            now = hours + " " + minutes + " " + seconds;
            flashOn = true;
        }
        clockText.text = now;
        dayText.text = days[time.getDay ()];
    }, 1000);
```

"That's what I was after," Mazzy said. "Do you mind if I copy this code, Ken?"

"Go ahead, Mazzy," I said. "All of the files I brought in today are for you all to take away and dissect. I've commented all of them as much as possible so that you can try and make the best of them."

Easing and dragging

"I've got one," said Joe, excitedly. "I like the one where you drag the ball and it snaps back. I can imagine using it on the kiosk in my store. It would be great if customers could drag a picture of the item that they want into a virtual shopping trolley thing. The picture would then spring back to its original position, but the details of that item would be added to an array that keeps track of the running total. That would be so useful."

"I'm glad you're enthused by the possibilities," I said with a smile. "We'd better look more closely at how the file was made before the excitement gets too much for you. I warn you now, though, there's a bit of math in this one. To be honest, you don't *have* to understand it fully to be able to use it.

"Without further ado, let's take a look at the code:

```
xTarget = ball._x;
yTarget = ball._y;

ballcheck = function () {
    this.onPress = function() {
        this.startDrag();
    };
    this.onRelease = this.onReleaseOutside = function () {
        this.stopDrag();
        _root.snapBack.apply(this);
    };
};
```

```
snapBack = function () {
     this.onEnterFrame = function() {
          xDist = _root.xTarget-this._x;
          yDist = _root.yTarget-this._y;
          xDist /= 2;
          yDist /= 2;
          this._x += xDist;
          this._y += yDist;
          if(Math.abs(this.xDist)<0.2 && Math.abs(yDist)<0.2) {
               this.onEnterFrame = undefined;
          }
     };
};

ballcheck.apply(ball);
```

"The only thing you have on the stage is a small circle with the instance name `ball`. The text just holds the instructions, and it isn't really an important part of the movie:

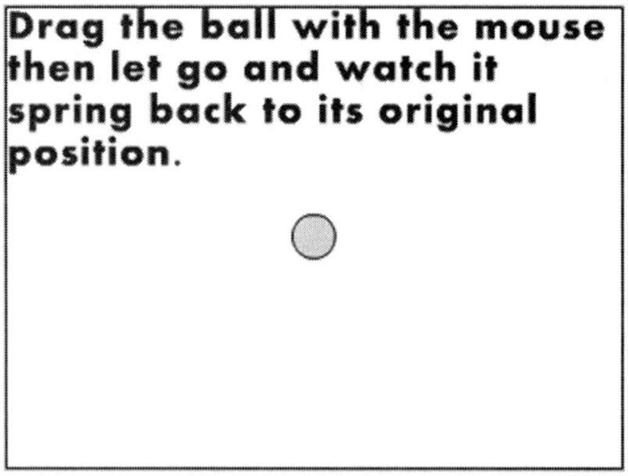

"Okay, the first thing that you do is record the initial position of the ball so that you know where you're trying to get back to. You store this position in the variables `xTarget` and `yTarget`.

"The next function, `ballcheck`, deals with the mouse interaction with the ball. Here, you encounter a couple of movie clip methods you haven't seen before but are extremely useful: `startDrag` and `stopDrag`. These two commands let you tell Flash that you want to be able to click the movie clip and drag it somewhere. You just need to tell Flash this, and it will do all of the work for you.

"The other interesting thing that you're doing here is assigning two events on one line:

```
this.onRelease = this.onReleaseOutside = function () {
```

"It may seem illogical that you can click something to drag it and then be outside it when you release the mouse, but it happens quite often, because you can move the mouse faster than Flash updates the frames.

"To deal with this, it's common to define `onRelease` and `onReleaseOutside` handlers to do the same thing. Rather than having two separate callbacks for this, you can instead set both of them up to use the same callback.

"Within this callback, you apply your second function to the ball whenever you release the mouse. This second function contains an `onEnterFrame` handler, and all of the code for telling the ball to spring back to its original position. Without this function, the ball would just stay wherever you dragged it to.

"This function consists of more than just simple movement, though. If you look closely when you release the ball, you can see that it starts off moving quickly toward the center and then slows down as it gets closer to it. This effect is called **easing**.

"The way you achieve this effect is to work out the distance between the target position and the current position, divide that number by two, and then move the ball there. You then repeat this every frame, moving the ball a smaller and smaller distance each time as it gets closer and closer, so that it seems to slow as it approaches the target." I drew a diagram on the board:

A | | | |T

"The ball starts at A and is heading for T. The bars mark the positions where the ball stops each frame."

"Sounds like one of my dad's journeys home on Saturday night," laughed Carl. "His movements are always defined by the bars that he stops at."

"Thank you, Carl, I'm sure he'd appreciate that," I said, smiling. "Now that you know what you need to do, let's look at how you do it. First, you need to find the distance to travel by subtracting the target position from your current position:

```
xDist = _root.xTarget-this._x;
yDist = _root.yTarget-this._y;
```

"You then want to divide this distance by two to find the amount that you want to move:

```
xDist /= 2;
yDist /= 2;
```

"Remember that X /= Y is just shorthand for X = X / Y. Now that you know how far you want the ball to move, you just need to add that distance to the current position:

```
this._x += xDist;
this._y += yDist;
```

"You could test the code now, and it would work perfectly except for one thing: if you tried to drag the ball again after it had returned to its position, you would find that it started moving again before you released the mouse.

"This is because you've set the `onEnterFrame` event handler, but you haven't stopped it after the ball has returned. Now, you could set up an `if` condition to test when the ball has returned to exactly where it started and then stop the handler, but when the ball gets close to the target position, its movements are so infinitesimally small that to the naked eye you'd probably think that it had stopped. Of course, this means that you'd be back to square one and the handler would still be running.

"The solution to this problem is to test when the ball is near enough to the original position that it looks like it's the same, but far enough away for it to quickly be picked up by the condition. I find that 0.2 is a good amount for this distance.

"This, though, opens up a new problem. You can drag the ball anywhere you want before releasing it, so you'd have to test if it was +/– 0.2 from the X position, and if it's +/– 0.2 from the Y position. Of course, it's possible to do that, but four `if`s looks like a lot.

"You could cut that number in half if only you didn't have to test for positive and negative numbers. You know by looking at the code that there's a way you can do this. The `Math.abs` method converts any number into an absolute, or positive number. For example, –3 would become 3, but 4, because it's already positive, would remain 4. This satisfies the `if` condition, and you now just need to turn off the event handler. You can do this by setting it to be `undefined`. `undefined` is a special keyword that Flash uses to denote that something is literally nothing—there's no value associated with the handler, so it performs no actions.

"That's it really for the code. There are a few different things that you can try with it, though. By changing the number that you divide the distance by, you can change the behavior of the ball. By setting it to a greater number, it will reach the target faster, and a smaller number will make it move slower.

"Try setting the x and y values to different numbers, and the ball will appear to curve as it springs back to the target. The real fun begins, though, when you set the number to a value between 0.5 and 1. This magical range makes the ball overshoot the target, and then snap back and wobble like a real spring. Try it, you just might like it."

Changing color

"How about this one, Ken?" asked Gemma. "I want to know how to get these beautiful colors." I looked over at Gemma's screen and saw that she was looking at my color-changing example. The screen was full of bouncing circles that changed color as they moved.

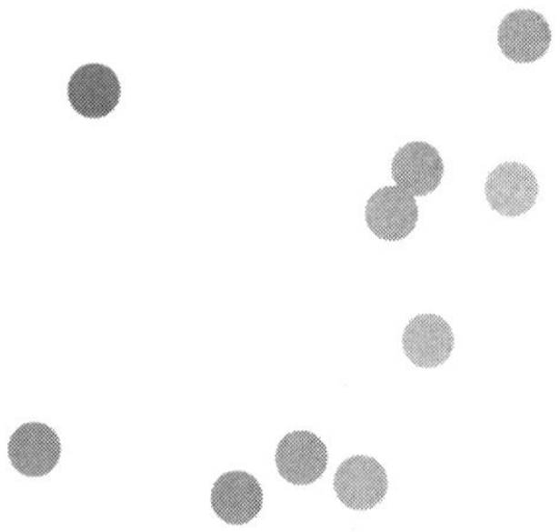

"Okay, no problem," I said. "Let's take a look at the code, shall we?

```
colorFunc = function () {
    this.onEnterFrame = function() {
        this.ballColTrans.rb = this._x-255;
        this.ballColTrans.bb = this._y-255;
        this.ballCol.setTransform(this.ballColTrans);
        this._x += this.xPower;
        this._y += this.yPower;
        if (this._x>=510 || this._x<=1) {
            this.xPower *= -1;
        }
        if (this._y>=510 || this._y<=1) {
            this.yPower *= -1;
        }
    };
};

for (i=1; i<=10; i++) {
    curBall = _root.attachMovie("ball", "ball"+i, i);
    curBall.xPower = 3;
    curBall.yPower = 3;
    curBall._x = Math.random()*510;
    curBall._y = Math.random()*510;
    curBall.ballCol = new Color(curBall);
    curBall.ballColTrans = new Object();
    colorFunc.apply(curBall);
}
```

"The only thing that you have in the Library is a small blue circle with the linkage name, `ball`. The other thing to note is that the size of the stage is set to 510x510. I'll start with the—"

"Don't worry about the bouncing ball code. I already understand how to do that," Gemma interrupted. "I just wanted to know how to do the colors."

"Okay, then, whatever you say," I said. "There's one thing that I want to mention about the positioning, though."

"Make it quick," smiled Gemma.

"I've used another method of the `Math` object to create random start positions for each of the balls," I started. "The `random` method is easy to use, but one important thing to remember about it is that it gives you a number between 0 and 1, so you have to multiply it by the top of your required number range to get a random number. If you want this to be a whole number, then just encase the whole thing within a `Math.round` statement to round the figure to the nearest whole number, like so:

```
X = Math.round(Math.random() * Y);
```

"Okay, that's the positioning over, I trust it was quick enough for you?" I asked. Gemma nodded that it was. "All right, then, let's move on to the `Color` object.

"The **`Color`** object is used for controlling the color of an asset in Flash. Just as with the other objects that you've seen, you first have to construct a new `Color` object using the `new` keyword.

"The difference between this and the other objects that you've seen is that you pass a parameter to the `Color` object when you create it that consists of the name of the target that you want the `Color` object to affect. In this case, it's the movie clip path variable, `curBall`.

```
curBall.ballCol = new Color(curBall);
```

"You can then change the colors of your object, but if you want to use the `setTransform` method to alter the colors, then you need to create a new `Transform` object to carry all of the parameters.

"The **`Transform`** object is another object that's set up almost like an array that holds only specific values. The `Color Transform` object looks complicated because it takes eight strangely named values, but once you can decode these names, then the whole thing starts to make more sense. The values each consist of a pair of letters like so: ra, rb, ga, gb, ba, bb, aa, ab. What do these mean?

"Well, the first letter of each pair pertains to the color: r = red, g = green, b = blue, and a = alpha. I know alpha isn't really a color; it's the amount of transparency that the color will have. The second letter means one of two things: 'a' is a percentage of color running from 100 to –100, and 'b' is the color offset running from 255 to –255. The offset is akin to the

RGB value of a color in Photoshop. That's not what it is, that's just what it's like, and then the percentage controls the amount of that color.

"Although you can set all of these attributes to get a specific color, you don't have to set them all. Here you can see that you're only setting the red and blue offsets of each ball. If you do leave any of the attributes out, then Flash will just leave them as the current color of the object.

"Once you've set the attributes of the Color Transform object that you want to change to, you then have to apply them to your Color object, which will in turn automatically apply them to the target. The way that you do this is to use the setTransform method of the Color object, and you pass it the name of the Color Transform object that you want to apply to it, like so:

```
this.ballCol.setTransform(this.ballColTrans);
```

"Here, ballCol is the name of the Color object, and ballColTrans is the name of the Transform object. Once this is done, the target should change color. I made the colors constantly shift by setting them to the current position of the ball.

"I set the stage to specific dimensions –510x510, so that I could get the full range of color values from –255 to 255 by just subtracting 255 from the current position.

"That's pretty much it. Remember that all you're doing here is transforming the color, so the resultant color depends on the initial color of the target. The original ball in the Library is blue, so the colors are more biased toward the blue end of the spectrum. Have a go at changing the code if you like. Try changing one of those values to green to get a different color range."

Just then, there was a knock at the door, and Randy poked his head around the corner. "Have I come in time?" he asked.

"Aha, my mystery guest," I said. "Come in."

"Aw, I was expecting more of a mystery than Randy," said Carl, looking glum.

"I hope I haven't disappointed you," replied Randy. "I still have a surprise in store for you, though. But first, am I allowed to see what I came here for?"

"Of course," I answered. "Who'd like to do the honors?"

"Gem . . . Jim . . . Car . . .!" came back the garbled cries of the students. They talked among themselves for a moment, but it was decided that Mazzy should be the one to unveil the site.

She'd rooted for Gemma, but Gemma had firmly said that she'd already done one presentation today, and she wasn't doing another.

Mazzy made her way to the front of the class and began her dramatization of the story of the gallery. Five minutes later, it was all over and the students were waiting with bated breath for Randy's reaction.

"Honestly, folks," he began, "I love it. It's perfect."

"And I'll be on hand to help you out with the updating or troubleshooting," Mazzy cut in.

"Well, what more could I ask for?" Randy asked. "A fantastic product, and free technical support to boot!"

"Who said anything about it being free?" joked Mazzy, and raised a laugh from the class.

"I can't thank you enough," said Randy once the tittering had died down, "so I thought I'd show my appreciation by doing what I do best and taking a photo." He reached into his bag and pulled out a camera. "Come on, all of you, line up in two rows in front of that window at the back of the class. I'll get this developed and send a copy out to you all."

After a little consternation and jostling, the students lined up along the window. Randy put his eye behind the viewfinder, but then stood up again. "Hang on," Randy said, "there's one missing." There were a few calls of "Ken!" before Carl dragged me out from where I was hiding behind a cupboard door.

"Come on, Ken. You didn't think we'd let you get out of it that easily, did you?" asked Carl.

Actually, I'd hoped they would, but I knew as the flash blinded me that with a class that good, I had no chance.

Appendix A
Class 1 Handout: Flash Tools

Tools reference (shortcut keys in parentheses)

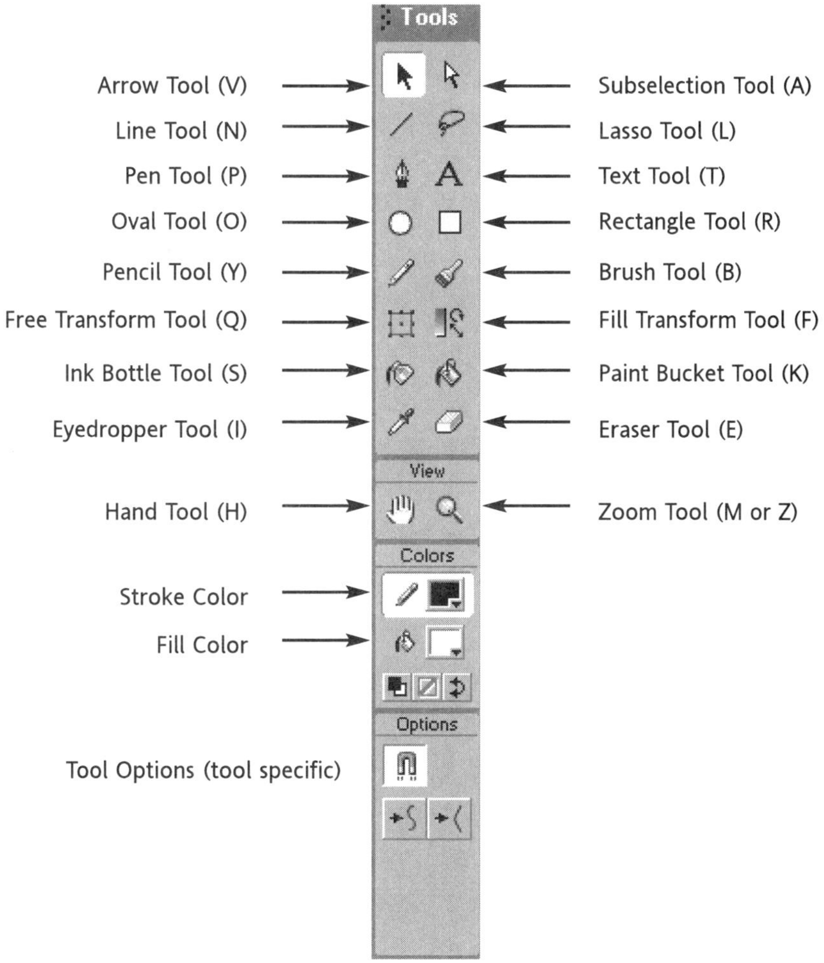

The Arrow tool

The Arrow tool is used to select objects on the stage for editing, and to move and place those selected objects.

The Arrow tool works very closely with the Property inspector, which displays information about the object you've chosen.

The basic operations of the Arrow tool work like this:

1. Select an object by clicking it:

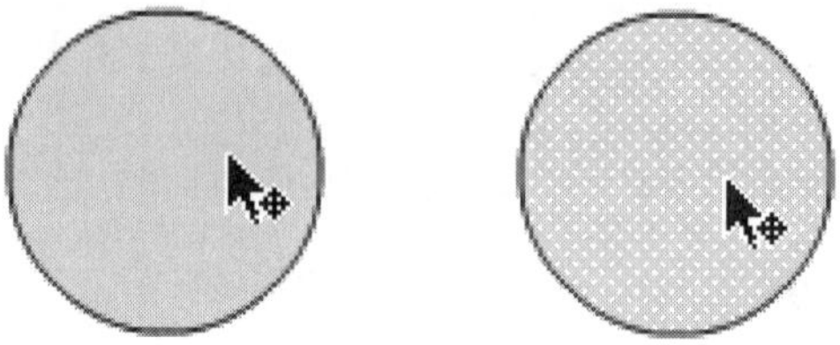

2. Select part or the whole of an object by drawing a box over it:

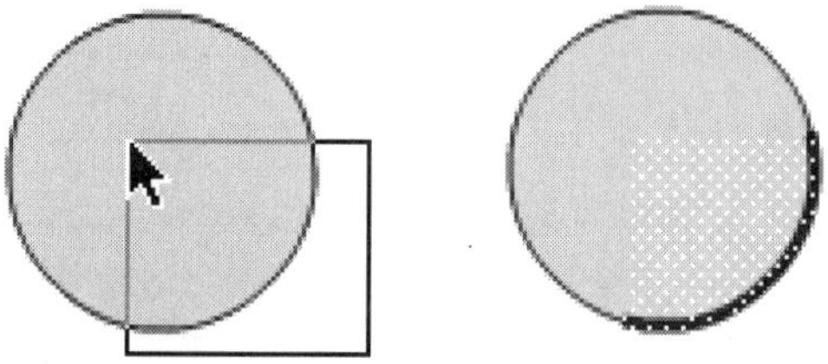

   (Hold down the SHIFT key to make multiple selections.)

3. Manipulate or reshape an object by clicking and dragging from its edge:

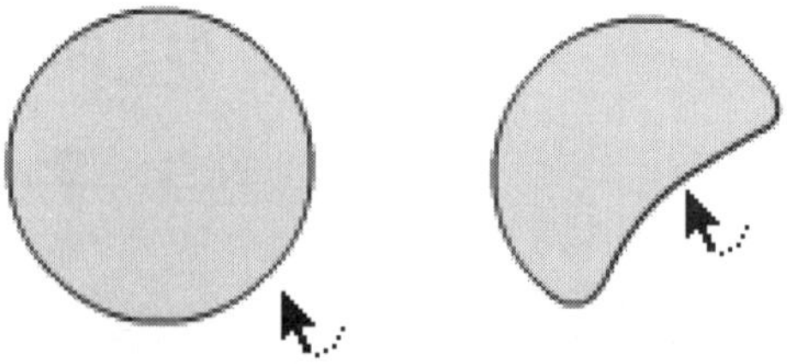

4. Move an object by clicking and dragging it. Release the mouse button to drop it:

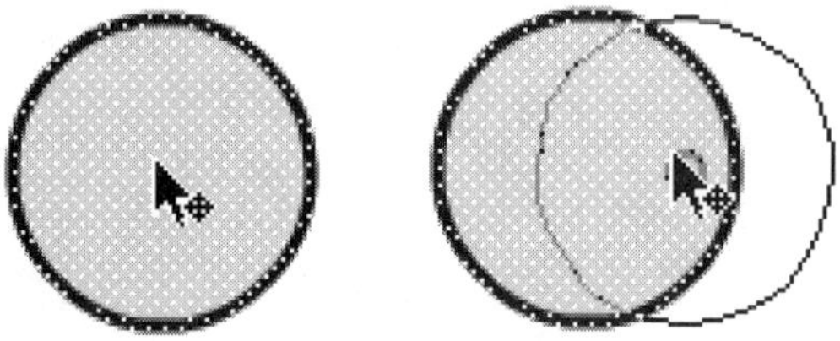

The Subselection tool 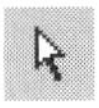

The Subselection tool allows you to select and alter specific points on a vector shape.

Select the Subselection tool and click a vector shape to reveal its vector points. The Subselection tool can do a couple of things:

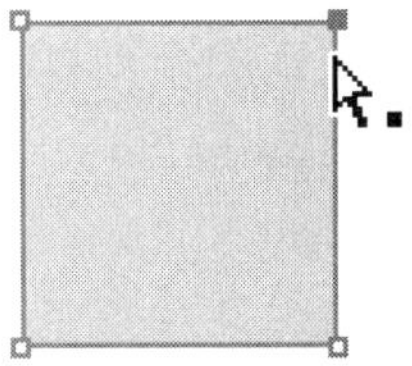

- Reshape an object.

  Click and drag a point to reshape the object:

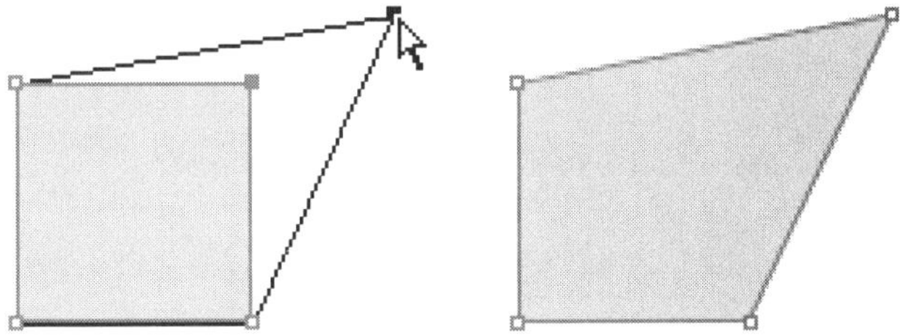

- Modify a curve.

  Click to select a point:

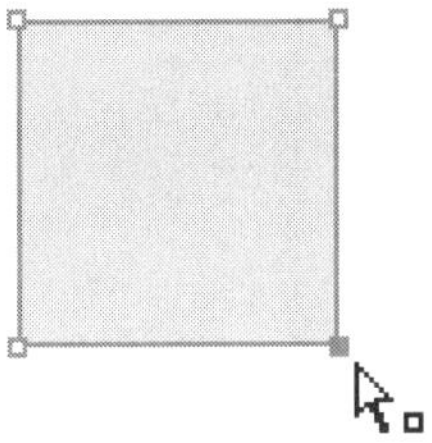

  Then hold down the ALT key and alter the curve with the Bezier curve handles:

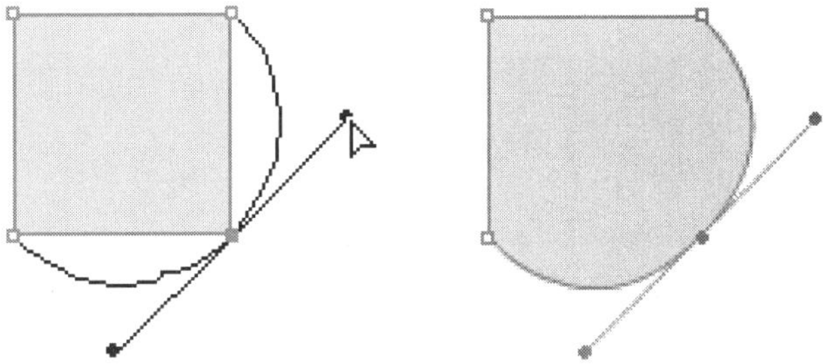

The Line tool 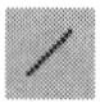

The Line tool is used to draw straight lines (strokes).

To use this tool, click at the start point of your line, then drag the mouse and release the button to confirm the end of the line.

Use the Property inspector to alter the stroke style and thickness of your line.

The Lasso tool 

The Lasso tool is a tool used for making irregular shape selections, allowing you to draw a selection.

The Lasso tool is used by "drawing" a selection:

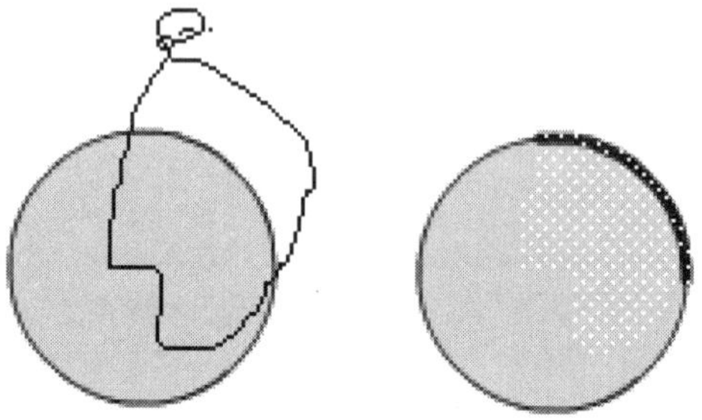

If the Polygon Mode option is switched on, straight, rubber-banded lines can be drawn with the Lasso:

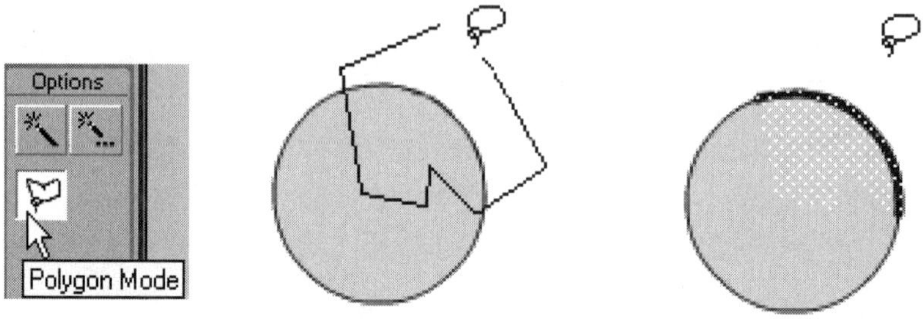

The Pen tool 

Although the Pen tool is complicated enough for its own handout, in short it's a tool to draw stroke curves and complicated shapes. The Pen tool is usually better known in other applications as the Bezier tool, because it draws Bezier curves (invented by Monsieur Pierre Bezier).

The best way to learn how this tool works is to experiment with it.

First, when you click from point to point, the Pen tool allows you to create vector shapes:

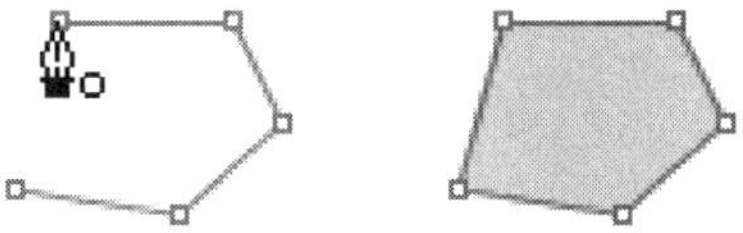

But this isn't what it was made for! Start afresh, then click once to draw a point. Now click elsewhere and move the mouse:

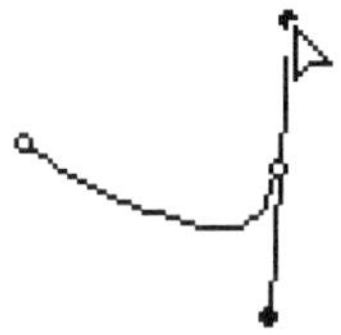

This time a curve appears, and by moving the mouse you affect its shape. This is a Bezier curve (but some people like to refer to it as a "bow tie"). When you release the mouse button you're left with a shape:

You can continue the overall shape by pressing the mouse button and/or sculpting curves from this new point:

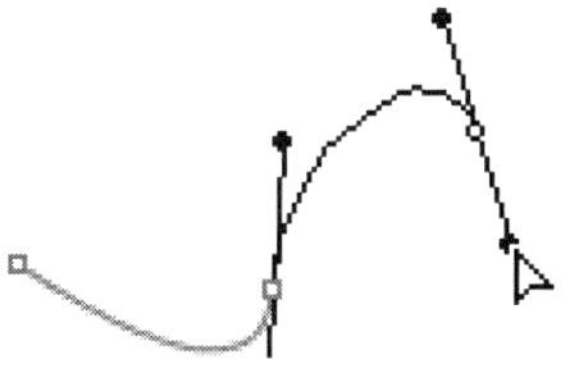

To close a shape, place the cursor over the start point so the cursor has an "O" attached to it and click.

If this all sounds a little confusing, just play with the tool until you're comfortable with it. It really is worth experimenting with.

The Text tool 

The Text tool is used to type and edit text in text fields.

Click anywhere to create a new text field.

The Text tool is best used in conjunction with the Property inspector.

The Oval tool 

The Oval tool is used for creating oval and circle shapes.

To draw an oval, click and drag the shape. Release the mouse button when you're satisfied with your shape.

To create a perfect circle, hold down the SHIFT key.

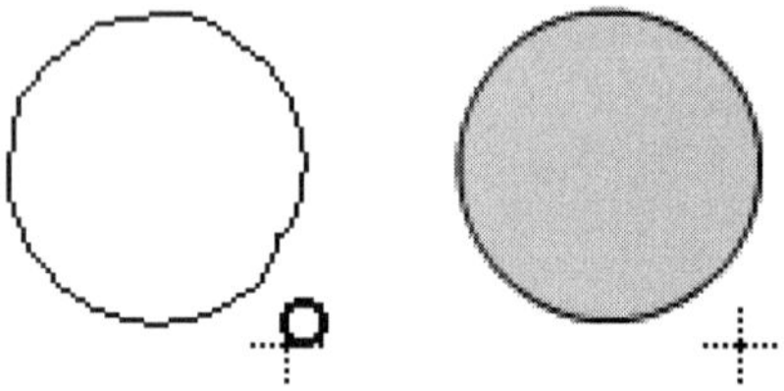

The Rectangle tool 

The Rectangle tool is used for drawing rectangles and squares.

To draw a rectangle, click and drag out the shape. Release the mouse button when you're satisfied with it. (To draw a perfect square, hold down the SHIFT key.)

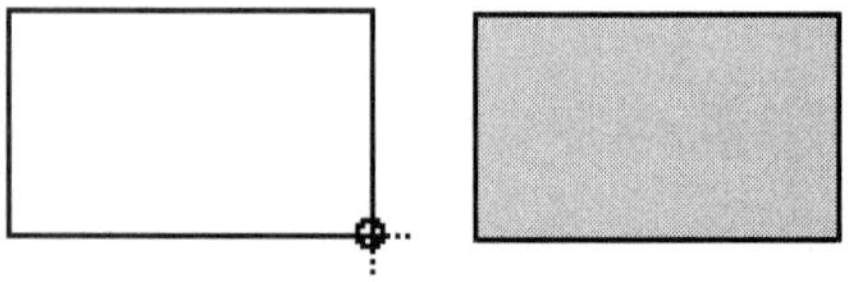

You can soften the edges of your rectangle shapes using the Round Rectangle Radius option. This option will allow you to modify the rounding of the edges.

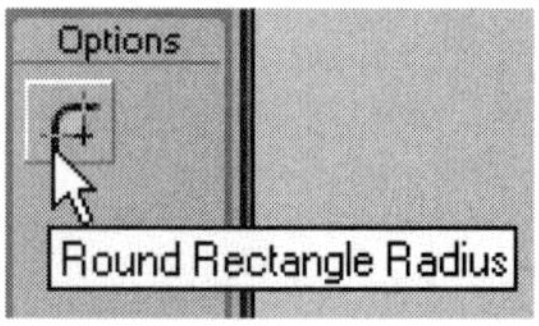

The Pencil tool 

The Pencil tool is a freehand drawing tool for drawing strokes.

To use the Pencil tool, just press the mouse button and move the mouse. Release the mouse button to stop drawing:

The Pencil tool allows you to cover up any personal weaknesses by optionally straightening or smoothing out your lines. The Ink setting will show your weaknesses!

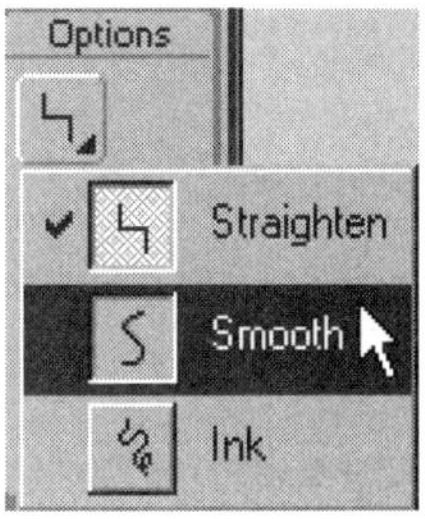

The Brush tool 

The Brush tool is used to paint chunky fills.

To paint with the Brush tool, just press the mouse button and move the mouse. Release the mouse button to stop painting.

The options for the Brush tool allow you to change the thickness of the brush, its shape, and the painting mode:

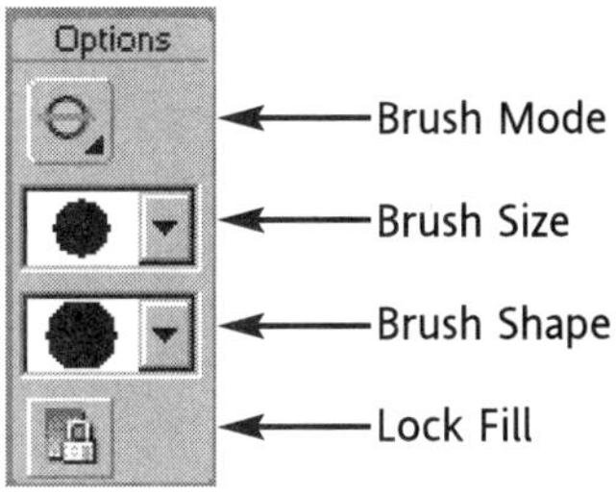

The Free Transform tool 

The Free Transform tool is used to manipulate the physical properties of objects. This tool allows you to perform actions from resizing to rotation to distortion.

To transform an object, select the Free Transform tool and select an object. The available transform modes then appear in the Options section of the tools panel.

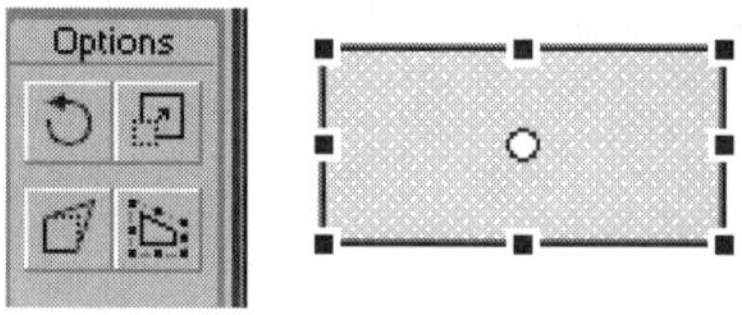

These options are as follows (reading from the top left clockwise):

- Rotate and Skew
- Scale
- Distort
- Envelope

Select a transform mode and then transform the object.

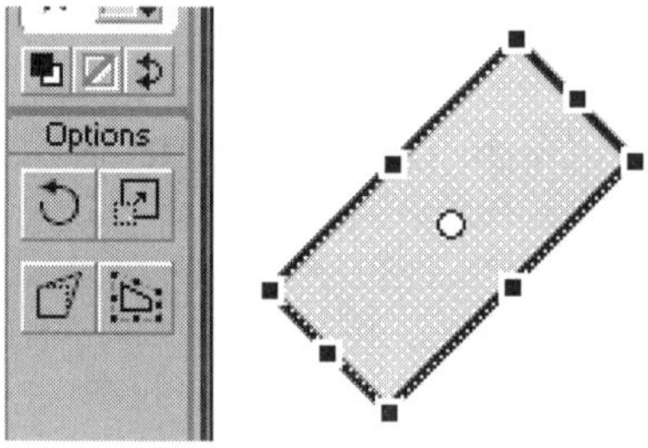

The last two modes here might not be that useful, but they are pretty wild, so give them a try.

The Fill Transform tool 

The Fill Transform tool allows you to modify a paint fill by scaling, rotation, or otherwise. This tool is particularly used for modifying gradient fills.

This tool functions differently for linear and radiant gradient fills. Select the Fill Transform tool and select the object that you wish to change the fill of. The following options will appear, depending on the gradient type.

Linear gradients

The following points will appear:

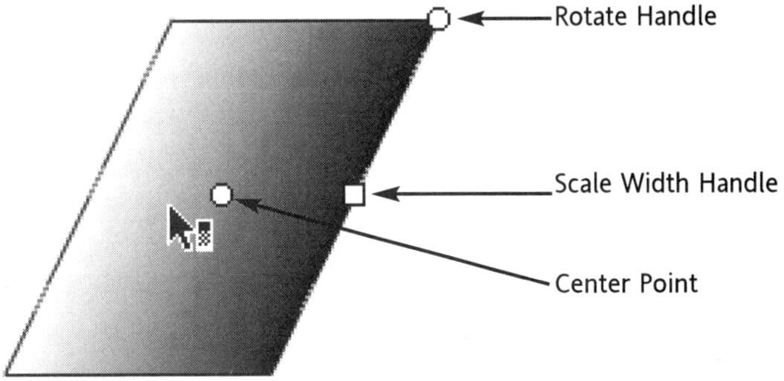

Click any of these points to change any of these attributes. Here's a change with the rotate handle:

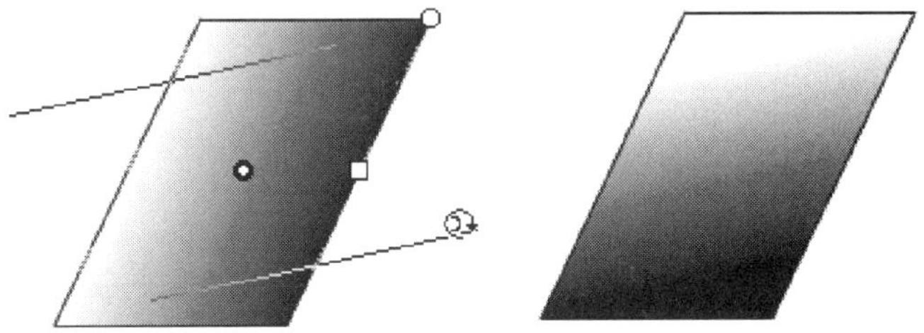

Radial gradients

The following points will appear:

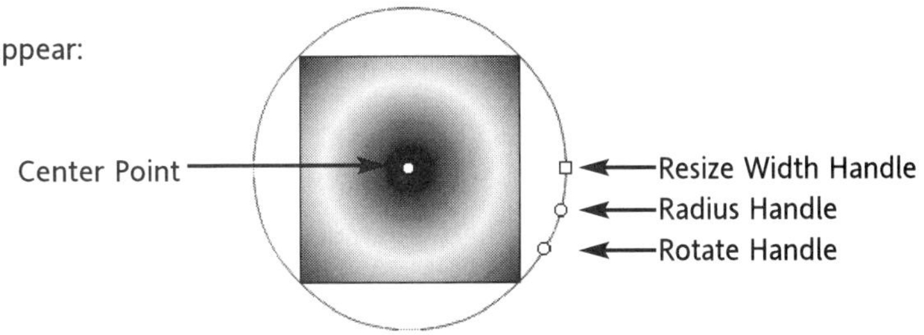

Click any of these points to manipulate that property. Here's what a change made with the Radius Handle looks like:

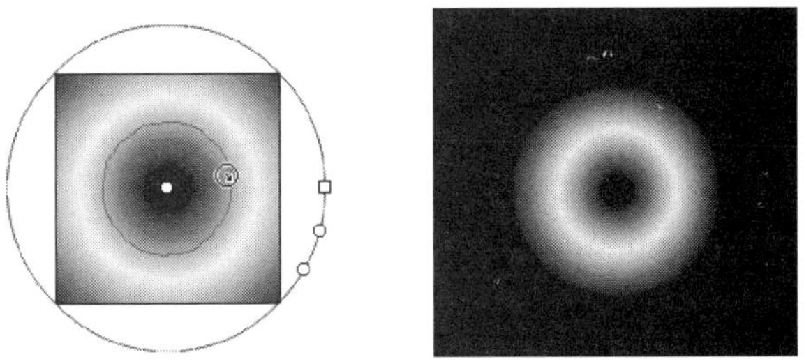

The Ink Bottle tool

The Ink Bottle tool is a very useful tool used to give a fill a stroke outline.

Select the Ink Bottle tool and click a fill object without a stroke (or with a partial stroke). Flash will then give the fill with a stroke outline:

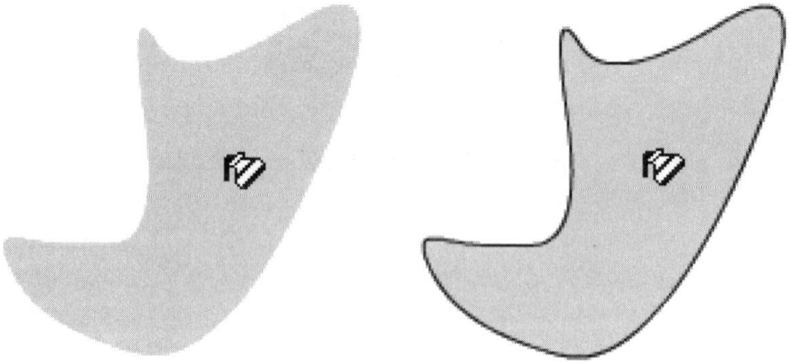

The Paint Bucket tool

The Paint Bucket tool is used to paint fills.

Select the Paint Bucket tool and choose a color to fill with. The Paint Bucket tool can paint over other colors:

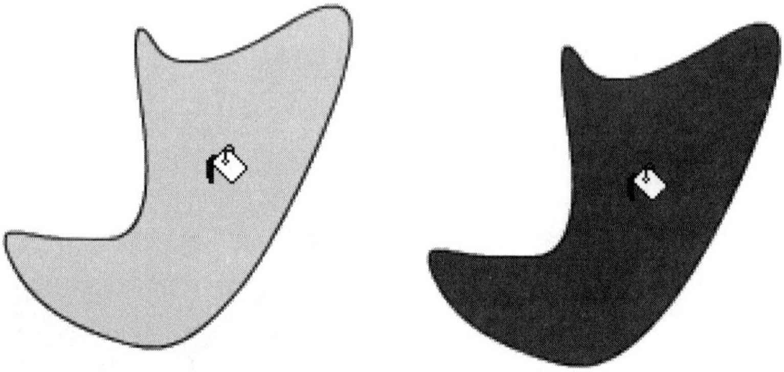

Or it can fill complete stroke shapes without fills:

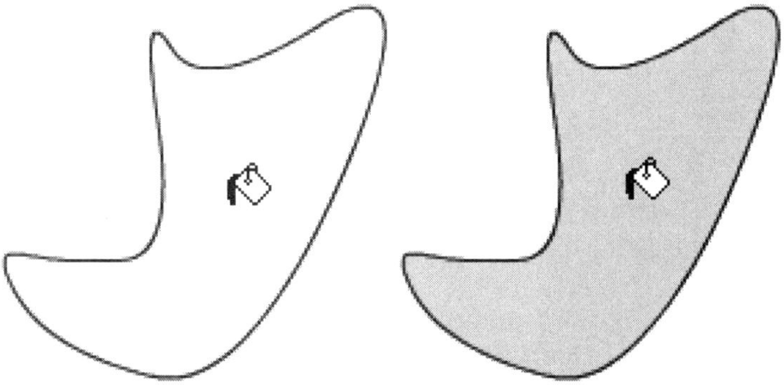

This tool can also fill in incomplete stroke shapes—that is, shapes with breaks in them. One of the options for this tool allows you to specify the size of the break that Flash is allowed to fill:

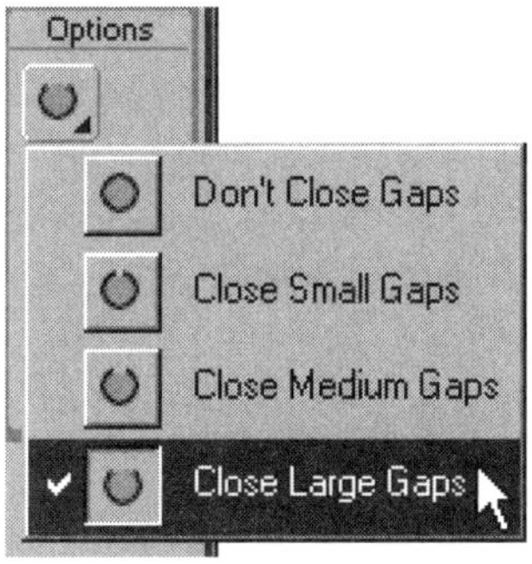

However, Flash considers a gap of this size to be a Large one!

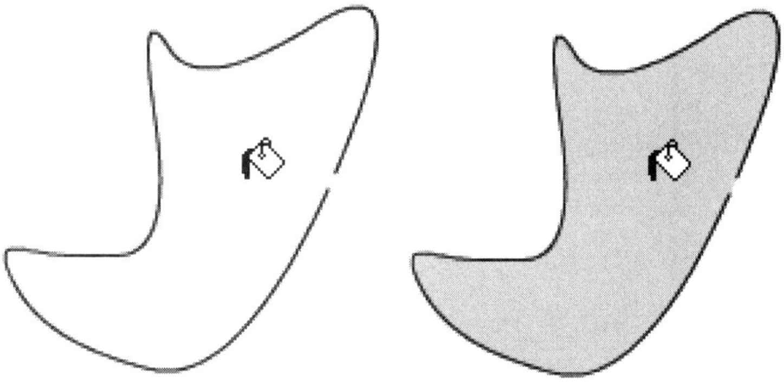

The Lock Fill option allows you to apply a single fill to a number of shapes. This is useful for gradient fills:

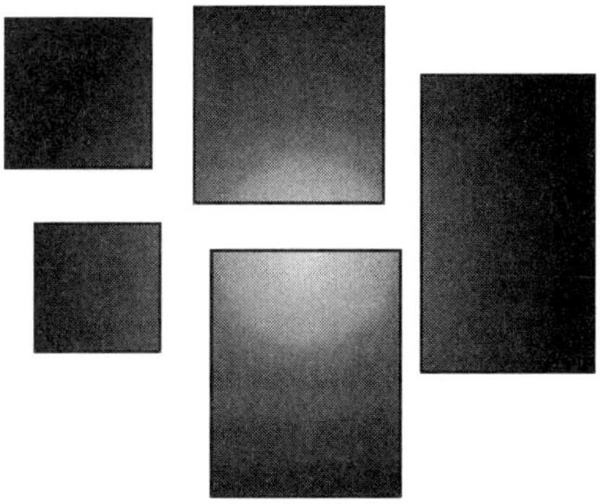

The Eyedropper tool 

This tool is used to take a sample of any color on the stage or screen.

Select the Eyedropper tool and click to sample a color from the screen. The sampled color will then be stored in the stroke or fill color area of the tools panel.

The Eraser tool 

The Eraser tool is used to rub out areas of content.

It has a number of options and modes to make rubbing out a little easier:

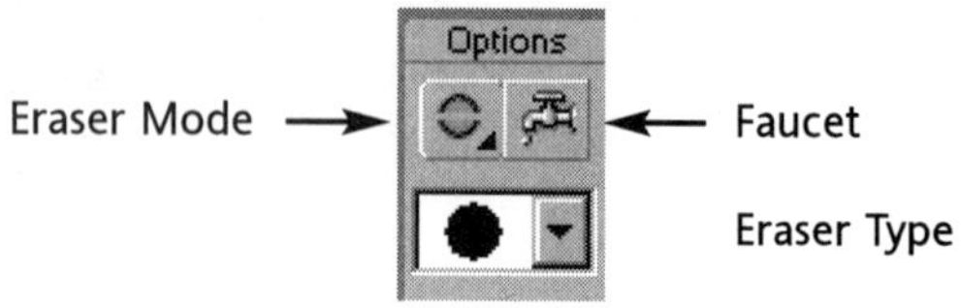

The Faucet tool

The Faucet tool will allow you to remove whole sections of content at once. These sections can be connected strokes, fills, or sections of color:

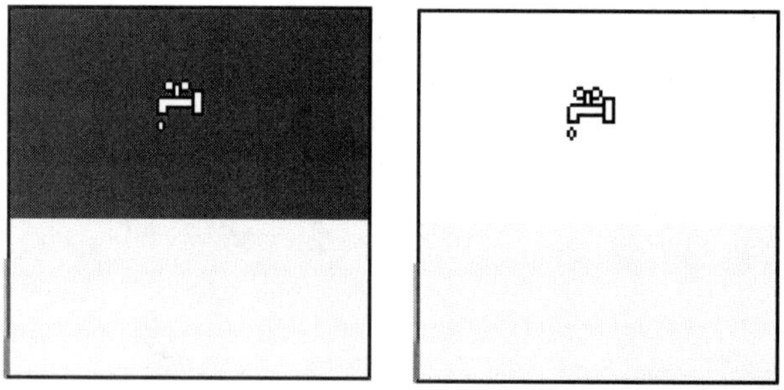

Brush types

If you prefer a more hands-on approach, you can erase freehand by pressing and rubbing out. The variety of brushes here will allow you to remove content using a different brush size or type.

Eraser mode

This option allows you to erase freehand given specific constraints. This option would have been useful for coloring books when you used to stray outside the lines!

Erase Normal will remove anything in the eraser's path.

Erase Fills will only remove fills and leave strokes alone.

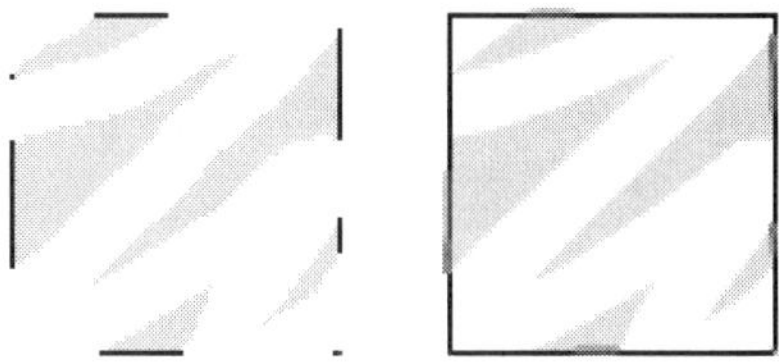

Erase Lines will only remove strokes.

Erase Selected Fills will rub out from any fills that are currently selected.

Erase Inside will erase within a stroke shape. The initial click will define where inside actually is.

View tools

The Hand tool 

This tool allows you to move the stage around in the view area.

Select this tool and click and drag around the stage area.

The Zoom tool 

This tool is used to zoom areas of the stage up to a maximum of 2000%. Each click of this tool will double the zoom in the area of the cursor.

The options section of this tool allows switching between zooming in and out.

Appendix B
Class 1 Handout: Shape Tweening

Like any animation, Flash animation is based on the simple principle of representing change over time. Unlike traditional animation, though, Flash can help you out through **tweening**. When Flash "tweens," it draws the frames in between two significant moments of action, as defined by the contents of keyframes. The replayed sequence of "keyframe, in-between-frames, keyframes" is the essence of Flash animation.

There are two types of animation in Flash: the **shape** tween and the **motion** tween (you'll learn about the latter type in week 3). A shape tween is a morphing operation, where the original object is transmogrified into a different object. Here's how a square morphs into a circle in a shape tween:

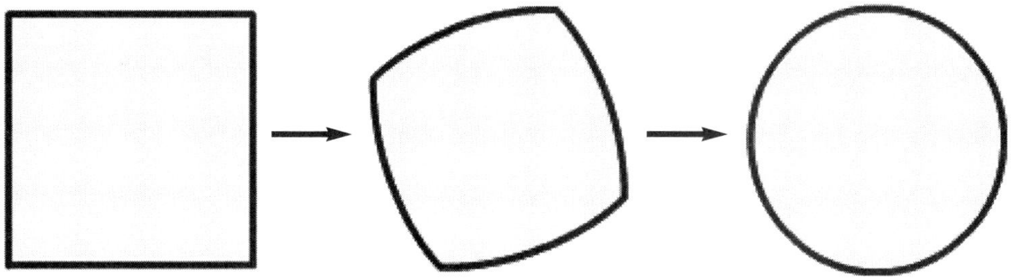

The most basic shape tweens requires two keyframes of content, with a tween set between them. The content on the two keyframes must be primitive shapes: strokes and fills only.

Let's run through a simple shape tween.

1. Open a new Flash movie and draw a square using the Rectangle tool. Hold down the SHIFT key to constrain the shape to a square.

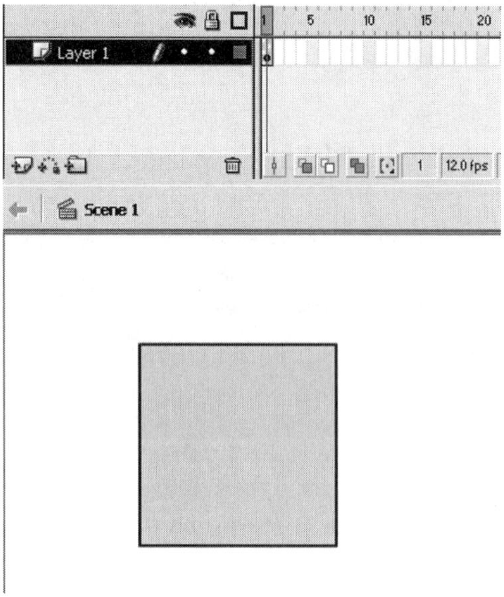

2. Select frame 20 of the timeline and insert a new keyframe using **Insert > Keyframe** or F6. The shape tween will take place between the keyframes on frames 1 and 20.

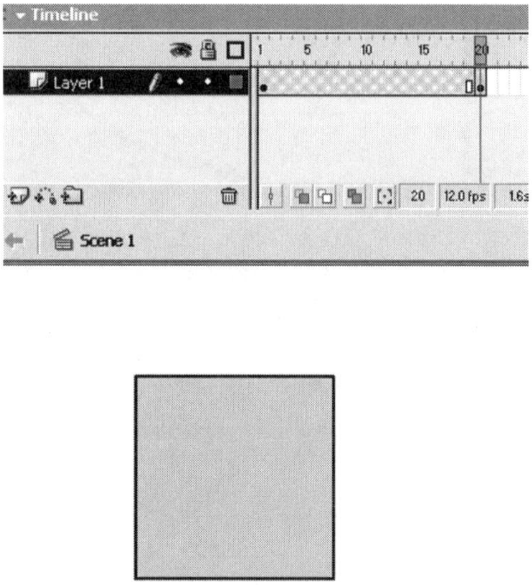

3. Select the Arrow tool and deselect the square on keyframe 20 by clicking away from it.

4. With the Arrow tool still selected, place your cursor over the corner of the square so the cursor changes like so:

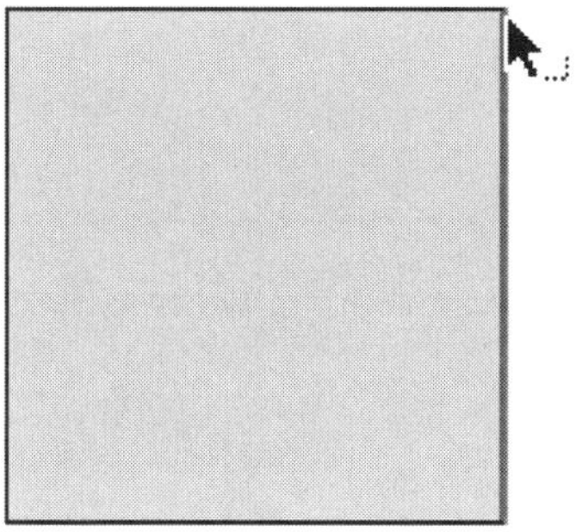

5. Now click and drag the corner to reshape the square. Release the mouse button when you're satisfied.

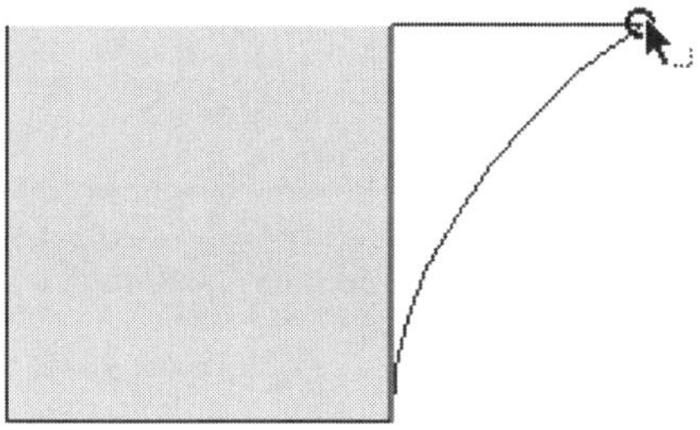

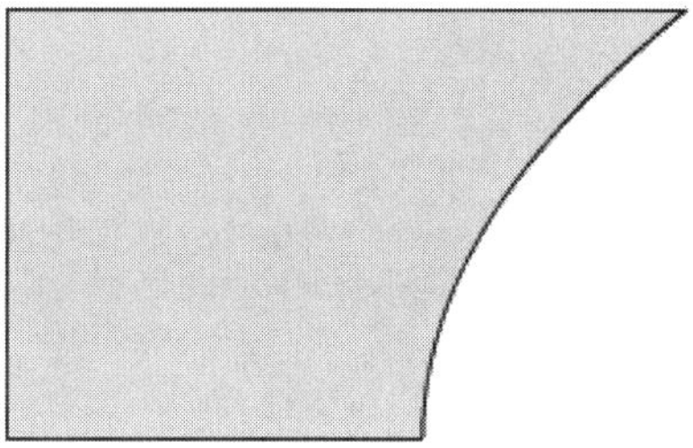

6. Repeat the last step, changing the square a little more, until it no longer resembles the original shape.

7. Once you're happy with the new shape, select a frame between the two keyframes

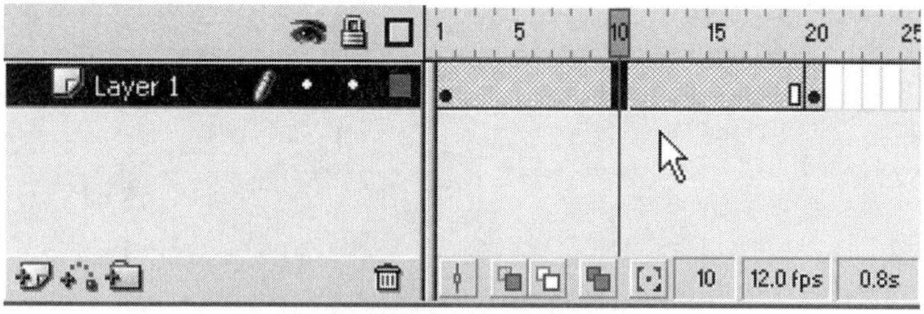

and select **Shape** from the **Tween** drop-down in the Property inspector.

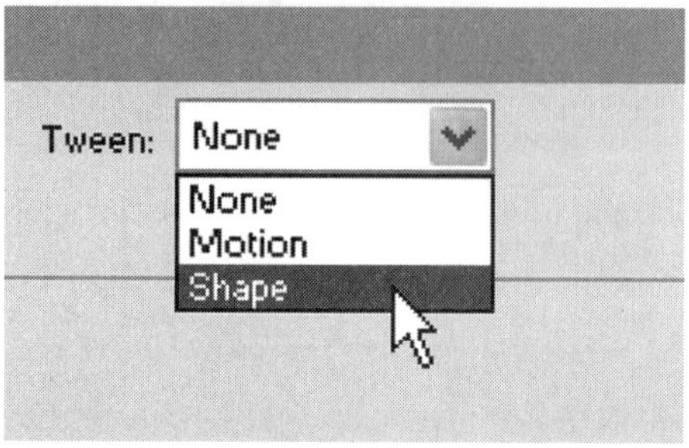

This will set a shape tween between the two keyframes. An arrow should now be drawn between the two keyframes, and the frames will be pale green. It should look like this:

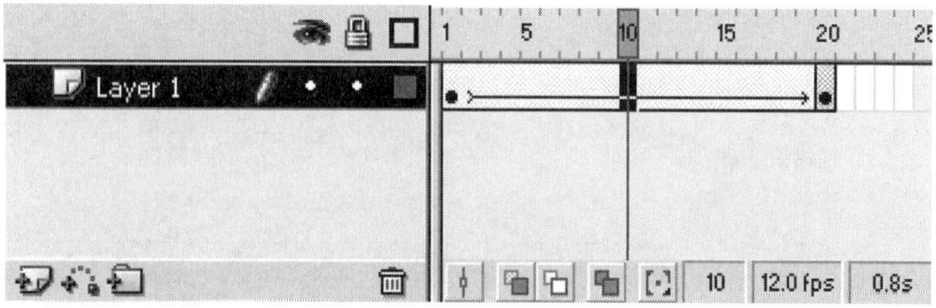

8. Now drag the playhead along the frame sequence and view the shape tween. You'll notice that the square morphs into the new shape you've created. To view the animation running, select **Control > Test Movie** to view it. Close the **Test Movie** window to return to the Flash application.

Besides morphing fills and strokes, the color of a shape can be tweened. Let's see how.

9. With the Arrow tool, select the squares fill on keyframe 1 and change its color using the Color Palette selector.

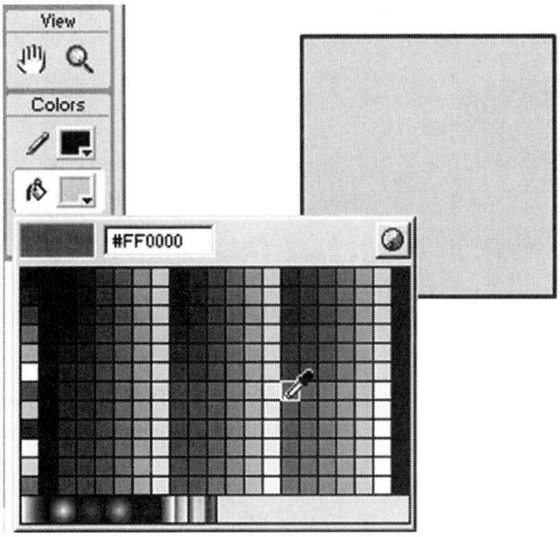

10. Test the movie again using **Control > Test Movie**. This time the shape will tween, but the color will change too.

Even though you've only done a two-keyframe shape tween here, you can add more keyframes as necessary. You could, for instance, insert a keyframe at frame 10 of this animation. This would result in a shape tween from frames 1 to 10 and 10 to 20.

Shape tweening with text

If you'd like to create a shape tween with text, you'll have to break the text into Flash vector primitives. To do this, select the text and select **Modify > Break Apart** not once, but twice!

Text Box Individual Letters Vector Primitives

Once you have primitive text, you can tween with them in the usual way.

Appendix C
ASCII and Key codes

ASCII Chart

This is a list of the first 127 ASCII characters. Some of the early characters have been removed because they are for special characters not used in Flash.

8	Backspace	54	6	81	Q	108	l
9	Tab	55	7	82	R	109	m
10	New Line	56	8	83	S	110	n
13	Carriage	57	9	84	T	111	o
	Return	58	:	85	U	112	p
32	Space	59	;	86	V	113	q
33	!	60	<	87	W	114	r
34	"	61	=	88	X	115	s
35	#	62	>	89	Y	116	t
36	$	63	?	90	Z	117	u
37	%	64	@	91	[	118	v
38	&	65	A	92	\	119	w
39	'	66	B	93	]	120	x
40	(	67	C	94	^	121	y
41	)	68	D	95	_	122	z
42	*	69	E	96	`	123	{
43	+	70	F	97	a	124	|
44	,	71	G	98	b	125	}
45	-	72	H	99	c	126	~
46	.	73	I	100	d	127	Del
47	/	74	J	101	e		
48	0	75	K	102	f		
49	1	76	L	103	g		
50	2	77	M	104	h		
51	3	78	N	105	i		
52	4	79	O	106	j		
53	5	80	P	107	k		

Key codes

These are the key codes that Flash can use instead of ASCII characters. This table was taken from the ActionScript dictionary that ships with Flash MX.

Letter or number key	Key code	Letter or number key	Key code
A	65	S	83
B	66	T	84
C	67	U	85
D	68	V	86
E	69	W	87
F	70	X	88
G	71	Y	89
H	72	Z	90
I	73	0	48
J	74	1	49
K	75	2	50
L	76	3	51
M	77	4	52
N	78	5	53
O	79	6	54
P	80	7	55
Q	81	8	56
R	82	9	57

Numeric keypad key	Key code	Numeric keypad key	Key code
Numbpad 0	96	Multiply	106
Numbpad 1	97	Add	107
Numbpad 2	98	Enter	108
Numbpad 3	99	Subtract	109
Numbpad 4	100	Decimal	110
Numbpad 5	101	Divide	111
Numbpad 6	102		
Numbpad 7	103		
Numbpad 8	104		
Numbpad 9	105		

Function key	Key code
F1	112
F2	113
F3	114
F4	115
F5	116
F6	117
F7	118
F8	119
F9	120
F10	121
F11	122
F12	123
F13	124
F14	125
F15	126

<table>
<tr><th>Key</th><th>Key code</th><th>Key</th><th>Key code</th></tr>
<tr><td>Backspace</td><td>8</td><td>Right Arrow</td><td>39</td></tr>
<tr><td>Tab</td><td>9</td><td>Down Arrow</td><td>40</td></tr>
<tr><td>Clear</td><td>12</td><td>Insert</td><td>45</td></tr>
<tr><td>Enter</td><td>13</td><td>Delete</td><td>46</td></tr>
<tr><td>Shift</td><td>16</td><td>Help</td><td>47</td></tr>
<tr><td>Control</td><td>17</td><td>Num Lock</td><td>144</td></tr>
<tr><td>Alt</td><td>18</td><td>; :</td><td>186</td></tr>
<tr><td>Caps Lock</td><td>20</td><td>= +</td><td>187</td></tr>
<tr><td>Esc</td><td>27</td><td>- _</td><td>189</td></tr>
<tr><td>Spacebar</td><td>32</td><td>/ ?</td><td>191</td></tr>
<tr><td>Page Up</td><td>33</td><td>\Q ~</td><td>192</td></tr>
<tr><td>Page Down</td><td>34</td><td>[{</td><td>219</td></tr>
<tr><td>End</td><td>35</td><td>\ |</td><td>220</td></tr>
<tr><td>Home</td><td>36</td><td>] }</td><td>221</td></tr>
<tr><td>Left Arrow</td><td>37</td><td>" '</td><td>222</td></tr>
<tr><td>Up Arrow</td><td>38</td><td></td><td></td></tr>
</table>

Special Key Codes

These properties of the Key object allow you to use English words instead of codes to detect certain characters.

Property	Description
Key.BACKSPACE	Constant associated with the key code value for the Backspace key (8).
Key.CAPSLOCK	Constant associated with the key code value for the Caps Lock key (20).
Key.CONTROL	Constant associated with the key code value for the Control key (17).
Key.DELETEKEY	Constant associated with the key code value for the Delete key (46).
Key.DOWN	Constant associated with the key code value for the Down Arrow key (40).
Key.END	Constant associated with the key code value for the End key (35).
Key.ENTER	Constant associated with the key code value for the Enter key (13).
Key.ESCAPE	Constant associated with the key code value for the Escape key (27).
Key.HOME	Constant associated with the key code value for the Home key (36).
Key.INSERT	Constant associated with the key code value for the Insert key (45).
Key.LEFT	Constant associated with the key code value for the Left Arrow key (37).
Key.PGDN	Constant associated with the key code value for the Page Down key (34).
Key.PGUP	Constant associated with the key code value for the Page Up key (33).
Key.RIGHT	Constant associated with the key code value for the Right Arrow key (39).
Key.SHIFT	Constant associated with the key code value for the Shift key (16).
Key.SPACE	Constant associated with the key code value for the Spacebar (32).
Key.TAB	Constant associated with the key code value for the Tab key (9).
Key.UP	Constant associated with the key code value for the Up Arrow key (38).

Index

The index is arranged hierarchically, in alphabetical order, with symbols preceding the letter A. Many second-level entries also occur as first-level entries. This is to ensure that you will find the information you require however you choose to search for it.

F

K

L

M

N

O

URLs